BRITISH SOLDIERS AMERICAN WAR

BRITISH SOLDIERS AMERICAN WAR

Voices *of the* American Revolution

DON N. HAGIST

with drawings by Eric H. Schnitzer

Yardley

Frontispiece: Professional British soldiers adapted rapidly and skillfully to the demands of warfare in America. For many, the eight-year war was part of a career that lasted thirty years or more. Depicted here is a corporal of the 9th Regiment of Foot on campaign north of Albany in 1777. He wears a uniform modified for wilderness campaigning: his coat has been shortened and his hat has been converted into a cap with a horsehair crest and a brass numeral on the front. Linen canvas trousers extend snugly over his shoes. Besides a cartridge pouch and bayonet belt, he wears a canteen and a haversack bulging with foraged apples.

First Westholme Paperback, February 2014

Westholme Publishing, LLC
904 Edgewood Road
Yardley, Pennsylvania 19067
Visit our Web site at www.westholmepublishing.com

ISBN: 978-1-59416-204-6
Also available in hardcover and as an eBook.

Printed in the United States of America.

For my parents,
Norma Hench Hagist and Warren M. Hagist,
who taught me the value of learning

CONTENTS

INTRODUCTION

It was one of America's longest conflicts. The government's professional army sent volunteer career soldiers, accustomed to overseas deployments, to fight in a land that was not well understood by many of the policymakers overseeing operations. Supplying and supporting the faraway army was difficult and expensive; a government divided over the merits of the war and the policies that led to it only worsened the logistical challenges. The military faced an enemy force that was not backed by a recognized government and was abetted by foreign fighters and supplies. Tactically, the army was hampered by an amorphous enemy and the unpredictably shifting loyalties of the local population. At the outbreak of war the government expected the army to be welcomed by the majority of the population as the instrument that would restore order and safety; instead, local inhabitants were often suspicious of the army and saw it as an exacerbating rather than mitigating influence. Although the officers and soldiers adapted superbly to local conditions and executed many outstanding feats of arms, frequent battlefield victories failed to develop into momentum toward an end to hostilities. Worse still, neither the government nor the regional army commanders were able to devise and execute a strategy for successful war termination. When the army was finally withdrawn, the failure of policies and politics was widely regarded strictly as a military defeat.

The war was in America, and the soldiers were British. Prior to hostilities the British government funded a small professional army composed of volunteer soldiers for whom military service was a career rather than a temporary commitment. Regiments were sent to posts in all corners of Britain's global empire, spending several years at a time garrisoning cities, forts, and outposts. When full-scale war broke out in Massachusetts in 1775, between five and ten thousand British soldiers were already in America, Canada, and the West Indies. As the war progressed this number increased more than fivefold, including additional career soldiers and recruits raised under shorter wartime enlistment terms. The British army was further bolstered by Loyalist corps raised in America, supplemented by German regiments and supported by Native American allies. Throughout this massive increase, however, the nucleus of the army continued to be Britain's career soldiers, the British regulars, the redcoats.

An estimated 50,000 individuals served in British infantry regiments during the war in America.[1] A substantial portion of these experienced the entire eight years of hostilities as one aspect of careers that lasted twenty years and longer. Many enlisted after the war began and were eligible for discharge when it ended, but chose instead to remain in the army. The length and complexity of the war, coupled with the greater length of typical military careers, ensured that most careers were unique if they were not truncated prematurely by death or desertion. Men joined the army for their own personal reasons, experienced varying amounts of training before being sent overseas, transferred from one regiment to another for various reasons, left the army through capture or desertion and returned to it by escape, exchange, apprehension, or surrender, were advanced and reduced in rank, practiced military specialties and pursued outside avocations, all before reaching an age and physical condition that warranted discharge from the army. Each man's course was guided by a combination of military demands and personal choices; the result was a distinctive career for each soldier, filled with shared experiences but nonetheless unique to each man.

The British army, and each regiment within it, was composed of soldiers from many regions and nations, from diverse social standings with a broad range of pre-military backgrounds and occupations, who had enlisted at different ages and had varying amounts of military experience. They didn't even all speak the same language. Yet there is a tendency to try to characterize British soldiers by finding common denominators, factors that they had in common which can be used to understand the army as a whole. Not only is this effort futile; it obscures the diversity of the army and the individuality of the soldiers themselves. The key to understanding the army is to recognize its effectiveness in bringing together such a varied amalgam of men and achieving a very high standard of operational success. Even though the war was lost, the performance of the British men at arms was generally excellent. That these men were not bred from common stock but assembled from all facets of society makes the caliber of their accomplishments all the more remarkable.

This book uses personal accounts of nine British soldiers to showcase the diverse nature of the army. Nothing teaches us about history like the voices of those who experienced it; to learn about the experience of British soldiers in the American Revolution, then, we should simply consult their writings. This brings up the immediate difficulty that, considering the number of common soldiers who served in the war, only a handful of personal accounts are known to exist. Accounts by officers are more plentiful, but those of common soldiers are hard to come by. Until this writing, only two such memoirs were in print, widely available, and readily identifiable as accounts by British soldiers.[2] Those two are very useful, but are not enough to give a broad view or provide a sense of the variation from one military career to another. Several others have been published but are either long out of print or are not titled in such a way as to make their content obvious.[3] Some of them are too short to warrant republication on their own, while others are lengthy memoirs of which only a portion pertains to British military service. The nine writings presented here, added to the two book-length memoirs that are in print, are all of the autobiographical accounts by British common soldiers who served in America between 1770 and 1783 known to exist at this time.

The original intent of this book was simply to bring these writings together in a single volume with some annotation to put each one into context. As work progressed, however, it became apparent that each writer emphasized aspects of his career that illustrate more general facets of the military life and structure. The very uniqueness of each account provides a vehicle to study attributes of the army as a whole, a portrait painted with diverse elements rather than broad strokes. Looking at these nine soldiers provides a perspective on the British military that is not apparent when studying any one man, and which is in fact impossible to discern by looking at any one man because no individual is typical of the army as a whole. This group does not tell us everything, but it provides an important basis for further study. The challenge to putting individual stories into context is, of course, establishing the context. Although we do not have a statistically significant number of memoirs to compare with one another, various sources provide a sufficient quantity of information about individual common soldiers to assemble a general picture from the small amounts of information available on each. Besides the muster rolls that tell their names, an assortment of additional military records, newspaper accounts, personal writings, and other sources reveal specific events in the lives and careers of thousands of soldiers. Using this material well means discerning generalities against which to compare individual soldiers. For example, some soldiers featured in this book became noncommissioned officers (that is, corporals and sergeants); analysis of muster rolls shows the overall proportion of men who achieved this advancement during their careers, thus giving a sense of whether the individuals under study were typical or remarkable in this one regard. Similar analysis can be done on attributes such as nationality, age, pre-military occupation, length of army service, literacy, and a host of other details. The result is a series of generalities that typify military life in the era. No one generality applies to all soldiers, but each individual career contains elements that were common to many others. The value of each of the narratives in this book is enhanced by understanding which aspects were experienced by what portion of the men in the army as a whole.

This book relies almost exclusively on primary sources to avoid the bias that is prevalent in secondary literature. Looking closely at each story and the hundreds of vignettes used to put it in into perspective, it is difficult to avoid a new bias, for each life garners sympathy when studied in detail. The goal is not to be an apologist for the policies of the

British government or the strategies of using military might to enforce them. Rather, it is to show the soldiers as the individuals they were, working for a living in the profession of arms, motivated by the daily concerns of human existence rather than the principles of government. They were soldiers, professional soldiers who chose the army over other career options and, as we shall see, reevaluated that choice as their lives progressed.

This is not a campaign history. There are plenty of those available already that tell the operational history of the war in terms of the policies, strategies, and campaigns. In most of these, the soldiers upon whose performance the operations hinged are represented as mere numbers, the sizes of armies as told by the numbers of men they contained with little significance placed on aggregate qualities much less individual characteristics. The views provided in this book are those of the men in the ranks; a basic understanding of the flow of the war is helpful but not necessary to fully appreciate their accounts. Their narratives give an appreciation for what the men themselves considered important, regardless of the scale of events in which they each played a part. The men featured in this book served in almost every campaign and theater of the war in America and Canada, and yet they tell us very little about the experience of battle. Details of life in the field are seldom mentioned unless they factored directly into the overall narrative, leaving us to wonder whether the events that are so memorable today had as great an impact on the men who participated in them as they did on history. To be sure, the events that affected the course of each soldier's life were seldom the same ones that affected the course of the war. From the perspective of an individual soldier, a great battle could be the same as a small skirmish and an hour of exposure to gunfire might be less a threat to life than a six-week voyage on a stormy ocean. These first-hand accounts do not give a perspective on the war itself, but on the lives and concerns of those who were a part of it.

Two of these men did not actually fight in the 1775–1783 war. One died in Boston shortly before hostilities began, while the other was sent to the West Indies in a newly raised regiment late in the war. Their accounts are included because each illustrates important aspects of the composition and operation of the army. The remaining seven participated in a variety of operations large and small, illustrating the nature of the soldier's operational experiences in America. With so few personal accounts available we cannot be choosy about which years and campaigns to represent, but instead we let the accounts themselves drive the overall narrative. None of these first-hand accounts stand alone very well, particularly as studies of soldiers; these men were not gifted writers and each of their narratives were intended to tell how they came to be the type of person they were rather than to fully recount their life experiences. Their value to the study of the British army is in their effectiveness as case studies when put into context with extensive support from other primary sources. The facets of each career provide a basis for analysis of what was typical, what was unusual, and how well each of these nine soldiers represents the generality of men who served in America.

Most of the military terminology used in this book is defined in the text or notes, but it is helpful to understand the basic component of military structure within which soldiers lived, the regiment. The British army was composed primarily of three disciplines: infantry, cavalry, and artillery. Within each of these arms, the soldiers were organized into regiments; for the infantry and cavalry, the regiment was the primary administrative and deployable entity. Each regiment received its own funding, managed its own recruiting, had distinctive elements to its uniform, and was moved from place to place within Great Britain and overseas as an operational element. Each infantry regiment was divided into ten companies of equal size consisting of three commissioned officers, five or six non-commissioned officers (sergeants and corporals), one or two drummers, and thirty-eight to seventy private soldiers – the numbers varied at different times before and during the war. This represents the established size, that is, the number of men that was funded by the government for a regiment at full strength. Normal operational attrition saw to it that actual numbers of both officers and men were usually somewhat below this, and regiments were always carrying on some form of recruiting to remain as close as possible to full strength. Although regiments were deployed as entities, and the companies of a regiment might be distributed among different posts in a region, the common soldier was not operationally isolated to his own company and regiment. In garrison and on campaign, soldiers of different companies and regiments regularly served together in small groups on all manner of duties from posting guards to foraging to building fortifications. As will be seen in this book, this gave opportunities for soldiers of different regiments to know one another. The exigencies of war sometimes diluted the apparent organization of regiments and companies. The memoirs presented here will show examples of soldiers serving away from their regiments, transferring from one regiment to another, leaving their regiments entirely and returning again.

The peacetime strength of a regiment consisted of 35 commissioned officers (including five staff officers in addition to the 30 company officers), 20 sergeants (two per company), 30 corporals (three per company), 10 drummers (one per company), 2 fifers in one of the companies, and 380 private soldiers. After the American war began in 1775 the government took measures to increase the size of the army. For the infantry regiments on service in America, this meant an increase in established strength of 200 men in the form of one sergeant, one drummer, and 18 private soldiers per company. To raise these men, two more companies were established for each regiment. Called Additional Companies, they were actually administrative vehicles for recruiting in Great Britain while their regiments served in America. Each of these companies, on paper, had the same strength as the companies on service, that is, three officers and sixty-six other ranks, but typically only the officers, sergeants, corporals and drummers served with any permanence. These men operated as recruiting parties in Great Britain, "beating up for recruits" wherever likely men were to be found. When enough recruits had been raised, they were sent to join their regiments in America. As the war progressed, the size of companies in America was increased again to seventy private soldiers, then reduced to fifty-eight; at the end of the war another reduction occurred, this time in the number of companies. These aspects of army structure will be discussed in more detail throughout this book when they are important to the narratives. For the general reader, it is sufficient to think of a regiment as an entity of four hundred to six hundred men (typically), and a company as a tenth of that, with a contingent recruiting new men in Great Britain.

Each of the nine autobiographical accounts in this book has been published before in some form. As such, each has been filtered in some way, either by a publisher or a transcriber. In no case do we have the original manuscript as written by the narrator. For this reason, we are bounded to editorial choices made by previous publishers when it comes to conventions of spelling, abbreviations, and other aspects of how the text is presented. We have no way of knowing how accurately these accounts reflect the words, written or spoken, of the people who related them. In most cases this book faithfully reproduces the text as it was first published, except to correct occasional blatant typographical errors. The sources are always given so that the inquisitive reader can review the material as it was first published to verify anything that may be in doubt. Five of the accounts presented here are extracts from longer memoirs in which the authors wrote at length about their lives after leaving the army. While interesting in their own right, the portions that do not pertain to their military careers, or the events leading to them, have been omitted.

In each chapter, each personal story, there is much more that could be said. More about the background, the policies, the strategy, the campaigns, the commanders, the logistics, the personnel, the clothing and equipment, the implications and aftermath. But those details are for other books and studies. This book is about individuals, and their lives as soldiers.

ONE

The Volunteer Soldier

John Robert Shaw, 33rd Regiment of Foot

Introduction

It was October 1774 and Edward Hall was in trouble. The Yorkshire native, a private soldier in the grenadier company of the 43rd Regiment of Foot, had been wandering in the countryside a few miles outside Boston when he ran into an army officer. The British army had been having problems with desertion abetted by local inhabitants who made a sport of inveigling soldiers to drink and then spiriting them away into the colonies. On suspicion of attempted desertion, Hall was put on trial for his life. Testifying in his own defense, he lucidly and earnestly admitted his unauthorized absence but asserted his intention to return to camp by morning. He read from a statement he'd prepared to convince the court of his dedication to the service, assuring them "that his Family being in very independent Circumstances he first entered into the Service not from Want, but Inclination" and "that he has always met with Treatment that left him no Reason of Complaint."[1] This testimony by a common British soldier directly states what we must infer about most of his peers, that service in the army in America during the 1775–1783 war was a voluntary career choice made by men who were, by the standards of the day, well enough treated that they served dutifully for decades.

British soldiers were volunteers. In the years preceding the American Revolution and for most of the war itself, men joined the British army voluntarily and in fact had legal recourse if they were brought into the service any other way. There were exceptions (discussed in Chapter 6), but their numbers were few. That military service was voluntary is a critical point because it underlies the proper perspective on many other aspects of the soldier's career including his motivation, his governance by military law, his need for and response to military discipline, and his behavior under conditions of adversity including combat and imprisonment. The popular perception that these men were coerced into enlistment, pressed from the dregs of society, or drawn from prisons directly contradicts the actual service records of the common men who chose the army as a career and became the professional soldiers who formed the backbone of the British regiments on service in America.

There is a favorite perception that British recruiting parties preyed on unsuspecting innocents by finding them in taverns, plying them with liquor and taking advantage of their inebriation to bond them into a life of military servitude. This quaint image of a bygone age fits in with a general impression of the army as a highly undesirable profession. As compelling as this recruitment scenario is, it is not supported by direct evidence. Recruiters did frequent taverns, but it would be surprising if they had not: taverns were the social centers of agrarian Britain where people met for business and pleasure. This made them, along with events such as markets and fairs, the most likely place for recruiters to find concentrations of eligible men. If any temptation was routinely used by recruiters it was the bounty money to which a recruit was entitled. This immediate payment, along with the promise of regular food and clothing and the prospect of travel and adventure, was more than enough to entice laborers and tradesmen whose circumstances might otherwise be trying and tedious.[2] Some lads are known to have accepted the invitation to enlist while insensible of their actions, accepting a shilling or other coin as partial payment of the enlistment bounty.[3] Many more, however, are known to have sought out recruiters as will be seen throughout this book. As described below, any who were unscrupulously compelled to enlist had opportunities to renege.

If it is a revelation that most soldiers enlisted voluntarily, then it is natural to wonder what would induce so many men to enter a career characterized by poor pay, brutal discipline, slim chances for advancement, and disregard by the government at the end of a lifetime of service. The motivation is impossible to understand if these bitter perceptions of the army are factual, but the perceptions are inaccurate. None of these notions is completely baseless, but they are all founded on the assumption that what happened to a few must have happened to the majority. Examination of primary sources reveals that the army was a reasonably attractive career compared to other choices available to young men of the era, offering its own temptations and rewards when compared to other professions. There were many different reasons why men enlisted, but for most it was a choice among many rather than a last resort or act of desperation.

While very few of the British soldiers who served in America left written records of their path to enlistment, those who did generally tell similar stories. John Robert Shaw (or Robertshaw) is presented first in this volume not only because he goes into detail about his enlistment and training but also because his circumstances were common. He was a rebellious teenager who was not inclined to follow the path that his father dictated. He argued, he disobeyed, he ran away from home, and he enlisted as a way to find his own direction. The fact that the American war had been in progress for two years did not deter him; the recruiting party that he joined belonged to a regiment already in America, so the potential dangers of service were as great as could be. His narrative discusses in plain terms two very important details about his entrance into the army: he volunteered, and after doing so he had the opportunity to change his mind. Far from being coerced by an unscrupulous recruiter, he traveled some distance to find a recruiting party and then had to convince the sergeant to accept him. And he was not in desperate straits; he left a career as a tradesman, and his father attempted to buy him out of his enlistment and take him home, but Shaw flatly refused in the presence of the recruiting sergeant. He was zealous in his determination to enlist in spite of having ample opportunity to choose otherwise. He may have had unrealistic visions of the career that awaited him, or perhaps he had no preconceptions at all, but he was no victim of false promises.

Shaw's experience is echoed by other soldiers whose writings are not presented here. Roger Lamb[4] enlisted in Dublin in 1773; years after leaving the army he wrote more extensively of his service than any other soldier of the era. Well-raised by loving parents, Lamb pursued a variety of endeavors other than employment until he had exhausted all of his options except returning home or joining the army. Like John Robert Shaw, he sought out a recruiter even though his parents likely would have forgiven him and afforded him other opportunities. Lamb's voluminous commentary on the army gives no hint whatsoever that he or his comrades entered the service involuntarily or unwillingly.[5] For both Shaw and Lamb, parental admonishment was a significant threat that strongly influenced their decisions to enlist, but they were moved to enlist by their own dispositions and not by force of the army or the government.

Thomas Sullivan, another soldier who wrote extensively of his service,[6] had a more direct reason for enlistment that was not influenced by domestic conflict. Although raised by a father who "took as much pains as possible to have me Instructed, in any thing that my inclination laid me to," the young Irishman was "strongly bent upon rambling" and had a desire "to travel and traverse a stretch of the Seas." He satisfied his disposition by enlisting in a regiment that he knew was going abroad and would not return to Great Britain for some years. The 49th Regiment of Foot was already preparing to embark for America when Sullivan enlisted at Cork in February 1775. He was twenty years old at the time, beyond the age of parental conflict but very much old enough to have tried his hand at other professions before choosing the army; although he does not mention his pre-military work, it is clear that he sought something more active and adventurous. In an era when travelers brought back tales of foreign wonders but most working-class professions were local and potentially monotonous, life as a soldier or sailor must have appealed to

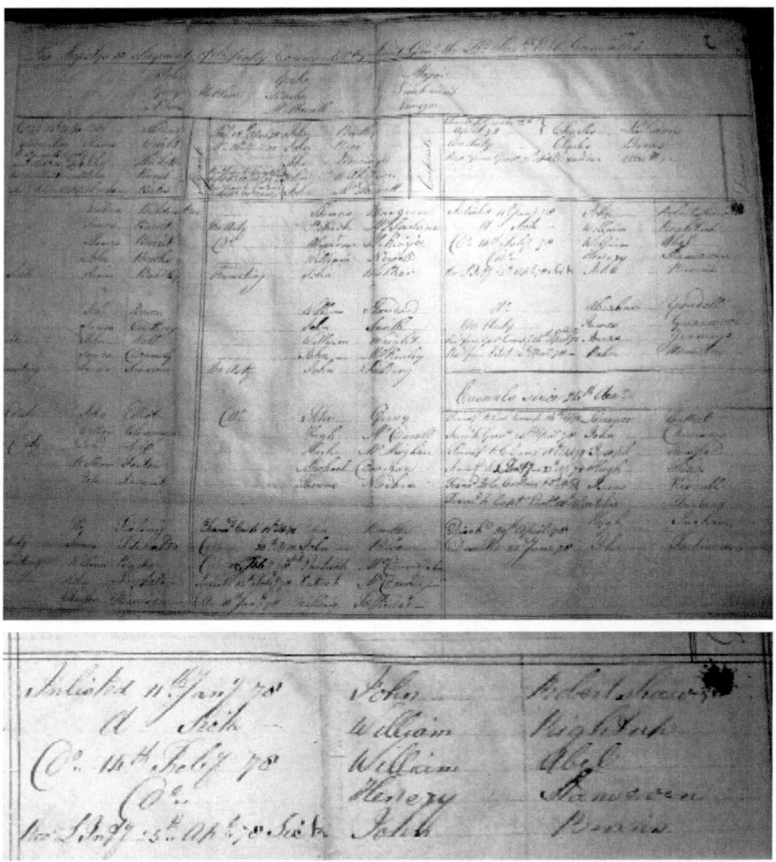

The muster roll of Major John Yorke's company, 33rd Regiment of Foot, top, recording the enlistment of John Robertshaw [Robert Shaw] to the left of the ink blotch on the far right, with a detail, below. The date written is actually when Robert Shaw boarded a transport for America. (*The National Archives. Photo by René Chartrand*)

many young men and was perhaps the single most prevalent reason for men to join the army.

William Pell did not serve in America but did join the army in 1779 while the war was raging. The story of his enlistment is even more benign than Shaw's and Lamb's, in that Pell was gainfully employed at the time. The young farm laborer was walking to his place of employ in Northamptonshire in January after spending the holidays with his family in Buckinghamshire. He chanced upon a sergeant and a recruit going the same way; as they walked they conversed about London and army life. It was not long before Pell expressed a desire to enlist, which the sergeant immediately facilitated. After settling affairs with his employer, Pell went with his new comrades to London where the formalities of enlistment were completed over several days. Far from being coerced into the army, Pell was fully aware that he had ample time to renege on the agreement and explicitly stated that "nothing was done in a hurry."[7] An article based on Pell's narrative shows the remarkable bias of modern literature, presenting Pell as having been entrapped into enlistment even though Pell himself describes it as his own impulsive decision and gives no hint of duress.[8]

Yet another similar experience was that of a teenager known to us only as "W. Griffith." He had been raised as a foundling and put to work as a farm hand to a cruel master when he was nine years old. In his early teens, feeling himself old enough to earn his living, he set out on his own and found several jobs but was not content at any of them. At around the same time that Shaw was insisting on being taken as a soldier, Griffith made a similar determination:

> One day, while musing in my mind what to do, I thought I would go for a soldier. I told my fellow-servant of it; he said I was foolish, and if I knew as much about soldiers as he did, I should do no such thing: but it laid so much on my mind, I could not resist it, though I could give no particular reason, for so doing, and what he said made no difference with me. I got up the next sabbath morning and went to Doncaster, about four miles off, there I saw a soldier, and told him my business: he said I had better go home again, for if I knew as much about soldiers as he did, I should not come here. I told him if he would not enlist me some one else should, for I was bent upon going. He then said if I was determined upon going, he might as well have half-a-guinea as any one else.[9] The man behaved well to me, told me I should not be sworn in till the fourth day, and then, if I paid the smart money, which was twenty-four shillings, I should go free. There were farmers in the place that told me they would employ me if I would go with

> them. I thanked them, but I was determined to go for a soldier, let the consequence be what it might.[10]

Griffith enlisted in the 65th Regiment of Foot, which had recently returned from service in America, spending five years as a soldier before receiving his discharge in 1783.

Pell and Griffith made clear an important detail that John Robert Shaw omitted from his enlistment story, that of attestation. The law required recruits to be taken before a magistrate or justice of the peace at least twenty-four hours but no more than four days after accepting the bounty, to either protest against or formally swear to enlistment. If the recruit agreed to enlistment, the recruitment process could continue; if he did not, he had the opportunity to state his dissent and be discharged upon returning the bounty plus a fee for the recruiter's costs.[11] The magistrate confirmed the man's identity, his availability to the army (insuring that he was not under apprenticeship, an escaped criminal, a deserter from another regiment, or otherwise disqualified from service), and provided an opportunity for the recruit to dispute his enlistment. The military understood that coerced men were unlikely to be good soldiers, the law did not allow conscription, and the population would not tolerate widespread unscrupulous recruiting practices. The isolated known cases of unwilling enlistment do not—indeed cannot—be taken as representative of the majority of British soldiers in the 1770s and 1780s. The British army was a volunteer force, and most of the men who served in it did so by choice.

The writers cited above are but a minuscule sample of the thousands of soldiers in the army during the 1770s and 1780s. They are distinctive in that they wrote of their experiences; maybe they were also distinctive in how they enlisted, and do not represent the most common experience. Additional information about enlistments can be found in the records of general courts-martial, military tribunals for soldiers who had committed major crimes. A common component of the prosecutorial examination by the court, especially in cases of desertion, was whether the soldier had been properly enlisted and attested. In all of the trials of British regular soldiers conducted in America from 1775 through 1783 (for which records survive), in the vast majority of cases proper enlistment was simply declared by a witness such as an officer or fellow soldier who was in the regiment at the time the soldier was enlisted, and was not questioned or argued by the defendant. If a soldier on trial, sometimes for his life, had anything to grasp for in his defense he usually did so; if proper enlistment was in doubt it could bring an acquittal, so there is every reason to believe that improperly enlisted soldiers would speak up when on trial.

A few soldiers did argue that they had come into the army against their will. When tried for desertion in February 1777, John Ingram of the 6th Regiment of Foot testified "that he was in liquor, when he was inlisted, and did not know that he was so, 'till they came and carried him away."[12] Ingram was a sailor on a trading ship in port in St. Vincent before the war began when he joined the 6th Regiment; in New York he made his way onto a British transport ship to pursue his former profession. The court did not accept his argument and sentenced him to be lashed.[13] George Hartly had served in America since 1766, transferring from the 34th to the 59th to the 38th Regiment before finally being discharged in early 1777. He took a ship back to London where, according to his testimony, he immediately fell in with a recruiting party who got him drunk, brought him before a magistrate for attestation while still intoxicated, and put him on a transport for America. In New York again by June of the same year, he was put on trial for desertion and theft. Although found guilty of the latter crime because he had left a guard post a few days before, he was recommended as an object of mercy because "the court being acquainted with many circumstances of his Past Life, tho' not produced in Evidence, Consider him a Wretched, Unhappy Man, whose Conduct carries with it, Evident marks of Insanity."[14]

John Walker of the 10th Regiment, tried for desertion and robbery in 1778, claimed that he was never attested. A fellow soldier, however, testified that "he heard the Articles of War against Mutiny & Desertion read to the Prisoner & saw him take the usual Oath of Fidelity, before the Bailiff of the Town of Inverness in Scotland."[15] John Alexander of the 4th Regiment, tried for desertion in 1778, also claimed not to have been attested and also heard a comrade in his regiment testify to the contrary.[16] Charles Toomey was drafted from the 59th Regiment into the 40th Regiment from which he deserted in late 1777. When put on trial, he claimed that he was never attested but gave the caveat that "being a Soldier's Son, the Recruiting party of the 59th Regiment with whom he enlisted, thought it unnecessary." The court did not investigate the accuracy of this statement; perhaps they thought it immaterial because, after deserting from the 40th, Toomey had enlisted in a Loyalist regiment from which he also deserted.[17] In desertion trials of 148 British soldiers in America between 1775 and 1783 fewer than 10 claimed irregularities in their enlistment,[18] and in all of these cases credible counter-testimony was offered. The remainder did not call their recruitment into question and a few, such as Edward Hall whose case is related above, asserted their voluntary enlistment.

Besides being one of only a few men who recorded their reasons for enlisting, John Robert Shaw is the only writer who described in detail the training he received before joining his regiment. During the era of the American Revolution, British regiments did their own recruiting rather than relying on an army-wide recruiting infrastructure. There were no restrictions on where a regiment could recruit; the system of regimental county titles and regional recruiting did not begin until 1782, too late to affect the composition of regiments serving in the American war, and even then was a recommendation rather than a mandate.[19] During the 1760s and 1770s it was recognized that regiments could recruit effectively by developing a rapport with the citizenry of specific regions, taking advantage of the relationships between friends and relatives to make military life more attractive,[20] but regiments on the regular establishment were nonetheless quite cosmopolitan in terms of the nativity of their soldiers.[21]

Among other places, regiments recruited locally from the areas that they were serving. In the British Isles, routine service in peace time saw regiments moved from place to place in England, Scotland, and Ireland, and the national makeup of the regiment reflected these movements. Regiments serving overseas recruited locally as well. During peace time, a regiment on service in a hospitable climate like the middle colonies of North America might need up to fifty new men each year to replace those who were discharged, died, or deserted.[22] Hostile climates like Florida and the West Indies caused significantly more casualties and therefore increased demand for recruits. Not every location could provide willing and able men to satisfy this attrition, so local recruiting alone was not sufficient to maintain the strength of a regiment. Whether in Britain or overseas, a few officers of each regiment led recruiting parties—generally consisting of a non-commissioned officer, a drummer, and sometimes one or a few trustworthy experienced soldiers—to locations throughout the British Isles where recruits were likely to be gotten. These recruiters followed seasonal patterns to be at markets and fairs where men gathered, and economic trends to find unemployed tradesmen and itinerant laborers in search of steady work and a change to their prospects.

When a soldier enlisted into a regiment serving in his local area, his training began immediately within the regiment itself. There were no boot camps and no army-wide training regimens to which new recruits were subjected. Although the government published a manual of arms governing the basic handling of the musket and bayonet, and describing "Plans and Explanations of the Method generally Practis'd at Review and Field-Days," procedures for everything from personal hygiene to tactical doctrine were the purview of the individual regiments as directed by the commanding officers and their subordinates. Corporate retention of this vast body of knowledge was supplemented by regimental standing orders but passed on primarily by experienced officers and soldiers directly training the new ones. Formal annual inspections, periodic visits by general officers, peer pressure from other regiments, operational requirements, and a general sense of duty insured that most regiments maintained an acceptable measure of discipline and readiness most of the time.[23]

Men enlisted by recruiting parties, either for regiments in other parts of the British Isles or for regiments serving overseas, had a somewhat different experience. When enlisted by a recruiting party, a man was under the direction of the recruiting officer and his small cadre for an indefinite time. He began his training immediately while under their care;

without uniform or equipment, the recruit learned hygiene, military deportment, and various procedures while also helping the recruiting party in its important business. The officer generally provided some clothing items, a knapsack, combs, and other essentials, but not a full regimental uniform. The recruit stayed with the recruiting party anywhere from weeks to a year or more, until an opportunity arose to journey to the parent regiment, usually in the company of other recruits and a noncommissioned or commissioned officer. If the regiment was overseas, recruits from several regiments might make the journey together. Only when the recruit joined the parent regiment did he receive a full regimental uniform, a set of accoutrements, and a stand of arms with which to complete his training as a soldier.

Contrary to much popular literature, the British army adapted rapidly and effectively to the conditions of the war in America. The first adaptation came almost immediately after news reached England of the outbreak of hostilities. In October 1775 the government ordered that each regiment on or destined for service in America be increased significantly in size both to insure adequate strength on the field and to enhance the recruiting and training infrastructure to accommodate wartime attrition.[24] The nominal size of each regiment's ten companies was augmented by about half, from 38 to 56 private soldiers plus an additional sergeant and drummer. Two further companies were added for the purpose of recruiting and training. Called Additional Companies, these were administrative vehicles to sustain six officers and a cadre of non-commissioned officers, drummers, and soldiers in Great Britain, as well as the recruits that they enlisted. Operationally, the members of the Additional Companies spread out all over Great Britain just as the informal recruiting parties had done in peace time.[25] Newly enlisted men began their training with these recruiting parties, again just as in peace time, but instead of eventually sending the recruits directly to embarkation they were sent to training depots in Chatham outside of London, Portsmouth in the southwest of England, or Cork in Ireland.

At least one Additional Company officer from each regiment was posted at the depot for the supervision and administration of the recruits for his regiment. At the depot the recruits received temporary uniforms consisting of caps, jackets, and trousers. They received arms and accoutrements for the first time, along with training on their handling, care, and maintenance. The men having already learned the basics of martial posture and marching while with the recruiting parties, the depot officers taught them to march in formation and fundamental tactical discipline. Their training regimen continued as new recruits trickled in. Once or twice a year, when enough recruits were at the depot, sufficient shipping was available, and favorable sailing conditions existed, the recruits boarded transports to join their regiments in America.

The precise length of John Robert Shaw's training is difficult to determine because we do not know his exact enlistment date; unfortunately no comprehensive collection of documents exists to reveal this information. The muster rolls that survive show the dates on which men began drawing pay from their parent regiments rather than from the recruiting parties, leaving a difference ranging from weeks to years between the actual enlistment date and the date given on the muster roll. Shaw says only that he enlisted in 1777. He also relates that he embarked from England in time to arrive for an interim stop in Ireland in February 1778; the muster rolls for the 33rd Regiment indicate that he joined on 11 January 1778, a date which correlates roughly to the day of his embarkation in England. He also suggests that he spent many weeks with his recruiting party, had an eight-week furlough to visit his home town, then spent "almost a year" at Chatham. Either he actually enlisted late in 1776 (a distinct possibility given that he relates hearing of the 27 August 1776 battle of Long Island after he had been enlisted for some time) or he overstates the duration of his stay at Chatham. Regardless, Shaw spent approximately a year in training before embarking for America.

The scant records available for other wartime recruits confirm that Shaw's experience was typical enough. Comparing the enlistment dates of 64 wartime recruits for the 22nd Regiment with the muster rolls shows that 22 of them spent over two years in Great Britain before joining the regiment in America, and a further 22 spent one to two years. This leaves only 20 with less than a full year of training before being sent overseas; of those, 15 had five months or more.[26] What this reveals is an army that managed attrition quite well. Going into the conflict as a volunteer force of professional soldiers, wartime expansion and losses were made up not by hastily deployed green recruits but by men methodically trained at least for the basic demands of military service.

John Robert Shaw tells us many remarkable and useful details about the life of a British soldier subsequent to his arrival in America. His enlistment and training experience, however, are what distinguishes his narrative in particular as a first-hand account that supports information in the textbooks, returns, and other documents from the era. The narrative that follows is Shaw's own account of his early life and service as a British soldier, to the point when he left the service during a campaign in America. A few portions have been omitted where Shaw recounts events that he himself did not experience.

The Narrative of John Robert Shaw

I was born on the 19th day of August, 1761, in the town of Manningham,[27] in the parish of Bradford, Yorkshire, Old England. My father was by occupation a stuff weaver, and I was put to the same business at the age of 12 years.

About two years after, I unfortunately formed an acquaintance with a certain Thomas Fields, who used every artifice and device in his power to draw me into vicious company, in order to bring me to ruin, which he too easily effected.

The first "great adventure" in which he engaged me was this: having learned of me that a certain old gentleman, with whom my father was particularly intimate, was in good circumstances, and had always money at command, he addressed me as follows:

"Now, John," says he, "let us go and borrow some money of this man in your father's name."

Accordingly through a long persuasion he prevailed upon me, and putting a plausible story in my mouth, off we went, and borrowed two shillings (sterling).

Being as yet a novice in wickedness, and altogether unpracticed in the profligate ways of the town, I was entirely at a loss, how to dispose of my ill-gotten treasure. But friend Tom soon found the way to the tavern, where to my shame I got drunk for the first time.

"Well, Tom," said I, having somewhat recovered my senses, "what is to be done now? My father, it seems, has discovered my roguery—there he comes."

Poor Tom made no reply, but slipped out the back door like a thief and left me to answer for my misconduct to my father, who led me off by the shoulder like a criminal. This broke the way for my total overthrow.

My next offense was sabbath breaking, to which my father was much opposed, being a strict churchman, and called by his neighbors a sober, moral man.

But as one bad practice generally brings on another, the blush of innocence being worn off, I soon transgressed again, which induced me to apply to my old friend Tom and other new comrades, for advice what to do to avoid the effects of my father's displeasure. Upon this, Tom and Jack immediately proposed that we should all go and enlist for soldiers, get clear of work, and be gentlemen at once. So we all concluded to go and enlist the first opportunity that offered. And lest this should come to my father's ears and I should thus be prevented from accomplishing my design, I determined to lose no time.

Accordingly in a few days I made my escape to a place called Leeds, a considerable town in the west Riding of Yorkshire, and 10 miles from my father's house, where I hoped to be secure and spend my hours more agreeably. But the keeping of bad company is a growing evil, by which my situation was rendered so unpleasant that I began to entertain serious thoughts of returning home, having found by experience that my uncle John Hall's house was not my home. Accordingly I returned to my father, like the repenting prodigal, and lived with him contentedly for some time.

But as old habits are hard to be relenquished, I again relapsed into my former irregularities and grew weary of labor.

In 1777 I ran away a second time, being, as I fancied, ill-treated by my stepmother. Though the true motive for my elopement was this: Early on Monday morning my father went to Bailden mill. He told me before he set off that if I did not finish my last week's work, when he came home he would give me a trimming. This being too hard a task, I put on my best apparel and directed my course to Shipley and thence to Windal to a magician to have my fortune told.

After that I pursued my journey to Coverly; and on Coverly moor I seriously deliberated with myself what was best to be done. At first I thought of returning home again, but the dread of paternal chastisement and the ridicule of my acquaintances, to which I must be exposed in case I came back the second time, banished all thoughts of domestic concerns and firmly fixed my resolution of enlisting as a king's soldier.

So on I went to the place of destination and arrived there late in the evening. No sooner had I entered the town than, to my great joy, I met one of the 33d regiment's recruits, who, when I told him my business, gladly gave me his hand and said, "Come, my fine lad, the king wants soldiers. Come on, my fine boy, I'll show you a place where the streets are paved with pancakes and where the hogs are going through the streets carrying knives and forks on their backs and crying 'Who will come and eat?'"[28]

I accompanied him to the recruiting party's place of rendezvous, at the Sign of the Leopard, behind the Shambles in Bridget Street, and was introduced to the recruiting sergeant, whose name was James Shackleton,[29] and also to the corporal, whose name was Goggell.[30]

Says the sergeant, "Well, my fine lad, will you enlist for a soldier? Where did you come from?"

"I came from Bailden."

"What is your name?"

"My name is John Robert Shaw."

"Are you willing to serve the king?"

"Yes, sir."

"Well, here is a shilling to serve King George III in the honorable 33d regiment of foot, commanded by the honorable Lord Cornwallis, knight and baronet of the star and garter. Well, my lad, you must go to the captain."

So we went to the captain. Says the sergeant, "Here is a young lad who wishes to enlist for a soldier."

"Well, my lad," says the captain, "how old are you?"

"Fifteen or sixteen."

"Well, sergeant, bring the standard."

It was brought, and I measured five feet and one inch, without my shoes.

"Well, my lad," says the captain, "you are too low and under size and I cannot take you. But here is a shilling and I'll give you a new hat and a cockade and a new suit of clothes, and go home and be a good boy and go to school and come to me two or three years hence and I will enlist you."

The name of this generous captain was Carr.[31]

"No," said I, "if you will not take me, I will go and enlist for a drummer in the 59th regiment." For recruits were being taken in at Leeds to fill up that regiment which had been cut off at the battle of Bunker Hill.[32]

"Well, then," said the captain, "since the lad is determined to be a soldier, and appears to be a promising youth, I will take him. Here are three guineas and a crown to drink His Majesty's health. Now my fine lad, be a good boy and I will take you to be my waiter. Sergeant Shackleton, you must take this young soldier under your care, and provide a billet for him, and get him good quarters. And tomorrow go with him to buy such necessities as you think he will stand in need of to make him appear like a gentleman."

"Come on, my fine Bailden lad," says the sergeant. "Come to my quarters."

And when I arrived there among my jolly companions, "Drummer, beat the point of war," was the word. For which a crown bowl of punch was called for to drink His Majesty's health. So we spent that night merrily and all retired to bed at 12 o'clock.

I was put to bed to a naked man, which I thought strange. But this is a common custom with soldiers in order to save their linens, as it is the policy of soldiers to preserve their clothing; for we had to appear three times a day dressed and powdered.[33]

Meanwhile, my absence occasioned a great deal of concern in my father's family, and much solicitude to know what was become of me. It was at length learned that I had gone to enlist for a soldier at Leeds. About two weeks after my elopement my father accompanied by my uncle set out in search of me, and having arrived at the place of rendezvous, inquired for me of the sergeant.

"Would you know your son if you saw him?" said the sergeant.

My father answered in the affirmative.

The reader will please to observe that at the time I was then setting between my father and uncle. "What is your son's name?" asked the sergeant.

"His name is John Robert Shaw from Bailden."

"Well, there he sits between you."

As soon as my father had composed himself, he proposed to me to be bought off and return home, but I obstinately refused it and replied, "If you buy me off today, I will enlist tomorrow for a drummer."

Here I cannot avoid reflecting on the shamefulness of my conduct; and among the numerous errors and improprieties of which I have been guilty this must be considered as none of the least. Ingratitude—that blackest of vices—steels the heart against all noble and exalted emotions and obliterates the finest feelings of the soul.

But to proceed with my narrative—my father finding me inflexibly determined to continue in the army, gave over all entreaties and departed in tears, leaving me to pursue the bent of my inclinations; for my situation, surrounded by giddy, thoughtless wretches like myself, effectually precluded all serious reflection on the improprieties of my conduct.

The next day I was sent with a billet to the Sign of the Cross-keys on Quarry Hill and there treated like a gentleman.

In a few weeks, however, the militia was called to do duty in the town of Leeds, and all the recruiting parties of the different regiments were to be billeted out in the country villages. It fell my lot to go to Bromley, from which once a day I was obliged to go to Leeds in order to march around with the recruiting party and exercise myself in running, jumping and learning to walk straight.

One evening as I was returning to my quarters, having rashly attempted to leap over a fence, I stuck a tenter hook in my leg, which so lacerated the same that I was obliged to hobble back to town as well as I could, where a surgeon was called in to dress the wound. I was then billeted at the Sign of the Eagle and Child in Cawe Lane and there treated very well. But not being satisfied, I was sent to the hospital at the upper end of the town, where having remained for eight weeks, I was discharged by the surgeon and sent with a billet to my old quarters at the Sign of the Cross-Keys on Quarry Hill.

After some time I obtained a furlough for eight weeks to go home to Bailden to visit my father. During this period I became acquainted with one Samuel Crabtree, an old soldier and lately from Minorca. From this man I received great encouragement concerning the military life, and was highly delighted on hearing him recount the particulars of the many sieges and battles in which he had been engaged.

While at Bailden I had frequent visits from several of my relatives and neighbors, all endeavoring to persuade me to be bought off and abandon the army. All their arguments and expostulations were in vain, though my grandfather, who was in tolerable circumstances and willing to assist me in case of good behavior, repeatedly declared that if I persisted in my contumacy, he would leave me only a shilling to buy a halter, as no better fate could be expected by such a graceless and undutiful youth. Yet, regardless of consequences, my resolution remained unshaken. Still I was determined to be a "gentleman soldier."

The term of my furlough being expired, I returned to the recruiting party at Leeds, and was received with expressions of great applause for my constancy.

We afterwards spent a considerable time in recruiting at the country villages, and with a good deal of success. While thus employed we had an account of the battle of Long Island, and of the gallant and soldier-like behavior of the 33d regiment, commanded by Lieutenant Colonel William Webster,[34] for which, as a mark of distinction an additional riband of the orange colour was bestowed: the whole consisting of the red, blue, white and yellow. These colours composed our cockade.[35] Four guineas more were given as a bounty to each recruit, which, with the 3 guineas and a crown, which they received at the time of enlisting, as already mentioned, amounted to seven guineas and a crown.

Shortly after, having gained a sufficient number of recruits, we received orders to march. Accordingly, we marched on through Wakefield, Blackbarnsley, Sheffield, Northampton, Nottingham, and so on to London.

We halted a few days in London in order to take some refreshments, for there was a Yorkshire man in the city, who made it a constant rule to treat all the Yorkshire recruits enlisted for the 33d regiment, having himself been an old soldier, and served the king in that regiment formerly in Flanders. So we all ate and drank heartily, and parted with our generous host in high spirits, and marched on to Greenwich, about five miles east from London, where we remained for three days, and viewed the curiosities of the place.

Among these nothing so much engaged my attention and commanded my admiration as the Royal Hospital.[36] It was formerly a royal palace, built by Humphrey, duke of Gloucester, enlarged by Henry VII, and completed by Henry VIII. The later often made this his place of residence, as also did the queens, Mary and Elizabeth, who were born in it. It was greatly improved and embellished by Charles II, who spent 36,000 pounds on that part of it which is now the first wing of the hospital toward London.

King William III, in 1694, granted it, "with nine acres of ground thereto belonging, to be converted into a royal hospital for old and disabled seamen, the widows and children of those who lost their lives in the service, and for the encouragement of navigation." Upwards of 2,000 old disabled seamen are maintained in this hospital—they are vulgarly called the king's beef eaters. The buildings are undoubtedly the finest in the world.

From Greenwich there is a fine view of the city of London, and the Thames with the shipping of almost all nations. The royal observatory commands a most delightful prospect—charming indeed beyond description.

Having spent our limited time in amusing ourselves with the curiosities of the place, we marched on to Chatham barracks, the finest garrison in old England. Chatham is the principal station of the royal navy and the yards and magazines are furnished with all sorts of naval stores, as well as materials for building the largest ships of war. Here are at least 1,000 ship carpenters working every day. They work 12 hours in a day, i.e., from 6 o'clock in the morning until 6 in the evening. Everything here is conducted with the utmost regularity.

We were now in barrack quarters, 16 or 20 privates in a room, with a sergeant to keep good order, and purchase provisions, and see it divided, when cooked and prepared according to the laws of the place.

Four pence a day for each private soldier are laid out for provisions at market; a half-penny to the doctor; the same to the chaplain and a penny for clothing; the whole pay of a soldier being six pence per day, with the queen's bounty of 19 shillings a year, and a complete suit of clothes consisting of 1 hat, 1 vest, 1 pair of breeches, 1 shirt, 1 pair of shoes, 1 pair of stockings, and 1 stock and stock buckle.

While we lay at Chatham, we were constantly exercising and learning the military evolutions under corporal Coggell, whose experience and skill in such matters were equalled by few in the army. There were 19 in number in the 33d regiment, who after only six months practice, challenged the whole garrison to contend with them in military discipline.

The garrison then consisted of 80 additional companies,[37] besides the first regiment of the Royal Scotch, (as they were called) who had been in practice for many years.[38]

A review of clothing was then and probably yet in practice every Monday morning: each soldier on the parade, with his knapsack on his back, and his firelock and accoutrements in complete order[39]—drums beating and colours flying; and to crown the whole the instrument called the cat and nine tails tipt with brass wire and constantly displayed.[40] The review being ended, if any clothing is missing, a circle is formed, and a drumhead court martial is called and the delinquent is tried and punished according to his desert.

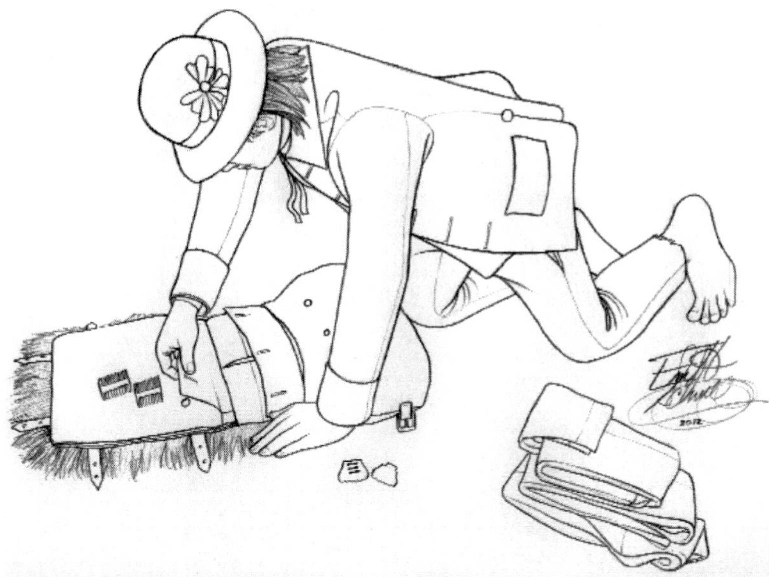

John Robert Shaw enlisted in England for a regiment that was in America. He spent months with the recruiting party in Yorkshire before being sent to join his regiment, a common experience for recruits in peacetime as well as wartime. The recruiting party provided enlistees with shoes, stockings, shirts, neck stocks, a military cockade for the hat, and items for neatly dressing the hair such as combs and ribbon ties. Sometimes spatterdashes were included to keep debris out of the low-topped military shoes. The recruit received a knapsack to carry these goods. Besides these items, he wore his civilian clothing unless parts of it were unserviceable, in which case more suitable garments were provided. Maintaining proper dress was part of his initial instruction in hygiene and military bearing.

In this illustration, a recruit wears mostly his own clothing while exploring the knapsack and other items provided by the army. His personal hat bears a cockade of colored ribbons as described in Shaw's narrative and depicted in period artwork portraying recruits, quite different from the black cockade that was part of the regimental uniform. The canvas knapsack is covered with hair-on goat skin for waterproofing. Two combs, a set of brass clasps for a neck stock, and a quantity of shirts and stockings will find places in the knapsack that already bulges with a pair of shoes that the recruit has yet to try on. This recruit's hair is not yet long enough to dress in a military style.

After lying in Chatham barracks almost a year, a draught was made, and four hundred of us deluded out under the pretense of doing duty at Portsmouth. The next morning a sergeant was dispatched to prepare the barracks, as we supposed, for our reception. We accordingly marched on to Portsmouth in good spirits, hoping to spend a few happy years in that place.

But how great was our disappointment when we arrived at Portsmouth and found the streets lined with old pensioners to guard us safe on board a ship![41] The boats were ready to convey us all on board of the ship *None-such,* which then lay at anchor in the port. The cries and lamentations of the poor, raw country soldiers were sufficient to have excited the compassion in the breast of the rudest barbarians; and, as for myself, I thought I was going to the Devil, when they rolled us down the hatchways like so much lumber.[42]

Having each received some bedding and an allowance of provisions, we lay promiscuously, and crowded together in the utmost confusion. The next day we weighed anchor and sailed for the Isle of Wight, where we lay four weeks; after which we set sail for Ireland, favoured at first with a pleasant breeze; but we had not been sailing more than 12 hours, before we were surprised with a thunderstorm and a contrary wind.

It was, I think, about 11 O'clock at night, when a man on the forecastle espied a rock, close ahead of the ship; upon which he called out to the steerman at the helm, "about ship"; which was done with all possible speed and so by the skill and dexterity of the mariners & the mercy of Providence, we were preserved from being wrecked on the rocks of Scilly.

Thus extricated from danger, we proceeded on our voyage and soon anchored in the harbour called the Cove of Cork, which is perhaps the most spacious and commodious haven in the world. The entrance is safe, and the whole navy of England might ride in it, secure from every wind that blows. Ships from England, bound for all parts of the West Indies, take in here a great deal of their provisions; and for the same purpose the Cove of Cork is visited by the vessels of many other nations.

Ships of burthen, however, are obliged to unload at a place called Passage, five miles and a half from the city, the channel not admitting vessels of above 150 tons. This port we entered in the beginning of February, 1778, and were all separated and put on board of different vessels.

It fell my lot to go on board the *Alexandria* of 24 guns; and she was called "a letter of marque."[43] There were 19 Englishmen and six Irishmen who were brought on board in irons, and 24 Hessians, making in all 49 in number, to do duty as marines. Our ship's crew consisted of 60 able-bodied seamen, besides officers, one captain, 1st, 2nd, and 3d mates, one boatswain, one carpenter and a cook and cook's mate.

A fleet of transports then lay in the Cove of Kinsale repairing their rigging, and embarking provisions for America. Kinsale, especially in time of war, is a place of much business, and frequented by rich, homeward bound fleets, as also by ships of war. The cove is a convenient and beautiful harbour, and lies about seven miles from the city of Cork.

The town is defended by a strong fort called Charles's Fort; and on the opposite shore there are two villages called Cove and Scilly; the inhabitants of which are generally native Irish and live in low built houses, made of mud, on a beautiful eminence, ranging with the barracks, and facing the inlet of the harbour. The barracks are capable of lodging and containing 12 companies of foot, besides a regiment at Charles's Fort. The garrison, however, then consisted of only four companies, with 16 or 20 pieces of cannon, and deemed sufficient to protect the town and harbour.

We lay eight weeks on board before we were ready to sail, during which time we were visited by the bomb ketches,[44] in order to sell and buy all sorts of necessities; for we had no liberty to go on shore, except two men at a time. We weighed anchor April 7th in company with upwards of 20 transports, (besides two letters of marque) laden with provisions, as well as men to assist in carrying on the unjust and unhappy war against the American colonies.

We met with nothing extraordinary during the voyage; only we were born off our course on the roads of certain islands, which I think belonged to Portugal, where we got in exchange for such necessities as we could spare, oranges, coconuts and pineapples. Continuing our voyage from thence, we arrived safely in America, and landed on Rhode Island, in the space of three months from the time of our setting sail from the coast of Ireland.

We remained on Rhode Island doing duty, while the British army were on their march from Philadelphia.

I joined the 33d regiment on Long Island at Graves-ends; and then we marched to Bedford,[45] where we lay until the beginning of autumn, when a detachment was called out to perform, as we supposed, some great exploit.[46] This detachment consisted of the 33d and 42nd regiments, with two companies of the body guards,[47] commanded by the colonels Webster and Frazer.[48] We went on board the flat bottomed boats just as it began to grow dark, and pursued our expedition, and landed on the beach about four miles from Elizabethtown point, with our pilot, or guide, as we thought.

We had marched a mile through the marsh before we discovered the trick;—our pilot had left us in the snare; sometimes up to the middle in mud and water; sometimes over head and ears in the ditches, crawling over one another in the greatest confusion.

At length with much difficulty we made our appearance near Elizabethtown just at daybreak, in woeful pickle, all bedaubed with mud and mire, as black as chimney sweepers; we looked more like frightening the people of the town than making them run for fear of the sword and bayonet. In this plight we advanced up to the town and took it.

And as a further instance of British inhumanity, the barracks were set on fire and burnt down with about ten or twelve poor sick soldiers in them.[49]

This being the day the continental troops were to draw their provisions, the English officers called on the bakers for their bread, but the bakers very boldly answered: "this bread is for gentlemen and not for you d——d bloody backs." Bread was therefore taken by force.

We then marched on to form a line between the river and the town, leaving two companies for a rear guard; but the Americans being reenforced with 4,000 troops, got between us and the river; now who dare say the English never turned their backs, or fled from an enemy? Colonel Webster was, it is true, for charging on the enemy, but Colonel Frazer, who was the oldest officer, and had the command, gave orders to face to the right, and make the best of our way to the boats.

That moment the enemy fired with their artillery, and killed two men of Captain Campbell's company, of the 33d regiment, whose names were Proctor and Keith;[50] and according to our colonel's account, these men "died in glory." And so, pursuant to our orders, we took to our heels and made our way to the boats in the utmost disorder.

The bakers of Elizabethtown had now the satisfaction of seeing the English scattering and leaving behind them the bread which they had forcibly taken away at the point of a bayonet. On this occasion, we had two killed, as already mentioned, two wounded, and five taken prisoner; besides a considerable number wounded as we made our escape from the East River.

We hurried down with all possible speed, landed at Brooklyn ferry opposite to New York, and proceeded on to Bedford and lay there for some time.

Not long after, an army was called forth to go on an expedition up the East River.[51] We all embarked and sailed some distance above Bedford, where we landed, marched to the town, plundered and burned it, with all the shipping in the harbour. Such predatory excursions, of which this is but a small specimen, reflect dishonor on the British name, and consign the reputation of the British officers who conducted them to eternal infamy.

The next day we marched into the country without opposition, except for a few of the militia who brought on a skirmish; but they were soon dispersed, and we proceeded on our march without further interruption. In this excursion, among other plunder, we took a store of molasses, the hogsheads being rolled out and their heads knocked in, a soldier's wife went to dip her camp kettle in a hogshead of molasses, and while she was stooping in order to fill her kettle, a soldier slipped behind her and threw her into the hogshead; when she was hauled out, a bystander then threw a parcel of feathers on her, which adhering to the molasses made her appear frightful enough. This little circumstance afforded us a good deal of amusement.

We then returned to our ships, well satisfied with our booty, and soon arrived at our former quarters on Long Island.

A few weeks after this, a most inhuman massacre took place near Tappan in New Jersey.[52] A farmer and his son living near each other, it happened that a small regiment of light horse (raised a short time before in Virginia and known by the name of Lady Washington's regiment)[53] quartered at their houses and barns in number about 300; the son being a true born American and the father a detestable tory; the latter went to New York and gave information of those unhappy soldiers, and offered to lead us to the place where they lay.

Accordingly General Grey undertook the barbarous task, and ordered out 1,000 troops, marching them one half to the right and the other to the left, with this hard-hearted tory and one of his associates to pilot us to the unhappy spot, where the shocking scene commenced.

When the advanced guard came up to the yard gate, the sentry was asleep. One of the officers of the grenadiers instantly cut off his head, without a word. The 33d regiment, to which I belonged, was about three miles off when the cruel carnage began; but as we approached, the shrieks and screams of the hapless victims whom our savage fellow soldiers were butchering, were sufficient to have melted into compassion the heart of a Turk or a Tartar.

Tongue cannot tell nor pen unfold the horrors of that dismal night. Some were seen having their arms cut off, and others with their bowels hanging out crying for mercy.

To preserve, however, some appearance of clemency, 43 were admitted prisoners of war; seven of the whole regiment, being out reconnoitering, escaped. The killed and wounded amounted to 250. How destitute of natural affection must have been the heart of the father, who could invite an enemy to murder his own son in cold blood!

And how contrary to the principles of honor it was in the enemy to accept such invitation![54] Let Britain boast no more of her honour, her science and civilization; but with shame hide her head in the dust; her fame is gone; Tappan will witness against her. Having performed this ignoble exploit, the few prisoners that were spared being conducted to New York by a guard of British soldiers, and the wounded sent off in wagons, we returned to Long Island to be ready for another scene of British barbarity.

In 1779 we marched up the North River to Verplanck's Neck, commonly called the King's ferry. There was a bombproofed blockhouse in the fort,[55] which mounted two sixpounders[56] opposite to Stony Point. The fort at Verplanck's stood on the east side of the river, where were stationed the 33d regiment, colonel Robertson's corps,[57] colonel Fannen's corps,[58] and major Ferguson's rifle company,[59] making in all about 700 rank and file, able-bodied fighting men, commanded by lieutenant colonel Webster.

We formed a blockhouse one mile from the fort, on a piece of rising ground. This blockhouse mounted two three-pounders, and was well set with pickets,[60] and commanded by one captain, one lieutenant, one ensign, two sergeants, four corporals, with a drummer and fifer, and fifty private soldiers, with a picket 100 yards in front,[61] the guard consisting of one sergeant, one corporal and twelve privates, forming a line of four sentinels.

When this was completed, a range of batteries were erected, with two blockhouses, one on the right and the other on the left side of the batteries, so as to command both the land and the river. These works mounted six six-pounders and one long 18-pounder, with a great deal of swivels.[62] There was a deep ditch in front of the works with three rows of abatis 40 yards apart,[63] and three large piles of tar barrels between the rows of abatis, where stood a man with a slow match ready[64] to set fire at the approach of the enemy.

During the building of these fortifications, the regulation was, one half on duty and the other on fatigue. While we continued there, which was nearly four months, we generally lay at night with our accoutrements on and with our firelocks in our arms.

Stony Point was a strong post on the west side of the river, nearly opposite to Verplanck's. The works had been completed and repaired with the utmost assiduity; so that they were now in a very strong state of defense, and were garrisoned by the 17th regiment of foot, one company of the 71st regiment of grenadiers, and a part of Fannen's corps, the whole being commanded by lieutenant colonel Johnson.[65]

General Wayne paid a visit to Stony Point about 12 o'clock at night; and first from the picket a running fire was heard, which occasioned some alarm. A general silence followed for some time, during which the American officers held a council; and the English soldiers were dismissed to their tents.[66]

But woe to the simple commander of Stony Point! When that undaunted hero general Wayne tickled their ears with "Remember the Paoli and the massacre of Lady Washington's light horse at the Tappan." The grenadiers, in particular, of the 71st regiment, made for a while a gallant defense.

But neither the formidable rows of abatis nor the strong works in front and flank could damp the ardour of the American troops, who, in the face of an incessant and tremendous fire of musquetry, and cannon loaded with grape shot, broke their way through every obstacle until the van of each column met in the center of the fortress and obliged the surviving part of the garrison, amounting to upwards of 500 men, to surrender themselves prisoners at discretion.

But let us pass over to our side of the river at Verplanck's—there you will not find a colonel Johnson, lying smug in his tent as at Stony Point; but you will find old colonel Webster, the Scotchman, ready cut and dry for you when the action commenced at the opposite fort. Four men out of each company turned out for a reserve guard, to receive the enemy when they should come across the river, as we expected nothing else but to be engaged front and rear at once; for we soon found Stony Point was taken, by their turning their artillery against us at Verplanck's, and commencing a dreadful cannonade, which necessarily obliged the shipping that lay in the river, to cut their cable and sail down.

But the Yankee army lay in our front eating molasses instead of attacking us.

Two or three days after this, the Americans commenced the evacuation of Stony Point, by destroying the works, dismounting the cannon, and removing their military stores and prisoners of war.

Among the number of vessels that came to carry off the booty was a row-galley laden with cannon and other stores, on our side of the river. Against this galley we directed our artillery, and poured in a volley of grape and chain shot,[67] which obliged the officers on board to desist from loading any further, and finding it impracticable to save the vessel, they spiked their cannon,[68] and set fire to the galley which having burned to the water sunk with her cargo to the bottom.

The balance of the military stores were conveyed to West Point and the troops withdrawn. In ten days we also evacuated our fortress at Verplanck's and withdrew our troops to New York.

We lay that winter at a place called the Narrows on Long Island until Christmas Day, when an expedition was undertaken by Sir Henry Clinton and Admiral Arbuthnot, against Charleston in South Carolina; as the conquest of the southern colonies was not meditated and considered as impracticable.

Our shipping lay on East River with the troops on board until the breaking of the ice, when several regiments were in the most imminent danger of being lost, particularly the 42nd, who were driven ashore with eight or ten ships, great and small. It was sometime in the spring before we could proceed in our voyage, being prevented by rough seas and tempestuous weather.

We set sail in very low spirits—our prospects were gloomy indeed—the very elements seemed to conspire against us, and threaten us with destruction. The distance between New York and Charleston is sailed in two weeks; but we were eight weeks on the passage.

The ship on which I was, being accidentally separated from the fleet in a storm, we were all in danger of being lost. The tempest blew with violence for about six hours. We had 400 soldiers on board, and by the heaving and rolling of the ship, all the beds in which we lay broke loose from the sides of the vessel to which they were fastened, and the ship was so agitated by the wind and waves that she changed her position, so that our gunnels ran under water, and the guns on the same side broke loose on the quarterdeck.

The storm, however, having somewhat abated, we refreshed ourselves and cheered our hearts with a good can of grog, and pursued our voyage, hoping the worst was over and that we should soon get in sight of the fleet. But alas! all our pleasing expectations were frustrated; for after sailing a considerable time, we lost all hopes of ever coming up with the fleet.

A quarrel took place between some of the land and sea officers and a fight ensued in which the fire fell into the steerage and communicated into the hold, from which the smoke was immediately perceived to issue in curling volumes so that we expected every minute to be blown up. In this critical and perilous situation the cries of the women and children were truly distressing;[69] and to render our danger still greater we were again assailed with a violent squall; the waves rose like mountains and threatened to overwhelm us; the ocean seemed to open its bosom to receive us; the swelling surges broke in upon us until we had five feet of water in the hold; our pumps were choked, and for a while refused to perform their office. Our condition was desperate.

But it pleased God to prolong our existence,—the fire was extinguished; and by repeated attempts and strenuous exertions we at length brought the pumps to work; the tempest ceased and we continued on our voyage, still hoping to come up with the fleet. Many a tedious hour did I sit on the foretop, eagerly casting my eyes around to see if I could anywhere descry a sail.

At length the wished for moment arrived; we espied our fleet and soon joined it with joyful acclamations. The signal was given for the different captains to go on board of the Convoy,[70] and a general invitation on board of the admiral's ship, where a concert of music was held, and the soldiers and sailors got a double allowance of rum to banish sorrow and exhilerate their spirits.

We soon came in sight of land and took possession of St. John Island near Charleston; 5,000 men were sent forward to erect a right and left hand battery of 24 guns each. This was accomplished the first night; and a centre battery the second night.

An entrenchment was likewise dug in such a direction as to have a communication from right to left; during which operation we were played on by the batteries in the front of the town, by a well-directed fire of grape, round and chain shot, with a great number of bomb shells.[71] There was one line of batteries after another until we came close to the canal; so that I have stood many a time on one side of the canal, while the American sentinel was directly opposite to me on the other side.

Though the offensive operations of the siege was conducted with great spirit and success, yet the town had still kept up a communication with the country on the farther side of Cooper River, and some bodies of militia, cavalry and infantry began to assemble on the higher part of that river, who, by keeping possession of the bridges might, at least, by cutting off supplies and molesting our foraging parties, have considerably retarded and disturbed the operation of our army.

To dislodge these troops, our general, as soon as his situation would permit, detached the 33d and 23d regiments and Tarletons' light horse,[72] in all about 1,400 men, under the command of lt. colonel Webster. We came on the enemy by surprise in the night, at Monk's corner, and bloody work we had: being however victorious, we succeeded in our object of effectually stopping up the pass.[73]

We remained at Monk's corner until the capitulation of general Lincoln,[74] after which we marched for Camden under the command of general Cornwallis and Lord Rawdon, with 1,500 effective infantry and 150 cavalry. When we arrived at Camden, a detachment was ordered to Ninety Six; but it fell to my lot to continue at Camden, where I fell sick for the first and last time, that is, with common sickness; for I have been oftentimes indisposed with the bottle fever, and by wounds, bruises, and broken bones, and such like accidents.

While we continued at Camden we fared pretty well; only General (Horatio) Gates advanced to disturb our repose; and having encamped at a place called Ruggles, about 13 miles from Camden, he sent us word that "he would eat his dinner in Camden or in hell the next day." His forces were vastly superior to ours, at least in numbers, being computed at 5,000 to 6,000 men; the greater number of these consisted of militia, on whom little dependence could be placed.

Having received intelligence that general Gates had encamped in a bad situation, Lord Cornwallis mustered his troops and harangued them in words nearly to this effect:

"Now, my brave soldiers, now an opportunity is offered for displaying your valour, and sustaining the glory of British arms;—all you who are willing to face your enemies;—all you who are ambitious of military fame stand forward; for their are eight or ten to one coming against; let the men who cannot bear the smell of gunpowder stand back and all you who are determined to conquer or die turn out."

Accordingly we all turned out except a few who were left to guard the sick and military stores. We marched out of Camden about 10 o'clock at night, August 15, 1780; it being the intention of our general to surprise the enemy in his quarters at Ruggles.

But in this we were disappointed, for Gen. Gates had set out about the same hour, in hopes to surprise us at Camden. We came up with their advanced party about seven miles from Camden, when the light troops and advanced guards on each side necessarily engaged each other in the dark. In this blind encounter, the American cavalry being driven back on the van, occasioned some disorder in their ranks; and having thus repelled them, we were eager for a general engagement; but Lord Cornwallis finding that the enemy were on bad ground, was unwilling to hazard in the dark the advantages which their situation would afford him in the light.

We then lay on our arms until daybreak, when both armies formed their lines, and approached within 100 yards of each other, and the Americans gave the first fire, which killed and wounded nearly one half of our number. We returned the fire and immediately charged on them with the bayonet. The action became general along the lines, and was supported with great obstinacy. The haziness of the morning prevented the ascent of the smoke, which occasioned such a thick cloud that it was difficult to observe the effects of a well supported fire on both sides.

It was discoverable, however, that the British troops were pushing forward and the Americans giving way; and after an obstinate resistance, for about three-quarters of an hour, the latter were thrown into confusion. We then opened to the right and left and let Tarleton's light horse pass through. Victory declared in our favor.

We took 900 prisoners and more are said to have been killed and wounded, but the precise number probably never ascertained. All their artillery amounting to 10 or 11 brass field pieces, with about 2,000 stands of arms, six stands of colours and all their baggage waggons, to the number of 150 fell into our hands. The whole body of the militia (which constituted, as I have observed, the greater part of General Gates force) with the exception of only one North Carolina regiment, took to their heels the first fire, and though their general did all in his power to rally them, he could not persuade them to make a single stand, and so getting to the woods as fast as they could, they totally dispersed, leaving the continental regular troops to oppose the whole force of the British army.

It was a hard-fought battle, and the victory not very cheaply purchased on the side of the British; for even in one regiment (the 33d to which I belonged) not less than 116 out of 240 were killed and wounded.[75] The whole loss may be estimated between 300 and 400 killed, wounded and missing; among these were several brave officers.

Lt. Col. Tarleton who had distinguished himself in this battle, was detached the next day with his cavalry, and the light infantry of the 23d regiment, called the English Fusiliers,[76] in pursuit of General Sumter, who had retreated with a body of Americans and some cannon.

General Sumter, it seems, confiding in his distance from the enemy, was surprised in the middle of the day on the 18th of August, as his men were engaged in getting peaches in an orchard not far from the Catawba Fords. Sumter himself having taken a number of tories, with a hogshead of rum and some provisions which they were carrying to the English army, was employed in dealing out the liquor, and was generous enough to give a gill to each prisoner, when Tarleton came upon him, killed 150 of his men and took 300 of them prisoners, with two pieces of cannon and several wagons.

The prisoners were conducted to Camden, and there treated with civility, and from thence they were sent off to Charleston under a guard of mounted infantry; but several of them were rescued by their countrymen before they could be carried to Charleston.

We lay in Camden until our wounded recovered, and then we marched on to Salisbury in North Carolina in close pursuit of the enemy, who had abandoned the town, leaving only a few sick tories in jail to die for want of water; and all the provisions they had were a few pounds of salt beef. We were detained a few days in Salisbury in order to procure some provisions.

Had it not been for this delay, we might probably have overtaken general Morgan, and retaliated upon him for Tarleton's defeat, and rescued the prisoners taken at the Cowpens....[77] This defeat was very mortifying to Lord Cornwallis; and I myself was an eyewitness when at the first interview between him and Tarleton, the account of the disaster brought tears from Cornwallis's eyes; lamenting, no doubt, the loss of so many brave soldiers.

The Cowpens prisoners were pushed off toward Winchester in Virginia, and we pursued in hopes of overtaking Morgan before he crossed the Yadkin river, a few miles from Salisbury; but in this we were deceived, as we had been before in several of our bad undertakings.

We then returned back some distance and took a route by the Moravian towns, and encamped one night on a rising ground contiguous to one of these towns, the inhabitants of which were very generous in rolling out their whiskey barrels to make us drunk. The Moravians were always suspected of being tories, but on this occasion, we had reason to think differently, by their liberality in furnishing us so abundantly with spiritous liquors, as all the world knows that a soldier's chief delight is in drinking. And, I believe, had the Americans been vigilant, they would have succeeded in their insidious design, for it is my candid opinion that there were not fifty sober men among us, for it was a very rainy night and we had suffered for want of drink, as well as through fatigue.

But we fortunately escaped being discovered, and lay there secure for some time. We next directed our march toward Charlotte, and coming within two miles of the town, the enemy formed a line of battle; but we advanced on them and they retreated; and a running fight ensued, until we came to the town, where they made a stand for a while, but we rushed on them with the bayonet, and they again retreated. We pursued them for about 7 miles; but they were too swift on foot for us; so finding that we could not come up with them, we returned back to Charlotte.

The next day a guard was sent to Rigley's Mills in order to do duty there and I turned baker for the guard (and a little for myself).[78]

We continued there for some time—but now comes the trouble—the enemy got a reenforcement of 3,000 or 4,000 men and we had to run back faster than we came. We made our retreat like lost sheep, not knowing where to go, no forage, no provisions for our men, though marching day and night. At this time I saw an English guinea offered for a bit of cornbread not larger than my two fingers. Hard times with us indeed—16 days without a morsel of bread.

In this starving condition we made our retreat to Wynnesborough, 40 miles from Camden, where we fixed our winter quarters and sent to Camden for provisions which soon were brought us by water, and then we fared sumptuously; being plentifully supplied with all sorts of provisions, and having our back rations paid up.

In relating the various incidents of my life, I should deem myself guilty of an unpardonable omission, were I to pass on without mentioning the circumstances of a fist fight, which I had when we were quartered in Wynnesborough and the first that I ever had since I came to the years of discretion.

There was a certain Bill Airton,[79] a butcher, who was a mess mate of mine, and had often endeavored to provoke me to a fight; but as I always considered him a stouter man than myself, and being besides unacquainted with the art of boxing (as it is called) I had constantly declined his invitations, and endeavored to keep clear of all private quarrels.

It happened, however, one day, when myself and several of my companions made a fire before our wigwam,[80] that Mr. Airton, who had been absent while the fuel was gathering, came up to the fire, and in a very abrupt manner says to me, "Shaw, d—-n you stand back, you have no right here, d—-n you, stand back." Giving me at the same time such a blow to the eye as made my head sing psalms for some time.

The sergeant then coming up, and, understanding the circumstances, says, "Shaw, you must fight and whip him or else

I will whip you." So we buckled to it in our buff; and having a good second helped the cause very much on my side; for a good officer makes a good soldier. Inspired with confidence through the encouragement of the sergeant, I soon gave Mr. Airton an Irishman's coat of arms, i.e., two black eyes and a bloody nose, which made him a good friend ever after.

Poor John and the butcher then stript to their buffs,
Fell to work and engaged in what's called fisticuffs;
And so the big butcher that would be a brawling
And picking a quarrel, at last got a mauling.

It was early in the spring (1781) before we set out; and then we took our route to Hillsborough where we set up the royal standard; and our general by a proclamation invited all loyal subjects to repair to it and assist in restoring order and government. But though we had been led to believe that the king had many friends in that part of the country, yet the event did not answer our expectations. The royalists were but few, and most of them too timid to join the king's standard. A part of them, indeed, under the command of a certain colonel Pyle, had set out with a view of joining us at Hillsborough; but they were accidentally met by a detachment of the American army and most of them cut off.[81]

We staid at Hillsborough about a week and all got completely shod. We left town in the night and made a movement toward the Haw River, marching by the way of the Rocky Ford.

We came up with the enemy by the river side, and having formed a line, we exchanged a few shots, and then advanced to give them the bayonet; but they retreated and crossed the river, and then we had a standing fight; and though we had orders not to cross the river, yet the front line consisting of the 33d, 23d and 71st regiments, the Irish volunteers,[82] and the Yagers,[83] under Lord Rawdon, would not be stopped by anything.

So we crossed the Rocky Ford, and hot works we had; but we beat them off and formed a line on the same side of the river which they had occupied and soon put them to flight and pursued them for 14 miles, until we lost sight of them.

We then directed our march toward Guilford Courthouse and halted about three or four miles from town. At this time the scarcity of provisions was so great that we had but one pound of flour for six men per day with very little beef and no salt the half of the time.

With this allowance, my mess mates and I made two meals a day, which we managed by first boiling the beef, and then taking it out and having mixed our pound of flour with some water we put it into the kettle in which the beef had been boiled; and when sufficiently heated, we took it off the fire and let it stand until it cooled. This served us for breakfast and the beef we kept for dinner; and as for supper we were obliged to do without it.

On one occasion, the officers, having by some means neglected to put out sentinels on guard for three hours together, impelled by hunger we took the blessed opportunity of going out in search of something to satisfy our craving appetite.

A soldier of the 23d by the name of Tattesdell[84] and myself made a push for the country. We had not gone above a mile until we came to a house in hopes to get something to eat; but the house was already full of soldiers upon the same business; and I heard the woman of the house crying, "I will go and tell your officers."

Upon hearing these words, my comrade and I proceeded forward about three or four miles, until we came to a fine, open plantation, and an elegant framed house belonging to a major Bell of the American army. So we entered the house, where we found an old lady and her two daughters—we saluted them with as much politeness as our awkward manners would admit of; and the old lady very civily asked us to sit down.

We soon told her our business, that we wanted some flour; upon which she immediately filled our knapsacks; and invited us to stay until something could be made ready, which invitation we readily accepted; and I very well remember that I got some of the best Johnny-cake I ever ate in my life.[85]

While we were partaking of the delicious repast, for to us it was truly delicious, a conversation arose.

Says the old lady, "Now if you will go with what you have gotten, and join our boys, I will give you my two daughters, and a complete suit of clothes apiece."

"But," we argued, "the bad consequences of desertion, that it was death by the law, and that even if we could bring ourselves to act so dishonourable a part as to desert our colours, yet death by shooting or hanging was a thing not much to be desired."

But by the bye, I must inform the reader that for my part, if I could have entertained the smallest hopes of succeeding in gaining the affections of either of the young ladies, so lovely were they in my eyes, I would cheerfully have hazarded my life and taken the old lady at her word; for I thought them the most beautiful creatures my eyes ever beheld.

But as such good fortune was not to be expected, and we had no time to delay, my comrade and I, after we had finished our meal, took our leave of the old lady, thanking her for her charity, and immediately departed.

Scarcely had we gone half way up the lane when seven of Lee's light horse[86] made their appearance; my companion swore there was Tarleton's light horse coming, and, says he, "we shall be taken up on suspicion of plundering and get 500 lashes apiece."

"No," said I, upon observing their brown coats and white cockades, "no, my friend, you are deceived; these must be the rebels."

Having therefore discovered his mistake, he began to cry;—but for my part, I thought it very good fortune. As they were advancing toward us, we concluded to go and meet them; which we did, and falling on our knees, begged for quarter, which they granted us and said, "Come on, we will give you good quarters."

And so on we went past the house that had betrayed us—it was fine fun for the old lady to see how handsomely she had tricked us.

They brought us on a short distance beyond major Bell's, and there were Washington and Lee's light horse and Morgan's riflemen. These officers examined us as to the strength of Cornwallis's army and sent us under general guard to general Greene's encampment, and while the guard were conducting us thither, they suffered one of Morgan's subaltern[87] officers to strip us; against which conduct we remonstrated, my observing that no British officer would permit a continental soldier to be stripped while a prisoner of war.

But we were obliged to submit, for the officer drew his sword and swore if we did not comply he would run us through. So they took our clothes, not leaving us even our leggings or shoes; and God knows, they wanted them badly; for such ragged mortals I never saw in my life before, to pass under the character of soldiers.

We were then brought to the camp on the 11th day of March, 1781, and after being reexamined by General Greene, we were sent to the provost, where we found about 30 fellow prisoners who had been taken on straggling parties. From thence we were sent to Halifax courthouse, where we remained until after the battle of Guilford, which took place the 15th of March, and was one of the hardest fought battles that ever happened in America....[88] The British general remained master of the field, and consequently claimed the victory. But it was a dear bought victory; for the loss on the side of the British, according to the account of Lord Cornwallis himself, was 532 killed, wounded and missing. Several of their bravest officers fell in the action, and amongst the rest, my good old colonel Webster received a mortal wound—he was as gallant an officer as ever drew the sword—I served in his regiment five years and some months.[89]

General Greene, in the account he sent to congress stated the loss of the continental forces at 329 killed, wounded and missing; in which number, however, the loss of the militia was not included; it amounts to upwards of 100.

In this battle a few prisoners were taken by the Americans, and sent forward to join us at Halifax courthouse; and in a short time we were marched on to Winchester in Virginia, where we joined the Cowpens prisoners, and were put into barracks a few miles from the town, under a strong guard.

Here we suffered much: our houses had no covering to shelter us from the inclemency of the weather; and we were exposed to cold, hunger and want of clothing; and all manner of ill treatment, insult and abuse.

Having thus, for a considerable time (I cannot say with the patience of Job) endured many hardships, we formed a project for our escape, by means of one of the guard, who agreed for three half joes[90] to conduct us to New York. The time and mode of elopement being fixed upon, we parted with our uniforms and put ourselves in disguise ready for the journey.[91]

But when the appointed hour arrived, we found ourselves deceived by the fellow's wilful neglect in fulfilling his promise, but what better could we expect from a tory and traitor. He that would turn tory is worse than a devil; for, be the devil as bad as he may be is still said to be true to his party.

So we had to continue in our confinement as refugees. But some time in the summer, we were ordered to be ready to march at a moment's warning; and soon after a new guard was appointed to conduct us to Lancaster in Pennsylvania.

The cruelty of this new guard exceeded anything we had yet seen; their conduct was indeed shameful and altogether incompatible with the profession of either soldiers or christians; they drove us like so many bullocks to the slaughter.

Scarcely had we advanced three miles before the captain broke his broad sword by cutting and slashing the prisoners, who were too much weakened by hunger and former ill treatment to keep up in the march. The lieutenant, a snotty-nosed stripling, just from the chimney corner, came up, raging like a madman, with his small sword in his hand, and pushed it with such violence into the back of one of my fellow prisoners, that he broke it in the wound, where it remained until one of his comrades pulled it out.

Now such dastardly conduct towards poor prisoners of war, who had no weapon to defend themselves, was a disgrace, even to chimney-corner officers. However, we marched along as well as we could, consoling ourselves with the hopes of being delivered one day or other from such cruel bondage.

We came to a place where there was a mill turned by a stream, the source of which was not more than 100 yards above the mill;—here we expected to draw some provisions, but were sadly disappointed, as we had been three days without any, and through perfect weakness, I trembled like a patient in a severe fit of the ague. All we drew was but one ear of corn per man, and this was a sweet morsel to us; we softened it in water, and grated it on the lid of our camp kettle and made bread of it.

This we did until we came to Fredericktown barracks, where we drew provisions, and found the people more hospitable and kind; many of them having experienced the hardships and calamities of war; and at the same time they had several of their friends and relatives, then prisoners with the English, and suffering much greater hardships than I ever experienced while a prisoner with the Americans.

But it is natural for every man to think his own case the hardest; and though of ill usage I had my share, yet I enjoyed the fresh air, while thousands of soldiers lay languishing and dying in loathsome prison ships, stinking jails, and dark dungeons, deprived of the privilege of the fresh air, necessary to preserve health; and even excluded from the cheerful light of heaven, and having nothing for subsistence but damaged provisions, such as even a wretch starving on the gibbet and ready to eat the flesh off his own body with hunger, might turn from with disgust.

Such was the unhappy situation of those who were taken at Long Island, Fort Washington, Brandywine, Germantown, Monmouth, Camden and several other places. Indeed the treatment of the prisoners in general during the American war was harsh, severe, and in many instances, inhuman; except only with regard to those who were taken under a capitulation; for such were always treated well.

Burgoyne's and Cornwallis's men were treated like gentlemen, to my own certain knowledge, and why not the soldier who is taken prisoner in the field of action, or in any other way discharging his duty to his king or country?

We next arrived at Lancaster, where we had reason to expect good treatment, the inhabitants being in general remarkable for hospitality, and for contributing to the relief of objects of distress. While in Lancaster I became acquainted with a man in the army, belonging to the 44th regiment, whom I think proper to mention in this place on account of his piety.

I had frequently observed him retiring into a secret place, which at length awakened my curiosity to see what he was about;—I watched him, and found he went there to pray; he was remarkably reserved in all his conduct and conversation; was often alone, and seldom spoke, except when spoken to;

and from his general deportment, I firmly believe he was what is truly a phenomenon in the army, a conscientious christian.[92]

But this pious example had little influence on my conduct. One day, I very well remember, I got a quarter of a dollar from a Mr. John Hoover, by dint of hard begging; I now fancied myself as rich as a king, and immediately sent for a loaf of bread and a pint of whiskey, with which I and my comrades regaled ourselves, and sung some merry songs, being for the time as happy as princes.

Not long after, before we left Lancaster, we concerted another scheme for our release, by undermining, from one of the cellars under the barrack yard and stockades, about 100 yards, and coming out in the graveyard—conveying the dirt in our pockets, and depositing it in the necessary house[93] and other private places.

The next thing was to seize the magazine which contained a large quantity of ammunition and firelocks, with which we intended to arm ourselves, and being joined by a strong party of tories, set fire to the town, and so proceed to form a junction with the English army.

But our evil designs were entirely frustrated, by one of our own men belonging to the 71st regiment, of the name of Burk, who first made our plot known to the officer of the guard; and being conducted to General Wayne, who was then in Lancaster, gave in all the names of the non-commissioned officers.

The consequence of this was that about 11 o'clock at night, General Wayne came to the barracks with a guard of militia, and called out those unhappy men, and marched them down to the jail and put them in close confinement. And the commissary of prisoners, whose name was Hobley, ordered a ditch to be dug at the foot of the stockades, 7 or 8 feet deep, and filled with large stones, to prevent us from undermining; and had pieces of scantling[94] spiked along the top and bottom of the stockades.

The prisoners were employed to do the work, and they very cunningly cut the spikes in two, so as to go through the scantling and but slightly penetrate the stockades. These short spikes were put in at the bottom in order that the stockade might swing when cut off underground.

A day or two after this when Mr. Hobley the commissary of prisoners came to call the roll, a man of Lord Rawdon's corps,[95] whose name has slipped my memory, took the commissary aside, and offered to shew him all the private ways by which the prisoners went out and in. Accordingly he went around the stockades with the commissary, and made all the discovery he could.

When all was done, and the fellow wanted to be discharged, Mr. Hobley called the prisoners together and represented to them the bad policy of one prisoner turning traitor against the rest, and concluded with telling the fellow he ought to be hanged for acting so much like a scoundrel.

We accordingly held a court martial, and the fellow pleaded guilty, and was sentenced to receive 500 lashes on his bare posteriors, well laid on with a broad leathern strap.

Soon after this, two of my fellow prisoners and myself laid a plan for our escape, which we effected in the following manner: the night being appointed for the purpose, we procured a large knife, with which about 2 o'clock in the morning we had dug about two feet underground, where, to our great joy, we found the stockade rotten, or at least considerably decayed.

We cut away by turns until the stockade swung by the upper spike; so the boldest fellow went foremost, and the sentry fired at the hindmost; but we all escaped to a rye field where we lay hidden for a while, and then made the best of our way to a friend's house, two miles from town, and found there 30 or 40 more lying in a barn.

Next morning, each man taking his own road, I directed my course for the Moravian towns (as it is called) 8 miles from Lancaster, and there I met with a friendly reception from a certain Joseph Willey, one of the Moravian society, a wool weaver by occupation, and a native of the town of Putsey in Yorkshire, old England.

This man, though a friend to individuals, particularly those from Yorkshire, was notwithstanding a true republican in principle, and as warm an advocate for the rights and liberties of America as any man could be.

He recommended me to the brethren of his society as a prisoner of war belonging to a christian nation, and an object of compassion, and prayed for their assistance; which they granted and furnished me with what I stood in need of; but not until they had exacted a promise from me that I would return to my captivity, and wait with patience for the exchange of prisoners.

This promise I fulfilled, and accordingly returned to Lancaster barracks. And in a few days after my return, an officer of an additional company of the 33d regiment taken with general Burgoyne's troops,[96] came to Lancaster, and an application was made for some money, and each man received five guineas; there were 16 of us in a room together making ourselves as happy as possible, and we were determined to have a general feast or frolic.

Accordingly having laid in provisions of different sorts and procured a barrel of whiskey in the morning, I leave you to guess, my courteous reader, what an appearance we made by the middle of the day, when a pot-pie was proposed for dinner, and the preparation of it undertaken by a drunken old soldier who, in making up the crust of the pie, used whiskey instead of water; the dough being made and rolled out, and put in the pot.

The ingredients of the pie were added consisting of old rancid bacon, dried apples and onions and old chews of tobacco; and when sufficiently baked at the fire, the whole compound was next stewed in good old whiskey. And when ready a general invitation was given to the neighbors to partake of this "delicate" repast.

And we concluded the entertainment with a good bucket of whiskey, dancing with our shirts off while we were able to stand, and then we lay down promiscuously, and slept til morning.

Our frolic resembled so much the Irish feast, as described by Dean Swift, that I cannot forbear transcribing a few lines from the poet:

We danced in a round, Cutting capers and ramping;
A mercy the ground Did not burst with our stamping.
The floor was all wet With leaps and with jumps,
While the water and sweat Splish splash in our pumps.
Bless you late and early Laughlin O'Enagin
By my hand, you dance rarely, Margery Grinagin.

Bring straw for my bed Shake it down to the feet,
Then over us spread The winnowing sheet.
To show I don't flinch Fill the bowl up again,
Then give us a pinch Of your sneezing, a yean.

Next morning myself and a certain McGowan, after taking a little more of the usquebaugh,[97] determined to try our fortune; and accordingly made application for a pass for a few hours, and a sentry to go as a safeguard to bring us back at the expiration of the limited time.

Previously to this, we had made ourselves acquainted with a certain militiaman by the name of Everman, a tobacco spinner, who lived in Lancaster, and a notorious drunkard. We called on him, and he readily attended us to a certain Tom Mahoney's, who kept the Sign of the White Horse in Donnegal Street, near the barracks.

So now, Mr. Everman, "What will you please to drink?" "What you please, gentlemen," said Mr. Everman.

So a lusty bowl of punch was called for, and we all drank heartily together, until our sentry got drunk, and fell asleep on his guard.

We seized the favorable opportunity, and set out to push our fortune; and in order to avoid suspicion, we soon parted and took different roads. I came to a farmer's house and inquired for work. The farmer very readily agreed to give me employment.

"But what," says he, "can you do?" I told him I was brought up a stuff weaver. "Can you weave worsted?"[98] says he. "Yes, sir," said I. "Well, then," said he, "if you will weave a piece of worsted I have on hands, and continue with me five weeks, I will teach you to be a linen weaver."

I consented and fulfilled the contract, and he made me an indifferent linen weaver.

After that I parted with my new master and went to live with one John Bostler, a Dutchman. The family consisted of the old man and his wife and three daughters. I was very much at a loss to understand their language, as none of them could speak English but the old man, who spoke it in a very broken manner.

This circumstance was to me an insurmountable obstacle, as it prevented all conversation with the female part of the family; and to be candid, I should have had no objection to pay court to one of this Dutchman's daughters; for they were fine, hearty, industrious girls. But finding it impractical I left Mr. Bostler and set out with a view of going to Coleman's furnace. But before I got there I fell in with one William Cassel, who had a large store building on hand, at the Cross-roads, leading to Lancaster, Stickle's tavern, Grubb forge and Hornet's tavern.

Here was the second well I ever dug. It was 65 feet deep, and in digging we came to a cavern in the side of the wall in which we could have turned a wagon and team, and at the depth of 26 feet, with some other curiosities too tedious to mention here.

After completion of this well I went to work for Christopher Laby, a moneist by profession; and here was the first quarry I ever wrought in. After I had been at the quarrying business for some time, I had the misfortune to break three of my ribs.

To the Cross-roads there was a resort of all descriptions of men, from furnaces and forges; prisoners of war and deserters from both the English and continental army; and men of diabolical principles and practices from almost all quarters employed in card playing, cock fighting, horse racing, billiard playing, long-bullet playing,[99] fiddling and dancing, drinking and carousing, no matter what day of the week, though the Sabbath was the more frequently chosen for such practices.

A party of us had agreed to go one Sunday morning to Captain Huston's (commonly called Hornet's) tavern, in order to drink bitters and to take a game at long bullets close by the Dutch meetinghouse. And while the good people were at sermon and praying to the Great Author of all things to turn our hearts away from evil ways, I was chose to look out for the bullets, and on a sudden one of the bullets struck me on the head, and knocked me down, where I lay, to the great consternation of all, for some time before the company could tell what was best to be done with me.

But at length some signs of life appearing, they removed me to the tavern in a very dangerous situation; for by this unlucky accident a fracture was made in my skull which so disturbed my brain that ever after, if I drank spiritous liquors, a temporary frenzy was produced which caused me to conduct in a most extravagant and outrageous manner.

I was not the only person that received punishment for his immoral and irregular practices; for many of my acquaintances fell victim to the same, and among the rest were Curtis Grubb and Peter Grubb; the former of whom in one of his frolics jumped into the furnace in full blast; and the latter by putting a pistol into his mouth blew out his brains. These with several other instances of the ruinous effects of dissipation and of keeping bad company were, and perhaps justly, considered by the good people of the vicinity as a judgment from heaven upon those wretches for their impiety.

As soon as I was able to work, I finished the job I had undertaken, and went to live with a certain Hugh H-gg-y, a few miles from Lancaster, with whom I took up my winter quarters. Mr. H was very much addicted to getting drunk and lying out in the woods, which made his wife very uneasy; but as good luck would have it, he had a dog that always accompanied his master, and when any misfortune befell him, the dog would come running home and alarm the family.

Upon which occasion I had to set out in search of him, through the thickest woods, and frequently when it was so dark that I could not see my hand before me; my dependence being entirely on the dog. But he never failed to lead me to the place where his master lay.

During my stay here I fared pretty well, and lived with some degree of contentment until a circumstance occurred, which obliged me to leave the house. Mr. H. one night at home got very groggy, was in a very ill humor, and swore "he would have revenge that night" and accordingly he ordered his wife to bring him some more grog, which she did, and handed him the bottle and some water.

Having drunk what suited him, he began to curse and swear at his wife, calling her a d—d strumpet, and loading her with every opprobrious epithet which his indignation suggested.

She endeavored by mild words to pacify him and bring him to reason, but this only made him more furious. He knocked her down, and jumped with his knees on her breast, and then pulling out his knife, swore he would kill her on the spot.

Now I thought it would be wrong in me to stand by and see murder committed without endeavoring to prevent it; so I took him by the collar and pulled him off until she made her escape.

This interference of mine, which I thought perfectly justifiable, was likely to produce such domestic broils that for the peace of the poor woman I thought it most prudent to leave the house; which I did and went to live with one Captain Wilhelm, an inn-keeper who lived about three miles from Lancaster. I happened to be in one of my mad frolics one day when three continental officers came on a visit to captain Wilhelm's. I was pretty tipsy and caused the officers to inquire, who was I?

They were told I was a prisoner of war and by name John R. Shaw.

Being afraid therefore that such inquiries might lead to a detection, and that some person for a reward might deliver me up to the British who, at that time, offered a half joe for every British prisoner brought to them at Lancaster, I was brought to a stand what to do in this delicate circumstance.

Upon a little reflection, however, I was determined against having any further connection with the English army; but if I could by any artiface get enlisted in the American army, as the war was, in all probability, nearly at an end, I should soon get my liberty, and be released from the hardships of military duty, of which I was pretty well tired.

But there was an act of congress against the enlisting of prisoners of war, which made my undertaking rather desperate; however, as I knew that many others in the same condition had got admittance, and that there were several hundreds of prisoners, who now enlisted in the different corps of the American army, I resolved to try my fortune by inventing the most plausible fiction which I could devise in order to prevent suspicion and detection.

Epilogue

Shaw is listed as a deserter on the muster rolls of the 33rd Regiment of Foot.[100] In a strict sense, he was. His account, however, makes clear the situations that soldiers could find themselves in, situations in which the instinct for preservation and opportunism won out over whatever sense of duty and loyalty to country that a man may have had.

Many British deserters enlisted in the American army. Precise numbers cannot be determined, but individual accounts are many. It is easy to regard this turning of coat as symbolic of sympathy and support for the American cause. In most cases it was in fact a simple matter of pragmatism: British soldiers enlisted as career military men; when they deserted they needed employment and the military was their vocation. The immediate wartime demands for manpower meant ready work for anyone able to tolerate martial discipline. The American army had its own problems with desertion, and large numbers of British deserters who enlisted in the American army subsequently deserted, some to get away from the army altogether and some to make their way back to British-held territory.[101] Shaw's enlistment cannot be taken as anything more than what he describes: a way to limit his future military service by protecting himself from being discovered as a British soldier and returned to his life-long enlistment commitment.[102]

In spite of his disinclination toward military service, Shaw spent several years in the Continental Army both at the end of the American Revolution and in subsequent conflicts. He rambled about and eked out an existence in various ways until finally establishing himself as a stone quarrier and well-digger in Kentucky. These avocations involved the use of explosives, and it was an accident with these combustibles that took his life in 1813 at the age of fifty-two. Only six years before, he had penned his narrative while recovering from injuries sustained in another explosion. *The Life and Travels of John Robert Shaw: A Narrative of the Life and Travels of the Well-Digger; now resident of Lexington, Kentucky, Written by Himself* was initially sold by subscription in 1807, and Shaw continued to advertise it in local newspapers until his death.[103] The portion of Shaw's autobiography presented here comprehends about a third of Shaw's entire narrative. The remainder chronicles the many misadventures of his life in America, which must have provided ample entertainment to those who purchased it in the early nineteenth century.

That Shaw accurately remembered the names of fellow soldiers in the 33rd Regiment of Foot even though he forgot or mangled names of senior officers in the British army is a testament to his loyalties not to service or sovereign but to self and comrades. His departure from the army, recorded by the British as desertion but considered by the Americans as a capture, was incidental rather than deliberate, driven by want of food. His efforts to escape captivity were determined but his desire to rejoin the British army was half-hearted, his true focus being on comfort and socialization. Had he stayed in the British service, Shaw would have become a prisoner of war within a few months when the British army, including Shaw's 33rd Regiment, capitulated at Yorktown. His path to captivity was already determined, and he probably would have become the Kentucky well-digger and autobiographer even if he hadn't gone in search of food one day in March 1781.

TWO

Volunteering for American Service

William Crawford, 20th Regiment of Foot

Introduction

John Barry, a grenadier in the 46th Regiment of Foot, was on trial for committing a robbery. He and a fellow soldier were charged with holding up an inhabitant of Staten Island on a road in July 1776, just weeks after the British army had landed there to prepare for a campaign to secure New York City. Barry was "a very large, big man, not only tall, but well set, and had a hoarse strong voice" that made him recognizable to his accuser even though the incident occurred in darkness.[1] Grenadiers, one of the ten companies in an infantry regiment, were chosen partly for their physique; Barry was clearly a likely candidate. But experience was also required to serve in this elite company. The court heard testimony that Barry had been a soldier for nine years, but not in the 46th Regiment. He had been a cavalry trooper in the 2nd Regiment of Horse since 1767, but when men were needed to fill the ranks of infantry regiments bound for America he volunteered and was "turned over to the infantry."[2] He was one of many experienced soldiers who chose to leave their regiments in the British Isles to participate in a distant war.

Opportunities to volunteer did not end when a man enlisted in the army. Great Britain's army of empire had soldiers on service in many parts of the world; by the 1770s the army had established a rotation such that regiments were sent on foreign service for several years at a time and then brought home. When trouble flared and additional troops were required in a given location there were a variety of ways to accommodate this need. Simply sending more regiments to the trouble spot was a viable short-term solution but not always the most effective one for sustained operations. Wartime attrition could exceed the capacity of the regiment to furnish replacements through its own recruiting, particularly when the time required for training was factored in; although some relatively raw recruits were sent directly to serve in America, this was clearly not the ideal way to provide the majority of men required for wartime service. Most recruits went through a process similar to that described by John Robert Shaw in the previous chapter, receiving valuable training in military fundamentals that required time to properly administer. To supplement recruiting and get trained men quickly to places of need, the army routinely transferred men among regiments. Men so transferred were called drafts (or draughts), and the process of transferring them from one regiment to another was called drafting. Unlike the modern use of the term, during the era of the American Revolution drafting did not refer to conscription or any form of bringing men into the army. Instead, it was a method of redistributing seasoned men to locations where experience was required, leaving regiments on home service to do the work of recruiting and training.[3]

There were three circumstances in which large numbers of men were drafted during the American war, only one of which has received any significant treatment in the literature (for reasons that will be clarified below). Each had similarities in terms of the administrative process by which each soldier's person, clothing, equipment, and financial accounts were handed off from one regiment to another; in this regard all drafts were similar, that is, a transfer was a transfer. In general, the soldier kept the clothing he had acquired from his old regiment, which was logical because it was his own personal property purchased through deductions from his pay; each regiment received and distributed new regimental uniforms once a year, so the draft was expected to retain his old regimentals until the next annual clothing issue (although the receiving regiment had the option of providing new regimentals at any time if they were available). Sometimes each draft also retained his arms and accoutrements—the musket, bayonet, and associated leather goods. The considerations for whether this was done are discussed below. The receiving regiment paid to the contributing regiment a sum of money for each draft equivalent to what was provided by the government for new recruits; if the arms and accoutrements were transferred the receiving regiment also paid for them. The draft himself received a sum equal to the recruiting bounty. The contributing regiment settled the accounts of each soldier up to an agreed-upon day, so that the man started his career in his new regiment with a clean financial slate.[4]

The first instances of drafting began shortly before the outbreak of hostilities. At the beginning of 1775 it was clear that the army in America needed reinforcements. Eight regiments were ordered to prepare for embarkation in two waves that would sail in April and May. In preparation for deployment these eight regiments needed men to reach full strength, and the regiments already in America were also to be brought up to full strength. The numbers needed were not particularly large, only two or three dozen per regiment (5 to 10 percent of full strength),[5] but they were needed in a time frame that normal recruiting methods could not accommodate. Regiments on service in Ireland were ordered to provide drafts both to effect the schedule and to offset the inexperience of new recruits. Although this initial draft drew only a few men from each affected regiment,[6] it began a trend that would be repeated regularly throughout the next two years with its greatest impact in the first half of 1776.

We have already seen that the size of regiments on or bound for service in America was increased in June 1775 from 380 to 560 private soldiers. This meant filling the ranks of regiments already in America as well as those which would soon be sent there. Extensive recruiting ensued to reach the new established strength, but drafting was essential not only to achieve the numbers but to insure a reasonable proportion of seasoned soldiers to new recruits. Regardless of how it was done, increasing the size of regiments took time. The orders for expansion were not received and disseminated to the army in Boston (which had become the single major garrison in the colonies) until 10 November 1775.[7] By January 1776 the Additional Companies were in place and recruiting, but at the same time a major reinforcement was preparing to sail for America consisting of regiments requiring recruits and drafts to achieve the desired strength for deployment.

Those regiments remaining in Great Britain were ordered to provide large numbers of men to the ones bound for America. The 36th Regiment of Foot, for example, provided 124 men to four regiments sailing with Sir Henry Clinton's expedition to South Carolina in January 1776. Two months later, they furnished another 104 drafts to the 53rd Regiment bound for Canada.[8] Similar drafts were made from a number of other regiments, sending fit and experienced men to America and leaving the substantial burden of recruiting to those corps remaining in Britain. As the war progressed, drafts began to be made not only from regiments on home service but also from the Additional Companies of regiments overseas. Recruits were needed everywhere, but some locations warranted greater urgency than others. So it was, for example, that in 1778 when Spain entered the war and threatened Gibraltar that recruits raised for several regiments in America were diverted to regiments in Gibraltar instead.[9]

In America, meanwhile, another variation of drafting was begun in late 1775 and continued throughout the war. The British army routinely had regiments on service in North America for periods of seven to ten years at a time even before the war began. Because of this, at the outbreak of hostilities there were several regiments in America that had already been there for a long time and were due to come home. Within each of these regiments was a mixture of long-serving veterans who were nearing the end of their physical capacity for active campaigning, and those with shorter service who were still able to take the field. Rather than send able-bodied men back to Great Britain, these men were drafted into other regiments in America; the regiments that returned to Great

Britain were composed only of officers, non-commissioned officers, and those soldiers who were no longer fit for overseas service. It is this drafting that is well-known in the literature on the American war (to the extent that any information on drafting is available) and it is often misrepresented by statements to the effect that all of the men were drafted in America and only the officers returned to Britain.[10] Although this was largely the case, a cadre of veteran private soldiers was also retained. The 52nd Regiment of Foot, for example, was drafted in 1778 after having served in America since 1765. 280 private soldiers from the 52nd were drafted into other regiments, but 36 were retained; another 70 were discharged, and 15 men who were prisoners of war continued to be carried on the rolls even after the regiment returned to Great Britain.[11] The liberal press in Britain sometimes capitalized on the skeletal appearance of returning regiments to highlight the ravages of the war, overlooking the fact that serviceable men had simply been drafted and remained on service in other regiments.[12] A sensible military expedient was thus politicized by both contemporaries and their successors.

Drafting was also used as an expedient when individuals or groups of soldiers found themselves in places where their regiments were not. Inherent limitations in the speed of communication combined with wartime changes of events resulted in a variety of separations between soldiers and their regiments. Prisoners of war escaped and made their way to the nearest British garrison, which was often not where their own regiment served. Sick and wounded men were left behind in army hospitals when regiments redeployed from one theater to another. Parties of recruits arrived at one location in America only to find that their regiment had moved to another. In all of these situations, the displaced soldiers were liable to be drafted into a local regiment rather than sent on to their current regiment.

Drafting is presented in some literature as being widely unpopular and a cause of widespread discontent among the soldiery.[13] It did have the potential to undermine the solidarity that some regiments attempted to build by recruiting in specific regions so that men knew they would be serving with relatives and friends; there was no mandate to recruit in this manner and regiments were not assigned regional titles until 1782, but the value of regional recruiting was recognized and used by some regiments.[14] It cannot be assumed, however, that drafting inherently destroyed regimental cohesion. When drafts were taken from regiments in Great Britain to serve in America, it was often on a voluntary basis (as will be seen below), and often drafts were all put into the same receiving regiment rather than dispersing them, allowing relatives and comrades to move as a group from one regiment to another. When regiments in America were drafted, the men were indeed dispersed among several other regiments, but the number remaining was so small that solidarity within that corps could no longer be a consideration except among the officers. Another concern about drafting was raised by a writer of the era who questioned its legality, given that soldiers enlisted into specific regiments and their attestations swore them to serve specifically in that regiment rather than in the army as a whole.[15] There are a few highly publicized cases of unrest caused by drafting, particularly when men enlisted with the expectation of serving in a particular region, but emphasizing these incidents obscures the fact that drafting occurred extensively and usually uneventfully. During peace time soldiers enlisted as a career rather than for a fixed term of service; with overseas deployments for a regiment occurring every five or ten years it was quite common for a soldier to serve in more than one regiment during his career, either by being drafted into a regiment being sent overseas or out of one being sent home. A study of one regiment over a ten year period shows that almost half the men served in more than one regiment during their careers, many of them having been drafted several times.[16] Instances of protest are few given the overall numbers of men who were drafted throughout the American war.

The same author who questioned the legality of drafting advocated an aspect of it that was in fact employed by the army at least early in the war: volunteerism. He wrote,

> Should it be asked, how is any corps on foreign service to be otherwise recruited? the answer is, by volunteers from the different regiments at home, a measure never known to

> fail, and by which a corps gets rid of those restless spirits, who are best when employed on active service.[17]

The drafting orders given to regiments early in the war did indeed specify that volunteers were to be solicited first. Only if the required number of volunteers was insufficient were men to be ordered to go as drafts. Orders were explicit in the attributes required for a soldier to be chosen as a draft:

> Volunteers for the American Service are to have the preference to others. These draughts are not limited to age, or size, but they must have served four months at least in the regiment. They must have bodily strength for immediate service, & they must have been suffishently trained to the use of arms, to be fit for the common duty of a soldier. They are to have no bodily impediment.[18]

Because no records survive that enumerate which men volunteered to be drafted and which ones were ordered, it is impossible to say whether these explicit orders were followed in all cases. Drafting certainly presented an opportunity for regiments to divest themselves of poor soldiers, and there is evidence in some cases that they did just that.[19] Using muster rolls to trace careers of hundreds of soldiers, however, provides ample testimony that most drafts were reliable soldiers who met the demands of their duties and adapted to their new regiments.[20]

Muster rolls show us the numbers of drafts and the regiments through which they transferred, but do not distinguish which men volunteered and which were selected by their officers. The commander of the 69th Regiment enthusiastically wrote that he'd called for volunteers from his regiment to go to America, and "They expressed the greatest joy in going; and in answer to a speech I made them before the Regt. expressed the greatest regard for me, acknowledged their being pitched on as a favour, and said it should be their study by their behaviour to be a credit to the Regt. they were draughted from."[21] This could be bravado, but some muster rolls do indicate volunteerism. In 1775 and 1776, cavalry regiments in Ireland provided well over 100 drafts for infantry regiments serving in America.[22] In the muster rolls, many of these men are denoted simply as having been "drafted," "Turned over to the Infantry," or "Drafted for America," but some regiments used more colorful and specific notations such as "volunteer to America," "Volunteers to the Infantry," "Went a Volunteer," "Turned out a volunteer for America," and "Gone a volunteer to America." The number of drafts from each regiment varies, and the numbers taken from each troop within the regiment also varies,[23] which can be considered a further indication that these men were given a choice rather than filling a quota. Soldiers in the cavalry were paid more than the infantry, but this does not seem to have been a deterrent. Unfortunately no specific orders have been found to suggest whether a bounty or some other incentive was offered to offset the difference in pay. There is no evidence that any incentive was offered other than the opportunity to serve in the war; even the Secretary at War mused, "What is this Mystery of the willingness of Troopers, to serve as private Grenadiers? I can't Decypher it; however it's done."[24] Insight on the intentions of individual soldiers is rare, but a few of these men did leave direct confirmation that they volunteered for service in America. James Barry's trial, discussed above, suggests that volunteerism was an indication of character, showing verve for military service that was worth mentioning when facing the judgment of a court martial. Robert Young, whose story appears in Chapter 5, gave a deposition that he volunteered for America immediately after his infantry regiment had returned from several years in Gibraltar.

There are known cases of men who did not volunteer to join the army or serve abroad. In early 1781, a twenty-year-old named John Matson was approached by a friendly character who promised to help him find good employment. Matson had come to London from his native Yorkshire to improve his knowledge of the building trade that he had learned from his father. Besides receiving "plain education" he had pursued drawing, music, and various forms of mathematics on his own time, and aspired to have his own business as an architect and builder. He had worked for a few months in London until his employer died. The friendly promise of a steady position led him into a trap; the man who feigned to help him was an agent securing recruits for the 100th

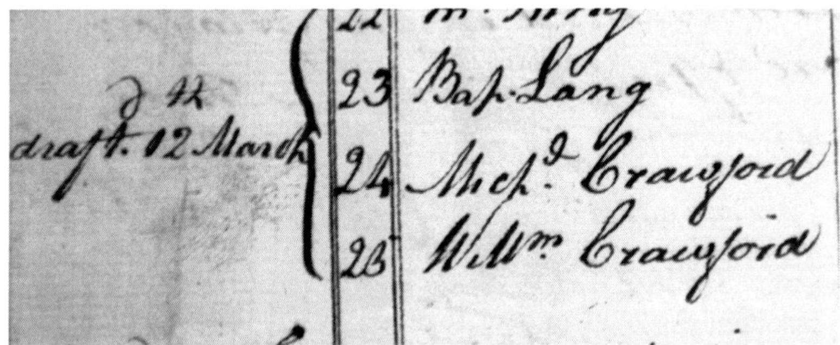
draft 12 March
23 Bap. Lang
24 Michl. Crawford
25 Willm Crawford

Detail from the muster roll of Captain Walsh's troop, 12th (Prince of Wales) Light Dragoons, recording the draft of William Crawford (*The National Archives. Photo by René Chartrand*)

Regiment of Foot, a new-raised regiment with orders to India. Matson was locked in a room with a few other young men who had been similarly kidnapped. They were sent to Hilsea Barracks in Portsmouth where they trained for a few weeks before embarking for India. Matson endured five years of campaigning and fighting in horrendous conditions before returning to London and being discharged in 1786.[25] Such unconscionable practices were not typical; as shown in Chapter 1, few soldiers complained about how they were enlisted when given an opportunity to do so in court. Matson's experience was the result of a long war that sapped the manpower pool, forcing new legal methods and inviting corruption; this is discussed in greater detail in Chapter 6.

The vast majority enlisted voluntarily during peacetime and volunteered yet again when war broke out. Among them was an Irishman named William Crawford, who joined the army in his early twenties after what he describes as a rather pastoral and frolicsome early life. He does not explicitly state his reasons for enlisting, but implies that he sought stability and direction that he was not finding in his life. He enlisted in a cavalry regiment, the 12th Light Dragoons. He claims to have enlisted when he was "quite young" and spent three years in this regiment, but the muster rolls do not bear this out; they give his enlistment date as 11 September 1775 when he would have been twenty-seven years old.[26] There is no obvious reason for this discrepancy, but Crawford nonetheless had at least a few months' experience in the army before answering a call for volunteers to serve in America. His motivation, probably the same as other volunteers for this service, was a desire to "satisfy my ardent disposition for adventure." He took the opportunity to join the 20th Regiment of Foot which sailed for Canada with five other regiments in May 1776.[27] News of the retreat from Concord and the battle of Bunker Hill had long since reached Great Britain, but spirited soldiers like Crawford confirmed an officer's observation that "there's nothing reconciles being shot at to one, so much as being paid for it."[28]

William Crawford's memoir of his service in America, written when he was seventy-four years old, is garbled in places (compared to other records of actual events) but nonetheless provides a number of useful insights. Of particular interest is his experience as a prisoner of war. Like hundreds if not thousands of other British prisoners he escaped incarceration.[29] Many of these escapees made their way back to British garrisons in New York, Rhode Island, Canada, or other places where they rejoined the army and continued service in other regiments. Many others, including Crawford, got waylaid by some circumstance or another which compelled them to remain in America. The story of his life was related by Crawford himself:

A Narrative of the Life and Character of William Crawford

I was born in the county of Fermanagh, in the parish of Killealy, near the town of Enniskillen, in the kingdom of Ireland, in 1748, and spent my youth partly in work and labor, and partly in attending fairs and horse races, and other scenes of festivity and pleasure, where I was fond of betting and gambling and the other diversions and amusements which we meet with on those occasions.—The race course was to me a place of extreme delight, and the licentiousness which prevailed there gave an agreeable excitement to my senses. I freely indulged in all the sport of the bucks and bloods, and the charms of the fair sex added to my imagination considerable fascinations to the other varieties of pleasure.

In these resorts of frolic and sport, when the passions had free play, it may easily be supposed that ideas of morality and religion seldom intervened to disturb our consciences, and we experienced less pain from having broke all the laws and commandments of God than from going home with a broken head. I can retrace my first sins of lust and avarice—my contempt for women and my love of gold and money to these scenes of youth, and I advise all young men to guard against the seductions of deceiving and alluring pleasures like these, where their hearts become corrupted, and they sacrifice their earthly happiness and their souls to violent passions and desperate courses.—The devil lays in wait at these times, and frequently wins a soul in the shape of a wager, and rides off with the heart and happiness of a sinner on the back of a favorite racer.—How many fine girls have gone to these sports and their accompanying dances, and jigged away their innocence and virtue!—They came like the fresh flowers of the morning, and returned miserable and deluded wretches. Some of them I have known after their fall to take to drink and thus seal their destruction both here and hereafter. But at that time I did my share, and left no remorse or pity for the horrid part I was acting.

Ireland was then a land of sport and fun, and it excited my warm feelings to be engaged as often as possible in these rows. But I soon after raised my views and laid aside my shillelah for a sword. The splendid uniform and glittering epaulettes, the beauty of the horses and grandeur of the parade, and above all, the king's golden guineas in form o' a bounty, won my heart, and I enlisted in the Prince of Wales' regiment of light dragoons. His present Britannic Majesty, George the fourth, was then quite young—his title was Prince of Wales, and he was the nominal colonel of this regiment of horse, which was called after his name. Here I remained some time and omitted no opportunity of seizing every pleasure that offered itself in the free and social kingdom of Ireland to a young and spirited soldier, for I was quite young when I enlisted. For three years I remained in this neighborhood where my father, whose name was Henry Crawford, resided. At length, to satisfy my ardent disposition for adventure, I determined to leave this regiment of light dragoons, which was then the 12th, and I volunteered in the 20th regiment of infantry, a marching regiment, which was ordered on foreign service, and was to be speedily embarked for America, against the provincial rebels to his majesty. This regiment was commanded by a brave and gallant officer, whose name was col. Lein,[30] under whose orders we marched forthwith to Cork, a seaport of Ireland, and in a few days set sail for the town of Quebec in Canada, and landed there after a dangerous voyage, in safety. Our regiment disembarked in fine order, and garrisoned part of those heavy and insuperable entrenchments until the celebrated battle of Quebec, when we were marched into the town and assisted in repelling the spirited assault of the Americans, in which we repelled Arnold with great slaughter, and killed gen. Montgomery and the greater part of his suite, aids-de-camp and staff officers. [31] The Americans were able to rally, and we were left time and opportunity to invade the province of New York. We accordingly were put under marching orders and ascended the great river St. Lawrence, and concentrated at a place called Les Trois Riviers, in Lower Canada, under the command of the brave general Carleton. Here we had some light engagements with the Americans, and defeated them. We then marched on to Sorrel River, and took the large town and island of Montreal, with all its stores and nunneries and monasteries, monks, friars, and some very pretty nuns and religious women. They were Roman catholics, though they were under his majesty's government. From this place we marched to St. Johns, which we also took possession of. After this we had frequent excursions and skirmishing with the rebels in a kind of light fighting and partisan, or as the French call it, petite guerre.[32] Sometimes we beat them, and sometimes we were obliged to retreat. We, however, penetrated into the state of New York, and after some time succeeded in retaking the strong positions and fortified barracks of Crown Point and Ticonderoga, which were yielded to his majesty's arms.[33] These were made temporary headquarters for gen. Carleton, and we extended our attacks on a number of small forts in the vicinity, which we carried with inconsiderable loss of lives on either side, until we were marched to a place called Freeman's Farm. Here we stood an engagement with the provincial rebels of six hours and three quarters. The fire was extremely heavy and the slaughter bloody. The Americans charged and re-charged, and his majesty's bayonets had full play. We contested with small arms and at the point of the bayonet for two pieces of cannon, which, with alternate slaughter on both sides, were taken and retaken twenty four times, and at last remained in our hands. The ground flowed with English and American blood, and the dead bodies of friends and enemies covered each other. The company to which I was attached consisted before the engagement of sixty three men, and out of them but eight remained.[34] I was the only officer that survived out of the whole complement of commissioned as well as non-commissioned officers. My rank in the company in this battle was that of a sergeant.[35]

After this we kept the ground so hardly fought for eighteen days, during which the Americans annoyed us continually with a loose and running fire, killing our men by single shots, and picking off every one who exposed himself to their rifles and buckshot, cutting down our sentries and outposts, and throwing shot into our lines, so that we were continually employed in watching them and returning their fire.

Gen. Carleton commanded us from the time we left Quebec, on our march up the St. Lawrence, Montreal, St. John's, and so on till we took possession of Crown Point and Ticonderoga, and then he retired in disgust on account of being placed under the orders of Gen. Burgoyne, who arrived from old England and overslaughed Carlton by maneuvering at home with the queen and her maids of honor and the ministers.[36] On his arrival general Burgoyne took the command, and proved but a poor soldier, and too nice to smell gunpowder.[37]

From this place of slaughter we marched to Schuyler's heights, where we lay fifteen days still tormented by the flanking and outlying parties of the Americans, who were always on the look out in every direction to intercept our foraging and watering parties, so that we got neither food for

William Crawford, a soldier in a cavalry regiment, volunteered for an infantry regiment preparing for service in America. Soldiers received new uniforms once a year and paid for them through wage stoppages; as such, they owned the uniforms. When a man moved from one regiment to another, he typically retained his existing uniform until the next annual clothing was received. This caused clothing variations in regiments that otherwise strived for consistency, an example of pragmatism taking precedence over stylistic considerations.

Depicted here is a soldier from the 12th Regiment of Dragoons who has just joined the 20th Regiment of Foot, wearing his cavalry clothing but armed as an infantryman. His cocked hat, issued to dragoons for wear when their distinctive leather helmets were not in use, lacks the white edging typically of infantry hats. His long hair is gathered, folded up on itself and tied in the military style called a club. Cavalry coats, although similar to the red coats of the infantry, differed in many details. The lapels, cuffs, and collar of the 12th Dragoons were black, while those of the 20th Regiment were yellow. The coat sleeves bear chevrons of worsted lace not found on infantry coats. The coat has two straps to secure shoulder belts for cavalry accoutrements, but infantrymen were equipped with only one such belt; the straps are more ornate than in most depictions of infantry coats. Although dragoons wore boots for riding, when dismounted they wore the same low-topped shoes and spatterdashes as the infantry.

Dragoons were armed quite differently from infantry. This soldier, therefore, has received arms and accoutrements from his new regiment. He carries one of the new short land pattern muskets received by the 20th Regiment in 1775, wears a waistbelt holding a bayonet scabbard and secured with an engraved brass buckle bearing the regiment's number in Roman numerals, and has a cartridge pouch slung over his left shoulder.

man or horse or water for either. Our suffering from hunger and thirst may be judged of by our ration being reduced to four ounces of pork, and eight ounces of bread per day, and afterwards to four of pork and six of bread. Gen. Burgoyne found it impossible to release us,[38] and as we were perishing by want of food and drink and were daily losing our men by the annoying fire and light parties of the enemy, we were at last obliged to surrender to the rebels under gen. Gates near Saratoga in the state of New York.

We were then marched to Prospect Hill near Boston in the state of Massachusetts, where we remained for several months, and found the inhabitants, or at least many of the principal people among them, not so friendly to the rebel cause, but favorable to the success of his majesty's arms, and well disposed to grant us as prisoners all the assistance in their power.[39] But we were ordered from this place to Rutland, and from Rutland to Albemarle in Virginia.[40]

At this place I was to winter with the rest of our British troops, all prisoners, and under guard of the Americans. I did not like such a place of inactivity and confinement, and laid a plan of escape which in a short time I was able to effect in the following manners—I cautiously observed the character of my fellow prisoners and fixed upon those in whom I could place confidence. Among those I selected sixty of the most trusty and thoroughgoing men. I required them to be secret and silent and had perfect confidence that they would not divulge the plot on which our liberty and hopes depended. We waited for a favorable opportunity which soon offered owing to our vigilance and the darkness of the night. A single sentry was posted at the point most suspicious to our views. He was at some distance from any other, and if I could kill him or silence him in any manner our road was open. I did not despair, I assembled and formed my men at a little distance and out of sight of the centinel, I gave the word as silently as possible:—We rushed upon him and finding it not necessary to kill him we captured him and carried him along with us.[41]

Having by threats and some little violence operated upon his fears and his love of life, we then made use of him to pioneer us about one hundred and six miles through the woods and mountains. When we had got thus far we thought ourselves safe from pursuit, and we were considerably fatigued and weary. We were also in want of food, and so we thought it necessary to change our plan of operations. For this purpose, we deemed it necessary to divide ourselves into small parties and to take different routes.

In all my adventures and services in his majesty's army, though I possessed no religion in my heart, I found it convenient to carry my prayer book about my person, because appearances of religion I have found to have great efficacy in the affairs of the world, by giving consequence to its owner and astounding the vulgar and ignorant, with the splendor of a jewel which they can never hope to own, and with the sublimity of a thing which they can never understand—besides, between the leaves of my prayer book I found a safe depositary for my money, which I won in battle by rifling the dead and wounded, or took from prisoners or got by any other fall speculation. Which money it is necessary to keep secret from the irreligious lovers of Mammon who frequent camps and armies. This prayer book I now put into requisition in his majesty's service, for I took it out and presenting it to our guide I obliged him to swear on it most solemnly—secrecy and royalty, and that he should not fight or be found in arms against his majesty the king of Great Britain, any more after that time. He took the oath and I then dismissed him with an injunction to make the best of his way home, and I have not seen or heard of him since.

Our parties then separated in different ways, and mine consisting of eleven or twelve persons marched on until we came to the borders of the Potomac River in the state of Virginia. Here our good fortune failed us and we saw our hopes of joining his majesty's standard about to expire. We were intercepted and arrested by an officer of the American service named col. Willis of the Virginia troops[42] and conducted to Martinsburg in Berkley county, and committed prisoners to the jail there. So that after traveling so many miles in a tough and woody country, we found ourselves separated from our comrades, and his majesty's troops and held in a rebel jail.

Here circumstances took place which I shall mention to show that no woman in this country can pretend to be my lawful wife, or her children legitimate, and therefore whatever I have done for them sprung from my kindness and good will, and not from any legal obligation. I have kept them and supported them, and given them property, and in return I have experienced nothing from them but the vilest ingratitude, and am at last brought by them to an ignominious death, the aggravating agony of which none can properly estimate but he who has felt,

"None sharper than a Serpent's tooth it is
To have a thankless child."[43]

I was now a prisoner in Berkley jail, and all my hopes of glory and promotion were likely to be at an end, unless I released myself from this place and I could see but a faint probability of any scheme of escape offering. But I was young, hearty, and handsome and fortune again befriended me, for I had not been confined more than twenty-four hours in Berkley jail, when the sheriffs daughter came into the prison with a case bottle of brandy. She poured it out for us and treated us in so kind a manner, that I immediately laid a plan in my own mind to make her subservient to my schemes. I was a pretty good judge from my experiences in Ireland how much power I possessed over the heart of a young and beautiful woman who properly estimated her own charms, and longed for a proper object of affection and love, who could do honor to her beauty,

"Upon this ground I spake—
She loved me for the dangers I had pass'd,
And I loved her that she did pity them."[44]

In short, I recollected immediately, those scenes of my youth when the strolling players visited the vicinity of Enniskillen and it struck me that now an opportunity presented to forage upon the enemy and make the daughter of a whig my companion and accomplice in my escape. I was further confirmed in my resolution by the heroic temper of the rebel's wife and daughters, in those days. I therefore lost no time in professing my determination to leave his majesty's service, if she would reccompence me with her charms. I told her the dangers I had encountered, the battles I had fought, the tempests I had escaped, the moving "accidents by field and flood," the comfortless life I led in jails and camps and campaigns, and countries without a friend but my rough and rude comrades, and I exaggerated in my strongest blarney the happiness which I might hope to find in her arms and in the enjoyment of domestic peace with her for a companion. With her I imagined I might perhaps be induced to relinquish my hopes of promotion in the British service, and I confess I found the heart of this daughter of a rebel so amiable and so tender, that I pleaded half from nature. I soon discovered that I had excited an interest in her mind, because

"She quick returned, and with a greedy ear
Devour'd up my discourse."[45]

She then inquired particularly and minutely of our names and places of birth, and stayed to lengthen out our conversation as long as she could. I seized the opportunity to impress on her my own name, birth and connections, and waited anxiously for the result.

Lydia Coburn, for that was her name, was a tall and beautiful girl and her nature was as tender and affectionate, that the tear of pity stood in her eye as she teased us in the jail. But her spirit was equal to her beauty, and in those times of civil war she participated in the feelings and sympathies of the soldiers she lived among.

She grew warm and animated in the cause of her country and the rebels and she heard me with increased interest when I promised to abandon the cause of Great Britain and become a citizen of her country. I of course conceived great hopes of success with this warm hearted and beautiful girl. Nor was I long deceived or doubtful.

The next day, which was the third of our imprisonment, she came again into the jail and asked me to walk out with her. I found she had been in the meantime inquiring particularly concerning me. I immediately took one of the prisoners with me and she conducted us to a tavern at a small distance and treated us to a bottle of wine. In the presence of both, she begged me to leave his majesty's service and proposed marriage to me, which I agreed to immediately and with all my heart, and requested liberty to send a present of liquor to those in jail. She assented to it with a frankness and liberality that heightened to my mind the effect of her charms, and I thought myself fortunate in meeting with such a spirited and beautiful girl, who could so suddenly conceive a sincere attachment for me, while a prisoner and an enemy. I gave up partly my idea of deceiving her, and was not determined what to do. But in a few days, she came to me with a license of marriage, which she forged in her father's office, and put it into my hands. I then conceived myself bound in honor to marry her, and accordingly we immediately arranged a plan of escape from the prison for me and carried it into execution that next day.

In the evening, accompanied by one of the prisoners, I waited impatient for Lydia. The sun set, and the gates were about to be closed, but the keeper had not yet appeared, though half an hour after his usual time. I began to give up all hope, but was again restored to strength when Lydia herself appeared with the keys. She came to us and told us to walk outside the door and wait for her, and we did so accordingly. She then arranged the other prisoners and locked up the doors, hanging the bunch of keys on a nail in the front entry or hall of the jail. She took my arm, and we sallied out in the dusk of the evening. It was just dark enough to prevent any particular observation and Lydia having my arm and leaning on it, we passed several persons without scrutiny. After we had gone out of town, we walked on without difficulty about three miles to a certain tavern, still accompanied by the prisoner whom I had selected as our companion. This tavern belonged to a captain in the Virginia militia whose name was Bolan.[46] He was absent, but Lydia introduced me to the family as her husband. He returned in the middle of the night and asked no questions as far as I know about me, and had not an opportunity to see me. We were all well received by the family and stayed all night. And here was the first matrimonial engagement in which I ever acted, and though I was in a manner made prisoner in spite of my own plans, I was quite satisfied with my bargain.

Early, however the next morning the alarm was given, and Lydia's family were on the hunt for their lost daughter. Her mother came to captain Bolan's accompanied by several attendants. She sent up for me, and I was obliged to get up and dress myself. I went down stairs and presented myself to the mother of my Lydia. I found her very angry and I thought at first infuriated. But I presented myself with a bold front and I was already so much in love with her daughter that she could hardly doubt my innocence. Mrs. Coburn asked me if I wanted to marry her daughter, and I answered with equal plainness and sincerity. Yes! The old woman found that I was a man of my word, and instantly relented and accepted me for a son in law. This was the first and only time in my failing in my allegiance to the crown of Great Britain, and nothing but the innocence and beauty of the royal spirit which she showed could have bound me so strongly.

The mother of Lydia then determined to have her daughter's marriage celebrated in conformity to law and old customs, and made arrangements to have it solemnized accordingly. But I had a haunting religion about me which induced me to determine that if I was married at all it would be according to the Church of England, the service of which I had in my Prayer Book, and so I requested the old mother to have a clergyman of the Church of England, which she agreed to. He was therefore sent for and came in due time, and Lydia and myself were married according to the rites and ceremonies of Old England.

Epilogue

Crawford called his earliest days of marriage the happiest of his life, but they did not last long. He admitted that a "restless spirit" possessed him. In spite of his admission that he did not have the "lamblike disposition" necessary to be truly spiritual, he practiced his own Anglican religion and did not embrace the religious diversity of his adopted country. He was all too outspoken in his disdain for the various other denominations in his region. Initially he was embraced by his wife's family and friends to the extent that he was appointed deputy sheriff and keeper of the very jail in which he had recently been confined. His happy life began to unravel when he became acquainted with local Tories who urged him to join them in seeking out the British army campaigning in Virginia. Although he opted against this, suspicion was aroused in his town and in his family; his pride and arrogance only aggravated this tension, as did his refusal to divulge the names of those disloyal to the cause of independence. He was soon separated from his wife and their two young children. Disheartened, he moved farther into the frontier of southwestern Pennsylvania where he settled to "farm and still."

His subsequent life was plagued by alcohol produced by his own still. He entered a relationship with a local woman and had children with her, but the entire family imbibed heavily and indulged other local inhabitants with the spirits as well. As the years passed, dysfunction brought all manner of infighting in the family. In a forty-year downward spiral of discord, Crawford remained proud of his British origins, and his adult children taunted him for it. He sang a song that he had learned in his youth called "Old Britannia" and this name became the children's derisive sobriquet for him. He became convinced that his common-law wife and their children would try to murder him. In 1822, during a whiskey-induced rage (it is not clear which parties involved were the more intoxicated), the seventy-three-year-old Crawford shot and killed one of his sons. His trial for murder was well-publicized in the rural West Virginia area where he lived; he was found guilty and executed by a public hanging on 21 February 1823.

Before he was executed, William Crawford wrote a memoir of his life for publication by the printer of the local newspaper.[47] The account presented here is approximately the first half of that narrative, up to the marriage that ended his connection to the British army. The remainder of *A Narrative of the Life and Character of William Crawford* describes in great detail the gradual disintegration of life that led to his capital crime. It is a rambling account that attempts to explain his behavior and provide some vague cautionary advice for others to avoid his plight, but ultimately does little more than present a picture of a proud and arrogant alcoholic who failed to find contentment in his life. This old soldier met his end not from the sting of battle or the effects of hard campaigning but from antagonism within his family that was fueled by his own restless disposition. Had he remained a soldier, he may well have met a more dignified end.

THREE

Wanderlust and Roving

Valentine Duckett, 65th Regiment of Foot

Introduction

The enlistments of John Robert Shaw and William Crawford both suggest elements of spontaneity. Shaw enlisted after a quarrel with his parents, and Crawford with an air of wanderlust. Roger Lamb, William Pell, and W. Griffith, discussed in the introduction to Chapter 1, describe similar sentiments. None of these men seems to have enlisted after long and careful consideration. The army was probably an option of which they were always aware, but the decision to enlist appears to have more to do with being discontent with immediate circumstances, down on luck or in need of a change. This theme is quite common among those few soldiers who have left us specific information on their decisions to enlist, and it is a theme which will recur throughout this book. Rather than zeal for the military or ardor for the political cause, many soldiers, perhaps the majority, enlisted in fairly immediate circumstances as a way to change their current situation. Given that the army was a lifelong career, at least for the peacetime enlistees (all of those mentioned above except Shaw), this may seem haphazard, but it probably reflects the normal way that working-class people chose careers during this era—by taking opportunities that were readily available.

It is, then, noteworthy that both Shaw and Crawford left the service when other opportunities arose. Could it be that men who had enlisted spontaneously were just as likely to desert spontaneously, and were therefore soldiers of questionable reliability? Shaw and Crawford each served dutifully and bravely enough for several years so their devotion to immediate duty cannot be questioned; moreover, both were prisoners of war in trying situations when they made their decisions to leave British service. In circumstances such as theirs, outside influences were much stronger at the moment than that of their officers, comrades, or national allegiance. Their desertions are in some measure excusable for the sake of self-preservation, even though men such as Roger Lamb and countless others in the similar circumstances remained loyal to the army.[1]

The army solved a key problem faced by legions of laborers and tradesmen in eighteenth-century Great Britain: it was stable. There were military expansions and contractions with the cycles of war and peace, there were extended periods overseas sometimes in harsh climates, and there were periods of hardship and danger; these disadvantages were offset by food, clothing, and pay, commodities which were occasionally interrupted but much more steady and certain for the soldier than for many itinerant workers. Labor markets were subject to their own uncertainties, from changing yields in agriculture to change in demand for manufactured goods to the earliest encroachment of industrialization. A soldier who enlisted during times of peace when the army was small could count on greater career stability than any other avocation could offer; the wartime enlistee could count on at least a few years' worth of steady compensation with the possibility of remaining in the army or even settling overseas at the end of the war. Besides employment stability, however, there was a contract for guaranteed service accompanied by regularity in duty and discipline. This was no problem for the majority of men, but there were some who were itinerant by nature, not just because of the realities of their civilian avocations. Men who wandered sometimes wandered into the army, and it is these men who were just as likely to wander out of it.

This is not to suggest that these roving souls were miscreants, vagabonds, or criminal by nature. Restlessness and discontent have run through the veins of young men since time immemorial, regardless of class, upbringing, or education. Young adults protested against their families, their immediately career prospects, or regimentation in general. The glamour of military regalia and the promise of overseas adventure painted the army as an alluring escape. While it did in fact provide a new life and (often) the adventure that goes with travel and rigor, regimentation was a fundamental facet of military life. Soldiers did have free time for nonmilitary pursuits, as will be discussed in Chapter 5, but the itinerant nature of military life made steady attachments difficult to maintain. For many men, the primary respite from duty was vice in the form of drink, gaming, and other pursuits of the unsettled. For those men who were already averse to discipline, the combination of on-duty regimentation and off-duty debauchery destroyed any possibility of a productive military career.

The storied strictness of British military discipline was a direct response to the tendency of restless soldiers to seek deleterious pastimes. Drunkenness and the resultant "riotous" behavior were a constant challenge, and the lash was not spared to keep problems in check. It is essential, however, to recognize that harsh punishments were characteristic of civilian professions as well. The army at least had a formal justice system, whereas apprentices, servants, and laborers were apt to be beaten by their masters without trial or recourse.[2] The common soldier's perception of treatment must be weighed in context of what could be expected from a demanding employer in a largely laboring population. For example, a young man named Thomas Cranfield left an apprenticeship as a tailor at the age of fourteen due to his own restless nature. He found two stations of steady employment during the next five years. First he agreed to work with a tailor just for food, but received so little that he was "half-starved" and obliged to share meals with the employer's dog. He then struggled for three years as an apprentice to a tailor who "was extremely severe and unmerciful, and frequently compelled him to work from four o'clock in the morning till eleven or twelve at night for many days together; while he was but badly clothed and fed, and never allowed a single penny for pocket-money. Upon the slightest offence, and sometimes for no offence at all, he was horse-whipped in the most severe and degrading manner, although he strove to the utmost of his power to serve his master."[3] More of Cranfield's life is presented in Chapter 5.

Another example comes from the memoir of W. Griffith, whose enlistment was discussed in the previous chapter. At the age of nine he was sent to work for a farmer whose treatment he remembered only too clearly:

> I never knew during the four years that I was with him, what it was to be free from sores and scars; he once broke my head with the thick end of a carter's whip; he once thrust a key into me head; by the force of his arm he would take me by my two ears and throw me down, and stamp on me, and whatever he had in his hand, if he could lift it, he would strike me with it; he would take my heavy nailed shoes, and beat my poor head with them; he would beat me with the iron end of the drag; he once struck me on the head with it, I fell senseless to the ground; he once beat me with the handle of the potatoe hoe, about the size of a broom handle, till my body was black in several places; he has taken me by the hair of my head, and thrown me into hedges, ditches, and where he pleased; thrown hard clod at my back when I have been in the fields, so that I have been scarce able to walk; he would knock me down, and kick me, and horse whip me, with no covering by my shirt: he was a strong powerful man, about six feet high. We were once at work in the harvest field, setting up shocks of corn; I did not set up mine as fast as he, he took a stick and beat me terribly, wore out the stick, knocked me down and kicked me, and I asked him if he meant to kill me; this was on a Sabbath morning, when the wind and rain had beat down the corn in the night.[4]

Situations like Cranfield's and Griffith's may have been extreme but nonetheless show the hardships to which common workmen might be subject.

Also critical in assessing the harshness of corporal punishment is an understanding of which men actually ran afoul of it. Military law required the sentence of a court-martial before corporal punishment, almost exclusively in the form of lashes with a whip called a cat-of-nine-tails, could be administered.

After sentencing, punishments were often remitted (that is, pardoned) either in part or completely. A number of surviving records list the men tried by regimental courts, describing the crimes, sentences, and extent to which each sentence was inflicted or remitted. Comparing these with muster rolls reveals the proportion of men who were brought to trial and that suffered the lash. The 44th Regiment of Foot tried 398 cases between 1778 and 1784, but many of the men were repeat offenders who were tried twice or more; the actual number of men tried was 213, or between 25 and 30 percent of the estimated 700 to 800 in the regiment.[5] Not all men convicted were sentenced to corporal punishment, and some of those sentenced were pardoned; taking these things into account, 133 men were actually lashed. The 44th was in Canada during the years covered by the punishment records; a similar set of records concerning four infantry regiments in Ireland during the years 1774 through 1777 show that between 20 and 25 percent of the men were brought to trial while only 10 to 15 percent were actually punished.[6] A corps composed of portions of the 18th and 65th Regiments of Foot serving in Boston held 91 trials for cases concerning 62 individuals (several of whom were repeat offenders) between October 1774 and May 1775, but only 43 suffered corporal punishment, about 19 percent of the detachment's approximately 228 men.[7] The consistency of these samples gives some measure of confidence that they can be extrapolated to other regiments for which no records are known to exist.[8] The key point is that punishment was harsh only for the minority of soldiers who were found guilty of crimes. Whether due to ethics or intimidation, the majority of British soldiers maintained sufficiently good discipline to avoid the lash.

One soldier whose temperament conflicted with military discipline was Valentine Duckett. Although he did not actually fight in the American war, he was a contemporary of many who did and his experiences as a soldier in America from 1768 through 1774 are instructive in understanding the wandering nature of many young men of the era. His memoir was recorded shortly before his death in circumstances that will be related below. The early part of his story echoes that of John Robert Shaw, in that he was an educated young man from a well-off middle-class English family who left home because of conflicts with his parents. His mother died when he was young. Characteristic of many adolescents, he could not abide his father's remarriage. Since he had an older brother serving in the army in London, he went there and availed himself of a position arranged by his brother. His age at the time is not clear, but he was probably in his early teens and too young to enlist. His self-described "inclination being on roving" led him from one employment to another and then back to his family in Derbyshire. Duckett's family business is not known, but his brother's service in a cavalry regiment and his own work as a postilion[9] and with a coachman suggests experience with horsemanship and animal husbandry. When he could not get along with his stepmother, however, he chose to enlist in the infantry. In early 1768 he signed with a recruiting party of the 65th Regiment of Foot which was then in Ireland but under orders to sail for America.

Duckett must have been a physically well-developed, "likely" young man, for he was accepted as a recruit at a young age, right around his fifteenth birthday.[10]. This was unusual; surviving recruiting instructions typically say that recruits were to be between the ages of seventeen and twenty-five, and military guidebooks expressed the importance of enlisting young men who were fully grown.[11] Recruiting officers were, however, allowed to use their judgment concerning teenagers who were of good stature and looked like they would develop into likely soldiers.[12] The fact that the 65th was preparing to go overseas perhaps gave the recruiters additional incentive to fill the ranks with native Britons while the opportunity was available. Duckett joined the regiment in Limerick but soon marched with it to Cork where they boarded transport ships bound for America.

The 65th Regiment of Foot arrived in Boston on 10 November 1768 and went into quarters on Castle Island rather than landing in the city proper. They did not stay long. On 21 June 1769 they were ordered to remove to Halifax, Nova Scotia, another important base of British military operations. The regiment immediately embarked on two warships, conditions that were surely crowded but sufficient for the short journey, and sailed from Boston on 24 June.[13] It is not known whether Duckett ever set foot in Boston during this eight-month stay on Castle Island, but he would make his own way there soon enough.

Duckett claims to have initially been "a good soldier" and the limited environment of Castle William in Boston harbor probably helped him to maintain that character. In Halifax, however, he acquired the bad habits that befell many soldiers. During two years in this remote seaport city he took to drinking and keeping bad company. Many inhabitants of North America felt great disdain for garrisoned troops, an attitude that was inflamed by drunken and bawdy behavior of soldiers. Seducing men away from the service became a common practice, one for which men like Duckett, already disposed toward restlessness, were easy targets. A sea captain name Live persuaded Duckett to join his crew, and the young soldier absconded from his regiment to pursue a life at sea. Duckett attributes his desertion to the effects of liquor, but certainly his self-described disposition to roving was a contributing factor.

Duckett was taken by Capt. Live to Mahon Bay, a port town a few miles south over land from Halifax. It was here that the young deserter had second thoughts. He was well within reach of patrols that might be sent from Halifax in search of deserters, and the offense he had committed by abandoning his regiment was a capital one. Fearing capture and the consequences of a court-martial, he absconded once again in a stolen boat. Not quite eighteen years old in the summer of 1771, Valentine Duckett was on the run.

The next year and a half were spent in a spree of deleterious activities which seem impossible to fit into the time span, yet Duckett's detailed descriptions of dishonorable acts does not suggest dishonesty. He signed onto a ship in spite of having no background as a mariner, but was able to learn the occupation sufficiently to take other seafaring opportunities. He sailed the American coast but was ever-wary of being recognized as a deserter, a trepidation justified by close calls and confinements from which he managed to escape. This fugitive existence became ever more criminal as he turned to theft and kept company with other vagrants, fugitives, and deserters, committing robberies in several cities and towns, sometimes

Valentine Duckett served with the 65th Regiment of Foot in Halifax, Nova Scotia, before hostilities broke out in America. He probably spent some of his time on formal garrison duties, primarily consisting of guard duty every few days. Orders given in Boston and Dublin during the same era indicate that soldiers on guard wore regimental uniforms with their hair dressed in a uniform style, neat and well groomed.

Here a soldier of the 65th Regiment is wearing the infantry uniform prescribed by Royal Warrant in December 1768. Coats, waistcoats, and breeches like those shown were issued to a soldier once a year and retained by him, in various states of repair and modification, until they were no longer serviceable; on formal duties the soldier wore his newest and best-maintained clothing, retaining older and worn garments for harsher activities. The military cocked hat, formed by folding up the brim of a broad-brimmed felt hat, bears a black horsehair cockade signifying the house of Hanover, a reference to King George III. White woven tape sewn to the edge of the brim guards against fraying. His red woolen coat is trimmed with white cuffs, collar, and lapels. The coat tails, called skirts, are folded back and secured at the corners with hooks and eyes or sewn together with straps of cloth and lace. He wears a white woolen waistcoat and breeches; a return of stores that the 65th lost in a fire in Boston reveals that the breeches were secured by a buckle at the knee. Knee-length gaiters of blackened canvas keep debris out of his low-topped shoes, while leather tops on the gaiters protect the knees. Closely spaced buttons on the coat, waistcoat, and gaiters keep the clothing snug to prevent dirt and cold air from penetrating. Worsted lace reinforces the coat buttonholes; each regiment had its own pattern of colored stripes woven into the buttonhole lace. No regimentally marked waistbelt buckle for the 65th Regiment survives, so an open brass buckle is shown here.

alone and sometimes in concert with various vagrant comrades. He was repeatedly imprisoned and escaped, until finally in Boston he was taken up as a deserter and extradited to his regiment in Halifax. His description suggests that this occurred around the beginning of 1773.[14] Tried and lashed for desertion, but apparently not for any of the other crimes he committed, he claims to have resolved to change his ways. There is other information, however, indicating that he again deserted and was recaptured, but was this time pardoned. No records of these trials survive among existing general court-martial proceedings, but desertion was sometimes tried by a regimental rather than a general court;[15] records of regimental courts are extremely scarce and are not known to exist for the 65th Regiment during the time of Duckett's service.[16]

Duckett's final desertion occurred in the spring of 1774, motivated by another age-old inducement of absented men. Having spent some time with "idle women" during his time away from the regiment, his thoughts turned again to them, although he doesn't appear to have had a specific plan. He set out over land through the wilds of Nova Scotia, eventually finding work once again as a mariner. After a few months, however, he made his way to Boston. On 9 July a general pardon had been proclaimed for any deserters who turned themselves in before 10 August.[17] Such pardons were offered from time to time as a way to recover men who were repentant but would not return for fear of punishment; the amnesties were not, however, particularly effective.[18] Indeed, Duckett had already been pardoned once for desertion based on just such a proclamation.

Valentine Duckett was apprehended in Boston on 20 August 1774, ten days after the pardon expired. A local resident was writing a letter at the time and took note of the event: "Am this instant interrupted by a chace of four soldiers after a deserter through the market. He proves to belong to the 65th, and left 'em two or three years since. He seems to be a smart, stout fellow, dress'd in a short jacket and long trousers. Am amaz'd he should [be so] stupid as to appear in so publick a place. They have lug'd him to the camp, from whence they will send him to his regiment, where I suppose a thousand lashes at least will be his portion."[19]

The writer based his assumption about punishment on recent desertion trials. A court-martial that sat in Boston on 4 August sentenced three men to various numbers of lashes for desertion or other forms of absence.[20] But there had been many other deserters that summer who were not caught and brought to trial.[21] It was high time for the army to set a harsher example. Furthermore, this newly apprehended deserter from the 65th Regiment was a repeat offender who had already been spared punishment. He would not be an object of mercy again.

Valentine Duckett was tried by a general court-martial for desertion, found guilty, and sentenced to death. This sealed his fate as a soldier and a living soul, but opened the way for his story to be recorded in history. It was the custom of the era to allow condemned men to make a public statement before their execution. The "dying speech," "last words," or "last speech" was sometimes confessional and cautionary, and if it was sufficiently eloquent or informative it was also marketable.[22] As occurred with several such testimonials, Duckett's dying speech was recorded (it is not known whether he himself wrote it down or just delivered it orally), transcribed by a Boston printer, and offered for sale.[23] A few copies survive,[24] giving us Duckett's own account of his life and rare insight into his motivation for joining the service, deserting, and attempting to return. The proceedings of the trial that condemned him also survive and help corroborate his memorial in addition to providing details of his capture and further testimony from the man himself.

Although the dying speech was given after the trial, for the sake of chronological continuity we present the speech first, in which Duckett describes the events of his life.

The Dying Speech of Valentine Duckett

The Life, Last Words, and Dying Speech of Valentine Dukett; Who was shot for Desertion, on Boston Common, Friday Morning, Sept. 9, 1774; agreeable to the Sentence of a

General Court-Martial held in Boston Camp, the 30th Day of August, 1774, Major Spenlow, President, Lieutenant Knight, of the 4th Regiment, Judge-Advocate, Captain Farrington, of the Royal-Artillery, the Captains West, Holmes, and Farrier, of the 4th Regiment, Captains Downe, Marsdin and Battier, of the 5th Regiment, Captain Graves, of the 23d Regiment, Captains Lumm, and Coker, of the 38th Regiment, Captains Thomson, and Hatfield, of the 43d Regiment.

I being now fully sensible that all events whether merciful or afflictive, are under the superintendency of God, who governs the universe of nature with the most perfect wisdom and rectitude, I desire most humbly to prostrate myself before this Almighty Being, imploring his favour and forgiveness and submissively acquiesce in the punishment assigned me.

I am now to finish a life, which by the equitable laws of my country I justly forfeited, though in a different manner than which I am this approaching morning to suffer; to prevent others arriving at so great a pitch of *debauchery, drunkenness, profligacy*, and other most attrocious and detestable actions as I have been guilty of, though but 21 years of age (which makes me tremble at the recollection) is a sufficient motive for giving a narrative of my past life, though many attrocious actions that I have committed will doubtless escape my recollection at this dismal hour of night.

I, Valentine Dukett, was born in St. Peter's Parish, Derbyshire, in England, August 10th, 1753; my father's name was William Dukett, I received good education of my parents, who lived credibly and were of good report, but my mother dying when I was but 9 years of age, my father married again, which was very disagreeable to me; I then left my father and went to London, where I had a brother in the Life guards, who put me to be postillion to one 'Squire Every; but my inclination being on roving, I left the place my brother had provided me, and refused his advice as I had done my father's before; I then hired myself to a stage-coachman, whose employment I soon left, and returned again to my father's, in Derbyshire; but my step-mother and I could not agree, and there being a recruiting party of the 65th regiment in that place, I listed with them for a soldier, and went to

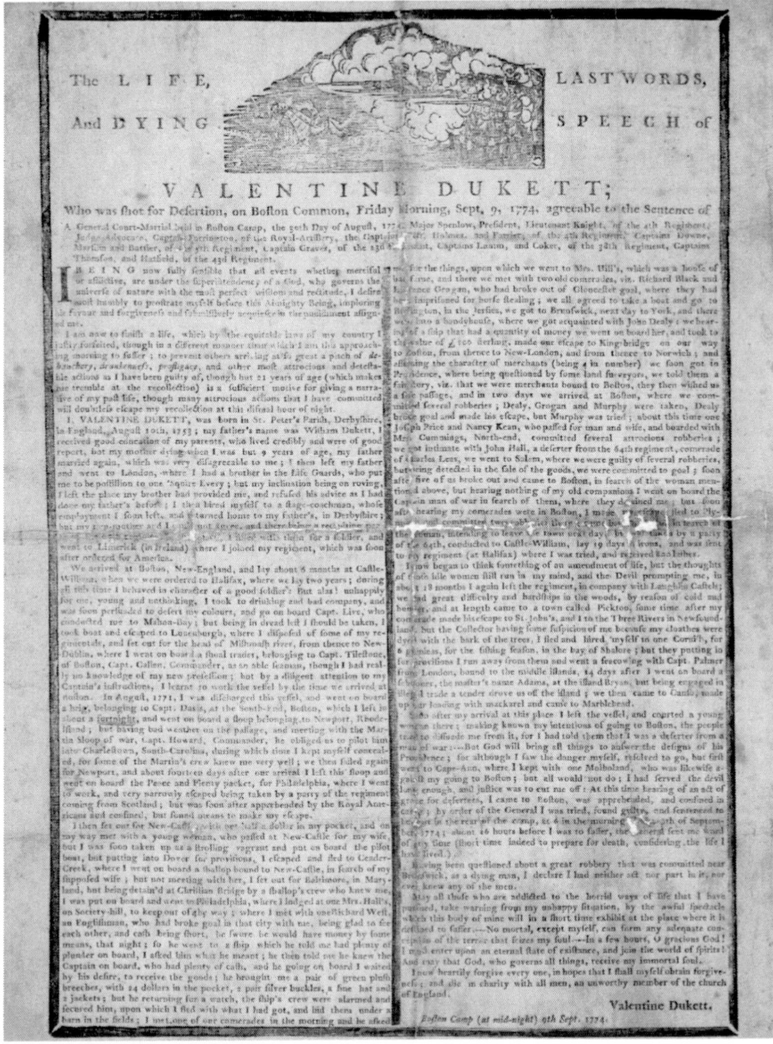

The LIFE, LAST WORDS, And DYING SPEECH of

VALENTINE DUKETT;

Who was ſhot for Deſertion, on Boſton Common, Friday Morning, Sept, 9, 1774, agreeable to the Sentence of

A General Court-Martial held in Boſton Camp, the 30th Day of Auguſt, 1774. Major Spenlow, Preſident, Lieutenant Knight, of the 4th Regiment, Judge-Advocate, Captain Farrington, of the Royal-Artillery, the Captains [illegible], Holmes, and Farmer, of the 4th Regiment, Captains Downe, Marſim and Battier, of the 5th Regiment, Captain Graves, of the 23d Regiment, Captains Lamm, and Coker, of the 38th Regiment, Captains Thomſon, and Hatfield, of the 43d Regiment.

I BEING now fully ſenſible that all events whether merciful or afflictive, are under the ſuperintendency of a God, who governs the univerſe of nature with the moſt perfect wiſdom and rectitude, I deſire moſt humbly to proſtrate myſelf before this Almighty Being, imploring his favour and forgiveneſs and ſubmiſſively acquieſce in the puniſhment aſſigned me.

I am now to finiſh a life, which by the equitable laws of my country I juſtly forfeited, though in a different manner than which I am this approaching morning to ſuffer; to prevent others arriving at ſo great a pitch of *debauchery, drunkenneſs, profligacy*, and other moſt attrocious and deteſtable actions as I have been guilty of, though but 21 years of age (which makes me tremble at the recollection) is a ſufficient motive for giving a narrative of my paſt life, though many attrocious actions that I have committed will doubtleſs eſcape my recollection at this diſmal hour of night.

I, VALENTINE DUKETT, was born in St. Peter's Pariſh, Derbyſhire, in England, Auguſt 10th, 1753; my father's name was William Dukett, I received good education of my parents, who lived credibly and were of good report, but my mother dying when I was but 9 years of age, my father married again, which was very diſagreeable to me; I then left my father and went to London, where I had a brother in the Life Guards, who put me to be poſtillion to one 'Squire Every; but my inclination being on roving, I left the place my brother had provided me, and refuſed his advice as I had done my father's before; I then hired myſelf to a ſtage-coachman, whoſe employment I ſoon left, and returned home to my father's, in Derbyſhire; but my ſtep-mother and I could not agree, and there being a recruiting par[illegible] I liſted with them for a ſoldier, and went to Limerick (in Ireland) where I joined my regiment, which was ſoon after ordered for America.

We arrived at Boſton, New-England, and lay about 6 months at Caſtle-William, when we were ordered to Halifax, where we lay two years; during all this time I behaved in character of a good ſoldier: But alas! unhappily for me, young and unthinking, I took to drinking and bad company, and was ſoon perſuaded to deſert my colours, and go on board Capt. Live, who conducted me to Mahon-Bay; but being in dread leſt I ſhould be taken, I took boat and eſcaped to Luneburgh, where I diſpoſed of ſome of my regimentals, and ſet out for the head of Miſhoaſh river, from thence to New-Dublin, where I went on board a ſhoal trader, belonging to Capt. Tileſtone, of Boſton, Capt. Callen, Commander, as an able ſeaman, though I had really no knowledge of my new profeſſion; but by a diligent attention to my Captain's inſtructions, I learnt to work the veſſel by the time we arrived at Boſton. In Auguſt, 1771, I was diſcharged this veſſel, and went on board a brig, belonging to Capt. Davis, at the South-End, Boſton, which I left in about a fortnight, and went on board a ſloop belonging to Newport, Rhode-Iſland; but having bad weather on the paſſage, and meeting with the Martin Sloop of war, Capt. Howard, Commander, he obliged us to pilot him into Charleſtown, South-Carolina, during which time I kept myſelf concealed, for ſome of the Martin's crew knew me very well; we then failed again for Newport, and about fourteen days after our arrival I left this ſloop and went on board the Peace and Plenty packet, for Philadelphia, where I went to work, and very narrowly eſcaped being taken by a party of the regiment coming from Scotland; but was ſoon after apprehended by the Royal Americans and confined, but found means to make my eſcape.

I then ſet out for New-Caſtle, with but half a dollar in my pocket, and on my way met with a young woman, who paſſed at New-Caſtle for my wife, but I was ſoon taken up as a ſtrolling vagrant and put on board the pilot boat, but putting into Dover for proviſions, I eſcaped and fled to Cender-Creek, where I went on board a ſhallop bound to New-Caſtle, in ſearch of my ſuppoſed wife; but not meeting with her, I ſet out for Baltimore, in Maryland, but being detain'd at Chriſtian Bridge by a ſhallop's crew who knew me, I was put on board and went to Philadelphia, where I lodged at one Mrs. Hall's, on Society-hill, to keep out of the way; where I met with one Richard Weſt, an Engliſhman, who had broke goal in that city with me, being glad to ſee each other, and caſh being ſhort, he ſwore he would have money by ſome means, that night; ſo he went to a ſhip which he told me had plenty of plunder on board, I aſked him what he meant; he then told me he knew the Captain on board, who had plenty of caſh, and he going on board I waited by his deſire, to receive the goods; he brought me a pair of green pluſh breeches, with 24 dollars in the pocket, 2 pair ſilver buckles, a fine hat and 2 jackets; but he returning for a watch, the ſhip's crew were alarmed and ſecured him, upon which I fled with what I had got, and hid them under a barn in the fields; I met one of our comerades in the morning and he aſked me for the things, upon which we went to Mrs. Hill's, which was a houſe of bad fame, and there we met with two old comerades, viz. Richard Black and Lawrence Grogan, who had broke out of Glouceſter goal, where they had been impriſoned for horſe ſtealing; we all agreed to take a boat and go to Burlington, in the Jerſies, we got to Brunſwick, next day to York, and there went into a bawdyhouſe, where we got acquainted with John Dealy: we hearing of a ſhip that had a quantity of money we went on board her, and took to the value of £100 ſterling, made our eſcape to Kingſbridge on our way to Boſton, from thence to New-London, and from thence to Norwich; and aſſuming the character of merchants (being 4 in number) we ſoon got in Providence, where being queſtioned by ſome land ſurveyors, we told them a fair ſtory, viz. that we were merchants bound to Boſton, they then wiſhed us a fair paſſage, and in two days we arrived at Boſton, where we committed ſeveral robberies; Dealy, Grogan and Murphy were taken, Dealy broke goal and made his eſcape, but Murphy was tried; about this time one Joſeph Price and Nancy Kean, who paſſed for man and wife, and boarded with Mrs. Cummings, North-end, committed ſeveral attrocious robberies; we got intimate with John Hall, a deſerter from the 64th regiment, comerade of Charles Lees, we went to Salem, where we were guilty of ſeveral robberies, but being detected in the ſale of the goods, we were committed to goal; ſoon after five of us broke out and came to Boſton, in ſearch of the woman mentioned above, but hearing nothing of my old companions I went on board the Captain man of war in ſearch of them, where they detained me; but ſoon after hearing my comerades were in Boſton, I made my eſcape, fled to Plymouth [illegible] committed two robberies there [illegible] in ſearch of the woman, intending to leave the town next day, [illegible] taken by a party of the 64th, conducted to Caſtle-William, lay 19 days in irons, and was ſent to my regiment (at Halifax) where I was tried, and received 800 laſhes.

I now began to think ſomething of an amendment of life, but the thoughts of thoſe idle women ſtill run in my mind, and the Devil prompting me, in about 18 months I again left the regiment, in company with Laughlin Caſtels; we had great difficulty and hardſhips in the woods, by reaſon of cold and hunger, and at length came to a town called Pickton, ſome time after my comerade made his eſcape to St. John's, and I to the Three Rivers in Newfoundland, but the Collector having ſome ſuſpicion of me becauſe my cloathes were dyed with the bark of the trees, I fled and hired myſelf to one Corniſh, for 6 guineas, for the fiſhing ſeaſon, in the bay of Shalore; but they putting in for proviſions I run away from them and went a ſeacowing with Capt. Palmer from London, bound to the middle iſlands, 14 days after I went on board a ſchooner, the maſter's name Adams, at the iſland Bryan, but being engaged in illegal trade a tender drove us off the iſland; we then came to Canſo, made up our loading with mackarel and came to Marblehead.

Soon after my arrival at this place I left the veſſel, and courted a young woman there; making known my intentions of going to Boſton, the people tried to diſſuade me from it, for I had told them that I was a deſerter from a man of war:—But God will bring all things to anſwer the deſigns of his Providence; for although I ſaw the danger myſelf, reſolved to go, but firſt went to Cape-Ann, where I kept with one Molholand, who was likewiſe againſt my going to Boſton; but all would not do; I had ſerved the devil long enough, and juſtice was to cut me off: At this time hearing of an act of grace for deſerters, I came to Boſton, was apprehended, and confined in camp; by order of the General I was tried, found guilty, and ſentenced to be ſhot in the rear of the camp, at 6 in the morning [illegible] of September, 1774; about 46 hours before I was to ſuffer, the General ſent me word of my ſate (ſhort time indeed to prepare for death, conſidering the life I have lived.)

Having been queſtioned about a great robbery that was committed near Brunſwick, as a dying man, I declare I had neither act nor part in it, nor ever knew any of the men.

May all thoſe who are addicted to the horrid ways of life that I have purſued, take warning from my unhappy ſituation, by the awful ſpectacle which this body of mine will in a ſhort time exhibit at the place where it is deſtined to ſuffer.—No mortal, except myſelf, can form any adequate conception of the terror that ſeizes my ſoul.—In a few hours, O gracious God! I muſt enter upon an eternal ſtate of exiſtence, and join the world of ſpirits! And may that God, who governs all things, receive my immortal ſoul.

I now heartily forgive every one, in hopes that I ſhall myſelf obtain forgiveneſs; and die in charity with all men, an unworthy member of the church of England.

Valentine Dukett.

Boſton Camp (at mid-night) 9th Sept. 1774.

Broadside recording the life and last words of Valentine Duckett. (*Massachusetts Historical Society*)

Limerick (in Ireland) where I joined my regiment, which was soon after ordered for America.

We arrived at Boston, New-England, and lay about 6 months at Castle-William, when we were ordered to Halifax, where we lay two years; during all of this time I behaved in character of a good soldier: But alas! unhappily for me, young and unthinking, I took to drinking and bad company, and was soon persuaded to desert my colours, and go on board Capt. Live, who conducted me to Mahon-Bay; but being in dread lest I should be taken, I took boat[25] and escaped to Lunenburgh, where I disposed of some of my regimentals,[26] and set out for the head of Mishmash River, from thence to New-Dublin, where I went on board a shoal trader, belonging to Capt. Tilestone, of Boston, Capt. Callen, Commander, as an able seaman, though I had really no knowledge of my new profession; but by diligent attention to my Captain's instructions, I learnt to work the vessel by the time we arrived at Boston. In August, 1771, I was discharged this vessel, and went on board a brig, belonging to Capt. Davis, at the South-End, Boston, which I left in about a fortnight, and went on board a sloop belonging to Newport, Rhode-Island; but having bad weather on the passage, and meeting with the Martin Sloop of war, Captain Howard, Commander, he obliged us to pilot him into Charlestown, South-Carolina, during which time, I kept myself concealed for some of the Martin's crew knew me very well; we then sailed again for Newport, and about fourteen days after our arrival, I left this sloop and went on board the Peace and Plenty packet,[27] for Philadelphia, where I went to work, and very narrowly escaped being taken by a parry[28] of the regiment coming from Scotland; but was soon after apprehended by the Royal Americans[29] and confined, but found means to make my escape.

I then set out for New-Castle, with but half a dollar in my pocket, and on my way met with a young woman, who passed at New-Castle for my wife, but I was soon taken up as a strolling vagrant and put on board the pilot boat, but putting into Dover for provisions, I escaped and fled to Ceader-Creek, where I went on board a shallop[30] bound to New-Castle, in search of my supposed wife; but not meeting with her, I set out for Baltimore, in Maryland, but being detained at Christian Bridge by a shallop's crew who knew me, I was put on board and went to Philadelphia, where I lodged at one Mrs. Hall's, on Society-hill, to keep out of the way; where I met with one Richard West, an Englishman, who had broke goal[31] in that city with me, being glad to see each other, and cash being short, he swore he would have money by some means, that night; so he went to a ship which he told me had plenty of plunder on board, I asked him what he meant; he then told me he knew the Captain on board, who had plenty of cash, and he going on board I waited by his desire, to receive the goods; he brought me a pair of green plush breeches, with 24 dollars in the pocket, 2 pair silver buckles, a fine hat and 2 jackets; but he returning for a watch, the ship's crew were alarmed and secured him, upon which I fled with what I had got, and hid them under a barn in the fields; I met one of our comrades in the morning and he asked me for the things, upon which we went to Mrs. Hill's, which was a house of bad fame, and there we met with two old comerades viz. Richard Black and Lawrence Grogan, who had broke out of Gloucester goal, where they had been imprisoned for horse stealing; we all agreed to take boat and go to Burlington, in the Jersies, we got to Brunswick, next day to York, and there went into a baudyhouse, where we got acquainted with John Dealy; we hearing of a ship that had a quantity of money we went on board her, and took to the value of £100 sterling, made our escape to Kingsbridge on our way to Boston, from thence to New-London, from thence to Norwich; and assuming the character of merchants (being 4 in number) we soon got to Providence, where being questioned by some land surveyors, we told them a fair story, viz. that we were merchants bound to Boston, they then wished us a safe passage, and in two days we arrived at Boston, where we committed several robberies; Dealy, Grogan and Murphy were taken, Dealy broke goal and made his escape, but Murphy was tried; about this time one Joseph Price and Nancy Kean, who passed for man and wife, and boarded with Mrs. Cummings, North-end, committed several attrocious robberies; we got intimate with John Hall, a deserter from the 64th regiment, comerade of Charles Leas, we went to Salem, where we were guilty of several robberies, but being detected in the sale of the goods, we were committed to goal; soon after five of us broke out and came to Boston, in search of the woman mentioned above, but hearing nothing of my old companions, I went on board the Captain man of war in search of them, where they detained me; but soon after hearing my comerades were in Boston, I made my escape, fled to Plymouth and committed two robberies there; came back to Boston in search of the woman, intending to leave the town next day, but was taken by a party of the 64th, conducted to Castle William, lay 19 days in irons, and was sent to my regiment (at Halifax) where I was tried, and received 800 lashes.

I now began to think something of an amendment of life, but the thoughts of those idle women still run in my mind, and the Devil prompting me, in about 18 months I again left the regiment, in company with Laughlin Castels; we had great difficulty and hardships in the woods, by reason of cold and hunger, and at length came to a town called Picktoo, some time after my comerade made his escape to St John's, and I to the Three Rivers in Newfoundland, but the Collector having some suspicion of me because my cloathes were dyed with the bark of the trees,[32] I fled and hired myself to one Cornish, for 6 guineas,[33] for the fishing season, in the bay of Shalore; but they putting in for provisions I run away from them and went a seacowing[34] with Captain Palmer from London, bound to the middle islands, 14 days after I went on board a schooner, the masters name Adams, at the island Bryan,[35] but being engaged in illegal trade a tender drove us off the island; we then came to Canso, made up our loading with mackarel and came to Marblehead.

Soon after my arrival at this place I left the vessel, and courted a young woman there; making known my intentions of going to Boston, the people tried to dissuade me from it, for I had told them I was a deserter from a man of war:—But God will bring all things to answer the designs of his Providence; for although I saw the danger myself, resolved to go, but first went to Cape-Ann, where I kept with one Mulholland, who was likewise against my going to Boston; but all would not do; I had served the devil long enough, and justice was to cut me off: At this time hearing of an act of grace for deserters, I came to Boston, was apprehended, and confined in camp; by order of the General I was tried, found guilty, and sentenced to be shot in the rear of the camp, at 6 in the morning of the 9th of September, 1774; about 16 hours before I was to suffer, the General sent me word of my time (short time indeed to prepare for death, considering the life I have lived.)

Having been questioned about a great robbery that was committed near Brunswick, as a dying man, I declare that I had neither act nor part in it, nor ever knew any of the men.

May all those who are addicted to the horrid ways of life that I have pursued, take warning from my unhappy situation, by the awful spectacle which this body of mine will in a short time exhibit at the place where it is destined to suffer.—No mortal, except myself, can form any adequate conception of the terror that seizes my soul.—In a few hours, O gracious God! I must enter upon an eternal state of existence, and join the world of spirits! And may that god, who governs all things, receive my mortal soul.

I now heartily forgive every one, in hopes that I shall myself obtain forgiveness; and die in charity with all men, an unworthy member of the church of England.

Valentine Duckett

Boston Camp (at mid-night) 9th Sept. 1774.

Eleven days passed between Valentine Duckett's capture and his military trial. Courts-martial were tribunals that followed judicial procedures in many ways similar to those familiar today. Charges were brought against the prisoner, prosecutorial witnesses gave depositions and then were examined by both the prosecutor and the defense, then the prisoner presented his defense and called his own witnesses. The composition of the court, however, was different from modern civil trials. The court was composed of commissioned officers who heard the evidence, questioned witnesses, deliberated, and passed the verdict. One of these officers also presided over the court. Another officer with the administrative assignment of Deputy Judge Advocate was responsible for planning the court, assisting the prisoner in preparing a defense, arranging for the appearance of witnesses, ensuring that proper military judicial procedures were followed during the trial, and handling the documentary aspects of the trial and the verdict. Regimental courts consisted of five officers from within a single regiment and tried crimes associated with the regiment's internal affairs—disorderly conduct, petty theft, disobedience, and a host of other minor disciplinary infractions.

Regimental courts could hand down sentences no more severe than corporal punishment, usually in the form of lashes. Higher crimes for which capital punishment could be sentenced required a general court-martial. These courts consisted of thirteen officers (plus the Deputy Judge Advocate) from several regiments, of a mixture of ranks none below lieutenant.[36]

Valentine Duckett's trial lasted three days, beginning on 31 August and ending on 2 September. Part of the formal nature of general courts was that the proceedings were recorded and copies sent to the War Office in London. There, the proceedings were transcribed into bound record books that survive to this day. The complete proceedings of Duckett's trial are as follows.

The Court Martial of Valentine Duckett

Proceedings of a General Court Martial held at the Camp near Boston on the 31st day of Augst 1774 by Virtue of a Warrant from His Excellency The Honble Thos Gage, General & Commander in Chief of all His Majesty's Forces in North America &c, &c, &c. dated Head Quarters at Boston Augst 30th 1774 and directed to Major Roger Spendlove of the 43d Regt of Foot.

Major Roger Spendlove President

Members

Capt Geo Thompson 43 Reg^{t}
Capt Grey Grove R. W. Fuziliers
Capt Anth^{y} Farrington R. Artillery
Capt John West King's own Reg^{t}
Capt William Holmes King's own Reg^{t}
Capt Charles Lumm 38th Reg^{t}
Capt Willm Law^{nce} Coker 38 Reg^{t}
Capt John Hatfield 43d Reg^{t}
Capt John Ferrier King's own Reg^{t}
Capt Patr^{k} Downes 5th Reg^{t}
Capt Fran^{s} Marsden 5th Reg^{t}
Capt William Battier 5th Reg^{t}
Lt Jo^{s} Knight of the King's own Reg^{t} of Foot Dep Judge Advocate

The Warrant being read & the Court & D. Judge Advocate being duly sworn they proceeded to the Tryal of Valentine Ducket private Soldier in His Majesty's 65th Reg^{t} of Foot confined by Lieu^{t} Colonel Bruce of the same Reg^{t} for Desertion.

Capt John Roberts of the 65th Reg^{t} was duly sworn.

Q: by the Court Do you know the Prisoner to have received pay & to have done Duty as a Soldier in the 65th Reg^{t} of Foot.

A: I do

Q: How long has he been a Soldier in said Reg^{t}.

A: Since the beginning of the Year 1768.

The Deponent declares that the Prisoner Valentine Ducket some time this last Spring absented himself without Leave from the Regt then lying at Halifax Nova Scotia & that the Reg^{t} had never received any acco~~ts~~ of him since till a few days ago when he was apprehended as a Deserter by a Serj~~t~~ of the 5th Reg^{t} & some Soldiers of the Artillery—that the day the Prisoner was taken the Deponent went to see him at the Quarter Guard of the 5th Reg^{t}, where he was confined, that he then told him his Intentions were to have Surrendered himself if he had not been so soon taken up that he had seen him (the Deponent) that day & meant to have given himself up to him.

Q: by the Court. Do you know if the Prisoner Valentine Ducket was ever guilty of a Crime of the same Nature of that for which he is now Tried.

A: I know him to have been twice guilty of it before.

Q: Was the Prisoner tried & punished for his former Desertions.

A: For the first he was tried & punished but on his Trial for the second offence it appearing that he had intentions of returning to his Regiment and there being also about that time an Act of Grace published he was pardoned.

John Andrew Soldier in the 65th Reg^{t} of Foot being duly sworn deposeth, that he knows the Prisoner Valentine Ducket to have recd pay & done duty as a Soldier in the 65th Reg^{t} farther that the said Ducket deserted some time last Spring from the Reg^{t} which was then lying in Hallifax Nova Scotia, that he knows him to have deserted twice before for which he was tried.

Serj^{t} George Kirk of the 5th Reg^{t} of Foot being duly sworn deposeth, that being standing in the Market Place at Boston on Saturday the 20th ins^{t} one Nicks a Soldier in the Royal Artillery came & tapped him on the Shoulder, on his turning round the said Nicks inform'd him that the Man who was then conversing with a Corp^{l} of the 5th Reg^{t} was a Deserter from the 65th Reg^{t} there being more than one in Number he ask'd him which of those was the Person, Nicks answer'd the Man with check Trowsers. The Deponent farther asked him how he came to know that he was a Deserter, he answered by his lying in the same Quarters at Hallifax, he ask'd him then the reason why he did not apprehend him himself. Nicks gave him to understand that he was some way doubtful they were not Sufficient in Number to do it. The Deponent then said if he would engage him to be a Deserter that he & the other Soldiers wou'd answer to take him. The Deponent advanced toward the Person whom he understood to be the Deserter, the Prisoner then quitted the Corporal & walk'd very quick. The Deponent followed him with a smart pace & came up with him—he immediately ask'd him whether he was ever in the 65th Reg^{t} he answer'd no he never was. The Corp^{l} & the two Soldiers of the Artillery then joined them & one of them said that was the Person which the Prisoner still deny'd. The Deponent then told the Prisoner that he would apprehend him as a Deserter from the 65th Reg^{t} & that he should go to Camp before Lord Percy, who commanded, upon which he brought him away; & in bringing him along thro' the Market the Prisoner run off & the Deponent with the other Soldiers pursued and overtook him & conducted him to Camp.

Q: by the D^{y} J A Was the Prisoner disguised when you apprehended him

A: He was

Q: How was he disguised

A: I do not recollect the particulars of his Dress but there was no part of it Military

Joseph Nicks Matross[37] in the Royal Artillery being duly sworn deposeth that on Saturday the 20th Ins^{t} being in the

Market place in Boston along with Richd Crampton of the same Corps, Crampton pointed out a Man to him & said he believed that was Ducket, upon which he look'd & saw a Man whom he knew to be Ducket talking to a Corp^{l} of the 5th Reg^{t}, that they then walked toward him & he left the Corporal. There being a Serj^{t} of the 5th Reg^{t} standing by he thought it proper to acquaint him who Ducket was in order to get his Assistance to apprehend him fearing that if he & his Companions were to attempt it themselves, the Towns people of whom there was a great Number present would prevent them. The Serj^{t} then went up to Ducket & enter'd into Conversation with him & the Deponent & Crampton join'd them just as the Serj^{t} had ask'd the Prisoner if he did not belong to the 65th Reg^{t} which he deny'd. The Deponent then told the Prisoner that his Name was Ducket & ask'd him if he did not know him & appealing to Crampton if he did not know him likewise to be Ducket, Crampton replied he knew him very well, upon which the Deponent desired he might be secur'd & taken to some place of safety. Ducket then desired they would not pull him about for that he was ready to go with them quietly any where, they let him walk with them without holding him, and after they had gone a little way the Prisoner, seeing an Opening, sprung off & run about thirty Yards. The Serj^{t} of the 5th Reg^{t} calling out Stop thief & Crampton pursuing the Prisoner he was again apprehended & conducted to Camp without his making any further Resistance.

Q: by the D J A Did you know the Prisoner Valentine Ducket to have been a Soldier in the 65th Reg^{t}

A: I did very well

Q: Did you know anything of his having deserted from the 65th Reg^{t} this last Spring

A: I did from the general report of the Men of that Reg^{t} at Hallifax, where I was at that time quartered

Q: Was the Prisoner disguised when he was apprehended on the 20th ins^{t}

A: He was so much disguised that had I not Recollected his having deserted I should not have known him

Richard Crampton Soldier in the Royal Reg^{t} of Artillery being duly sworn confirms in every Respect the Evidence of Joseph Nicks.

The Court then Adjourned 'till tomorrow Morning 10 o'Clock

Sept 1st 1774

The Court met according to adjournment President & Members the same as Yesterday

The Prisoner Valentine Ducket being brought on his Defence delivered a paper to the Court which being read by the Deputy Judge Advocate is as follows.

Gentlemen,

Hearing there was an Act of Grace, when I came to Marblehead, I left the Vessel I belong'd to & came to Boston, where I was informed the time of the Act was out, on which I went to the house of Patr^k Carrol & told him I came on purpose to Surrender myself to my Colonel in Boston. I also went to the house of Mrs Rea & told her the same, who advised me to wait an opportunity of meeting my Colonel. I likewise inform'd my Shipmates, Richard Barry & Morris Mullowney of my intention of Surrendering, but soon after in looking for my Colonel, in the Town of Boston I was met with by two of the Train[38] & two of the fifth Regiment, who enquired of me, was I not a Deserter from 65th I was much suppris'd at it, I being a little in Liquor, & sprung towards two Officers that was near, on purpose to acquaint them of my Intention, & told Corp^l Crawley of the 5th before I came to Camp that I was a Deserter & was not willing to be taken, as I was come to Town with no other intent than to give myself up to my Colonel who was in Boston.

Richard Barry Marriner being called upon by the Prisoner being duly sworn deposeth that he belongs to a Schooner in which the Prisoner Ducket had sailed for some Time before he was apprehended, that a few weeks ago Ducket acknowledged to him he was a Deserter from the 65th Reg^t and told him he came to this part of the Country in order to surrender himself to his Officer.

Mary Davis being called upon by the Prisoner & being duly sworn deposeth that she lives as a Servt with one Carrol who keeps a publick House in Boston, that the day before & the Morning of the Day on which the Prisoner was apprehended he had been at the House & mention'd his Intentions of Surrendering himself as a Deserter, that upon somebody's saying that if he meant to deliver himself up he should lose no time in doing it, he replied he would amuse himself for two or three days & then give himself up as afterwards he must expect to be confined to the Reg^{t}.

The Deponent farther says that her Mistress is ready to give Evidence to the same purpose, but she is too much indisposed to attend the Court.

John Andrew[39] being duly called upon says he heard the wife of Carrol declare the Prisoner Ducket told her before he was apprehended that he had Intentions to surrender himself.

Daniel Martin being duly sworn deposeth that he is part owner of the Schooner mentioned in the Evidence of Barry, that the said Schooner arrived at Marblehead from a Fishing Voyage as well as he can recollect on the 6th Augst that on the 20th the Prisoner Ducket (whom he had seen at Marblehead on the 10th) came to him in Boston & ask'd him for some Money on Acco^{t} of Wages, & upon the Deponent's wanting to put him off to another Time the Prisoner told him he was a Deserter, but does not recollect hearing him say he had any Intentions to surrender himself.

The Court then adjorn'd till tomorrow 9 o'Clock

Sept 2d 1774

The Court met according to adjournment President & Members the same as Yesterday

The Court having deliberately and duly considered and weighed the Evidence against the Prisoner Valentine Ducket and his Defence do find him Guilty of having deserted His Majesty's service some Time about the Month of April last which is a Breach of the 1st Article of the 6th Section of the Articles of War, they therefore sentence him to suffer Death.

Jos Knight Rog^{r} Spendelove Presid^{t}

Depy Judge Advocate Brevet Major in the 43d Regiment

Boston August 8th 1774[40]

I approve of the above Sentence of the General Court Martial upon Valentine Ducket of his Majesty's 65th Regiment and order the same to be put in Execution.

Thos Gage

Commdr in Chief

Epilogue

Capital sentences required the approval of the commander in chief, approval which was five days in coming but which brought orders for the sentence to be carried out by a firing squad the following morning.[41] Duckett had just hours to receive the news and compose his dying speech. The purpose of a military execution was not so much to punish the offender as to show a stark example to the rest of the army; as such, a portion of the garrison was ordered to witness the event. The local population was also able to witness the gruesome spectacle, and John Andrews, who had made note of Duckett's capture, was among those who rose early to attend the 6 A.M. proceedings on the strand of beach behind the British army encampment on Boston Common. He described the final hour of the "smart, stout fellow" including the presentation of the dying speech. Duckett's initial composure may have stemmed from a continued expectation of mercy, for the military often pardoned capital offenders at the last moment. No reprieve, however, was forthcoming:

> Neither prompted by a brutal gratification, nor destitute of tender feelings, but led by a curiosity natural to most men, early this morning I attended the execution of the poor fellow whom I mentioned in one of my former letters to have been taken up in y market for desertion. After the Parson had pray'd with him, and while his grave was digging, he address'd himself to the Soldiers (who were drawn up from all the Regiments around him): he spoke for half an hour very fluently and compos'd, but when he was fix'd to the spot from which he was not to remove but into an awfull eternity, his spirits were much agitated, and after another exhortation and prayer, which continued about a quarter of an hour, he received the discharge of six muskets from about eight yards distance, and least that was not sufficient, a fourth stepp'd up and presented his gun close to his head and discharg'd it, which put a period to his life, he was then laid upon the lid of his coffin and expos'd to the view of the whole Army, who were made to march in a slow, solemn step close on one side his body, as an example in terrorem, I suppose; though I imagine it will have a quite

> contrary effect (unless they are lost to all sense of humanity) and create in them an utter detestation to remain subordinate to a set of men, who were instrumental in committing such an unjust act of cruelty.[42]

Had Duckett been pardoned and remained in the army, it is difficult to predict where his career might have taken him. Part of the 65th Regiment came to serve in Boston while the rest stayed in Halifax, and two companies of the corps fought in the famous actions on 19 April and 17 June 1775. After Boston was evacuated and the British army reorganized in Halifax in April and May 1776, the able-bodied men of the 65th were drafted and a small cadre returned to Great Britain to recruit anew. Duckett, young and stout, probably would have been among the drafts who were distributed into almost every regiment that campaigned through New York, New Jersey, and Pennsylvania during the next two years and in various locations for the remainder of the war. These men had careers of all descriptions, some dying or deserting in America and others living out their lives as soldiers and then as pensioners.[43] But Duckett's career and life were ended a month after his twenty-first birthday.

While the army to some brought satiation for wanderlust and satisfaction for an adventuresome spirit, men like Duckett sought a kind of stability and belonging that no career could provide. Unlike some of the rovers who passed through the army in their lifelong journeys, Duckett seems to have been ever conflicted. He left home but returned again, he left the army but returned again, content neither with a structured life nor satisfied with wandering. Perhaps his tragic end brought him peace.

FOUR

Literacy and Education

Thomas Watson, 23rd Regiment of Foot

Introduction

Like Valentine Duckett, Thomas Watson rambled during the early parts of his life. Indeed, there are aspects of his story that are remarkably similar to Duckett's and which also echo John Robert Shaw and Roger Lamb. Watson was unable to reconcile spending his life at any occupation he tried, and is yet another example of a young man who left home because he could not get along with his family. There are some marked distinctions in Watson's character and experience, however, that make him an example of the path and opportunities followed by another category of soldier: those who turned to the army not only for stability and adventure, but to better themselves.

Conventional wisdom holds that most soldiers were illiterate, a reflection of the low literacy among the segment of society from which they were recruited. Each soldier that we have studied so far, though, makes a point of mentioning their education. This can be interpreted in two ways, either as showing that education among the low classes was common, or that the army included a broader range of people than widely believed. It is outside the scope of this study to examine literacy among the working classes of Great Britain, but it is clear from the men presented here that many British soldiers were from comfortable, "middle-class" families rather than the dregs of society.

Although we have seen from the example of John Robert Shaw that not all soldiers were from the working classes, there is no doubt that the majority were, even if we cannot precisely quantify the proportion that constituted this majority. There is a category of surviving documents that allows us to test this conventional wisdom and offers a thought-provoking perspective on literacy in the army. When soldiers were discharged from the army they were given a document, aptly called a discharge, that provided legal proof of the completion of the man's military obligation. A substantial number of discharges survive. These documents will be described in detail in a later chapter; among the important information that they hold is the soldier's signature, or his mark if he was unable to write his own name. Surveying a substantial number of discharges of soldiers who served in America during the 1775–1783 war, we find that roughly half bear signatures rather than marks. This suggests that half of the men in the army were literate if we accept the debatable postulates that all men who could write their names were literate, and that the surviving discharges are an accurate random sample of the army as a whole.[1]

Regardless, however, of proportion of recruits that were literate, we know for certain that Thomas Watson was not. Born in a village in Cheshire, England, in 1753, Watson's father died when Thomas was only a few months old, leaving him and five siblings to be raised by his mother. These impoverished conditions induced Thomas to take work in the coal mines when he was just seven years old where he was "amongst a very wicked company" and soon "became as bad as any, according to my age." He became addicted to card playing and acquired a foul vernacular. As his older siblings left and pursued their own lives, young Thomas stayed at home and cared for his mother until she died shortly before his fifteenth birthday. He then went to London to live with one of his sisters.

Watson's stay in London apparently was short. Affected by a sore leg that had afflicted him from youth, he returned to his hometown to live with another sister. Finding that he disliked her husband, he soon departed and went to Lancashire. He stayed there for about a year but does not relate his activities. Again he returned to his home village but once more "could not make it seem like home." Restless and without direction, he did what many wandering youth did: he determined to go to sea. He went to Liverpool and signed on to a ship bound for Virginia, but was unable to bear conditions on board ship; it is not clear whether he made one voyage or simply stayed on the ship in port for a time. His aspirations as a mariner quashed, he returned to the Lancashire coal mines.

Wanderlust or discontent soon led him to Staffordshire where he worked at an unspecified pursuit, probably mining again, before moving on to the city of Wolverhampton. It was there that he found a recruiting party of the 23rd Regiment of Foot which was then under orders for deployment to America. Watson said that he was "persuaded" to enlist, a term that could be interpreted as meaning that he was coerced into the army. It is likely, however, that the impressionable young man was a willing volunteer. Compared to the life he had been living as an itinerant miner, service as a soldier was an attractive proposition.

That the 23rd's recruiters enlisted a miner shows that they were not deterred by a common notion that men of this profession were poorly suited to the army and were likely to desert.[2] Perhaps imminent overseas service gave the recruiters confidence that men of this background would not have the opportunities to desert that they might if remaining in Britain.[3] This particular recruit, approaching his twentieth year, would never again enter a British mine.

Watson does not give the date of his enlistment, but it clearly was in late 1772 or early 1773. Apparently Watson's sore leg, if he had not outgrown it, was not severe enough to prevent him from traveling or to cause the regimental surgeon to reject him as a recruit. Watson's enlistment in the 23rd Regiment also provides yet another example of the wide-ranging recruiting conducted by British regiments during this era. Although the 23rd held the title Royal Welch Fusiliers,[4] they followed the normal practice of recruiting from all over Great Britain, drawing men from where ever they could be gotten.[5] And, contrary to any notion that people did not travel much, Watson had ventured through many parts of England in his youth before joining the army a considerable distance from his original home in Cheshire.

Watson the soldier went to Chatham Barracks outside of London and embarked for America in early April 1773; the 23rd Regiment went on four transports. Watson was on the *Friendship*, which also carried one of the most prolific British military diarists of the American war, Captain Frederick Mackenzie. This officer described the voyage in great detail in a letter home.[6] The regiment's transports and a few other ships rode at anchor in the Catwater, an inlet of Plymouth Sound, waiting for favorable winds to take them into open water. Fair winds came on the 25th and the ships proceeded through the English Channel and into the Atlantic Ocean. On the first few days seasickness was rampant, exacerbated by strong swells. On 2 May a child of the regiment died, and on the same day a child was born to a soldier's wife; that child died about two weeks later "due to bad management." On 7 May, gales arose and continued intermittently for the next five days. Rigging was damaged, sails split, but most fearful for the soldiers were waves breaking over the deck and rolls that put the gunwales underwater, forcing the soldiers below under battened hatches. The heavy weather scattered the ships, but within days they were together again. When the weather calmed, it was discovered that the main mast had been overstressed and could not be rigged with its full complement of sails for the remainder of the voyage.

Not everything was going poorly. After three weeks seasickness had largely abated and the regiment's men and women were generally healthy. The soldiers were divided into four groups, one of which kept watch on deck at all times. Each day the berths were cleaned and sprinkled with vinegar. The routine was healthful but challenging to maintain when seasickness induced lethargy. Several times men were literally dragged with ropes from their berths to the deck. In spite of the damage to its masts and rigging, the *Friendship* was able to outsail the old ship used by the commodore in charge of the little convoy. The master asked for, and was granted, permission to continue alone rather than keep pace with the flagship. Over the next few days they lost sight of the remaining ships in the convoy. They encountered other ships and, as was the custom, bore close enough to communicate by speaking trumpet, discussing their reckoned positions and exchanging news. Flying fish and sea turtles were frequently observed, and officers made sport of shooting at porpoises that swam along with the ship. The soldiers tried to catch fish but failed. Another gale buffeted the ship for a day, followed by fair winds and fast sailing. On the morning of 3 June they attempted to speak to a sloop, but it bore away after getting close enough to discern soldiers on board the *Friendship*. This suggested to the British that the sloop was out of Boston, "as they are remarkable for their aversion to people with red coats on." When they believed themselves near land, they began to take depth soundings.

The eastern end of Long Island was sighted on the evening of 8 June and by evening of the 9th they were at the mouth of New York harbor. Before nightfall they brought a pilot on board who, in spite of a dark windy night, guided them to a city wharf by 11 P.M. Due to the darkness the ship touched the wharf before the sailors could drop an anchor to wait out the night. When dawn came they learned that they were the first of the transports to arrive. On 11 June the soldiers disembarked and went into barracks in the city. Two more transports, the *Henry* and the *Pallas*, arrived on the 12th. The *Henry*'s voyage was relatively uneventful, but smallpox broke out on board the *Pallas* which took the lives of four children. Two soldiers were similarly afflicted and recovered, but two died of other illnesses. The last transport, the *Brudenell*, came in on the 17th, having been slowed by taking on water and by a damaged mast. The voyage to America experienced by Watson was typical enough in both duration and hazard. Time at sea traveling from east to west could be as little as four or five weeks, but soldiers often spent several additional weeks on board ship waiting for favorable winds before departure and at their destination ports. Bad weather characterized part of almost every voyage, and military men making the passage for the first time were usually afflicted by seasickness, frightened by the tumbling of the vessel, and quickly indoctrinated to the arduous routine of maintaining order and cleanliness in cramped conditions. In spite of the dangers and difficulties, the vast majority of British soldiers arrived in America safely and in reasonably good health. A few disasters occurred, but not enough to seriously impact the effectiveness of the army.[7]

Thomas Watson's own writings provide very little detail on his life as a soldier, but make it clear that he underwent significant changes during his time in the army. One of these, particularly remarkable in the context of this study, was his transformation from illiteracy to a level of education that would allow him, eventually, to write his own memoir. In this he brings to light a little-known aspect of the military that forces us to rethink stereotypes of British soldiers. Describing his shift from the mines to the military, Watson wrote: "I found that I had bettered myself in regard to bad company. This may seem strange to some, but it is no more strange than true, for my education, while young, at the coal mines, was far worse than in the army. I was now twenty years old, and scarce knew my letters. I was now, therefore, resolved to leave off my bad language, and endeavor for learning, which I measurably did, while in the army."

The notion that a man could "endeavor for learning" in the British army of the eighteenth century sounds peculiar, but is borne out by other military writings. One of the most widely read guidebooks for army officers included this discussion of the importance of education to the management of a regiment:

> From the common people (the English in particular) employing their children very early, in works of labour, their education becomes totally neglected, and as the Soldiery is in general from that class, many of them (although otherwise properly qualified for Non-commission-officers) can neither read nor write, which being absolutely necessary for those employed as such, it would be of infinite improvement, if (as is the case, in some of the Corps of Scotch Hollanders)[8] every Regiment was to establish a school, under the management of an old Soldier qualified for such an undertaking, and to be supported by voluntary contributions from the Officers; by which means, not only the Soldiers, who were desirous of improvement,

> might be taught to read and write, but also the children of the Regiment, which institution, besides the advantage it must always be, to have a number of men so far well qualified for Non-commission-officers, would likewise be a real charity, by educating children, who from the poverty of their parents, must ever remain in a state of ignorance.[9]

Another prolific author included a similar recommendation in two of his works, suggesting that "A Serjeant, or Corporal, whose sobriety, honesty, and good conduct, can be depended upon, and who is capable to teach writing, reading, and arithmetic, should be employed to act in the capacity of school-master, by whom soldiers and their children may be carefully instructed: a room or tent should be appointed for that use; and it would be highly commendable if the Chaplain, or his deputy, would pay some attention to the conduct of the school."[10]

That these recommendations were followed by at least some regiments is proven by orders given in several regiments, worth repeating here verbatim:

> A School to be establish'd in the Barracks at the Mess Room for instructing the younger Men in Writing & Arithematick 2 Hours in the Forenoon & 2 in the Afternoon. … The Men who attend the School may have Paper by applying to the Qr. Mr. Serjeant. … A Return to be given in Immediately of each Compy the Names of the men who Attend the School.[11]
>
> The Regimental School now Established to be kept up in all Quarters and duly attended. The Serjeant who has the direction of it to report any who shou'd be bad behaved, Remiss or Irregular. At the end of every 2d Month, he will give in a return to the Commanding Officer of the Names of those, who attend the School of each Company, what they learn, whether to Read or write &c. and the progress they make. If they are any way remarkably well behaved, &ca he will Notice them.[12]
>
> In consequence of the Non Commisd Officers being Ordered to put themselves to school, for their improvement in Writing and Arithmatick, such of them as are at present under a greater weekly stoppage than the usual

> Arrears, Officers Commanding Companys will augment their weekly Pay, to whatever sum they may think sufficient to pay for their Schooling & to furnish them with Paper, pens and Ink.[13]

These passages from regimental orders prove that some regiments maintained schools, but we cannot say whether the practice was universal. Regimental orderly books are quite rare, and we do not have enough of them to accurately deduce whether regimental schools were commonplace.

There are other indications of the value the army placed on education. Roger Lamb, a well-educated young soldier who became a schoolmaster after leaving the army, earned extra money by teaching writing and arithmetic to a sergeant's child in the 9th Regiment.[14] A schoolmaster in Rhode Island included among his receipts a payment for "Schooling Soldiers Children" while the place was a British garrison in 1777.[15] We do not know if the 23rd Regiment had a school during Watson's service, or if he sought his own tutelage from within or without the regiment. We can be confident that his efforts to better himself were supported by his officers. That he was eventually able to pen a memoir is testimony to the success of his efforts.

Thomas Watson wrote his brief memoir in 1803 at the age of fifty.[16] He had lived half his life since leaving the army and had other things to focus on besides his youth and time as a soldier. He wrote fewer than one thousand words describing his early life and military service, and yet this short account is invaluable both for the aspects that corroborate other narratives and for the new insights that he introduces. The entire narrative from the beginning until Watson's departure from the army will be presented here, but Watson omitted an important chapter of this part of his life. A military document fills in some important details. For chronological flow, we present the first portion of Watson's memoir, which will be followed by a discussion of events as given in other sources, before continuing with the remainder of the memoir.

Watson's own autobiographical narrative begins:

I have had it on my mind for some years, to leave something in writing, of the Lord's dealings with me from my youth, and now I am in my fiftieth year, I begin. I was born in the year of our Lord 1753, in a small village, called Nessholt, in Cheshire, of England, seven miles from Chester. My father's name was Joseph, who died when I was but a few months old. My mother was left with six children, whose names were George, Mary, Nancy, Joseph, William and Thomas. We were brought up in the way of the Church of England. When I was about 7 years of age, I was put to work at the coal mines, amongst a very wicked company, and soon became as bad as any, according to my age. For which I felt the judgments of God at that early age, for my wicked ways, and when I turned therefrom, I felt his love to my soul. I lived with, and had the care of my mother, as long as she lived: when she died, I was nearly fifteen years of age. I then went to London, to live with a sister. While in London, I was troubled with a sore leg, which I had from my youth. So I returned home again, and found my other sister married to a man I disliked. I soon left my home again and went to Lancashire, and stayed there about a year, and then returned home again, and stayed a while, but could not make it seem like home to me. I was then resolved to go to sea, and went to Liverpool to accomplish the same, and went on board a ship bound to Virginia; but she smelt so strong of tobacco, I was sick all the time I was on board. So I returned, and went to my old occupation in the coal mines, at the Duke of Bridgewater's Works, at Worsley Mills, near Bolton, in Lancashire. I stayed there a while, and then went to Staffordshire, and worked there for a while, and then went to Wolverhampton, where there was a recruiting party, that persuaded me to enlist for a soldier, to go to America, to be stationed at New-York, for the space of five years. This opportunity I embraced, and enlisted accordingly, and set sail for America, the 25th day, 4th month, 1773, and arrived at New-York the 9th of 6th month following, having a good passage. I found that I had bettered myself in regard to bad company. This may seem strange to some, but it is no more strange than true, for my education, while young, at the coal mines, was far worse than in the army. I was now twenty years old, and scarce knew my letters. I was now, therefore, resolved to leave off my bad language, and endeavor for learning, which I measurably did, while in the army. And whilst here, I felt many visitations of God's love to my soul, yea, and some loud calls, insomuch that I often promised obedience; yea, I often felt the light of Christ to shine in my dark heart; yea, and did discover it to be the light of Christ that enlightens every man that cometh into the world.

The 23rd Regiment of Foot, with Thomas Watson in its ranks, served for about a year in New York before sailing to Boston in July 1774. Watson wrote nothing about his time in New York, but the publisher of his memoir noted in the introduction that "Whilst stationed in New-York, he has often been heard to say, that the sin of intemperance had so far gained an ascendancy over him, as scarcely to allow him to go to sleep sober for months together." Watson apparently acquired some acquaintances among the local population whom he left behind but did not forget when the regiment embarked for Boston.

On 17 March 1775 Thomas Watson and a fellow soldier of the 23rd Regiment, Jacob Jones, disappeared from the Boston garrison. Jones was new to the regiment since its arrival in America but appears on the muster rolls with no annotation to suggest where he came from. It is possible that he enlisted in America and deserted to return to his family, but this is only speculation based on his appearance on the muster rolls and information that will be related below. Watson was absent from his regiment when hostilities broke out on 19 April 1775, and he did not witness the Pyrrhic British victory at Bunker Hill two months later. He did not experience the winter of deprivation in Boston, the evacuation of that city, and the army's reorganization in Halifax, Nova Scotia. He did not participate in the dramatic British victories that led to the fall of New York City in the late summer and autumn of 1776.

Thomas Watson came to America with the 23rd Regiment of Foot, or Royal Welch Fusiliers, shortly before the war began. Originally formed to escort the artillery, by the time of the American war fusilier regiments were identical to other infantry regiments. As an homage to their original role fusilier soldiers wore black bearskin caps, a style worn only by grenadiers and drummers in other regiments. It is not clear whether these caps were worn frequently or only on special occasions and otherwise replaced by cocked hats.

This illustration draws on a picture rendered by an officer of the 23rd Regiment in Boston showing a sentry of the regiment wearing a fur cap with the Prince of Wales's three-feather badge on the red back panel. His hair is braided and tucked into his cap in the style called a plait. The coat lapels, cuffs, and collar are the very dark blue called royal blue. This soldier is dressed for a march into the countryside in the months preceding the 19 April 1775 expedition to Concord. The troops wore knapsacks on these day-long marches for exercise and training; they may have also worn canteens or haversacks but none is mentioned in orders for these marches. The soldier wears calf-length spatterdashes, which were favored in America over knee-length gaiters. The cartridge pouch slung over his left shoulder, secured by a strap on the coat, bears a cast-brass three-feather badge. His waistbelt and bayonet, worn over his other shoulder for greater comfort on the march, are not visible. The hooks and eyes that clip the corners of the coat skirts together are reinforced with cloth ornaments in the popular shape of hearts. The coat buttons are in pairs, consistent with a light infantryman drawn by the same officer upon whose work this illustration was based; many regiments had paired buttons including two other fusilier regiments, the 7th and 21st.

2012

But the fall of New York brought about Thomas Watson's return to the British army and the 23rd Regiment of Foot.

On 21 September 1776 Watson was apprehended in New York City by a corporal of the 43rd Regiment who recognized him, having seen him during their service in Boston. Eleven days later he was brought to trial for desertion by a general court-martial. The trial proceeded as follows:[17]

Thomas Watson, private Soldier in His Majesty's 23d, or Royal Welch Fusileer Regt. of Foot, was brought before the Court and accused of having deserted from the said Regiment.

Sergeant Robert Laithwait of the 23d Regt. of Foot being duly sworn, deposed that he knows the prisoner to have been duly inlisted, and to have received pay as a Soldier in His Majesty's 23d Regt. of Foot, and that he deserted in the beginning of March 1775, from the said Regt. then at Boston.

Corporal Thomas Hunter of the 23d Regt. of Foot, being duly sworn deposed that he was Corporal of the same Company in the 23d Regt. that the prisoner belong'd to, and that he deserted from the said Regiment, the latter end of February or beginning of March 1775.

Q. Does he know him to have been duly inlisted and to have received pay as a Soldier in that Regt?

A. Yes he does.

The Prisoner being put upon his defence, declared that he had no intention of deserting, but was kidnapped away; that there was one Jones a Soldier in the 23d Regt. who had a Brother that lived at Dorchester point; and this man came one day to see his Brother the Soldier when he ask'd him—(Watson) to go and drink with him, and he accordingly went to a public house, with the two Brothers; that the one who lived at Dorchester, ask'd him afterwards if he would not go and see him into the boat, which he assented to; and upon his coming to the Wharf, a man knock'd him down, and the two Jones's assisted by two others, tied him, and put him into the boat, and slapping a pistol to his head, swore that if he made a noise that they would shoot him; that the boat then rowed over to the opposite shore, and they then endeavour'd to

Pacify him, and perswade him to join them, but this he refused to do, and they then threaten'd to tar and feather him, that they carried him, with his Arms tied behind him, five and thirty miles that night, and conducted him thus from town to town, and then put him into Harford goal amongst those they called Tories; that he was confined there upwards of three Months; when he broke out and endeavour'd to come to Boston; that he one night in particular passed the lines of Roxbury, and had gone, as he imagined through all the Sentries, when some men, whom he afterwards found to be riflemen, but at that time he thought to be English Soldiers, got up and called out to them not to kill him, as he was coming in to them, that they then seized him and lodged him in the Provost Guard that night, and the next morning he was sent with another man towards the mines at White Plains in Connecticut; that being a miner by trade, he worked there all last Winter; and as he knew his business very well he was appointed as a Deputy to make the other men work, and was permitted to go out, whereas the others were kept confined; that he made his escape from them in March last, and having travelled two days, he came to a town called Pittsfield or Plainfield or some such name, that he inquired if there were any lories there, and a large house was pointed out to him, to which he went, and having told his case to the Master of it, he gave him five dollars and a coat; that he then set out for New London, and work'd as a labourer there for about a month; that he wanted to go to Boston but hearing that the Army had left it, he set out for New York, and here he arrived about the latter end of May; that upon his arrival at New York he found that the Asia Man of War lay below; he got a canoe and endeavour'd with one, White, who said that he was a Deserter from the 59th Regt. to go down to the Asia, but they were hailed from Staten Island, and the canoe brought to by some riflemen; who brought them up prisoners to the Town; that they were then examined by a Colonel Reid of the Rebel Army, whom they told that they went with an intention to catch Oysters, and were then released; that he then went to one Jonathan Smith, whom he knew to be a Friend to Government, and told him that he wished to get on board the fleet, and Smith proposed that they should take a Boat of his

Master's and attempt it, but his Wife said that they had shot a man in making the attempt, and therefore advised them against it, but recommended him to hide himself till the Rebels abandon'd the town; that he accordingly concealed himself, till the Army took possession of it, when he intended to surrender himself to his own Colonel; that hearing he was not on Shore, he wrote to Governor Tryon, telling him where he was, as also his name and the Regt. he belonged to, and sent the letter by Mrs. Smith, but in the meantime he was apprehended by a Corporal of the 43d Regt.

Mary Smith being duly sworn was examined.

Q. (By desire of the Prisoner) Did not the Prisoner mention to her his intention of going to the fleet?

A. Yes.

Q. Whether she did not get him a place to conceal himself in, till the rebels had march'd out of town, and afterwards carry a Letter for him to the Governor, acquainting him, where he (the Prisoner) was?

A. She did get him a place to conceal himself in, and carried a Letter to the Governor, but was told by his butler, that he was not well enough to see anybody; and whilst she was out with that letter the prisoner was taken up.

Q. Who was in the house at the time he was apprehended.

A. A hired Servant Girl.

Q. Did she leave the letter at Governor Tryon's?

A. No. She did not.

Q. When did the prisoner write the letter?

A. A day or two she thinks, before she carried it but she cannot positively say.

Q. What was her reason for not leaving the letter that she carried to Governor Tryon?

A. Because the Butler told her there was no occasion as there could be nothing done till he was settled a little.

Q. Where was the Governor or the Butler when she attempted to deliver the letter?

A. She first saw the Butler at the house of one Walker a Cooper to the Artillery, whose wife first mentioned the matter to him, and the Witness meeting him afterwards—in the Street said that she hoped he should not forget what Mrs. Walker had said to him, and told him that she had a petition to the Governor, but he said that he could not deliver it then, but would mention the matter to the Governor who was then on Long Island as soon as he went over.

Q. How long was the prisoner concealed in her house?

A. He was concealed in her father-in-law's house and did not come to her house till after the rebels had left the town.

Q. What became of the Letter?

A. The Prisoner told her, after he was apprehended, that it w'd be of no service then, and therefore she destroyed it.

Q. Where was the prisoner from the 16th of September, the day the Army took possession of the town, till the 21st when he was apprehended?

A. He was in the house but not concealed; and she went out several times to endeavour to find his Colonel.

Q. How long has she known the prisoner?

A. Since last Summer.

Q. Does she know the prisoner to have been in the rebel Army?

A. All she knows of that is that the prisoner came one day into her house with one Jones, who was a Drum Major in the Rebel Army; that the young woman whom she had in the house, and who had known the prisoner when he was in the 23d Regt. ask'd him if he did not wish to have his old Coat on again, upon which he turned round to Jones and said, if it had not been for that Villain, I should have had it on.

Q. How was the prisoner dressed then?

A. He was in one of the rebel uniforms.

Q. Did she ever see him under arms or with accoutrements?[18]

A. She never did.

Q. What station was he in, in the rebel Army?

A. She does not know

Q. Did she ever hear the prisoner say how he had left his Regt.?

A. She heard him say that he had been to drink with Jones and his brother, and that they had tied him and carried him off by force.

Q. Does she know any thing of the prisoner's attempting to go in a Canoe on board the Asia, and being taken prisoner by some riflemen?

A. She knows no more of it than what he told her.

Q. Had the prisoner the coat on that he now wears, when she went with the letter?

A. No, he had a Coat of her husbands on then, which she has since sent for.

Q. When did she see him last in the rebel uniform?

A. He wore it till the day that she carried the letter—and then he put her husband's Coat on.

The Court Adjourned till 8 oClock next morning

Thursday Oct 3d 1776

The Court being met pursuant to Adjurnment

Mary Smith was again examined.

Q. What arms were there in her house?

A. A sword which her husband has borrowed from a Mr. Lispenard.

Q. Were there no firelocks[19] or bayonets?

A. There were not.

Q. What ammunition was there in the house?

A. None but a small bag which her husband or the Apprentice of her father-in-law had found, and brought in; the rebels would often, when it rained, bring their arms and ammunition into the house, and hang them up, without her leave, but they always took them away again.

Q. (by desire of the prisoner) Did she not hear the prisoner say that he would rather die by his own Regt. than stay in the Country with the rebels?

A. She did hear him say so, before the King's troops arrived in Town; and she heard him say, since they came in, that if he was restored to his Regt. that he wish'd immediately to be engaged with the rebels, that he might have satisfaction of them.

Q. (by the Court) Does she recollect her husband and the prisoner, proposing to go off to the fleet in a Canoe, and her perswading them against it?

A. Yes she does.

Q. What conversation pass'd on that occasion?

A. The prisoner and her husband often talked of it, till she beg'd of her husband not to leave her in the hands of the rebels, as they would soon be relieved; and she added that he might possibly be killed from the batteries, or from the shipping, from their not knowing his intent of coming off.

Q. What conversation had she with Mrs. Walker concerning the prisoner, and at what time?

A. She had a conversation with Mrs. Walker concerning him, before the King's Troops came into town, and another the morning she attempted to carry the Letter to the Governour; knowing that she had some interest in the Governour's family, she ask'd her if she cou'd do any thing for the prisoner, and when the butler came in, Mrs. Walker took him aside into another room, to mention the prisoner (as she supposed) to the butler, and Mrs. Walker afterwards told the Witness that she had mentioned it, and the butler promised to do all in his power.

Benjamin Johnstone, Butler to Governor Tryon being duly sworn, was examined.

Q. (by desire of the prisoner) What conversation pass'd between Mrs. Walker and him in relation to the prisoner?

A. About a fortnight ago Mrs. Walker called to him and ask'd him, if he thought a young man, who had deserted from the 23d Regt. would upon application to General Howe or any of the officers, be cleared, and desired that he would make enquiry, as the Man was very desirous of returning to his Regt. but was apprehensive that he could not do it with any safety, the Witness intended to have mentioned it to the Governor, but forgot it through the hurry of business; he recollects that Mrs. Walker said that she would keep him prisoner, till she saw the Witness; he ask'd her what sort of a Character the man had & she answered a very good one, and that he had been enticed away.

Q. Had he any conversation with Mary Smith?

A. No, he had not; he does not know Mary Smith.

Q. Did not a woman in the Street speak to him about the prisoner?

A. Yes, but she was a stranger to him.

Q. Did that woman make mention of a petition to the Governor, in favour of the prisoner?

A. Yes, but he told her that would have no effect, as the Governour had so much other business, and advised her to apply to some of the officers in the town.

Q. When was it that this strange woman spoke to him?

A. He thinks it was about four or five days after Mrs. Walker had spoke to him.

Q. When did Mrs. Walker mention the affair to him?

A. Four or five days after the Army came into town, she told him that the prisoner had concealed himself, that he might not go with the rebels, and that he wish'd to deliver himself up.

Q. Was it before the Town was set on fire that Mrs. Walker spoke to him?

A. Yes.

Mary Walker being duly sworn was examined.

Q. (by desire of the prisoner) Did not the prisoner desire her several times to apply in his behalf to the Governour or some other officer, telling her where he was and what Regt. he belonged to?

A. Yes, and she was four times at the Governour's House, to endeavour to speak to him about the prisoner.

Q. Upon seeing some rebels returning in boats from Powlie's-hook[20] did not the prisoner desire her to conceal him, that he might not get into their hands?

A. Yes.

Q. Does she know any thing of the prisoner's endeavouring to take two field pieces[21] from the rebels?

A. She knows that her husband and he went down to see how many men were with these field pieces, and if they could have got any men to assist them, they would have taken them.

Q. What clothes did the prisoner used to wear?

A. A blue coat faced with white or buff.

Q. Did she ever see the prisoner bear arms in the rebel service?

A. She never did.

Q. Did she know him to be in the rebel service?

A. She saw him go about with the rebels, and she heard him lament, that he quitted the King's service.

Q. What Regt. in the rebel service did the Prisoner serve in?

A. She does not know the names of any of the Regts.

Q. Did she not look upon him to be as much in the rebel service as any other of the Rebels that she saw in Town?

A. No, she did not.

Q. What reason had she to think so?

A. Because he never explained himself with any bitterness against the King, as others frequently did, but wish'd to serve his King and Country.

Q. Did she see the prisoner in the course of the 15th Inst.

A. It was in the morning of that day, that the prisoner desir'd her to conceal him.

Q. Did he ever desire her to conceal him before that day?

A. Yes, frequently.

Q. What trade or occupation did the prisoner follow?

A. She does not know.

Q. Did she ever hear him say in what manner he had quitted the King's service?

A. She heard him say that he had got in Liquor, and was carried away by another man, and that he wish'd very much to get back, if he could find an opportunity.

Q. Did she ever hear him say that he had been carried away by force?

A. She don't remember that she ever did.

Q. Does she know a man by the name of Jones who was a Drum Major in the rebel Army?

A. There was a man dressed in red, who used often to pass by her door, and who said that he had been in the King's service, but she did not know his name.

Q. Did she ever hear Mrs. Smith mention how the prisoner had quitted the King's service?

A. She never did.

The Prisoner concluded his defence with declaring that he had not the least intention or desire of deserting, for he liked the profession of a Soldier so much better than the trade he had been brought up to, that he would not have taken his discharge, if it had been offered to him.

The Court having duly considered the evidence for and against the prisoner Thomas Watson, together with what he had to offer in his defence, is of opinion that he is guilty of the crime laid to his charge, in breach of the 1st Article of War of the 6th Section, and doth sentence him the said Thomas Watson to receive seven hundred lashes on his bare back with a Cat of nine tails.

J.Gunning

Lt. Col. in the Army
Approved W. Howe
Step:P: Adye
Deputy Judge Advocate

Unaccountably, neither the corporal who apprehended Watson nor anyone who spoke to him after his capture appeared before the court; in most desertion trials, circumstances of the man's capture figured heavily (including, for example, the trial of Valentine Duckett described in the previous chapter). It is also curious that no testimony was offered to verify the identity or plausibility of Watson's claims about his abductor, Jacob Jones. Although Watson had a fine story and witnesses to back it up, the court surely must have noticed inconsistencies in the deponents' testimonies—a letter mentioned by one but not by another, the failure to produce this letter and an allegation that Watson wanted it disposed of, the ambiguity of Watson's concealment, a suggestion that Watson had claimed to have "quitted the service," a butler who only brought out inconsistencies in the stories of the other witnesses. The trial was held only a week after Watson was apprehended, so the events should have been fresh in the minds of the participants. Clearly Watson had gotten to know these people while serving in the area in 1773 and 1774, and was more likely to have gone to them by choice than to have gone through the series of events that he presented to the court.

That Watson was found guilty does not mean that they discounted his tale, however unlikely it may have seemed. Even if Watson had been forcibly carried off, he was intoxicated at the time and therefore had made himself vulnerable to abduction. Many soldiers pleaded that they deserted when alcohol left them bereft of their judgment if not their senses, and the army could not allow this as grounds for acquittal lest they condone drunkenness that deprived them of effective soldiers, not to mention afford a blanket alibi for every deserter. Sentencing him to corporal rather than capital punishment was probably the result of several factors. Although the court had ample reason to doubt Watson's story they heard nothing contradicting it. There was no evidence that he had borne arms for the Americans or done any particular service for them. The court heard nothing on the critical point of how Watson was actually apprehended. Deserters tended to resist or attempt to flee, while an abducted man could be expected to willingly deliver himself. No one testified to Watson's character as a soldier, and the thirteen-member court included no officers from his regiment to provide such information off the record. With no record of the deliberations of the court, we cannot know the rationale behind their relatively lenient sentence.

Watson waited in prison for nine days, no doubt pondering his impending punishment. On 12 October, the commander-in-chief announced in general orders that "in Consideration of some Circumstances in favor of Thomas Watson, he has thought proper to Remit his punishment, But he is to Continue in the Provost till a proper Opportunity offers of Sending him to his Regiment."[22] There is no record of what the favorable circumstances were, whether General Howe was sympathetic to Watson when he reviewed the trial or whether someone intervened on Watson's behalf. Whatever the reason, Thomas Watson was a soldier again. At this time the 23rd Regiment was campaigning north of the city in a drive that would include the battle of White Plains. We have no indication of when a "proper opportunity" allowed Watson to rejoin the regiment, but assume that it was some time later in 1776 or early 1777. The only mention of Watson in battle comes from the publisher's introduction to the memoir, concerning the October 1777 Battle of Germantown: "as before he had but witnessed the trappings and the order of a British army, he now had to behold and witness the horrors of war; the shrieks and the moans of the wounded and the dying, heretofore his companions; some pleading with Heaven for reconciliation, and some belching forth curses to keep these from repentance."

Watson's life in the army included much of the "debauched and drunken way of life" that he had experienced in the mines. In his own words he "was afflicted many ways, both in body and mind." He drank, he played cards, he was sentenced to a lashing which, although never administered, must have been dreaded. It is unclear whether he deserted or was forcibly taken from the army, and equally unclear whether he returned voluntarily or was captured. As his memoir continues, he presents himself as constantly conflicted between habit and conscience, and although the information from his trial does not directly reflect this internal conflict his apparent inability to either settle in America or rejoin the British army (until, that is, the army came to him) are consistent with his rambling, unsettled nature:

I think to mention a remarkable instance I saw in the army: I warned a man for guard.[23] He told me he could not go; for, said he, I am in hell; which words seemed to strike me with terror. I asked him what he had done? He said he had had many visitations, and three loud calls, to turn unto the Lord; but, he said, I am now in hell; and many times he put his hand on his breast, and said, Oh, I feel the torments of hell! I asked him where he came from. He said he was born in Philadelphia, and educated amongst the people called Quakers, and his mother was a Quaker Preacher. This stopped my career a little; but it was not long before I was as bad as ever again. This man said he should die in a few days; and so he did, and I was at his funeral. He complained of no bodily sickness, except crying out, Oh, I feel the torments of hell! I was now in the height of my wickedness, endeavoring to stifle the just witness of God in my heart. But the judgments of the Lord did follow me; yea, and I had to acknowledge it was just for me to be thus afflicted. Oh! I was afflicted many ways, both in body and mind; and I can say that, as wickedness abounded, the grace of God did superabound; and in the beginning of the year 1778, I was convinced that wars and fightings were from the wicked one. "From whence come wars and fightings!" Come they not hence from the lust in man? Oh, it is the very height of wickedness! I now began to call on the Lord to deliver me from the army; for at this time I did not know but that all men did fight. In a while it was made known to me, how and when to go away, and I likewise accomplished the same. It was when the army lay at Philadelphia, in the 3d month, 1778, and I came straight to

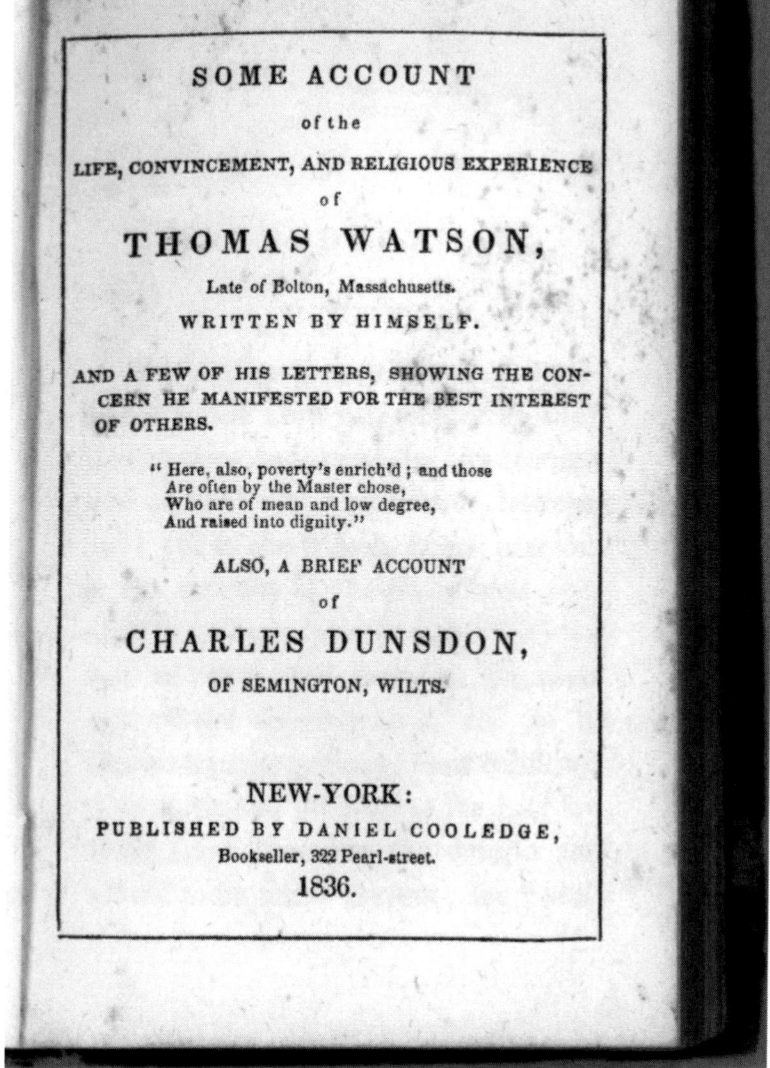
SOME ACCOUNT

of the

LIFE, CONVINCEMENT, AND RELIGIOUS EXPERIENCE

of

THOMAS WATSON,

Late of Bolton, Massachusetts.

WRITTEN BY HIMSELF.

AND A FEW OF HIS LETTERS, SHOWING THE CONCERN HE MANIFESTED FOR THE BEST INTEREST OF OTHERS.

"Here, also, poverty's enrich'd; and those
Are often by the Master chose,
Who are of mean and low degree,
And raised into dignity."

ALSO, A BRIEF ACCOUNT

of

CHARLES DUNSDON,

OF SEMINGTON, WILTS.

NEW-YORK:

PUBLISHED BY DANIEL COOLEDGE,

Bookseller, 322 Pearl-street.

1836.

Title page of Thomas Watson's memoir, published posthumously. (*Nantucket Historical Society*)

New-England; and when I got clear, it was brought before me what I had promised, providing the Lord would deliver me from the army. It was to amend my ways and serve him. Although I had left off some of my bad conduct, yet I found the evil root not wholly removed.

Epilogue

The rolls of the 23rd Regiment of Foot confirm Watson's desertion on 22 March 1778. No details of his elopement have been found, but the memoir's publisher wrote: "The officers seeing the sincerity of Thomas's convincement respecting war, and fearing he might proselyte others to his faith, told him if he would leave directly and secretly, no inquiry should be made for him." It is difficult to imagine British officers condoning a desertion in this manner, but we cannot discount it altogether. Perhaps Watson was poorly behaved and an agitator among his fellow soldiers. He wrote that he enlisted "for five years" but is not clear about whether he enlisted for a fixed term or he simply referred to how long he actually served. While peacetime enlistments were normally for life, there are known cases of men enlisting for fixed durations of service.[24] It is possible that he was denied discharge at what he considered to be the end of his obligation, a circumstance that surely would have turned him into a resentful soldier compelled to sour the morale of his comrades or persuaded him to desert—or both.

Regardless of his motivation at the time, Watson later attributed it to Divine deliverance that obliged him to "amend my ways and serve him." He immediately went to New England where he "went to work for my living." He attended a Calvinist church for a while, but was not satisfied with it. At twenty-six years of age he gradually slid back into his "corrupt nature"; he likened himself to the Israelites "who, after experiencing deliverance from under Pharaoh, and passing through the Red Sea, sang on the banks of deliverance, but soon forgot His works." He made many acquaintances who "would come to hear me tell stories, which I had a good knack at." He kept bad company, played cards, and drank. In spite of this lifestyle, in 1780 he married Elizabeth Taggart of Rhode Island, a woman from "a reputable family," and settled in Gloucester, Rhode Island. Soon after his marriage, a six-month illness again persuaded him to amend his ways, but he "began to make promises, day after day … but found it of little effect, for I generally broke them by night." He gave much consideration to religion, scripture, and spirituality. He sought out educated men and discussed these topics with them, and attended meetings of various religions. Much of Watson's memoir is devoted to his internal struggles as he sought spiritual direction. By 1785, he was convinced to become a Quaker, a decision that his wife vehemently opposed. He nonetheless adopted their ways of speech and clothing, which gave him a sense of peace. His wife fell into a long illness during which she continued to object to his religion, but suddenly gave herself over to it and asked him to raise their two young children as Quakers. A few days later she died.

Watson moved his family to Bolton, Massachusetts, where he remained for the rest of his life. He married again and had another child. When this wife died, he married yet again and had two more children. He managed to prosper, buying a farm and living comfortably. And he became an approved minister, traveling to Quaker meetings and attending services of other religions throughout the northeast. The latter part of his memoir is devoted to instances where he was able to bring peace and spiritual guidance to others. In 1803, Watson penned his memoir, but it was not published until 1836. The publisher notes that Watson's brother William settled on the island of St. Vincent and prospered as an agent for the government and master of a ship. In the 1790s, during a port call in Boston, William heard that his brother was living in Bolton and paid a visit. They had not seen each other since boyhood. William determined to relocate and brought his wife to Bolton, but after a few years they returned to the West Indies because of her preference for the climate there. William came once more to visit Thomas in the early 1800s, and they travelled throughout New England and New York visiting acquaintances and attending meetings. William returned to the islands having seen his brother for the last time. Thomas Watson was stricken with a fever that took his life on 2 June 1811. He was interred in the Friends' burying ground in Bolton two days later.

Five years as a soldier did not mitigate Thomas Watson's restless spirit, and may not have been the catalyst for his convincement and dedication to religion. Military service did, however, make his transformation possible. It got him out of the mines, providing him a career that, in his court testimony at age twenty-three, he explicitly stated that he preferred to the trade of his upbringing. The army brought him to America, a true land of opportunity for anyone willing to work hard and diligently. Although it took Watson some years after his desertion to establish such personal discipline, he was certainly in a place with more options for a nonlaboring life than he might have had as a discharged soldier in Great Britain. Perhaps most important, the army afforded him the opportunity to learn reading and writing, skills recognized as valuable for career soldiers that Watson instead used to learn his new discipline as a man of peace.

FIVE

Free Time for Industry and Mischief

Robert Young, 33rd Regiment of Foot

Introduction

The army needed more from its soldiers than the conventional duties that centered on carrying a firelock. Even during war, only a minority of a soldier's time was spent on campaign. When the army was not on the move there were always martial duties such as guards and training, but there was also equipment to be maintained, clothing to be prepared and repaired, barracks and huts to be constructed and fitted out, firewood to be cut and collected, fortifications to be built and improved, and innumerable other chores necessary to sustain military effectiveness. Although the army had departments to oversee these activities and hired civilian artificers for many tasks, soldiers were widely relied upon for a great deal of the labor associated with the military infrastructure.

Besides raw labor, however, many soldiers had valuable skills that the army took full advantage of. Given that most soldiers enlisted in their late teens or early twenties,[1] it is no surprise that many learned trades before choosing a career in the army. In most regiments, at least half of the soldiers had learned some trade other than "labourer" prior to enlistment.[2] We have seen that William Crawford and Thomas Watson had learned trades before enlisting in the army—but stone cutting and mining were probably seldom if ever required; neither man makes any mention of working at their trades while soldiers. Other trades directly filled military needs and allowed regiments to be in some measure self-sufficient in terms of maintaining their own readiness. Tailors fitted new regimental uniforms to soldiers and made supplemental clothing from scratch. Shoemakers maintained the footwear so vital to the infantry; they could also work with leather cartridge pouches, bayonet scabbards, and belting. Carpenters, sawyers, bakers, smiths, hatters, barbers, and others could all perform their trades to benefit their fellow soldiers.[3] Even gardeners found employment growing fresh vegetables for the use of regiments and military hospitals.[4]

One tradesman turned soldier who left a memoir was Thomas Cranfield.[5] He did not serve in America, but he did join the army while the American war was raging. His path to the army was in many ways similar to that of John Robert Shaw, Valentine Duckett, and Thomas Watson. His parents sent him to a parochial school at the age of seven where he studied for seven years in spite of being "averse to instruction and impatient of control." At fourteen he was apprenticed to a tailor where he learned much of that trade and also continued reading and writing, but "being weary of restraint" he absconded after fifteen months. The teenager determined to distance himself from his place of birth near London and rapidly made his way to the midland city of Birmingham. He lived as a vagrant performing what odd jobs he could until he found employment with another tailor, and then another to whom he agreed on an apprenticeship. Although ill-treated, he remained for three years and "made considerable progress" in the trade. Unable to bear his abusive master any longer, he fled in his nineteenth year, 1777. While on his way to Worcester that August he encountered a recruiting party from the 39th Regiment of Foot "and was by them induced to enlist into the king's service."

Only a month later the 39th marched for Portsmouth and embarked for Gibraltar, which place it reached in November. Cranfield's military training began in earnest only after arriving at that important garrison. In spite of his "high spirit and quick temper" he learned quickly and well. He was clean and attentive to orders, and his education was appreciated. He soon caught the notice of the commanding officer; once he had mastered the exercise of a soldier, "his regular duties as a private were discontinued; and he was employed in making clothes for the regiment, which added much to his income." This work provided constant employment and was of such importance that, when the garrison was besieged by the Spanish in 1779, Cranfield had to request "to take his share in the duties and dangers of the private soldier, from which, by his employment, he was excempt." He fought through the four-year siege; after it was lifted he returned to tailoring, and in 1783 at the age of twenty-five he was appointed master tailor to the regiment, "which employment was the means of furnishing him with an income superior to that of many of the commissioned officers." He accumulated some property, and married the daughter of a corporal in his regiment. At the end of the year he returned to England and took his discharge, having enlisted only for the duration of the war. His employment as a tailor in the army had allowed him to earn far more during six years as a soldier than he could have imagined when he enlisted.

In spite of the many demands of the military, British soldiers had free time. Whether this is counterintuitive or obvious depends upon one's preconceptions, but the factual record makes it clear enough that there were breaks in the military routine, in the duties and campaigns, which allowed soldiers to pursue their own interests at least within the context of their immediate situation and environment. Even Thomas Cranfield, during the siege of Gibraltar, found time to go fishing and was also in a card game that got crashed by an enemy shell.[6] The question worthy of study, then, is not whether these men had time to themselves but how they spent it. As with all questions about British soldiers, there are a great variety of answers that can be grouped into a few general categories. We cannot of course know how every soldier spent all of his free time, and no soldier spent all of it the same way. We can nonetheless document several common activities.

A primary leisure-time diversion for British soldiers was society's pastime of choice for millennia: drinking. The health benefits of alcoholic beverages including watered-down rum and spruce beer were well known to the army,[7] and the regular issue of these mild libations ensured that every soldier had a taste for alcohol. The rationed quantities of rum or beer were insufficient to provide the level of relaxation that hard military duty warranted, so the army also licensed vendors to operate canteens in close proximity to camps and garrisons. Called sutlers, these purveyors could offer for sale anything that soldiers wanted to buy, which meant that they sold mostly alcoholic beverages. Local commanders issued the licenses and regulated the operation of these businesses to the extent necessary for order to be maintained.[8] A further element of regulation was assured by the soldiers' having to use their own money for purchases. A soldier's finances were managed by his company commander, and the extent to which the soldier was allowed to have spending money depended upon his own good discipline; a soldier's pay could not be denied, but it could be withheld indefinitely.[9] In theory this meant that the only men with enough money to get into trouble were those disinclined to do so.

In practice, British soldiers in America regularly drank to excess and the attendant discipline problems were rampant. It is impossible to estimate the portion of soldiers that drank to excess, and we can be sure that at least a few did so under any circumstances. In Boston in 1774 and 1775, however, intoxication was such a problem that experienced officers commented on it and progressively stricter measures were taken to attempt to curb it.[10] For the alcohol-addicted soldier, lack of money was an obstacle but not a preventative; all manner of methods were used to obtain their tonic directly or find the funds to purchase it. Malcolm Campbell of the 38th Regiment took the simple approach of offering to help clean his comrade Luke Murphy's firelock and bayonet in return for liquor; this occurred after they had already been drinking and Murphy, unable to persuade anyone else to get the liquor needed to repay his debt, took a nonmilitary coat belonging to an officer's servant, tried to sneak out of camp, and was taken up on suspicion of attempting to desert.[11] Theft was an all-too-common method of obtaining alcohol. Benjamin Doran and William Lamb of the 63rd Regiment and John Cox and

John Woods of the 23rd Regiment used a skeleton key to get into a Boston storehouse and brought dozens of bottles of liquor to a nearby residence where one of their wives was quartered.[12] Bryan Sweeny and James Gardner of the 22nd Regiment chose to indulge immediately in wine that they liberated from a cask in a New York basement they'd broken into; when the homeowner went into the cellar, "the door of which had also been broke open they discovered the two prisoners, one of them hid away behind a Cask of bottled wine, and the other leaning over it, and the Cellar floor very wet, and many empty bottles broke and laying about; Gardiner, he thinks, had a bottle in his hand or between his legs; they were both very drunk, and one was vomiting when they took them." Through testimony in the trials of these and other men we see the ways that soldiers literally begged, borrowed, and stole to obtain liquor; that we know about these incidents suggests that they are but a few of countless many. Drunkenness was also a causal factor in a substantial number of regimental and general courts-martial, providing stark testimony both to the widespread use of alcohol in the army and wide variety of problems caused by intoxication.[13]

The problem continued in varying degrees throughout the war and has been sufficiently covered in the literature that it does not warrant detailed study here.[14] The perils of overindulgence are evident in the careers of Valentine Duckett, who was compelled to the desertions that led to his demise, and Thomas Watson, who struggled throughout his military career with the deleterious behaviors learned in his mining days.

Fortunately, there were other ways to spend free time besides drinking. As is the case with the modern military, British soldiers in the 1770s and 1780s were allowed to have part-time jobs. Many men had useful skills learned before joining the army, and those who did not could work at the variety of laboring tasks available in urban areas and the agricultural countryside. When they didn't interfere with army duties, nonmilitary jobs were beneficial to the army because they occupied the soldier's free time in a productive manner; military textbooks provided guidance for officers on discerning when it was appropriate to allow such work and how to regulate it.[15] The manpower available from garrisoned regiments could, however, saturate the local labor pool and drive down wages; this was one source of friction between soldiers and Boston townspeople that culminated in the Boston Massacre in 1770.[16] The ability to earn a living at a trade was also occasionally an inducement for soldiers to desert, as in the case of Evan Evans of the 52nd Regiment who, in June 1777, packed up his shoemaker's tools and made his way through fields towards the American lines near Piscataway, New Jersey. Although tried for desertion and sentenced to death, he was pardoned and discharged from the army the following year.[17] The itinerant nature of military life limited opportunities for long-term local employment of soldiers who remained faithful to the service.

There were other pastimes. Sports were a fairly common part of military life, from impromptu ball games involving a few soldiers to field days in which entire regiments participated in competitions.[18] Soldiers went fishing as a legitimate pastime that would supplement their diets;[19] they also found time to plunder produce and livestock for both food and income.[20] Occasional references are found to soldiers reading, including religious texts.[21]

In the previous chapter we saw that soldiers like Thomas Watson chose to better themselves through learning, and sometimes had the option of going to school. Thomas Sullivan of the 49th Regiment found army life gave him "many hours in which I could divert myself in Reading and Writing" which he filled "in putting in writing some few transactions which I could plainly and clearly testify, in order to divert myself and my Friends; as also not to have my name buried in Oblivion."[22] This resulted in an extensive narrative of his service in the British army blended with information about events and campaigns in which he did not participate; he wrote an introduction in 1778 that suggests an intention to continue it, but no further portions have been found. No other contemporaneous journal by a British soldier serving in the American war of 1775–1783 is known to exist, and there is no way to know how many soldiers passed their time in this manner. A sergeant of the 98th Regiment is known to have kept "a daily Journal or Diary of every thing that happened, besides many curious things agreeable to his own Ideas," but what became of this work is not known.[23]

What about Robert Young, the subject of this chapter? He spent his free time differently than any other soldier we've encountered, even though his background, enlistment, and career have many aspects in common with other soldiers presented in this study. He was born in 1750 to a merchant in Carrick-on-Shannon, Ireland. His father groomed him to the family business first by sending him to school until his mid-teens, and then to work as a clerk for a wholesaler in Dublin. He was thus possessed of everything necessary for a prosperous life except for his own personal predisposition. Free time, pocket money, and the natural inclinations of a teenager opened the way for vices; after less than a year his behavior put him at odds with his employer. After a brief trip to England he returned to Dublin and, for reasons unstated, he enlisted in the 2nd Regiment of Foot. A gap in the regiment's muster rolls prevents us from knowing the year that he joined. By 1768, he was in the regiment and serving in the British garrison at Gibraltar.[24] Young's own memorial indicates that he began working in Dublin at "about fifteen years of age," worked for about ten months, enlisted, spent a further ten months in Dublin followed by three years with a detachment on the Isle of Man before going to Gibraltar. Some parts of this time line must be inaccurate; a small detachment of the 2nd Regiment did indeed garrison the Isle of Man from 1765 to 1769, but Young would have had to enlist at about age fourteen to spend almost a year in Dublin, followed by three on the Isle of Man, and then be in Gibraltar by the first half of 1768. Such temporal inaccuracies are not unusual in personal recollections, however, and do not detract from the overall traceability of Young's story. What is clear is that he was only about sixteen or seventeen when he enlisted, a few years younger than most but not so young as to be remarkable or for the record to be questionable.

Young's seven years of soldiering in Gibraltar is duly recorded on the semiannual muster rolls. Since he left home this was the longest time that he spent in any one place. The isolated location gave him no choice, and his own brief mention of this long period suggests that it was an uneventful time which may have been good for him and certainly was good for the local population. Upon the regiment's return to Great Britain at the beginning of 1776, his career took a remarkable turn. Having just returned from abroad, the 2nd was not included among the regiments deployed to America but, like William Crawford, Robert Young answered the call for volunteer drafts to fight in the new war. By late spring most regiments on orders for America had already sailed, so Young entered an Additional Company, one of the recruiting organizations that remained in Great Britain to support regiments that were on service overseas. Unfortunately another gap in the rolls of the 2nd Regiment leaves us uncertain exactly when he changed corps,[25] but we can be sure that it was after March and before July 1776. We also do not know the process by which volunteers were assigned to deploying regiments, whether they had some part in the decision or were sent to regiments based on need or location. Whether by choice or by chance, Robert Young joined the Additional Company of the 33rd Regiment of Foot, a formation that was destined for a wartime experience completely unlike any other body of recruits sent to America.

The 33rd Regiment of Foot had departed for America at the end of 1775 as part of Sir Henry Clinton's abortive attempt to seize Charleston, South Carolina.[26] Like other regiments on American service, they left a cadre of officers and soldiers in Great Britain for recruiting, not only to offset attrition but also to accommodate the increased established strength for the regiment. Explicit recruiting of new men was supplemented by volunteer drafts such as Robert Young, but unfortunately we lack information on what portion of the new men was new recruits and what portion was drafts. Also joining the Additional Companies in 1776 were nearly 2,000 men raised in Germany, distributed among regiments according to need.[27] The 33rd received 101 of these German recruits, more than almost any other British regiment; their number included both newly enlisted men and soldiers with prior military experience in Europe.[28] By the middle of the year this disparate group of new 33rd Regiment soldiers was ready for embarkation under the command of Lieutenant George Anson Nutt. The exact number of men in Nutt's detachment is not known; it was certainly more than 155 and probably less than 175. It is also unclear whether it consisted entirely of men of the 33rd or included a smattering of recruits for other regiments. Regardless, the intent was for these men to join the 33rd Regiment (and any other regiments whose recruits may have been in the detachment) as soon as they arrived in America. This is what happened to most parties of recruits sent to America. But not those of the 33rd.

The Colonel of the 33rd Regiment was Major General Charles, Earl Cornwallis. Regiments were usually commanded in person by their second-ranking officer, the lieutenant colonel, because the colonel himself held higher offices. It was, however, fairly common for regiments to be sent to the theater of operations where their colonel was serving. Cornwallis had orders to go to Canada after Charleston was taken, and the 33rd Regiment was to go there as well and become part of the northern army.[29] But Charleston did not fall. Plans were changed. Cornwallis went not to Canada but to serve in the New York campaign. The 33rd Regiment also received orders to serve in the New York area. Lieutenant Nutt's detachment did not. The timing of the changing events was such that Nutt's detachment sailed with a convoy of recruits bound for Quebec, rather than with a similar convoy bound for New York. By the time they arrived in Canada, it was too late in the season to sail back down the St. Lawrence River and around the coast to New York.

In most cases, recruits separated from their parent regiment were simply drafted into other regiments in the area, where they were integrated into the army and subsisted locally.[30] When Lieutenant Nutt's men arrived in Quebec in late 1776, General Sir Guy Carleton initially intended to do just that. He soon reconsidered, however, because of the unique nature of the 33rd's recruits. He explained in a letter to the Secretary at War that

> it having been represented to me the English recruits for the 33d regiment, sent to Quebec with Lieutenant Nutt, were raised in the Neighbourhood of Lord Cornwallis's, and inlisted in Confidence of their serving in that Corps,

> therefore the disposing of the men otherwise than in his Lordships own regiment might prejudice its recruiting in those parts hereafter; that greater expense had been incurred in fitting them out than other Colonels might chuse to reimburse; and indeed uncommon pains had been taken with them in other respects; from these considerations, I shall therefore defer turning over both these and the German recruits, to the Regiments here, in hopes they may have an Opportunity of Joyning their own Regiment in the Spring.[31]

The Secretary at War responded in agreement to Carleton's overall plan. Because, however, over half of the recruits in Nutt's detachment were Germans assigned to, but not recruited by, the 33rd Regiment, the Secretary suggested that the Germans alone be drafted to other corps; he even indicated that the 33rd's Additional Company in Britain was already recruiting replacements for them.[32] This guidance was not taken, and the entirety of Nutt's detachment was maintained as a separate entity in the northern army. Those like Robert Young who were recruited in Britain had been trained and clothed in a manner that made then exceptional, while the Germans who composed over half the detachment may not have even received military clothing.[33] It was an unusual corps, and it is unfortunate that more details of its composition and operations do not exist.

For the winter of 1776–1777, all of the recruits for the army in Canada remained separate from their regiments because the season was too far advanced for them to make their way to the garrison posts that stretched from Quebec down through Montreal to Isle aux Noix. The several detachments of recruits were embodied into their regiments in the early summer, except of course for that of the 33rd Regiment. Robert Young, a veteran soldier in a strangely mixed detachment much farther away than others from its parent regiment, occupied his free time much as he had done while a merchant in Dublin and a recruit on the Isle of Man. He even had an offer to desert and remain in Quebec. Whether his loyalty was to the army or to his rambling inclination, he remained with his detachment as it prepared for the 1777 campaign season.

A substantial portion of the northern army was to travel south along Lake Champlain, over land to the Hudson River, and continue to Albany as part of a grand plan to end the war by isolating New England from the rest of the American colonies. Lieutenant Nutt's detachment was included in this expedition because it provided an excellent opportunity for them to move south; after arriving at Albany they could be sent to New York to finally be incorporated into the 33rd Regiment. Although too small and too inexperienced to be an autonomous fighting unit, Nutt's detachment could perform valuable auxiliary logistical duties. A return of Burgoyne's army dated 1 July 1777 reported that Lieutenant Nutt's detachment consisted of 154 men.[34] Having been in Canada for at least eight months; it is possible that the composition of the detachment had changed and that soldiers who did not belong to the 33rd Regiment were added to Nutt's detachment in order to send them to New York while others not fit for campaigning remained behind in Canada. The initial part of the campaign was a voyage in small craft down Lake Champlain, during which the men of the 33rd were ordered to serve "on board the fleet"; their specific duties are not known.[35] As the army disembarked and prepared for an assault on Fort Ticonderoga, the duties of Nutt's detachment changed. The expedition included a substantial quantity of artillery, largely for an anticipated bombardment of the fortification that had defied a British siege nineteen years before. By 1 July Nutt's detachment was assigned to serve with the artillery, taking on the arduous task of moving guns, equipment, and stores, freeing up trained artillerymen to handle more sophisticated tasks.[36]

The service of George Anson Nutt's detachment was unique among parties of recruits separated from their regiments in America, but they shared the same fate as the rest of Burgoyne's army. The demise of the campaign in September and October does not warrant retelling here; it is sufficient to say that the detachment of recruits for the 33rd Regiment was among the forces surrendered at the Convention of Saratoga. On 17 October, Lieutenant Nutt, four noncommissioned officers, and ninety-five rank and file surrendered, for a total of one hundred men belonging to the detachment.[37] No

Robert Young arrived in Canada with a party of recruits, only to learn that the 33rd Regiment was actually in the New York area. We can only speculate on how Young and his fellow soldiers may have dressed on the 1777 campaign because various sources suggest different possibilities.

An experienced soldier drafted from another regiment, Young may have retained his clothing from the 2nd Regiment of Foot for the journey to America and kept it for another year because his detachment could not get new clothing from their parent regiment. It is also possible that his detachment provided alternative clothing for him, for it was said of the 33rd's recruits that "greater expense had been incurred in fitting them out"; it is not known how their dress differed from the jackets, caps, and trousers provided to most recruits at training depots in Great Britain. A German officer who rendered pictures of soldiers on the 1777 campaign included one captioned "33rd Regiment" with red lapels, cuffs, and collar like those of the 33rd, but the buttonhole lace is rectangular rather than the distinctive curved style used by the 33rd and a few other regiments. Because of this lace style and the fact that it is a full regimental coat rather than a recruit's jacket, a case can be made that the picture actually shows the 53rd Regiment.

The soldier shown here conforms to surviving copies of the German officer's illustration, even though it does not accurately portray the warranted uniform of the 33rd Regiment. On the 1777 northern campaign hats were modified into caps by cutting off parts of the brim, reapplying them, and adding a fur crest. His hair is tied back in the style called a club. The coat skirts are cut short, and he wears typical breeches, stockings, and spatterdashes. The detachment was assigned to assist the artillery; this soldier has slung his musket and carries a hand spike, a stout wooden lever used to move gun carriages. His waistbelt, with a cast brass buckle bearing the number of his regiment, is worn over his shoulder for comfort; other straps hold the canteen and haversack that are not visible behind his back.

33
2012

details survive of the specific composition of the detachment at this time, but one British officer noted that the detachment's casualties were nine wounded and ten captured during the campaign.[38] It is certain that Robert Young was still serving in the little corps; he, along with William Crawford of the 20th Regiment and several thousand other British soldiers, were disarmed, put under guard, and marched across Massachusetts toward Boston. The terms of the Convention stipulated that they would be sent back to Great Britain, but differing interpretations of these terms led to internment of Burgoyne's army for the remainder of the war. Desertion was rampant, and Robert Young was among the first to go.

From Saratoga the Convention Army marched toward Worcester, Massachusetts, en route to Boston. This took them through the town of Hadley, north of Springfield. It was there that Robert Young deserted from the British troops in pursuit of his favorite pastime, one which took him to several different towns during the course of the next two years. Having been well educated in his youth he earned his living as a schoolmaster. This may not seem a likely vocation for a former soldier, particularly a deserter with a roving disposition, but keeping schools was a surprisingly common postmilitary profession. Besides prolific writer Roger Lamb, who kept the Free School in Whitefriar Lane, Dublin, there was Johann Philip Aulenbach, a German servant and musician who was among the European recruits sent into British regiments in 1776; after seven years of campaigning in America as a trumpeter in the 17th Light Dragoons, he and his wife took a land grant in Nova Scotia where they eventually settled in Lunenberg and he taught at a parochial school well into the 1800s.[39] Thomas Cranfield left the 39th Regiment and kept a Sunday school in Kingsland near London for some fifty years, and John MacDonald kept schools in Scotland after a military career of almost twenty years that began in 1778 and included service in the 73rd Regiment during the siege of Gibraltar; these two men wrote memoirs late in their lives, a likely inclination for a teacher.[40] Newspaper advertisements for deserters reveal some who kept schools before joining the army, including eighteen-year-old James Dougherty of the 3rd Regiment of Horse who was a "former schoolmaster at Letterkenny" in

Ireland and twenty-year-old John Waugh of the 13th Regiment who "once kept a School" in Kendal, county Westmoreland (today Cumbria).[41] A schoolmaster from Caithness in Scotland named Donald McGregor enlisted in the 54th Regiment in 1776 at the age of fifty-two during the flurry of early war recruiting, but was discharged after only two years because he was "disabled"; there is no evidence that he ever left Great Britain to join the regiment in America.[42] In addition to Robert Young, other British deserters in America went on to keep schools including Samuel Woodward who "lately kept school in Mifflin county above Lewistown" before joining the American army in 1795, and possibly Walter Graham of the 22nd Regiment.[43] Even a prisoner of war, William Ellis of the 10th Regiment of Foot, kept a school when allowed out of jail in Springfield, Massachusetts.[44] Having seen in Chapter 4 that regiments sometimes kept schools, we wonder if some of these men gained their experience in the army either as students or by teaching their fellow soldiers.

Although he was fully capable of steady employment, Young's personal habits caused him to move every few months, leaving behind schools in one town after another. Sometime in the middle of 1779 he settled in the town of Brookfield, Massachusetts. The previous year, Brookfield had been the scene of a remarkable murder; the daughter of a prominent Loyalist general had coerced a wayward American soldier and two British escapees from the Convention Army to murder her husband, for which she and her three abettors were all executed.[45] In this town already tainted by misdeeds of absconded British soldiers, Robert Young once again kept a school and once again pursued his pastimes, but here fate caught up with him. On 7 September he was arrested;[46] over the next two months he was brought to trial, found guilty, and sentenced to death.[47] Like Valentine Duckett five years before, Robert Young gave a dying speech which has survived in the form of a broadside. In his own words we learn of Young's early life, military career, and the personal pursuits that were his undoing.

The Dying Speech of Robert Young

The Last Words, and Dying Speech of Robert Young,
Who is to be Executed at Worcester this Day, November 11th, 1779, for a Rape committed on the Body of Jane Green, a Child, eleven years of age, at Brookfield, in the County of Worcester, on the 3d Day of September last.

I was born in Carrick on Shannon, in the County of Leitrim, in Ireland, and am now twenty-nine years of age.

My father was a merchant, and I being the youngest of his children then living, was intended for the same business, for which purpose I was kept at school until I was about fifteen years of age, and then my father thought proper, in order to have me well instructed in the business, to send me in quality of a clerk, to a wholesale merchant in the city of Dublin, Mr. George Reilly.

At that early age I was much inclined to the company of women, but an absolute hater of all sorts of strong liquor. I made large promises to one of my employer's servant maids, if she would yield to my unlawful embraces, to which, by constant importunity, she consented; afterwards, to prevent discovery, I studied all means to have her discharged, which I soon after got accomplished, being much in favour with the merchant and his wife. I then got acquainted with several lewd women, and being much in their company, in a short time learned to drink to excess.

I lived with Mr. Reilly about ten months, when he began to find out my way of spending my time and money when absent from the shop, for which he reprimanded me, and declared he would inform my parents of my conduct, if I would not quit such company, and apply myself to the necessary callings of my business; on which I left him, and went to Liverpool, in England, where I staid twelve or fourteen days, and returned to Dublin again.

Soon after my return to Dublin, I inlisted and joined the 5th regiment, and then gave myself up to all manner of debauchery. The regiment lay ten months in Dublin after I had joined it, during which time I was sent to the hospital, being bad with a disorder I had never before experienced, but was no stranger to it afterwards.

I was stationed for three years in the Isle-of-man; there I betrayed three girls, but after leaving them, have scarce thought of them to this fatal period. I was afterwards seven years in the garrison of Gibralter, and then went to England.

On my return to England, finding a body of troops that were bound to Canada, under the command of General Burgoyne, I joined them as a volunteer, and we were landed at Quebec, and there wintered. At Quebec I drew but little money, which induced me to study how I would procure more. At length I cast my eyes on a widow, paid her several visits, and strove to deceive her; she was for some time deaf to my protestations, but so closely did I pursue my purpose of deceiving her, that at length she gave heed to my request, and believed my falsehood: She supplied me with money, and I was enabled to get plenty of liquor, spending much of my time with lewd companions: The widow's affection became so great, that she requested me to stay behind; however, I left her, and went with the troops against Ticonderoga. I was then doing duty with the artillery, but belonged to the 33d regiment. I was in the two principal engagements, but received no wound.

After the surrender of the British army, I marched with them as far as Hadley, where I became acquainted with a girl, who advised me to desert; I spent a night with her, and agreed to go as far as Western, and then return back, which I accordingly did.

Afterwards I went to Pelham, where I lived three months, and then went to Shelburne, where I continued five months. At both these last mentioned places, I studied to deceive the fair sex, and betrayed a young woman in each of them. My rambling inclination continuing I soon left them as I had many others, and went to Greenfield, where I kept school to teach reading and writing. After keeping school here about two months, I began my old practices of seducing the young women, I gained the consent of one in particular who I often went to see in private; she liked me so well that she promised to go with me: Her parents tried all means to keep her from me, but to little purpose; they denied me admittance to their house; I tarried better than five months in Greenfield, and when I left that place, the girl left her friends in order to see me, which she often did. I afterwards lived in Montague, Sunderland and Greenwich, and kept school in several places to good acceptance.

Whilst I was keeping school in Greenwich, I was informed by Mr. Green's sister, that a schoolmaster was wanted in Brookfield: and when my time was out in Greenwich I went to Brookfield, and denied belonging to the British troops, in order to avoid as much as possible any discourse on that subject.

I opened a school at Mr. Samuel Green's, which I duly and faithfully attended: I was not long there before I got acquainted with Anne Green, and kept her company some time before her parents knew of it, knowing me then to be doing the same with others, and that I was many nights from home, I promised to quit all other company in that way, and offered marriage to Anne; she agreed: I then told her I belonged to the British army, but would never join it. Many arguments were used, and means tried, to diswade her from my company, but nothing would shaker her constancy: I loved her without deceit, and against much opposition we were published, and intended to be married in a few days. I now declare to the world, that I wronged her in court, and hope no one will think ill of her on my account. Her sister Jane was basely used by me; I humbly ask her forgiveness, and all others whom I have offended.

I freely forgive the world, as I hope for forgiveness through Christ Jesus and hope my unhappy end will be a warning to all others to forsake their evil ways, and seek the Lord while he may be found, and not persist in those pernicious courses that will inevitably end in the destruction of their bodies, and endanger their precious souls. Robert Young.

A quick attempt to corroborate Robert Young's dying speech invites the conclusion that it is a fabrication because it says that Young enlisted in the 5th Regiment of Foot, then served in Gibraltar before volunteering for service in America. This could not be true; the 5th Regiment is well known to have arrived in Boston in 1774 before hostilities broke out, and did not serve in Gibraltar during the preceding years. Closer examination reveals that the designation of the regiment is an error probably introduced by the printer. Young's service on the Isle of Man with a detachment from his regiment followed by several years in Gibraltar and a return to Great Britain in 1775 describes the deployment of the 2nd Regiment of Foot, and the muster rolls of the 2nd confirm his service in that corps. Although Young offers little detail about his military activities, everything that he describes correlates with the movements of the regiments and detachments in which he claims to have served, giving us confidence in the veracity of his story and the accuracy of its rendering.

Young's dying speech, like that of Valentine Duckett and others, was primarily confessional and also cautionary. There were criminals who were less repentant and uttered last words that were of no value to printers,[48] but educated, literate men like Robert Young provided valuable material for a ready market. Their skill at expression produced printable, readable copy and their misdeeds were shockingly entertaining. Robert Young went a step further. In addition to his confessional and repentant speech, he wrote a cautionary poem. In an era when political thinkers submitted versified commentary to newspapers and balladeers commemorated current events with new lyrics to popular tunes, Young's poetic composition was not wholly innovative. At least two other British soldiers of Young's era wrote verses. In America, Andrew Scott of the 80th Regiment composed "as many pieces as would have completed a small volume" but only two survived, presented in Appendix 1.[49] In Great Britain a young trooper in the 18th (Inniskilling) Light Dragoons self-published an eighty-four-page book of his own poems which prompted a critic to note that "he not only makes verses, but, which is more to his honour, performs the duty of a good soldier"; his work is featured in Appendix 2.[50]

Although certainly not the only soldier-authored poem of the era, Robert Young's verse is perhaps unique among the public writings prepared by the condemned. It was published and sold as a broadside separately from the speech but by the same printers.[51]

Robert Young's Cautionary Poem

The Dying Criminal:
Poem,
By Robert Young, on his own Execution, which is to be on this day, November 11th, 1779, for a Rape committed on the Body of Jane Green, a Child, eleven years of age, at Brookfield, in the County of Worcester, on the third Day of September last,
Corrected from his own Manuscript.

Attend, ye youth! If ye would fain be old,
Take solemn warning when my tale is told;
In blooming life my soul I must resign,
In my full strength, just aged twenty-nine.

But a short time ago, I little thought
That to this shameful end I should be brought;
But the soul fiend, excepting God controuls,
Dresses sin lovely when he baits for souls.

Could you the monster in true colours see,
His subject nor his servant would you be;
His gilded baits would ne'er allure your minds,
For he who serves him bitter anguish finds.

Had I as oft unto my Bible went,
As on vain pleasures I was eager bent,
These lines had never been composed by me,
Nor my vile body hung upon the tree.

Those guilty pleasures that I did pursue,
No more delight—they're painful to my view;
The monster, Sin, that dwells within my breast,
Tortures my soul and robs me of my rest.

The fatal time I very well remember,
For it was on the third day of September,
I went to Western, thoughtless of my God,
Though worlds do tremble at his awful nod:

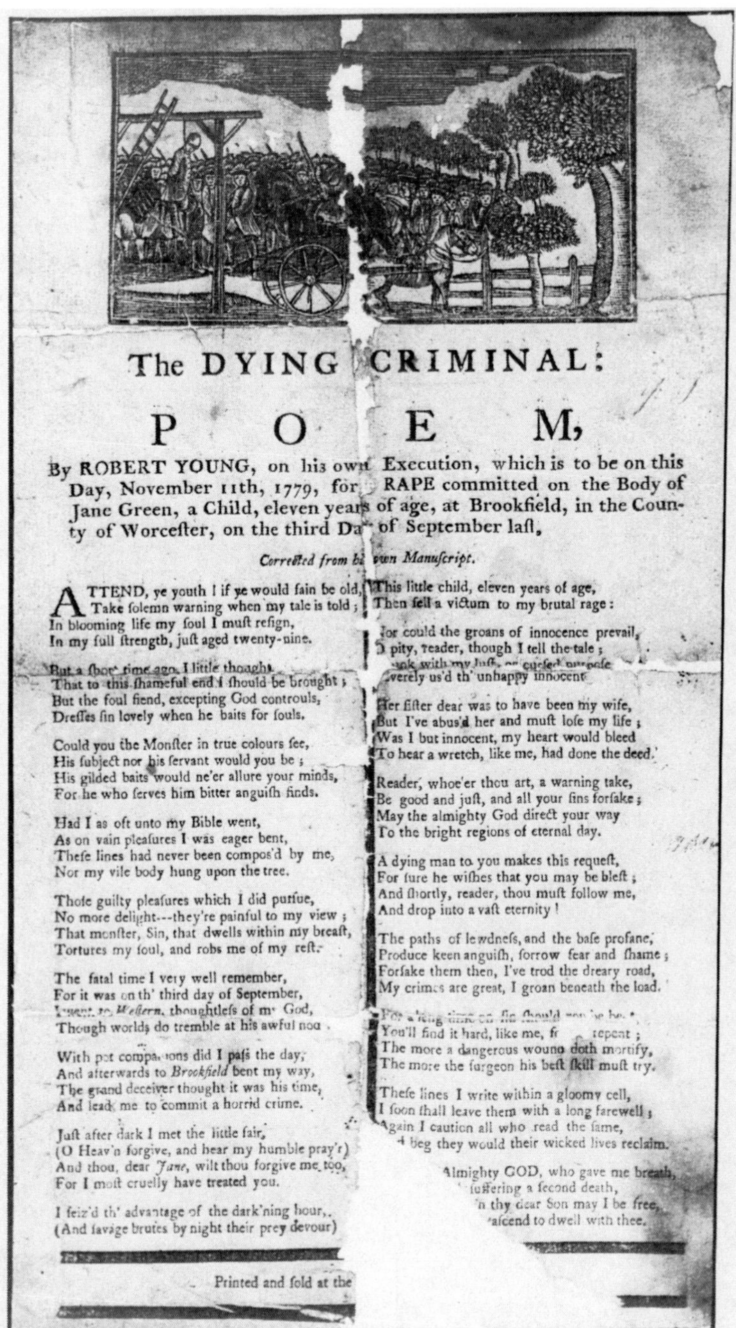

The DYING CRIMINAL:

P O E M,

By ROBERT YOUNG, on his own Execution, which is to be on this Day, November 11th, 1779, for RAPE committed on the Body of Jane Green, a Child, eleven years of age, at Brookfield, in the County of Worceſter, on the third Da[illegible] of September laſt,

Corrected from h[illegible] own Manuſcript.

ATTEND, ye youth ! if ye would fain be old,
Take ſolemn warning when my tale is told ;
In blooming life my ſoul I muſt reſign,
In my full ſtrength, juſt aged twenty-nine.

But a ſhor[illegible] time ago, I little thought
That to this ſhameful end I ſhould be brought ;
But the foul fiend, excepting God controuls,
Dreſſes ſin lovely when he baits for ſouls.

Could you the Monſter in true colours ſee,
His ſubject nor his ſervant would you be ;
His gilded baits would ne'er allure your minds,
For he who ſerves him bitter anguiſh finds.

Had I as oft unto my Bible went,
As on vain pleaſures I was eager bent,
Theſe lines had never been compos'd by me,
Nor my vile body hung upon the tree.

Thoſe guilty pleaſures which I did purſue,
No more delight---they're painful to my view ;
That monſter, Sin, that dwells within my breaſt,
Tortures my ſoul, and robs me of my reſt.

The fatal time I very well remember,
For it was on th' third day of September,
I went to *Weſtern*, thoughtleſs of m[illegible] God,
Though worlds do tremble at his awful no[illegible]

With pot compa[illegible]ons did I paſs the day,
And afterwards to *Brookfield* bent my way,
The grand deceiver thought it was his time,
And lead me to commit a horrid crime.

Juſt after dark I met the little fair,
(O Heav'n forgive, and hear my humble pray'r)
And thou, dear *Jane*, wilt thou forgive me too,
For I moſt cruelly have treated you.

I ſeiz'd th' advantage of the dark'ning hour,
(And ſavage brutes by night their prey devour)

This little child, eleven years of age,
Then fell a victum to my brutal rage :

[illegible]or could the groans of innocence prevail,
[illegible] pity, reader, though I tell the tale ;
[illegible] with my luſt, [illegible] curſed purpoſe
[illegible]verely us'd th' unhappy innocent

Her ſiſter dear was to have been my wife,
But I've abus'd her and muſt loſe my life ;
Was I but innocent, my heart would bleed
To hear a wretch, like me, had done the deed.

Reader, whoe'er thou art, a warning take,
Be good and juſt, and all your ſins forſake ;
May the almighty God direct your way
To the bright regions of eternal day.

A dying man to you makes this requeſt,
For ſure he wiſhes that you may be bleſt ;
And ſhortly, reader, thou muſt follow me,
And drop into a vaſt eternity !

The paths of lewdneſs, and the baſe profane,
Produce keen anguiſh, ſorrow fear and ſhame ;
Forſake them then, I've trod the dreary road,
My crimes are great, I groan beneath the load.

For a long time [illegible] ſin ſhould [illegible]
You'll find it hard, like me, fr[illegible] repent ;
The more a dangerous wound doth mortify,
The more the ſurgeon his beſt ſkill muſt try.

Theſe lines I write within a gloomy cell,
I ſoon ſhall leave them with a long farewell ;
Again I caution all who read the ſame,
[illegible] beg they would their wicked lives reclaim.

[illegible]lmighty GOD, who gave me breath,
[illegible] ſuffering a ſecond death,
[illegible]n thy dear Son may I be free,
[illegible]aſcend to dwell with thee.

Printed and ſold at the [illegible]

Broadside bearing Robert Young's cautionary poem. (*Library of Congress*)

With pot-companions did I pass the day,[52]
And then direct to Brookfield bent my way,
The grand-deceiver thought it was his time,
And led me to commit a horrid crime.

Just after dark I met the little fair,
(O Heav'n forgive, and hear my humble pray'r)
And thou, dear Jane, wilt thou forgive me too,
For I most cruelly have treated you.

I seiz'd advantage of the dark'ning hour,
(And savage brutes by night their prey devour)[53]
This little child, eleven years of age,
Then fell a victim to my brutal rage;

Nor could the groans of innocence prevail;
O pity, reader, though I tell the tale;
Drunk with my lust, on cursed purpose bent,
Severely us'd th' unhappy innocent

Her sister dear was to have been my wife,
But I've abus'd her and must lose my life;
Was I but innocent, my heart would bleed
To hear a wretch, like me, had done the deed.

Reader, whoe'er thou art, a warning take,
Be good and just, and all your sins forsake;
May the Almightly God direct your way
To the bright regions of eternal day.

A dying man to you makes this request,
For sure he wishes that you may be blest;
And shortly, reader, thou must follow me,
And drop into a vast eternity!

The paths of lewdness, and the base profane,
Produce keen anguish, sorrow, fear and shame;
Forsake them then, I've trod the dreary road,
My crimes are great, I groan beneath the load.

For a long time on sin should you be bent,
You'll find it hard, like me for to repent;
The more a dangerous wound doth mortify,
The more the surgeon his best skill must try.

These lines I write within a gloomy cell,
I soon shall leave them with a long farewell;
Again I caution all who read the same,
And beg they would their wicked lives reclaim.

O thou, Almighty God, who gave me breath,
Save me from suffering a second death,
Through faith in thy dear Son may I be free,
And my poor soul ascend to dwell with Thee.

Each of the narratives presented so far has showcased something about one British soldier that was common to many others; taking them together, we get a picture of how these men lived. Robert Young's story is difficult to fit into this schema. Like John Robert Shaw he left the life mandated by his father and instead enlisted in the army. Like William Crawford, he was a long-serving soldier who volunteered for service in America, was part of Burgoyne's army that surrendered in October 1777 and endured the hardships of a prisoner of war. Like Valentine Duckett, he was convicted of a capital crime and executed, leaving a dying speech which is the source of most of our information about him.

Young's behavior toward women, on the other hand, cannot be considered in any way typical. It was not unique; a soldier of the 61st Regiment named James Andrew was executed in Scotland in 1784 for robbery, and in his own last speech confessed to "disagreeable and unhappy schemes of seducing young women to supply my extravagances." Andrew had been raised by "honest parents, nigh to the city of Belfast in the Kingdom of Ireland" and moved to Scotland in pursuit of higher wages after completing an apprenticeship as a linen weaver, but his "extremes of vice, folly and dissipation" led him to enlist "to keep myself from being harassed by the clamours of women I had injured."[54] The deviance of Robert Young and

James Andrew was, however, rare in society never mind in the army. Rape was a capital crime in the military as well as in the civil justice system; as such, it was tried by general courts-martial, the records of most of which survive. In America 587 general courts held between August 1774 and August 1783 include only six soldiers (and two mariners) tried for rape.[55] This collection of records is known to be incomplete because it is missing some trials described in general orders, but these orders reveal only one additional rape trial.[56] Although a British officer on Staten Island in 1776 wrote about the army having "most entertaining courts-martial every day" because of complaints by local women of being ravished by soldiers,[57] a deserter from the 55th Regiment deposed to American authorities that "the inhabitants of Staten Island are well and no Soldier dare do any thing agt them."[58] Although several general courts sat on Staten Island to try crimes like plunder and robbery, there were none for rape or assaults on local women.[59] Some authors have argued that, even though rape was a capital crime warranting a general court-martial, other cases may have been tried at the regimental level. There is in fact an example of an attempted rape case being tried at the regimental level, but it is only one out of 1,400 trials in six regiments and detachments;[60] one additional case is known in a regiment for which comprehensive records are not available.[61] Even considering untried incidents, of which there were surely many, most perpetrators were probably one-time offenders; Robert Young's proclivity cannot be taken as typical behavior of soldiers.

Women were an integral part of the armies of the era.[62] As an army of empire, the British army infrastructure allowed soldiers' wives and families to accompany their husbands on overseas deployments to the extent that anywhere between 10 percent and 25 percent of the men in a regiment might have wives with them, many with children.[63] Accommodation varied from sharing space in barracks and tents to obtaining private housing in the vicinity of the regiment's post depending on specific circumstances. These women were provided with rations by the army (it is the victualing returns that provide most of the surviving information on numbers of women with the army) and supplemented their husbands' incomes by working at various jobs; many were employed directly by the army as nurses, washerwomen, and sutlers (purveyors of provisions). The result was an army in which women were an everyday fixture. Robert Young's predatory behavior cannot, therefore, be ascribed to a lack of exposure to the opposite gender or a general isolation of soldiers from women.

What it illustrates about the army is that it was composed of individuals, some with vices and some without, and among the former some much more severe than others. Every society has its fringe elements, people with problems that compel them to behavioral extremes. That Young could exercise his abuses shows us that soldiers in general had free time outside of their military duties. To have led the life he led and committed the acts that he did makes it clear that he was not constantly burdened with soldiering but had ample time for his personal pursuits, even on service in America.

SIX

Unwilling Volunteers and Criminals

Ebenezer Fox, 88th Regiment of Foot

Introduction

A study of British soldiers during the era of the American Revolution would be incomplete without some discussion of criminals conscripted into the army. This is not because convicts composed a significant portion of the army but precisely because they did not, and yet much literature and conventional wisdom suggests that they did.[1] Undeniably, British law made provisions for men to choose military service instead of jail time.[2] Given the conditions in British prisons the choice seems obvious enough, but it was not a decision to be taken lightly. Enlistment in the army was a commitment for life, no less for the civil malefactor than for any other enlistee; magistrates did not offer a few years in the army as an alternative to a few years in prison, but instead offered the army as a career choice to men who had made decisions that put them on the wrong side of the law. Those who enlisted after the war began had the option, like any other enlistee, of taking their discharge at the end of the war, but given that the vast majority of criminals-cum-soldiers were sent to harsh climates with high mortality rates[3] it was still in the individual's interest to carefully consider whether the army was truly a better option than prison.

In spite of the tendency to focus on recruitment of criminals, only one detailed and quantitative study on the subject has been published.[4] That study spells out both the conditions and the numbers quite plainly, albeit the latter not precisely for want of complete records. Once a man was convicted of a crime, only a royal pardon could commute his sentence and allow enlistment as an alternative. During the five years leading up to the American war no such pardons were granted, and during the period 1775–1781 only 764 pardons were granted in England and Wales (records for Scotland and Ireland are not available). During the same period, one hundred times as many men were enlisted into the army by other means. Pardoned criminals, then, made up only a tiny portion of the army as a whole. One such man, George William Berrepo, had voyaged from his native St. Eustatius to England, apparently as a sailor, but once on shore he squandered his money and fell in with bad company. He got involved in a scheme that earned him a conviction for forgery and he was incarcerated in Winchester jail. He was pardoned "through my Keeper's Christianity" after which he enlisted in the 18th Regiment of Foot; his own account that "he received his Majesty's most Gracious pardon, and I then enlisted for a Soldier" gives the impression that enlistment was not a condition of the pardon. Rather than seeing the army as a cruel alternative to a crueler fate, he saw it as a way to "Reforme my way of life and Reprieve my ill behaviour."[5] He enlisted in July 1776 when the 18th Regiment had just returned to Great Britain after many years in America.

There were other ways that criminals could be allowed into the armed forces. Judges and justices could reduce the sentences of men convicted of petty larceny or misdemeanors on the condition that those men joined the army. Quarter-sessions records show numerous instances of this practice both before and during the war, but the numbers still amount to only a handful compared to the overall volume of wartime recruiting. Between 1775 and 1781, for example, there were fourteen such cases in Essex, three in Hertfordshire, two in Shropshire, and none in London. If numbers like these were consistent across all counties it would yield barely a few hundred men. Another option was for men to opt for enlistment before sentencing. Several individual cases can be documented, and even in the absence of comprehensive figures for this type of proceeding there is no reason to believe that it contributed any more men to the military than did royal pardons or commuted sentences. It bears noting that the practice of judges or magistrates offering military service as an alternative to trial and prison was common practice well into the twentieth-century in many nations.

Just as important as the recruitment of criminals was the disposition of these men once in the army. During the 1770s and 1780s Great Britain's army operated in many parts of the world; while war was raging in America, British troops were also stationed and sometimes fighting in the West Indies, Nicaragua, Gibraltar, Minorca, West Africa, and India. Substantial forces were also required for the defense of the home islands, particularly after France joined the war in 1778. The climate in tropical locations had long been a bane for British troops, taking a horrendous toll on the regiments sent to those regions. It is no surprise, then, that the majority of criminals recruited into the army were sent to those undesirable and often fatal locations. While only a small portion of the army as a whole, social malcontents constituted a substantial part of the British troops sent to garrisons on the west coast of Africa; in this way military service was vaguely analogous to transportation, the practice of sending criminals to distant colonies. We can guess that somewhere between 1 and 5 percent of the army may have been either accused or convicted criminals, but the proportion in the army in America was certainly considerably smaller.

This is not to suggest that the remainder of enlistees were exclusively well-behaved, law-abiding citizens. We have seen that voluntary enlistment was often a means of escape from a man's social problems. Men like Robert Young are known to have committed crimes before enlisting, and men like Valentine Duckett turned to crime after deserting (which was itself a crime). There are a few high-profile cases of serial criminals who joined the army briefly during their storied lives. Perhaps the most famous was James Aitken, known as John the Painter, who enlisted and deserted at least twice during a rambling criminal life that ended with his execution for attempting to destroy the naval dockyards at Portsmouth.[6] A less storied example is James Fleyd or Lloyd, who was suspected of "having committed many villainies in different parts of Great Britain" when he was apprehended in Sherborne, Dorsetshire, after deserting from a recruiting party of the 40th Regiment a week earlier.[7] We do not know whether recruiters were aware of his criminal activities before enlisting him or learned of them only after his desertion.

When the war's scope broadened in 1778, a new measure was taken by the government to stimulate enlistment among a British population that was barely meeting the demands of the military. Besides the incentive of a limited term of enlistment that had been introduced in 1775, enlistment bounties were increased, physical standards decreased, and the maximum age increased.[8] A harsher measure came in the form of a press act which allowed justices of the peace and tax commissioners to force enlistment upon "able-bodied idle and disorderly Persons" who did not "exercise and industriously follow some lawful Trade or Employment" or have some other way to sustain themselves.[9] While this opened the way for abuses on the part of the recruiting machinery, it had strict limitations. It applied only in the London area and some other regions of southern England, not to Great Britain in general. The act expressly stated that pressed men must be fit for military service, and it allowed citizens pressed in this manner to plead their case before an examining official. The goal of the act was not so much to increase the army by conscription but to encourage voluntary enlistment as an alternative to being pressed. While either option landed the enlistee in the army, voluntary enlistment afforded the opportunity to choose the regiment and therefore, to some extent, the location of service; the threat of being pressed was the specter of being sent to a fatal tropical location.

The 1778 press act was not particularly effective. The following year new recruiting laws were enacted, raising the bounty for volunteer enlistment even more, facilitating the establishment of a career after discharge from the service, further relaxing the physical requirements and widening the eligible age range. In addition, a wider range of men were allowed to be impressed; the law was extended from "idle and disorderly Persons" to also include "incorrigible rogues," that is, repeat runaways who were supported by their parish. In addition, the regional restrictions were removed so that the law applied throughout Great Britain. There were temporary repeals in some regions so as not to interfere with the harvest, but in general this new law was in effect from February 1779.

The press act was repealed just over a year later, in May 1780; the incentives for volunteers remained in place, but it was no longer legal to force men into service. Impressment had been legal for the army for two years, after which it was deemed best to return to strictly volunteer enlistment. The press acts were repealed for two reasons. First, the practice was almost universally unpopular with both the general population and with the army. Those men eligible to be pressed certainly didn't want to be, ineligible men could be taken either accidentally or by unscrupulous officials, regimental officers did not for a moment assume that men brought into their corps unwillingly would somehow become good soldiers, and willing volunteers were not keen on having society's idle, disorderly, and incorrigible rogues alongside them in the ranks. A British militia officer described reaction to the press acts succinctly:

> An act for impressing soldiers took place in 1779, when all the thieves, pickpockets and vagabonds in the environs of London, too lame to run away, or too poor to bribe the parish officers, were apprehended and delivered over as soldiers to the regiments quartered in the very townes and villages where these banditti had lived and been taken; these men being thus set at large in the midst of their old companions and connections, immediately deserted, whereby the whole expence, by no means an inconsiderable one, was thrown away: nor did the soldiers of the regiments on which they were imposed, take the least pains to prevent their escape, or to retake them; as they justly considered being thus made the companions of thieves and robbers, a most grievous and cruel insult, and loudly complained of it as such, to their officers. Indeed it seems to have been a very ill judged measure, tending to destroy that professional pride, that esprit de corps which ought most assiduously

> to be cultivated in every regiment. The profession of a soldier has long ceased to be lucrative, if it ever was so. If it is likewise made dishonorable, where shall we get soldiers on whom we may depend? when the exigencies of the time make it necessary to take such men into the service, they should at least be sent to regiments quartered in a distant part of the kingdom, where they and their characters are equally unknown, or divided among the regiments on foreign service.[10]

Unpopularity and abuse were just two reasons for revoking the press act. The other was simply that it was not particularly effective. Complete figures have not survived for the entire two-year period during which impressment was allowed for the army, but there is detailed data for a six-month period from March through October 1779. During this time 1,463 men were pressed in England and Wales. Of these, however, 501 were discharged for one reason or another, died, or were for other reasons not incorporated into the army.[11] On average 50 recruits per year were required just to maintain the strength of each regiment on service in America,[12] and a large number of new regiments were being raised to defend the home islands and to serve in expanding theaters of war such as Gibraltar and the West Indies; in this context, 962 men pressed during this six-month period was a trifling number compared to the tens of thousands being recruited. In Scotland only 67 men were pressed from March through June, an insignificant contribution.[13] With the number of men pressed already small, the number that reached America was further diminished by a chance event. The initial press act became effective in May 1778, meaning that recruits obtained in accordance with the act were ready for deployment in early 1779. Embarking in March, delays prevented sailing until the following month and an unusually long passage ensued. Disease broke out on some of the transports. When they finally disembarked in New York in August many recruits were sick; a substantial number did not recover.[14] Although we don't know how many of these recruits had been pressed rather than voluntarily enlisting, it is clear that the overall proportion of pressed men in regiments in America could not have been large.

What all of this demonstrates is that, while it was possible for criminals to choose enlistment over incarceration and that, for two of the eight war years, men could be impressed into the army, only a small portion of the army was composed of men recruited in this manner. Even if they were poor soldiers, their numbers were too few to significantly impact the effectiveness of the army. But does a criminal record imply poor discipline and unsuitability for the military? The vast majority of judicial records that leave us names of men offered the opportunity to enlist do not identify specific regiments into which they entered, making it impossible to trace their careers in muster rolls. The few who can be traced prove that enlistment from prison was not a clear indicator of a man's overall character. In 1776, for example, "six very fine Lads now confined in Shrewsbury Goal for petty Offences" were enlisted by a lieutenant in the 46th Regiment, pending their royal pardon.[15] Three of them subsequently appear on the rolls for the 46th Regiment in America (unfortunately no comprehensive muster rolls are known to exist pertaining to the recruiting parties—the Additional Companies—of any regiment). The fate of the other three is not known; their pardons may have been denied, they may have been deemed physically unfit, they may have deserted while recruits in Britain, they may have been drafted into a different regiment, they may have died while recruits or during the voyage to America, or they may have been rejected as unfit after arriving in America. The other three arrived in America during the first half of 1777. One of them was still in the regiment in New York in August 1778 but does not appear on the next set of muster rolls prepared in St. Lucia, West Indies, two years later; this gap in the muster rolls leaves his fate unknown. The final two men not only continued serving in the regiment through its return to England in 1782, but both had by the end of that year become noncommissioned officers, one a corporal and one a sergeant.[16] We have not traced their subsequent careers, but it is clear that these "fine Lads" became fine and trusted soldiers even though they were among the relatively few known to have been recruited out of prison.

It is unfortunate that we do not have a narrative written by an enlisted criminal or an impressed man who served in

America. We do not even know how many such men there were, but the above discussion suggests that there were not likely more than a few hundred, if that many. Given the small number of personal writings of British soldiers that survive overall, the odds of one of them being from this small number of social malefactors is slim. But there is a memoir written by a young man who chose enlistment as the lesser of two evils. Ebenezer Fox was recruited out of a prison, but not a civil facility in Great Britain. Fox was an American naval prisoner incarcerated on one of the infamous floating hulks in New York harbor. When the opportunity arose, he chose to enlist in the British army as a means to escape the hellish conditions that he saw claiming lives of fellow prisoners every day.

Ebenezer Fox was born in January 1763 in Roxbury, Massachusetts, just outside of Boston. He was the son of a tailor, but at the age of seven was put to work on a local farm. At the age of twelve he and a companion resolved to run away and seek their fortunes at sea. They left for the seaport of Providence, Rhode Island, on the very eve of the outbreak of war, 18 April 1775. The war did not interrupt their plans and they each soon found their own engagements on merchant vessels; they never saw each other again. After two voyages and some significant adventure Fox returned to his family after an absence of six months. He spent the winter attending school, and when the siege of Boston was lifted in the spring he began working for a barber in the city. In late 1779, not quite sixteen years of age, he served for a few months in the militia as a substitute for his employer and trekked under arms to Albany and back. These disparate activities, sailing and schooling and soldiering and styling hair, were forging the chain of events that pulled Fox unknowingly toward the British army.

In 1780 Fox went to sea again, this time on a twenty-eight-gun frigate named *Protector* operated by the Massachusetts state navy. Their first cruise was reasonably profitable, so Fox signed on for a second that began in late 1780 and continued into 1781. After its moderate success interdicting merchant shipping along the American coast and in the West Indies, the fortunes of war turned against the ship. While cruising off of British-occupied New York it was overtaken and captured by the British warships *Roebuck* and *Medea* on 5 May 1781.[17] The crew of the *Protector* was taken in to New York harbor and imprisoned in one of the most deadly places of the war, the prison hulk *Jersey*.[18]

The British incarcerated large numbers of America prisoners on obsolete ships because the space was available and escape was difficult. Although widely censured by historians, the practice was common during the era and the Americans also employed prison ships in Boston and Providence. In the context of the day, it was not the concept of prison ships that was objectionable but the horrific conditions that prevailed on the prison hulks in New York harbor. The vessels were crowded, and poor sanitation was exacerbated by poor ventilation. In an age where prison conditions were expected to debilitate prisoners, the hulks in New York harbor killed them off in droves. The numerous narratives and memoirs of survivors provide vivid descriptions of the extraordinarily bad conditions that they endured.[19] Faced with gradual death from hunger and disease, the prisoners developed creative schemes for escape, but few are known to have succeeded and many ended in either death that was at least due to action rather than inaction, or capture and reinternment in the same awful place.

Fox spent the summer on board the *Jersey* watching desperate men die. He also saw an opportunity to depart of his own volition, albeit under conditions that he abhorred. From time to time, British army recruiting officers from the 88th Regiment of Foot came on board offering an alternative to the fatal squalor of shipboard imprisonment. They tendered tempting terms of food, clothing, pay, and even the honorable expectation of faraway service where they would not fight against their countrymen. A printed advertisement aimed at men "awake to the allurements of Glory and Riches" promised pay vastly superior to other regiments.[20] Even though the 88th was touted to be in the "most healthy Part of all Spanish America," lucrative perquisites were necessary because the island of Jamaica was in reality a harsh, unforgiving climate typical of destinations for enlisted malefactors. The regiment, called the British Volunteers, had been raised in 1778 and

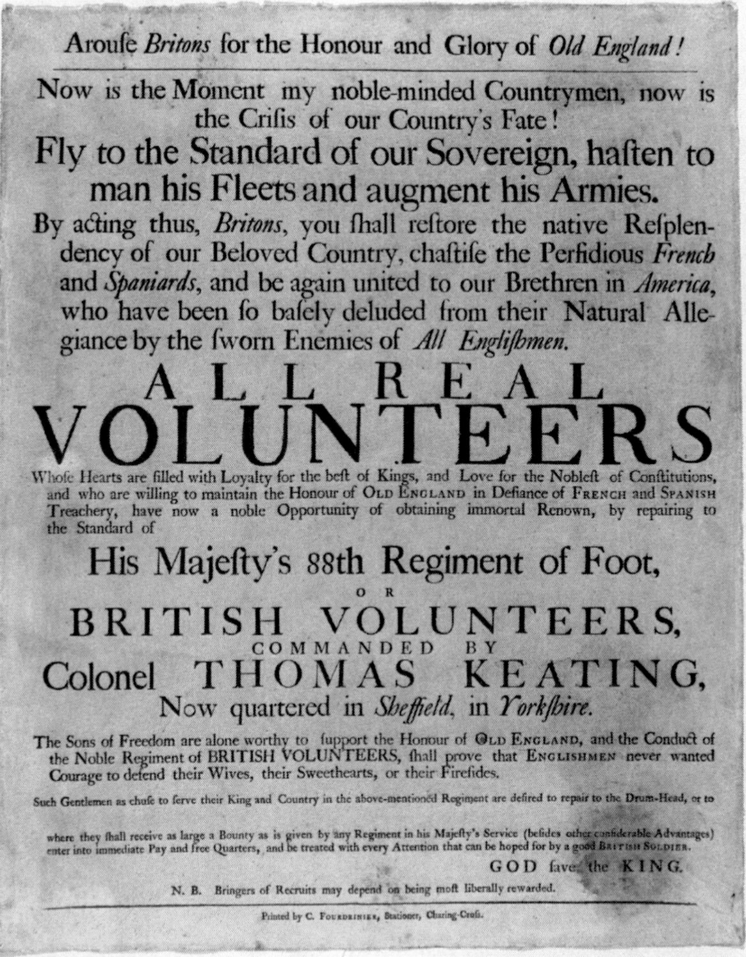

British recruiting poster for the 88th Regiment of Foot, 1779. (*National Army Museum*)

sent to the island a year later; ravaging tropical diseases demanded a steady stream of replacements[21] and American prisoners of war seemed like suitably expendable candidates. Calling enlistees "brave adventurers" with "an opportunity of signalizing themselves in serving their King and country," one advertisement appealed in particular to those "so prudent as to accept the Royal pardon."[22] The detainees on the *Jersey* at first shunned these offers, but as winter approached with its promise of freezing cold to augment starvation and illness, Fox and eleven others consigned themselves to the 88th Regiment of Foot knowing that they were otherwise liable to be impressed into the navy if they didn't succumb to illness. They also had in mind that they would have better opportunities to escape as deserters from the army than as prisoners on board a festering hulk. Faced with severely limited options Ebenezer Fox made the same choice that John Robert Shaw, William Crawford, Valentine Duckett, Thomas Watson, and Robert Young had made: he enlisted voluntarily. To be sure, it was the least of evils, but it was voluntary nonetheless and fully within the spirit of the army's recruiting policies. After all, each of the other volunteer soldiers we have discussed perceived enlistment as the best available option at the time, regardless of how genuinely dire his circumstances.

Fox and other enlistees from the New York area were soon on board a vessel bound for Jamaica in the waning months of 1781, and Fox despaired of ever seeing his homeland again. The ship was accompanied by a smaller vessel, a schooner; the ship's captain supplemented its crew with some of the newly enlisted American prisoners since most of them had seafaring experience. The American recruits devised a scheme to seize the schooner and make for the American coast, but one lost his nerve and threatened to betray them. In a matter of days they were docked in Kingston, Jamaica, where they were put in the care of a British sergeant and rapidly integrated into the routine of the military garrison.

Days of droll repetition of mundane drilling, duty, and military maintenance wore on the active minds of young Ebenezer Fox and his comrades. Their zeal to desert was unwavering, and although the challenges of getting out of the garrison and then off the island were daunting they diligently gathered information and evaluated schemes. Fox's fortune came when his skills as a barber were recognized. He was taken away from routine soldier's duties and made hairdresser to the regiment's officers. Here his education complemented his skills; he was able to ingratiate himself to the officers, earning their trust and assimilating information that they unwittingly passed on. He was given a pass to come and go as he pleased, and he had plenty of free time to use this privilege for learning the local roads and military posts. After a bit more than six months as a British soldier, he and several trusted comrades were ready to make their escape.

Fox's memoir tells the story of his reluctant British army service; we pick up his narrative at the time he landed in Jamaica.

Extract from the Memoir of Ebenezer Fox

We then landed, and with the sergeant at the head marched in single file through Kingston to a place called Harmony-hall, where the regiment was quartered, and were placed under the care of a drill sergeant. The next morning we were ordered out for drill, and received our uniform and arms, which we were ordered to keep bright and in good order for service. We had but little employment, excepting being drilled to our hearts' content by the sergeant, to make good soldiers of us for the service of his Majesty, King George the Third. The life of a soldier in a garrison is an idle one at the best; and, though the duties are not laborious, there is a monotony in them which is extremely irksome to the active mind of youth. But we could not reasonably expect to spend our lives in a garrison, if such a thing were desirable: after having had our share of it, we were aware that we should be called upon to perform some foreign service, we knew not where, perhaps to bear arms against our beloved country. With the fear of this in view, and the reluctance we experienced in serving what we still considered the cause of our enemy, our minds were constantly employed in devising ways and means to effect our escape.

It appeared to be the object of our officers to reconcile us to the service, by making our duties easy and agreeable. We were often indulged with the privilege of leaving our quarters to visit the town or wander about the country adjacent. Harmony-Hall, our quarters, was enclosed by a high fence, having two gates in front and one in the rear, at each of which a sentry was stationed. When a soldier wished to leave the Hall, it was necessary for him to obtain a written order called a "pass," to show to the sentry when he went out, and to give up when he returned. Several of us thought it a practicable thing to get on board some of the British merchant vessels in the harbor, which were in need of men, and whose captains would not hesitate to receive and secrete us, as they were frequently deprived of their hands by impressment on board of the ships of war. We availed ourselves of every opportunity we could obtain to get information respecting English vessels, their time of sailing, their destined ports, &c.; thinking that, if we could once get to England, we should find some means to get thence to France, whence we could return to our own country.

In our rambles about the town and country, we visited the grog-shops and taverns, places where sailors generally resort, and had got considerably acquainted with the keepers of these establishments. Our "passes" were signed by a commissioned officer, and they gave us permission to carry our side-arms, that is, a bayonet, and to be absent two hours at a time.

While I and one of my comrades were wandering about the town one day, we stepped into a house, where liquors and refreshments were to be obtained. We found one of the seats occupied by an English sailor, to whom we, rather too frankly for prudence, communicated our intentions; or, more correctly speaking, gave him some cause for suspecting our designs from the questions we asked him respecting the probability of obtaining employment on board of some merchant vessel, in case we could get released from our present engagements. The sailor was inclined to be very sociable, and discovered no objections to drinking freely at our expense; telling us that he belonged to an English ship that would sail in a few days; that his captain was in want of hands; and that, at his intercession, he would undoubtedly take us on board.

He appeared so friendly, and his manners were so insinuating, that he completely won our confidence. He asked us how we could obtain liberty to leave the garrison, and to pass in and out when we pleased? Taking my "pass" out of my pocket, I showed it to him, and told him that was our authority. He took it into his hand, apparently with an intention of reading it; and, after looking at it for some time, in a sort of careless manner, he put it into his pocket. I felt a little surprised when I saw him do it, and my companion expressed his fears by whispering into my ear, "Blast his eyes, he means to keep the pass."

Having allowed the fellow to get possession of the paper, I felt myself responsible for it, and that it was necessary for me to recover it, even if I were obliged to resort to violent measures. I therefore said to him, "My friend, I must have that paper, as we cannot return to our quarters without it." He replied, "You had better be peaceable about it, for I mean to see your commanding officer."

Matters had now come to a crisis. I saw that it was the sailor's object to inform against us, and to carry the "pass" as an evidence of our conference with him. I immediately drew my bayonet from its scabbard, and, thrusting it against his side with force sufficient to inflict a slight wound, put my hand into his pocket and took out the "pass"; and then, giving him a blow upon the head with the butt end of my bayonet, dropped him senseless on the floor. The noise of this conflict brought the landlord into the room, followed by his wife, with whom a previous acquaintance had made me somewhat of a favorite. The rascal had by this time recovered his senses and had got upon his legs, and began to represent the matter in a light the most favorable to himself.

We vehemently contradicted his assertions, and were stoutly backed up by the landlady, who was a considerable of a termagant, and declared that "the sailor was a quarrelsome fellow; that he had made a difficulty once before in the house; and that her husband would be a fool if he did not kick him out of doors."

The landlord, to prove that he was "compos mentis," and to appease the wrath of his wife, which waxed warm, complied with her kind wishes, and the sailor was, without much ceremony, hurried through the door, his progress not a little accelerated by a brisk application of the landlord's foot, which sent him spinning into the street in the manner prescribed by the good woman. We were then advised by our friends to return to our quarters as quick as possible, lest the fellow might make some trouble for us. We paid our bill, and gave the landlord many thanks, not forgetting the landlady, to whose kind interference we owed our fortunate escape. This circumstance made me more cautious in future of communicating my designs to strangers, how friendly soever they might appear.

About this time, I was unexpectedly released from the duties of a soldier. One day I attracted the attention of an officer, by the exercise of my skill as a barber in the act of shaving a comrade; and was forthwith promoted to the high station of hairdresser and shaver for the officers. This was very agreeable to me, as it gave me an opportunity of obtaining much information respecting the town and country around, and likewise much leisure time, and many indulgences not granted to the soldiers. I was assiduous in my attentions to my superiors, and thereby gained their confidence, and could, almost whenever I wished, procure a pass to go out when I desired.

But, although my duties were light and I experienced much kind treatment, I still felt myself in a state of servitude,—a prisoner, as it were, among the enemies of my country,—in a thraldom, from which I was desirous of being released. I was willing to incur any hazard to obtain my liberty, and to breathe once more the air of freedom. To visit my dear native land, my friends, and the scenes of my childhood, was the prevailing wish of my mind; to accomplish this desire I was willing to hazard my life. Many difficulties were to be surmounted before this could be effected. Friends were to be found, in whom confidence could be placed.

It was difficult to tell whom to trust. To impart my views to others might expose me to treachery; and, if betrayed, the consequences would be fatal. It was necessary to proceed with great caution in obtaining the opinions of those who were likely to embark in the undertaking I had in contemplation. Several must be found, possessing similar views and intentions, alike in courage and determination to carry through whatever plan might be formed. To desert from a military force, in an enemy's country, and that an island, seemed to be a desperate undertaking with little prospect of success. But I was resolved upon the attempt, and my thoughts were continually employed in devising ways and means to effect it. I

Ebenezer Fox was sent to the West Indies where he joined the 88th Regiment of Foot. It is likely that the warranted uniform was modified for service in this hot climate, but no information has been found describing their clothing on daily duties. Fox's work as a hairdresser for the regiment's officers is representative of the myriad jobs that skilled soldiers performed for the army.

In this picture, a private soldier prepares his commanding officer's hair for curling. He wears a linen canvas apron, an accessory used by many tradesmen to protect clothing. His red regimental coat has green lapels, cuffs, and collar. False pocket flaps help the coat retain its shape when items are carried in the pockets that are actually in the coat lining. The white lining is visible on the turned-back skirts; the coarse material is turned under to prevent fraying, exposing a narrow band of the more tightly woven red outer wool. Linen trousers, well-suited for the warm climate, were also popular summer garments in the American colonies; they are tailored to fit closely, preventing damp and debris from entering the low-topped shoes. He uses heated iron tongs to flatten individual tufts of hair. A comb is handily tucked into his own hair, which is just barely long enough to be folded up once and tied. In this informal setting, the soldier wears a cloth handkerchief tied around his neck rather than a stiff neck stock.

The officer's features are based on a portrait of William Gardiner when he served in the 45th Regiment prior to becoming the 88th Regiment's Lieutenant Colonel during Fox's service. The officer wears only his linen shirt, woolen breeches, and stockings, and is covered by a sheet protecting his clothing. He uses this idle time to catch up on news from London.

gained upon the confidence of the officers daily, and was indulged with opportunities of leaving the garrison whenever I chose.

Availing myself of this privilege, I became acquainted with all the avenues from the town as far as Rock-fort, which was situated at the distance of two miles from Kingston, on the right-hand side of the road. I ascertained that it was the custom to place a number of sentries on the left-hand side of the road, about the eighth of a mile from the fort, in the road to Rock-fort, at a place called the "Plum-tree." Deserters, who were ignorant of this circumstance, were often taken up by the sentries, and brought back to the garrison. The night before we escaped, five soldiers were caught in the act of deserting, and brought back in the morning while the regiment were on parade. The poor fellows looked the very objects of despair when they were delivered up, and put under guard to await their trial by a court-martial.

I had become acquainted with five soldiers, who had been released from military duty, because they were mechanicks, and could make themselves useful in the performance of various mechanical services. They enjoyed considerable liberty, but did not possess the confidence of the officers in so great a degree as I did, having made myself useful and agreeable to them by personal attention in contributing to their comfort and convenience. My knowledge of the town and its environs rendered me a valuable coadjutor, and gave me more consequence in the estimation of my comrades, than I should otherwise have had, and made me a sort of leader in the enterprise, though I was then but about nineteen years of age.

We had frequent opportunities of being together to digest our plan, and to make arrangements for putting it into execution. About this time, I had the good fortune to obtain a high degree of confidence, and to find great favor in the sight of the commanding-officer by the exercise of my professional skill in making him wonderfully satisfied with himself upon the occasion of a military ball. He was so much pleased with the improvement I made in his personal appearance, that, in the fulness of his heart, he gave me a "pass to go out whenever I chose till further orders." This was a great privilege, and I derived great advantages from the use of it.

The five comrades, with whom I had associated, as I have observed, were mechanicks, two of whom were armorers; and they had obtained from the arsenal two pistols and three swords, which were all the weapons we had: these, together with some articles of clothing, we had deposited in the hut of an old negro, whom we had bribed to secrecy. The regiment, stationed at Rock-fort, was designated as "Lord Montague's men," or the American Rangers, and had been recruited in North and South Carolina.[23] Their uniform was a short blue jacket with white facings. Having made all the preparations in our power, we appointed the time to commence the attempt. Our plan was, to travel across the island and trust to circumstances, which might providentially be thrown in our way, to escape to the island of Cuba. Our fears were not a little excited, when we saw the poor fellows brought back on the morning preceding the night we had fixed for our undertaking; especially when we heard the commanding-officer declare, "that, whatever might be their fate, the next, who should undertake to desert, should be hung."

I had a general pass, as I have before observed, for myself to go out at pleasure; but it was necessary to obtain a special one for my companions, and this duty devolved on me. In the afternoon, soon after dinner, I asked the commanding-officer to grant me the favor of a pass for five of my acquaintance to go out to spend the evening, upon condition of returning before nine o'clock. The officer hesitated for a moment; and then, as he signed the pass, said, "I believe I can trust you; but remember that you must not come back without them." This I readily promised, and I faithfully fulfilled the obligation.

About the middle of the week, in the month of July, 1782, our little party of six, five Americans, and one Irishman, an active, courageous fellow, left the town, and proceeded to the negro's hut, where we received our weapons and clothing and some little store of provisions which we had deposited. That afternoon, a soldier had been buried at Rock-fort, and part of the regiment had been out to attend the funeral. Seeing these soldiers upon their return at a distance, and fearing that our bundles might excite their suspicion, we concluded to separate and meet again as soon as the soldiers had passed. We escaped their notice, and fortunately met together a little time after, all but one who was missing. We waited some time, and looked in various directions for him, without success. We were afraid to remain where we were any longer, as it was now past eight o'clock; and we knew, if we did not return by nine, a party would be sent in search of us.

The man, whom we missed, was somewhat intoxicated, and the probability was that he had lain down and fallen asleep; or perhaps his courage had failed, and he had given up the undertaking, and might have gone back and given information against us. We were satisfied that we could wait no longer for him without exposing ourselves to great danger, and therefore concluded to proceed without him. What was his fate I have never been able to ascertain.

We pushed rapidly forward till we had got about a mile from Kingston, when we entered a small piece of wood-land, and divested ourselves of our uniform, which we had worn with much reluctance, and had never ceased to regret having exposed ourselves to the necessity of putting on; clothed ourselves in the sailor garments, which we had taken care to provide; cut the white binding from our hats; and were soon metamorphosed into much better sailors, than we had ever been soldiers.[24]

Having loaded our pistols, we again proceeded. We had advanced but a few rods, when we met a sergeant, belonging to a regiment called the Liverpool Blues,[25] who had been to Rock-fort to see some of his acquaintance, and was then upon his return. It was near the time for stationing the guard, as usual, at the place called the "Plum-tree." The sergeant hailed us with, "Where are you bound, my lads?" We answered, "To Rock-fort."

He replied, "I have just come from there, and found all well: how goes on the recruiting at New-York? and what is the news?"

A ship had arrived the day previous, from New-York, and he supposed that we were some of the recruits that she had brought over. We perceived his mistake, and adapted our answers to his questions, so as to encourage his delusion. We told him that the recruiting went on bravely, and we were going to join our regiment at Rock-fort. The fellow seemed to be in a very happy mood, and immediately declared his intention of turning back to show us the way to the fort.

Our situation was rendered very embarrassing by this kind offer; and to refuse it, we feared, would excite suspicion. Our generous guide thought he was doing us service, when he was leading us directly to destruction; and the idea of killing him, while he imagined that he was performing a good service for us, was very unpleasant; but it was our only alternative. In a few moments the deed would have been done; self-preservation made it necessary: but, fortunately for the poor fellow, and much to our satisfaction, he suddenly recollected that his pass required him to be back to Kingston by nine o'clock, and, bidding us good-night, and telling us that we could not miss the way, he left us, and pursued his route to Kingston at a rapid pace.

We thought it important that we should get as far from Kingston that night as possible, as we should undoubtedly be pursued in the morning; and the sergeant, from whom we had just parted, would give information of us, as soon as he arrived and ascertained that we were deserters. The danger, to which we had been exposed by our recent interview, cast a gloom over our spirits, and gave us a realizing sense of the difficulties and hazards with which we must contend. But go forward we must, for to go back would be death.

We proceeded at a rapid pace for about half of a mile farther, when we met with an old negro, who hailed us, saying, "Where be you going, massa buckra men?[26] there be a plenty of soldiers a little way a-head; they will take you up, and put you on board of man-of-war." We told him that we had got a pass. The negro replied, "Dey no care for dat, dey put you on board a man-of-war." He mistook us for sailors who were deserting from some ship.

I had become acquainted with several negroes in Kingston, and always found them kind and willing to give any information that was in their power to furnish. They appeared to feel a sort of sympathy for the soldiers and sailors; seeing some resemblance between their own degraded condition and that of the miserable military and naval slaves of British despotism. Whatever might be the cause, I always found the negroes in and about Kingston ready to give every facility to a soldier or sailor who wished to desert. We soon agreed with the old fellow for a dollar to guide us into a path through the woods, by following which we should avoid the guard at the "Plum-tree," in whose vicinity we then were. I had reconnoitred the ground sufficiently, previous to this, to be aware of the necessity of taking this path, and knew about where it was; but we were sensible that a faithful guide, who had a perfect knowledge of the ground, would be of great service to us, especially in the night.

After we had entered the woods, we had no fear of treachery on the part of our guide, as his life was in our hands. The fate that awaited him, should he attempt to jeopardize our safety, was clearly understood by him; but, the earnest and simple manner in which he declared the sincerity of his intentions in serving us, put at rest in our minds all doubts of his fidelity. We followed our guide about a mile, when he told us that we had got past the guard, and, giving us directions as to our future course, he left us, after having called God to witness that he never would inform against us. We had no reason to doubt that he faithfully kept his promise.

Our anxiety to escape pursuit determined us to use all the expedition we could through the night. About midnight, we came to one of the many rivulets with which Jamaica abounds. As we were unable to determine what its width or depth was in the darkness, it was necessary to proceed with caution. The tallest of our party was sent forward to try to wade across. The rest followed in single file, according to our respective heights; I, being the shortest, brought up the rear. Holding our arms and provisions and part of our clothing above our heads, we soon arrived on the opposite shore. When I was in the middle of the river, I found the water up to my chin, and was fearful at one time that I should be obliged to abandon my bundle, and resort to swimming. We travelled in our wet clothes the remainder of the night, and, towards daylight, we looked round for some retired spot, where we could secrete ourselves during the day, as we considered that it would expose us to great hazard, if not to certain detection, to travel by daylight at so little distance from Kingston as we then were. We soon found a secluded spot on the side of a hill thickly set with brushwood, well calculated for concealing us from the view of any who might pass that way.

In the course of the forenoon, we saw from our place of concealment a number of negroes pass by, carrying to the market at Kingston various articles of country produce upon their heads in baskets. We had provided for our sustenance a small quantity of bread and dried herring, sufficient to last three days, the time we thought requisite to travel across the island; of this provision we eat sparingly, but suffered much for want of water, as we were afraid of being seen if we ventured from our hiding-place till night, when we cautiously, one at a time, crept down to the foot of the hill, and quenched our thirst from a small rivulet.

As soon as it was dark enough to prevent discovery, we left our place of concealment, and proceeded on our second night's journey. We had been exposed to considerable danger the preceding night and day, and had suffered much from hunger, and more from thirst; our spirits were depressed, and we experienced the wearisomeness that arises from a want of sleep. Gloomy forebodings assailed us; and we moved on in melancholy silence. After having travelled three or four hours, we unexpectedly found ourselves near a hut, and were alarmed at hearing a negro female voice exclaim, "Here come a whole parcel of Buckra man." We immediately started from the spot, and proceeded with all practicable speed till we had travelled three or four miles, when we sat down to rest, and to refresh ourselves with some of our bread and dried herring.

After we had rested about half an hour, we renewed our journey with all the speed we could exercise; and proceeded without interruption till day-light approached, when we thought it necessary to find a place for concealment during the day. We entered the woods at a short distance from the road, where we spent the day, partially satisfying our hunger with a scanty portion of bread and herring, and some berries, which we found, of various kinds; and amusing ourselves with the relation of the dangers we had passed through, and speculations upon the nature of those which we might be called upon to encounter. The day passed without any alarm, and as night approached we prepared to re-commence our journey. Soon after dark, we issued from the woods, entered upon the road, and proceeded for several hours without meeting with anything to molest or make us afraid. We occasionally rested, eat sparingly of our nearly exhausted stores, and drank water when we could find it, and travelled without interruption till morning. A place for concealment during the day was again selected; and, as we had slept but little since we left Kingston, we concluded to get all the rest we could, and spent the greater part of the day in sleep, each one of us in succession keeping watch while the others slept. After several hours' rest, we found ourselves considerably refreshed; and as our small stock of provisions was nearly exhausted, and we had consumed nearly the time we had anticipated would be required to arrive on the opposite side of the island, we concluded that we would venture to travel by daylight.

We took the precaution to divide our party, three taking one side of the road, a little in advance, and two on the other side; keeping a vigilant look-out, in every direction. One of our men in advance gave notice, some time in the forenoon, that he discovered an object at a distance apparently approaching. We thought it prudent to retire from the road to a neighboring thicket, till we could ascertain what the object was. It proved to be a gentleman on horseback, who, by his dress, appeared to be an officer of high rank, followed by a servant.

The officer wore a large, gold-laced, three-cornered hat, and was richly dressed: both he and his servant were well armed. As soon as they had passed and were out of sight, we left our retreat with the intention of proceeding; but, finding ourselves in need of more rest, we penetrated farther into the woods to find a place of repose.

Our strength began to fail for want of food, and we found it necessary to take more frequent opportunities for rest and sleep. We gathered a few berries, and, having enjoyed a few hours of uninterrupted sleep, we felt refreshed, and returned to the road to pursue our journey. We travelled without interruption till about three o'clock in the afternoon, and, while ascending a hill, we were alarmed by hearing the sound of voices. We stopped, and collected together to consult upon what course to adopt. In a few moments, we saw coming over the hill three stout negroes, armed with muskets, which they immediately presented to us, and ordered us to stop.

Our arms, as I have formerly observed, consisted of two pistols and three swords; upon the pistols we could place but little dependence, as they were not in good order; and the swords were concealed under our clothes; to attempt to draw them out would have caused the negroes instantly to fire upon us.

They were about ten rods before us, and stood in the attitude of taking a deliberate aim at us. To run would be certain death to some of us; we therefore saw no alternative but to advance. One of our number, a man named Jones, a tall, powerful fellow, took a paper from his pocket, and, holding it up before him, advanced, with great apparent confidence in his manner, and the rest of us imitated his example. As we approached, Jones held out the paper to one of them, telling him that it was our pass, giving us authority to travel across the island. The negroes, as we very well knew, were unable to read; it was therefore immaterial what was written upon the paper,—I believe it was an old letter,—as manuscript or print was entirely beyond their comprehension. While we were advancing, we had time to confer with each other; and the circumstances of the moment, the critical situation in which we were placed, naturally led our minds to one conclusion, to obtain the consent of the negroes that we might pursue our journey; but if they opposed our progress, to resort to violence, if we perished in the attempt.

There was something very exciting to our feelings in marching up to the muzzles of these fellows' guns; to have our progress interrupted when we were, as we supposed, so near the end of our journey. Our sufferings had made us somewhat savage in our feelings; and we marched up to them with that determination of purpose which desperate men have resolved upon, when life, liberty, and everything they value is at stake—all depended upon prompt and decisive action.

This was a fearful moment. The negroes stood in a row, their muskets still presented, but their attention was principally directed to the paper which Jones held before them; while our eyes were constantly fixed upon them, anxiously watching their motions, and designing to disarm them as soon as a favorable opportunity should be offered.

The negroes were large and powerful men, while we, though we outnumbered them, were worn down by our long march, and enfeebled by hunger. In physical power we were greatly their inferiors. But the desperate circumstances in which we were placed inspired us with uncommon courage, and gave us an unnatural degree of strength.

We advanced steadily forward, shoulder to shoulder, till the breasts of three of us were within a few inches of the muzzles of their guns. Jones reached forward and handed the paper to one of the negroes. He took it, and having turned it round several times, and examined both sides, and finding himself not much the wiser for it, shook his head and said, "We must stop you." The expression of his countenance, the doubts which were manifested in his manner of receiving the paper, convinced us, that all hope of deceiving or conciliating them was at an end.

Their muskets were still presented, their fingers upon the triggers. An awful pause of a moment ensued, when we made a sudden and desperate spring forward, and seized their muskets; our attack was so unexpected, that we wrenched them from their hands before they were aware of our intention. The negro, whom I attacked, fired just as I seized his gun, but I had fortunately turned the direction of it, and the ball inflicted a slight wound upon my side, the scar of which remains to this day. This was the only gun that was discharged during this dreadful encounter.

As soon as it was in my possession, I exercised all my strength, more than I thought I possessed, and gave him a tremendous blow over the head with the breech, which brought him to the ground, from which he never rose.

I had no sooner accomplished my work, when I found my companions had been equally active, and had despatched the other two negroes in the same space of time. None of our party received any injury but myself, and my wound I considered as trifling.

The report of the gun we were fearful would alarm some of our enemies' comrades, who might be in the vicinity, and bring them to the spot. We accordingly dragged the bodies to a considerable distance into the woods, where we buried them under a quantity of leaves and brush. In their pockets we found a few biscuit, which were very acceptable to us in our famished condition.[27]

The best gun was selected, as we did not think it necessary to burden ourselves with the others, as they had been injured in the conflict. We took what ammunition we thought necessary, and then sought a place of rest for the remainder of the day.

The negroes whom we had encountered, belonged to a class called "Cudjoe men," who were free, in consequence of some services, which their ancestors, the Maroons, agreed to render to the government; and were permitted to inhabit the mountains and the northern part of the island. They were encouraged to exercise their vigilance by the promise of receiving a certain sum of money for every fugitive slave they restored to his master, or soldier whom they should arrest as a deserter. We had been apprized of the existence of these beings before we left Kingston, and were in constant fear of meeting with some of them. Their huts were scattered along the three roads from Kingston, viz., Rock-fort road, the County road, and the Spanish-town road. We avoided as much as possible all of these roads, and travelled circuitous paths in the woods; and, having no guide and an imperfect compass, we wandered a great deal out of the direct way; and much of the time travelled considerable distances without making any advancement.

The direct distance across the island is about forty or fifty miles, which we could have travelled with ease in two days; but, from the cautious manner we proceeded and the irregular course we pursued, we were nearly five days in accomplishing our undertaking. Considering our ignorance of the interior parts of the island, it has ever since been a matter of surprise to me that we succeeded in getting across the island; and that we did not perish in the woods. Had we travelled upon either of the before named roads, instead of threading our way through the woods, we should have been overtaken by the parties of soldiers, who were sent in pursuit of us. I received information, several years after our escape, of the exertions that were used to overtake us and carry us back to Kingston. A young man, by the name of Hunt, was carried into Kingston, as a prisoner, taken by a British vessel, the day after our escape. Previous to his sailing from Boston, he had heard that I was in Kingston; and when made a prisoner, he hoped to obtain some assistance from me in his captivity, as we had been formerly acquainted. He made inquiries of the sergeant of the guard, placed over him, respecting me. The sergeant replied, that "Fox was fool enough to run off last night, with five others; he had no military duty to perform; all he had to do was to shave and dress the officers, and he spent most of the time in walking about the streets. I suppose they think they will show us a Yankee trick; but they will find themselves mistaken, for there are three parties out after them, one on each road, and they had orders to bring them back before night, dead or alive." It seems by this account that we must have been taken, had we not pursued our journey in the woods instead of the road.

To return to my narrative: We lay down in the woods, languid and exhausted, after the excitement and fatigue from our contest with the negroes, and slept soundly for some time, when I suddenly awoke, and saw at a little distance from me the head of a monstrous serpent, raised several feet from the ground, and gazing earnestly upon us, with his mouth frightfully distended. I was so much alarmed that, at first, I imagined it to be the "old serpent" himself, and immediately awakened my companions. But I believe the serpent was more alarmed than we were, for he darted off among the bushes with so much rapidity that I could not ascertain his length, but was satisfied that the circumference of his body was of the size of a man's.

As it was now nearly dark, we thought we would venture again upon our journey. Having loaded our musket, the spoils of our victory, we entered the road, and, having looked around with great caution, and finding no obstacles in the way to excite any apprehension, we started forward. We knew not for a certainty where we were; but were satisfied, from the time we had consumed in our journey, that we could not be at a great distance from the northern side of the island.

We travelled all night, occasionally stopping to rest, and refresh ourselves with some of the hard biscuit, which we had found in the pockets of the negroes, and a draught of water from the springs by the road-side.

As daylight approached, we found ourselves on the summit of a hill, and in sight of the ocean. I doubt whether Columbus and his crew experienced more heart-felt joy when they saw the new world, than our little party did when we discovered the sea. We could hardly refrain from uttering a loud exclamation of joy. Here was an end to our wanderings, our fatigue, and sufferings. We gazed upon the watery expanse with feelings of unutterable delight, upon whose surface we were to be wafted from the shores of captivity.

After we had remained as long as we thought prudent upon the eminence, we retired to the woods, for concealment during the day. We needed rest, and slept the greater part of the day. We ventured out several times in the course of the day to take a peep abroad, but with great care that we should not be seen. We saw a number of negroes moving about in various directions, but were not discovered by any of them.

Our plan of operations for the future was the subject of much discussion; but we arrived at no definite conclusion, excepting to avail ourselves of any opportunity that should be offered to leave the island.

We had supposed, although perhaps we had no good reason for it, that we might find some merchant vessel on the coast, in which we might be received as sailors; as it was difficult to obtain men, and their wages were high.

Before sunset, we left our hiding place, after eating the remainder of our bread, and proceeded cautiously towards the shore, keeping ourselves concealed as much as possible behind the bushes.

We saw a number of huts, scattered along the shore, mostly separate, some in small clusters. Part of the time during the day, a fog had prevailed, which now cleared away, and our prospect was uninterrupted. The island of Cuba could just be seen in the horizon, at the distance of thirty leagues; between that and us lay the ocean, smooth and unruffled, and not a sail to whiten its surface.

Dejected and melancholy, we again sought our place of concealment, to reflect upon our situation, and form some determination respecting future operations. To remain where we were long, without starving or being detected, was impossible; but how to get away was the problem to be solved.

Undetermined what to do, we left our retreat again, and the first object that met our view upon the water was a sail-boat directing her course to the shore near where we were.

Here was a means of escape that Providence had thrown in our way. Our previous despair was now changed into hope, and, with spirits suddenly elated, we retreated to the bushes to come to some immediate decision.

We resolved ourselves into a committee, appointed a moderator, and proceeded to business. The question to be discussed was, whether we should attempt to make a prize of the boat, and escape to Cuba. Without spending much time, as we had none to spare, to discuss the question, or to hear speeches for, much less against it, we put it to vote, and carried it unanimously.

The wind was blowing from the shore, and the boat was consequently beating in against the wind. This was a favorable circumstance for us, if we could get possession of the boat. The undertaking was fraught with difficulty and danger, but it was our only chance for escape.

We left our council place, and crept cautiously down to the shore, keeping concealed as much as possible behind the bushes, till we arrived near to the point, at which we thought the boat was steering. As she was beating against the wind, we concluded, if the man at the helm could be brought down, the boat would luff, which would bring her near the shore, when we were immediately to spring on board. Jones, being the best marksman, took the musket, and seeing that it was well loaded and primed, crept as close to the edge of the shore as he could without being discovered by the crew, and lay down, to wait for a good opportunity to fire at the man at the helm. The rest of us kept as near to him as possible.

Every circumstance seemed to favor our design. The negroes were all in their huts, and everything around was quiet and still.

The boat soon approached near enough for Jones to take a sure aim; and we scarcely breathed as we lay extended on the ground, waiting for him to perform the duty assigned him.

In a few moments, bang went the gun, and down went the negro from the helm into the bottom of the boat; and, as we had anticipated, the helm being abandoned, the boat luffed up in the wind and was brought close to the shore, which was bold, and the water deep enough to float her. The instant the gun was fired, we were upon our feet, and in the next moment up to our waists in the water alongside of the boat.

No time was lost in shoving her about, and getting her bows from the land. There was a fresh breeze from the shore; the sails filled; and the boat was soon under a brisk headway. I remained in the water the last, and, as I attempted to get on board, my hands slipped from my hold on the gunwale, and I fell into the water. I heard an exclamation, "Good God! Fox is lost!" from one of our party; but as the boat swept by me, I caught with my middle finger in the noose of a rope that hung over the stern, and was seized by the cape of my jacket and drawn into the boat by the powerful arm of Jones, who was managing the helm. All that I have described was apparently the work of a moment. Never did men use greater exertions than we did at this time.

The report of Jones' gun alarmed the negroes, and brought them from their huts in all directions down to the shore, armed with muskets and clubs, and full of rage and fury. They waded out after us, up to their chins in the water; and fired volley after volley, as fast as they could load. The bullets fell thickly around us, but fortunately none of us were injured. Our progress was so rapid, that we were soon out of reach of their shot; but, as soon as we could find time, we loaded our gun and gave one parting salute.

Our attention was next directed to the disposal of the crew of the boat we had captured, consisting of three men and a boy. As soon as we sprang into the boat, they fled with terror and amazement into a sort of cabin in the bow, where they still remained.

It was no wonder that they were frightened, attacked so suddenly by an enemy, who, as it seemed to them, had arisen all at once from the bowels of the earth or the depths of the ocean.

Whether the head of the negro at the helm was bullet-proof, or whether the ball approached so near to it as to frighten him into insensibility, we never knew; but we found him prostrate in the bottom of the boat, when we entered it, apparently dead; but, to our gratification, we soon found that he was alive, and not a curl of his wool discomposed.

He was soon upon his knees, supplicating mercy, in which attitude and tone he was followed by the rest of the crew as we called them from their hiding place. Had we been disposed to do an unjust action, we had an opportunity of realizing a considerable sum of money, by carrying them to Cuba and selling them for slaves.

The temptation was great to men destitute of funds as we were; but our moral sense overcame the temptation, and we gave them their choice to proceed with us on our voyage, or expose themselves to the hazard of drowning by attempting to swim ashore. They accepted the latter proposition with much gratitude, and were soon swimming lustily for the shore, from which we were at the distance of more than a mile, where we saw them all safely arrive.

We felt some anxiety respecting the ability of the boy to swim so far; but, as he was desirous of going with them, two of our men took him by his arms and legs, and gave him a regular yo-hoi-ho heave; and we had the satisfaction of seeing the little fellow shaking the water from his curly pate upon the shore, before his companions had landed.

The negroes collected around them in great numbers after they landed, probably to hear their account of the transaction; and to obtain information concerning our intentions and destination.

We felt animated by our success. We found the boat in good order; and, with a fresh breeze, we made rapid progress. We found a plenty of provisions in the boat, with which, for the first time for five days, we abundantly satisfied our hunger.

Epilogue

Fox and his companions sailed their tiny craft to Cuba where they went ashore finally free of British incarceration and military service. From there they gained a passage to Haiti where they went on board an American privateer. It proved to be out of Boston, and Fox was acquainted with many of the crew. While his companions went their own ways, Fox signed on to the crew for a voyage to France. There he remained until the war officially ended in 1783. He secured a passage to Boston and arrived in May, seeing his family for the first time in four years. They had learned of his incarceration on board the *Jersey* and his subsequent enlistment; knowing that he had enlisted only as an alternative to a worse fate, family friends had taken up a subscription to purchase his release from the British army. Before the money could be directed to Jamaica, however, a letter that Fox had written from Haiti arrived informing his mother of his escape.

Ebenezer Fox returned to his employment as a barber, and when he turned twenty-one he pursued this trade on his own. He later opened a store selling hardware and other goods, remaining in this business until 1837. In his old age his grandchildren reveled in his stories of adventure during the war that gave birth to their nation; when they desired to hear his entire wartime experiences, he found that a cough he'd developed made a lengthy retelling impossible. We have this cough to thank for Fox's life becoming recorded history, for he determined to write a memoir for his grandchildren to read. He set to writing a few pages each day over the course of a winter, and was amazed as fresh recollections flowed into his mind. The resulting narrative was so much enjoyed within his family that they shared it with others, and at the age of seventy-five he prepared it for publication. It did not, however, go into print until four years after his death in 1843 under the title of *The Adventures of Ebenezer Fox in the Revolutionary War.*[28] Fox mentions in the text that readers may have cause to doubt some of his details because of the time elapsed between the occurrence and the telling, but he does not relate anything that defies our conventional wisdom or that does not stand up to verification from other sources.

SEVEN

The Pensioner

George Fox, 7th and 47th Regiments of Foot

Introduction

Deserters. Drunkards. Ramblers. Robbers. Rapists. Is this what the British army was made of? Each of the six narratives presented so far were written by men who committed some sort of crime during their military career; indeed, two of the accounts are repentant last words, the ultimate testimony to the disaffected behavior of their narrators. The one man who turned to divinity, Thomas Watson, had been a gambler and drinker as a soldier, and twice committed the capital martial crime of desertion. John Robert Shaw maintained a responsible career as a young soldier right up to the point where he chose to desert rather than remain a prisoner of war. William Crawford also deserted as a prisoner, and although his initial intentions were to escape and rejoin the army, his bond with the bottle was a lifelong liability that led to his demise. Valentine Duckett was persuaded away from service by contemptuous characters and turned to a life of rambling indiscretions and crimes. Robert Young's offenses against women require no discussion, and ten years of loyal service did not stop him from deserting almost immediately after becoming a prisoner of war. Ebenezer Fox was a rascally soldier simply because he was an unwilling one; although his desertion can be seen as an act of America patriotism and a logical result of the way that he was recruited, from the perspective of British military discipline he was just another schemer who absconded from his enlistment obligation. Some of these men's lives were characterized by opprobrious conduct while others committed singular acts that nonetheless categorized them as criminals in the eyes of the army. Although they left the majority of surviving narratives, they do not represent the majority of the army.

Chance, assisted by societal customs, has seen to it that we have more information on soldiers who committed crimes than on those who did not. Of the majority of British soldiers who served in America we know little more than their names. Names of individual soldiers, along with a chronology of their careers, are readily available on muster rolls, but these documents seldom give specifics beyond the date of entry into a regiment and the date of departure from it.[1] Description books recording each man's age, height, hair and eye color, and other distinguishing physical characteristics were fastidiously kept,[2] but very few survive; with a couple of exceptions, the only places where these descriptive details have survived are in newspaper advertisements and army orders concerning deserters, issued so that the local populace could keep an eye out for the fugitives. Duty rosters and other documents chronicling routine service are also extremely rare. In contrast, men who were charged with significant crimes were tried by general courts-martial; because the proceedings of many of these courts survive, we are able to gain valuable insight on the routine activities of the men tried, while similar information for the legions of dutiful, never-accused soldiers remains unknown. Profoundly few soldiers left memoirs of any kind, and by chance the majority of those who did were deserters. Perhaps they perceived their experiences as more interesting that most, or perhaps their memoirs provided them a sort of confessional catharsis. The dying speeches are self-explanatory; it is unfortunate that men who left the army on honorable terms were not compelled to write or narrate similar synopses of their services.

Seven of the nine men presented in this book deserted from the army. This proportion is not in any way representative of the army as a whole. Muster rolls show us that regiments in America had desertion rates on the order of 5 to 10 percent over the course of the war years.[3] Men absconded from garrisons, camps, and campaign trails for reasons that were wholly their own, from rambling dispositions to discontent with discipline, from fear of punishment to the temptation of external influences. In addition to those who left directly, a significant number of prisoners of war failed to return when repatriation orders came. These men are recorded as deserters on muster rolls even though their actual fate was unknown, and as we have seen we can only speculate on the reasons why men did not return.[4] The muster rolls are deceptive in some cases. There are men who were prisoners of war from regiments serving in Canada who escaped and joined other regiments in New York, but on the rolls of their original regiments they are written off as deserters simply because their whereabouts were unknown.[5] On occasion, men who deserted and then returned are not accurately annotated on the rolls, appearing as new enlistees rather than returned deserters.[6] This makes it impossible to determine a precise number of deserters even from sources as authoritative as muster rolls. The important point for this study is that the vast majority of soldiers did not desert, but instead served their obligations faithfully. That the majority of released prisoners of war did in fact return to their regiments, and a significant number escaped captivity and managed to make their way into other regiments, is testimony to the determination of most soldiers—90 percent or more—to remain faithful to their martial obligation.

Desertion was a major crime subject to capital punishment; there was also a plethora of lesser infractions for which a soldier could be accused. Deviations from duty, poor hygiene, loss or disrepair of clothing and equipment, drunkenness, disrespect, and disobedience all could land a soldier in front of a regimental court that had the authority to impose a sentence of corporal punishment. The literature generally focuses on the brutal and life-threatening nature of punishment without attempting to determine its prevalence. As discussed in Chapter 3, records of regimental courts-martial for six corps during the 1770s and 1780s show that only 10 to 20 percent of the men in a given regiment were likely to be subject to such harsh measures. Taking the numeric data on desertion and regimental courts together, we must assume that the overwhelming majority of soldiers were obedient and dutiful by nature rather than by intimidation.

The regimental court records that survive cover periods of five years or less, whereas the careers of soldiers often lasted more than twenty years. Several sources reveal that soldiers could serve for such long periods without infractions requiring military justice. The documents verifying the legal discharge of soldiers, discussed in more detail below, sometimes include language such as "during twenty two years service having never been brought to a Court Martial" and "not having been brought to a Court Martial for Twenty years."[7] Additional examples come, ironically, from other court proceedings. While the records of regimental courts cited in Chapter 3 give only a summary of each case, the full proceedings of many general courts-martial survive. These courts tried high crimes including desertion, murder, rape, and mutiny. These courts also sentenced offenders to lashes as corporal punishment and could give sentences of capital punishment. Although the proceedings of these courts reveal a great deal about the army—for example, the trials of Valentine Duckett and Thomas Watson presented in Chapters 3 and 5—they are not good indicators of discipline within a regiment because relatively few men were tried by general courts; most regiments in America during the 1775–1783 war had only five to ten men tried in this way.[8] Many accused soldiers called on officers or noncommissioned officers as character witnesses at their trials, revealing dozens of soldiers who "behaved as well as the common run of Soldiers,"[9] "never was Charged with any offence or misdemeanour whatever, never was confined,"[10] or had never had "any Irregularity or misbehaviour being ever laid to his Charge."[11] Testimonials such as these are quite common in general courts for soldiers with anywhere from a few to over twenty years of service. Although these statements refer to just a few soldiers among thousands, they prove that it was common enough for soldiers to have long careers typified by good and obedient behavior rather than being kept in line by harsh disciplinary practices.

Additional evidence comes from the large numbers of men who reenlisted immediately after being discharged at the end of the war. Although peacetime enlistments were not for a fixed term of service, men who enlisted after 16 December 1775 were entitled to be discharged at the end of the war if they had served for at least three years. Although they had the opportunity to settle in America, take a land grant in Canada, or return to Great Britain, large numbers of discharged soldiers chose instead to enlist in regiments remaining in service in Canada or the West Indies.[12] Rather than short-term soldiers, they chose to become career military men.

The long-serving soldier eventually reached a physical condition that rendered him no longer fit for active service. These men were discharged at the discretion of the regiment, but they had something to look forward to that no civilian trade provided. The British army awarded pensions to discharged soldiers who had merit based on long service or incapacitation due to service. The pension was not much—five pence per day for most pensioners—but it did afford subsistence and was truly better than nothing for men who could not work for a living. There was no guarantee of a pension, but a man who had made the military his career, as most of them did, stood a reasonably good chance of getting one if he was legally discharged at the end of his service—that is, if he did not die while in the army or desert from it. Examination of the careers of soldiers in the 22nd Regiment of Foot, for example, reveals that pensions were granted to at least half of those who were discharged at the end of their service.[13]

An alternative form of reward was a land grant. A gift of one hundred acres of land in an overseas colony was a substantial reward to British citizens who had no way to own land in their own country, and encouraged settlement on the frontiers of the empire. The tracts of land allocated for these grants, however, were on unsettled frontiers and required tremendous labor to convert into productive farmland. British soldiers discharged in America at the end of the 1775–1783 war were given the option of accepting a land grant in Nova Scotia or returning to Great Britain.[14] When those who took land grants are added to those who received pensions, nearly

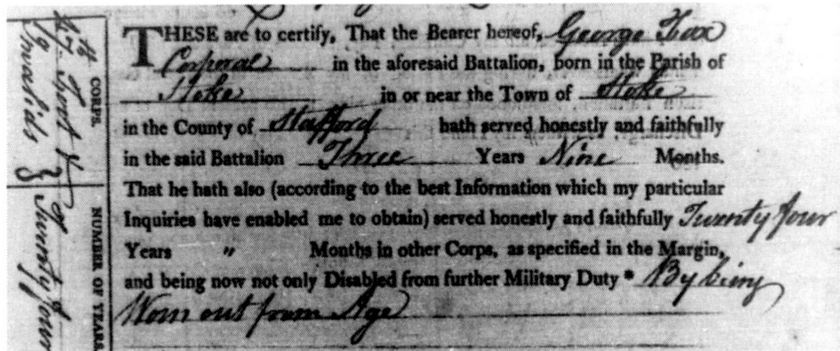

CORPS. | NUMBER OF YEARS.

THESE are to certify, That the Bearer hereof, George Fox
Corporal in the aforesaid Battalion, born in the Parish of
Stoke in or near the Town of Stoke
in the County of Stafford hath served honestly and faithfully
in the said Battalion Three Years Nine Months.
That he hath also (according to the best Information which my particular
Inquiries have enabled me to obtain) served honestly and faithfully Twenty four
Years " Months in other Corps, as specified in the Margin,
and being now not only Disabled from further Military Duty * By being
Worn out from Age

Detail (from a microfilm negative) of George Fox's discharge from the Royal Veteran Battalion. (*The National Archives. Photo by Michael Barrett*)

60 percent of discharged soldiers are known to have received some form of reward after their military service.[15]

Most pensions were administered through Chelsea Hospital. This institution was established during the reign of Charles II to accommodate old and disabled soldiers but was quickly filled to capacity. This brought about the establishment of out-pensions, that is, pensions for men who did not reside at the hospital itself. The system was refined during the early 1700s to the extent that it was running smoothly by the second half of the century. Discharged soldiers could go to London and appear in person before a board of commissioners, present their discharge along with any recommendations they might have from former officers, and make their claims for royal bounty in the form of a pension. The commissioners, appointed by the government, were bound to regulations that guided their decisions but had some leeway in their interpretation. They used their judgment to decide the merits of each claim, generally considering twenty years of service or a debilitating injury as sufficient to merit a pension.[16] The record books listing the date of examination of each claimant and whether or not the board awarded a pension do not include any information on the deliberations of the commissioners or the rationale for each decision.[17] We do not know the extent to which each soldier pleaded his case or presented evidence of distinguished service. If a pension was granted, the hospital retained a copy of the soldier's discharge, the document provided by his last regiment testifying that he had been legally released from service. Many of these discharges survive, providing valuable details about the man's service, albeit usually only a sentence or two.[18]

Pension funds were paid directly from tax revenues in an elegant manner. When a man was awarded a pension he informed the commissioners of his intended place of residence. The commissioners provided lists of pensioners to the collectors of excise throughout the British Isles, including each man's name, age, former regiment, trade, place of birth, and date of pension award. Twice a year the collectors of excise met with the pensioners in their districts and paid the funds due for the next six months of their subsistence.[19] Any man failing to meet with the collector of excise was presumed dead and struck from the list.[20] The collectors submitted detailed reports to the hospital commissioners of the funds paid out and the status of the pensioners in their districts. The commissioners were thereby removed from directly handling funds while retaining oversight of the pension rolls. In this way, between 10,000 and 20,000 pensioners were subsisted at any given time during the last quarter of the eighteenth century.[21]

There were variations. Chelsea Hospital carried a limited number of pensions that paid higher rates that the usual five pence per day.[22] Another hospital had been established at Kilmainham outside of Dublin, Ireland. Although it served essentially the same purpose, it had only a fixed number of out-pensions to offer. Because of this limitation, the vast majority of out-pensioners received their subsistence from Chelsea even if they resided in Ireland.[23]

Out-pensions were not without obligation. While infantry and cavalry regiments required men fit for active campaigning, the coast of Great Britain was dotted with fortifications that could be manned by men less physically capable. These posts were served largely by corps called invalid companies made up of veteran officers and soldiers who had been discharged from regular regiments. In times of peace these companies were small in size and number; when tangible threats existed the companies were reinforced and new ones created. Reinforcement was achieved by calling pensioners back to active service until they were no longer needed or no longer capable. When the need arose, a general call was made for out-pensioners to appear before officers appointed to determine their fitness for service in an invalid company.[24] Failure to appear before one of these boards, which sat in major population centers, was cause for being struck off the pension rolls. Men fit for service were sent to a garrison, sometimes near their place of residence and sometimes as far away as the islands of Jersey or Guernsey off the coast of France. In these garrisons thousands of veterans of the American war served many additional years, some into the second decade of the nineteenth century, before being discharged and returned to the pension rolls once again.[25]

The system was not without opportunities for corruption. Late in his army career Roger Lamb of the 23rd Regiment filled in personal information on the printed forms that discharged soldiers carried from their regiments to the Chelsea examination board, recording each man's service, maladies, and other details. In his personal notebook containing many passages not in his published memoirs, Lamb divulged the haphazard manner in which this was done in his own corps:

> In filling up the soldiers discharges which were signed by the Colonel before they were sent to me, the soldiers were asked "How long have you served" their answer would be seven or eight years more than they really were in the service, this they said in order that they might the more readily pass the Board by having a longer servitude. I then wrote the number of years they mentioned. But in filling up my own discharge I wrote Twelve just the number I really did serve. It is a false notion to think soldiers are served by putting down in their papers more years than they actually were in the service. No it is bringing a curse on them by lying and perjury! They are obliged to swear in a most solemn manner before a Magistrate every quarter of a year, that they have served the number of years specified in their discharge. And I do not wonder at the misery some of these poor old men undergo after leaving the Army seeing that the curse of lying and perjury are upon them.[26]

Lamb's allegations are plausible, but there is no evidence that such fraudulent practices were widespread.[27] Another approach to an ill-begotten pension required much more desperation on the part of the soldier. In 1770s Ireland soldiers were occasionally attacked and maimed by marauding citizens, apparently in protest of military presence. In a brutal practice called houghing (pronounced "hocking"), hapless soldiers walking alone at night were attacked and their Achilles tendons cut.[28] This was a crippling injury that rendered the man unfit for service and probably unable to earn a living. Knowing that disabilities incurred in the service could bring the award of a pension,[29] a soldier in the 11th Regiment of Foot used a razor to cut his own tendon and staged a scene so that he appeared to have been assaulted. His deception was found out, but his fate is not known.[30] It is unlikely that such grim self-inflicted measures were common. Injuries and health disorders such as asthma and rheumatism were usually certified by the regimental surgeon on the soldier's discharge.[31]

Exemplary of the out-pensioners who served long and dutifully is George Fox. He enlisted voluntarily at a typical age after having learned a trade, served in two regiments during peace and war, spent time as a prisoner of war, received an out-pension after the American war, then served ten more years in a veteran battalion in the 1790s and 1800s. He hailed from the town of Stoke, one of six Staffordshire towns known collectively as the Potteries after the ceramics industry that had been thriving there for over a century when Fox was born in 1745.[32] It is no surprise, then, that young Fox pursued this trade, becoming a pot maker, as did his younger brother Thomas. We have no details on the first two decades of his life, whether he worked diligently at his trade or had the wandering disposition that characterized other young men that we've studied. What we do know is that he changed careers at the age of twenty or twenty-one, when he enlisted in the 7th Regiment of Foot, known as the Royal Fusiliers, in the town of Newcastle-under-Lyme not far from his home town of Stoke.

A memoir narrated by Fox gives us his own story of his career as a soldier; we will discuss this narrative later on, but first summarize the events it recounts and provide additional details on the man who experienced them. Thanks to a rare document, we know something of George Fox's physical attributes. Regiments kept "description books" that recorded basic attributes of their men such as height, age, hair and eye color, and any other attributes that might aid in recognizing the man in the event of desertion. Very few of these are known to still exist, but one of Fox's company officers made up such a list in November 1772 in a notebook that also included standing orders, templates of commonly used military forms, and other utilitarian information.[33] From this we know that Fox stood five feet six inches (among the shortest of the thirty-seven men in his company), and had a "fresh" complexion, brown hair, and the pale blue eyes described in the era as "grey." His trade is given as "Potmaker." The thirty-seven descriptions show varied backgrounds of men in the company, including thirteen weavers, three cordwainers, two tailors, two pot makers, a brazier, a hairdresser, a button maker, a plasterer, a card maker, a laborer, a miller, and eleven men with no trade listed. Five of the men were from "North Britain" (Scotland) and one from Ireland, with the remainder being from "South Britain" (England).

According to this record Fox was enlisted by Lieutenant Rowland Mainwaring. His enlistment is recorded as February 1767, and the regiment's muster rolls give the date that he was "entertained" as 9 February.[34] Fox's own recollection was that he enlisted in 1766, an apparent ambiguity that is resolved by recognizing that the recruiting party was operating well away from the headquarters of the 7th Regiment. As we have seen with other soldiers, it was common for a new recruit to spend weeks or months with the recruiting party until an opportune time arose for him to travel to the main body of the regiment. So it was that Fox went to Edinburgh in early 1767.[35] His first eighteen months as a soldier were spent moving around Scotland with the 7th Regiment—from Edinburgh to Perth, then to Aberdeen, on to Fort George on the Moray Firth at the northeast end of the Great Glen, then to nearby Inverness, and finally southwest to the garrisons of Fort Augustus and Fort William at the other end of the Great Glen. Fox tells us nothing of this time besides the movements of the regiment. As a new soldier, he surely spent much of this time learning and training, performing the routines of the peacetime military, and marveling at locations undoubtedly new and strange to him. He must have shown some promise as a military man, for in October 1769 he was sent out on the recruiting service under Lieutenant Charles Cochrane. This party returned to the place where George Fox himself had enlisted, Newcastle-under-Lyme. There they found another willing recruit in George's younger brother Thomas.

The description list indicates that Thomas varied from his brother by three years of age and a half inch in height. Thomas was also a potter by trade and also enlisted at the age of twenty when he'd had ample time to develop a taste for or a dislike of the profession. The two brothers met up with the 7th Regiment again in March 1770 at the town of Berwick-upon-Tweed, in the very northeast corner of England just an hour's walk from the Scottish border. This was the end of the regiment's time in the North, however; in September they marched to the great army barracks at Chatham outside of London, there to spend two years in garrison. In September 1772 they moved to another major military center, Portsmouth, on the south coast. George then went on recruiting service once again, this time to Worcestershire, while his brother remained in the Portsmouth garrison. Service in two of the biggest military depots in Great Britain may have offered a sense of foreboding to the Fox brothers and their comrades in the 7th Regiment, for these places were staging areas for overseas deployment; or they may have continued their martial routine in ignorance of the future. Regardless of whether they knew it or not, they were going to America.

War had not yet begun, but by the time the 7th Regiment embarked in April 1773 troubles had been brewing. The Boston Massacre had occurred in 1770, and the burning of the revenue cutter *Gaspee* in 1772. Although they were sent to America as part of normal peacetime deployments, one wonders if there was any trepidation among the soldiers about serving in a land that was becoming more politically tense and tending toward violence. The 7th Regiment landed in Quebec in July, no doubt with an appreciation for the important British army victory that had occurred there just fourteen years before. Among the officers in Fox's company was a young lieutenant named John André who years later would become inexorably tied to the infamous Benedict Arnold.[36] Fox surely knew André but makes no mention of him. In fact, Fox says nothing of pre-war activities or events in the Canadian capital, perhaps because it was mundane compared to what followed. In January 1774 an officer of the 7th lamented that "Our Regiment is very sick, as we have lost 18 men within this last ten weeks, and 34 remains in hospital. Several of them have been taken ill on guard and died in great agonies within eighteen hours afterwards—three men died this morning. I imagine it is the Rum which they get for 21s. the Gall. The Garrison drinks and games very much."[37] A few months later "a soldier of the 7th Regiment was found dead, lying on his face in a puddle on the Road between St. Roch and Mr Grant's Windmill. It is imagined being intoxicated he had fallen in the Mud whereby he was unfortunately suffocated, as there was but very little water where he lay."[38] Fox made no mention of such follies, but the outbreak of war provided events significant enough to warrant his recollection; his memories become detailed in the summer of 1775 when the 7th Regiment was distributed among several posts along the waterways between Quebec and Lake Chaplain. Fox, however, was in a detachment of the regiment that remained in Quebec, a twist of fate that drastically altered his wartime experiences. While his brother Thomas marched with the regiment past Montreal to the post at St. John's in August, George Fox stayed behind with fifty-one other men of the 7th.

The following month a whirlwind of warfare swept up the waterways. American forces, encouraged by successes around Boston, attacked and seized British positions at Ticonderoga, St. John's, Chamblee, and Montreal. The bulk of the 7th Regiment was captured piecemeal, primarily at St. John's. George Fox's detachment was combined with a detachment of a newly raised regiment, the Royal Highland Emigrants, which made some abortive moves to reinforce the beleaguered posts before being ordered to Quebec, the linchpin of Canada. Holding Quebec was critical, and every available man set to preparing defenses against the seemingly unstoppable onslaught from the South. Having lost the principal parts of the two regular regiments in Canada, the 7th and 26th Regiments, General Sir Guy Carleton relied on the handful of remaining regular soldiers, local militia, and whatever sailors, townspeople, and refugees he could arm and employ. They dug in for a desperate defense of the prized capital of Canada.

In 1759, British forces had taken Quebec in one of the most revered battles in British military history. After laying siege to the cliffside town in the summer, British forces had worked their way around to the landward side of the town and drawn the French defenders out onto the plains to do battle. In 1775, a hastily assembled American army, carried by the momentum of repeated victories, attempted to unseat the under-strength Quebec garrison, but their boldness and enthusiasm was not matched by tactical prowess. With several factors pressing them to haste, they attacked the city in the winter, during a snowstorm, on the cliff side; an assault more opposite to that which had succeeded in 1759 would be difficult to conceive. The defenders crushed the attack, and although the broken American army managed to maintain a siege until spring, they had lost all hope of victory. Canada remained in British hands and would never again be threatened. Although Fox participated in the successful defense of the city, his account of the action lacks any details of his personal activities. This is unfortunate because the little detachment of the 7th Regiment "distinguished themselves" in the defeat of the American assault on the city,[39] and even in the funeral given by the garrison for the fallen commander of the attackers; an observer noted that "the regular troops, particularly that fine body of men, the Seventh Regiment, with reversed arms, and scarfs on the left elbow, accompanied the corpse to the grave."[40] They then endured significant hardship manning the defenses throughout the winter. While standing sentry, the eyes of one 7th Regiment soldier froze shut; he remained at his post, blind, until discovered by an officer who took him to a warm guardhouse to recover.[41] A few months later two imprisoned American officers bribed two soldiers of the 7th in an attempt to gain their assistance in escaping. When British officers questioned how the soldiers came to have an inordinate amount of money the soldiers revealed the plot, and the American officers were confined more closely. There is no record that the British soldiers were punished for accepting the bribes.[42]

The siege was lifted in May when British reinforcements arrived in Quebec as soon as the St. Lawrence River was sufficiently clear of ice to allow their transports to arrive from Halifax. Most of the newly arriving regiments had embarked in Ireland about two months before. Included in the powerful force were the 9th Regiment of Foot, whose ranks included the prolific author Roger Lamb;[43] the 20th Regiment with William Crawford whose narrative appears in this volume; and the 29th Regiment which still had men in its ranks who had figured in the Boston Massacre six years before.[44] One of the regiments did not come directly from Great Britain, but instead had arrived in America in 1773; the 47th Regiment of Foot had served in the New York area for a year, then moved to Boston where it was involved in the opening engagements of the war and the subsequent siege. When Boston was evacuated, the 47th was the only regiment shifted from the army destined to descend on New York to the army preparing to reestablish British dominance in Canada. There was a simple reason behind this transfer: the colonel of the 47th Regiment was Major-General Sir Guy Carleton, commander in chief of British forces in Canada; although regimental colonels seldom actually served with their regiments, it was common for their regiments to be sent to serve in places where their colonels held higher-level commands.[45] Because it had been in America for some time already, the 47th was somewhat under strength compared to the others that were arriving fresh from Great Britain. There was a straightforward way to recruit the regiment, for there was in Quebec a detachment of men whose regiment had been captured the previous year. So it was that George Fox and the other men of the 7th Regiment who had helped to defend Quebec were drafted into the 47th Regiment and immediately sent on the offensive.[46]

The string of British garrisons that had fallen in the fall were quickly retaken as British forces routed the weary American army that had come so close to winning Canada.

The chase continued all the way to Lake Chaplain where the armies took to the water in fleets of hastily built gunboats. Already dominant on land with seasoned professional soldiers, the British matched this dominance on the lake by assembling bona-fide warships that had been either prefabricated in England for the purpose or disassembled in Quebec and rebuilt at the northern end of the lake. Crewed by experienced sailors, mounting guns manned by artillerymen, and carrying soldiers from the army, this little navy outclassed that of the Americans in every way. As both fleets took to the water in earnest in early October the Americans managed to level the playing field by carefully choosing the location of the inevitable naval battle, sheltering themselves in a narrow passage behind Valcour Island that limited the ability of the superior British fleet to engage. Although the British won the battle, it bought time for the remains of the American army to escape intact to the fortress at Ticonderoga. This fort was to Lake Champlain what Quebec was to Canada, the key to controlling the entire region; the British had suffered disastrous losses attempting to take it from the French in the previous war, and were not about to risk another such debacle this late in the campaign season with an army that, although successful, was not equipped to besiege an entrenched position. The British withdrew and spent the winter in their string of posts extending from the top of the lake to Quebec.

George Fox's recollection of these events is chronologically garbled and lacking in significant personal details. He relates the next campaign more clearly, albeit with the early parts intermixed with some of the significant events from the previous year. Fox's account of the fateful 1777 campaign from Canada toward Albany led by Major General John Burgoyne is valuable not for new perspectives on the overall conduct of operations, but for its insights on the experiences of individual soldiers. It is in this part of his account that Fox finally interjects some personal experiences, including carrying a wounded officer to safety and having part of his equipment shot away by a cannonball. Although two other soldiers presented in this book, William Crawford and Robert Young, served on the same campaign, they touch only lightly on their personal experiences. Fox goes into detail, giving the perspective of a common soldier on this rigorous expedition that is exceeded only by soldier-cum-author Roger Lamb.[47] Fox was appointed corporal at some time after 1776 but the absence of muster rolls between early 1777 and 1782, and Fox's own silence on the matter, leave it unknown whether this occurred before or after the campaign.

When the campaign met its ignominious end at Saratoga in October, George Fox was in one of the eight companies of the 47th Regiment incarcerated (a portion had been left behind in Canada; these men were eventually either discharged or drafted into other regiments)[48] and marched with the Convention Army to barracks outside of Boston. During the next five and a half years, as this army of prisoners marched across the American countryside and whiled away time in stockaded cantonments, George Fox did something that only a minority of his comrades did: he dutifully remained with his dwindling regiment. Of about 375 men of the 47th captured, only about 75 remained with the Convention Army in the summer of 1781.[49] While men like Roger Lamb escaped and rejoined the British army in New York, men like William Crawford absconded with similar intentions but were diverted by local opportunities, and men like Robert Young deserted with no aspirations of remaining a soldier, Fox experienced every day of the lengthy captivity. His personal account of this period is the only one of its kind and provides an invaluable record of this interesting chapter in the history of the British army in America. Repatriation came at the close of hostilities in May 1783; Fox and the remaining prisoners of the 47th Regiment were escorted from Lancaster, Pennsylvania, to New Jersey where they crossed to Staten Island and rejoined their army. Soon after, they boarded transports and returned to Great Britain for the first time in eleven years.

Some time during the few years after his return to his native land, George Fox narrated his recollections of service in America to a nephew. Whether he conveyed his story in this way because he was illiterate, or for some other reason, is not known. It is fortunate that this record of his memories survives, but the nature of the manuscript is problematic. The nephew who wrote it did so in a rapid fashion that included

George Fox spent several years as a prisoner of war after the failed 1777 northern campaign. When he was captured he may have been wearing clothing from his original regiment, the 7th, or the 47th into which he had been drafted. Regardless, by 1781 it is unlikely that many of those garments remained serviceable. The British army sent clothing to its incarcerated soldiers, but not regimental uniforms. Advertisements for escapees and inventories of delivered goods make it possible to hypothesize how these long-term prisoners may have looked.

This prisoner of war wears a linen coatee described in some advertisements for escapees. His linen trousers, typical of those worn by British soldiers in America, have been repeatedly patched and darned to extend their life. Shirts made from coarse blue and white checked linen were widely issued to soldiers for work and off-duty use; around his neck is a tied handkerchief rather than a formal neck stock. The last vestiges of his regimental clothing are carried in a well-worn knapsack that shows various repairs and is missing some straps and buckles. He wears a woolen foraging cap made from cast-off cuttings of old coats; caps like these were widely used by the army, but no fixed pattern existed and they probably varied from one regiment to another. The number of the 47th Regiment is formed from cloth numerals sewn onto the cap's front flap. The soldier's hair has grown long and disheveled after years of lacking a military routine.

numerous abbreviations, rampant misspellings, some notes in the third person, and various other challenges to the reader. If the words were George Fox's own, there would be value in transcribing the manuscript verbatim because the handwriting conventions would give some insights into the man himself, but they are not; they are clearly reflections of the copyist. Also, the manuscript has already been transcribed and published verbatim, so a version is available to anyone wishing to refer to it.[50] For these reasons, we have chosen here to refine the manuscript into more readable text, in very much the way that the original publishers of the other narratives in this book must have done; the publisher of Robert Young's dying speech clearly states this, and the publishers of the other narratives most likely did likewise. The chronological discontinuities, just as likely to be caused by extemporaneous narration of the events as by genuinely inaccurate recollection of them, are largely preserved, but the abbreviations, fragmentary sentences, and other nuances of handwriting have been rationalized into modern prose.

The Narrative of George Fox

Listed in 7th regt. foot at Newcastle[51] Sep — 1766
Joined the regiment at Edinburgh March — 1767
went to Perth the same year
went to Aberdeen City
1768
went to fort George North
went to Inverness
1769
went to fort William & fort Augustus
Came to Newcastle recruiting October 1769
Joined the regiment at Berwick upon Tweed with Thomas March 1770
To Chatham (300 miles) the same year September & November 1770

To Portmouth.—September 1772 and then recruiting to Worcestershire October 1772
Joined the regiment. March 10 1773
Bound to Quebec left Plymouth April 16 1773—no hammock
Landed at Quebec 23 July 1773

Went into country cantonments for ten days. Quebec is situated at the head of the River St. Lawrence upon a high rock consisting of the upper & lower town. The lower is almost as large as the upper, and is walled; the port Louis gate is at the west end of the town, port St. John at the north west, Paris gate in the north, sallyport gate east going down to the lower town, Cape Diamond a strong fortified battery southwest, the grand battery north east. The governor with a deputy governor lived there, barracks for two regiments almost 1/4 of a mile square, three churches, two French and one English, other meeting houses (none in the lower town), a castle to the east.

The regiment went to St. Johns 25 miles above Montreal which is 200 miles above Quebec situated at the edge of Lakes, which are fed by the North river, on 27 August 1775. 52 men were left at Quebec. Went to Sante-gaine 70 miles south east in a detachment consisting of 20 men to watch the motions of rebels in Nova Scotia. Lived ten days upon fish. October, went to the relief of St. Johns with Maclean, Colonel in the 71st.[52] General Carlton went to Montreal. Took 4 field pieces 200 miles up to St. Denies, along with 1200 men with Canadians, and there we heard that St. Johns was taken and General Carlton defeated. We received orders to go to Quebec. Received a challenge from General Montgomery. With Carlton were landed 800 men that were pressed in. Maclean's had 52 of the 7th & 70 of 71st regiments.[53] At St. Denies we fired at the army across the river, and that night lay under arms. Received an express at 11 o'clock at night from Guy Carlton to retreat to Sorel 25 miles below, retreated that night, but before we had raised a breast work we perceived them following us, which made us take to our sloop of war and a brig. An express came from Quebec that General Arnold was besieging Quebec with 1200 men. Maclean went down the river with his 70 men and left us with the brig and sloop and we rode quarantine[54] for twelve days and the rebels opened a twelve pound battery upon us which made us cut our cables and make out for the sea. In our passage we took Guy Carlton on board. 12,000 of Americans passed on their road to Montreal.

Arnold came from Boston to Quebec 300 miles through the woods with 1200 men and 300 Indians. Through the fatigues of the march they deserted and fled to the woods; through the scarceness of provisions the men were obliged to cut the branches and bark of trees to eat, and coming down the river in bateaus they spoiled the greatest part of their powder so that they had but three rounds per man. When they arrived at Point Levi opposite Quebec they gave three cheers to alarm the garrison of their arrival and then crossed the river and went into country cantonments for winter quarters, and laid a regular siege to the town. When Maclean arrived at Quebec there was but two guns mounted in the town, but by the time we came down he had mounted several, and while Arnold went to Montreal to join Montgomery we were employed mounting guns and fortifying ourselves, expecting a battle about the middle of October. The rebels under Montgomery come and laid siege to Quebec. The first battery they erected against us was against St. Johns gate that leads to Abraham's plain mounting one mortar and four twelve pounders.[55] The next battery they erected was a fascine battery[56] over the river at Point Levi opposite the lower town, consisting of six twelve pounders; the third battery erected at Abraham plain port Louis of four nine pounders. The fourth battery was over the St. Charles River. They continued the siege till the 31st of December, playing their batteries night and day, and we the same, balls by day and shells by night. On that day by 5 o'clock in the morning they stormed the garrison. General Arnold with 800 men was at the north end of the lower town and took a battery consisting of 6 guns, 12 pounders. Montgomery with 1200 men intended storming the south end of the lower town but he lost his life in the attempt, with an orderly sergeant and corporal of artillery, from a canister shot.[57] Arnold was wounded in the leg at the beginning and his detachment was all killed and took prisoners. They still continued the siege all winter until the 7th May when the 29th Regiment came up the river to our relief and we sallied out upon Abraham plain. But the enemy refused us and they left all their heavy baggage behind them. The same day we pursued them 9 miles to a place called Cruse ferry towards Montreal and then came back to Quebec. They left their sick, a great many with the small pox, their old men and lads.

Soon after the 47th Foot came from Halifax and the 9th, 31st, 20th, 21st, 24th and 62nd Regiments and several light infantry and grenadiers from other regiments.[58] In a few days we all went by shipping to Pointe aux Trembles 21 miles away and there the 52 of us from the 7th Regiment were ordered to be drafted into the 47th Regiment on 24 March 1776.[59] Then 100 men proceeded to the Three Rivers and we lay at anchor for four days.[60] On that day the rebels came down by the woods intending to burn the town called the Three Rivers. On the 7th June we landed and drew up in line of battle, our left wing engaged them and we took and killed several of them particularly General Thompson their Chief.[61]

They retreated to St. Johns, then we set sail and landed at Sorel and marched to St. Dennis, and from there to Chamblee 18 miles above St. Denis. We halted there four hours to victual and then pursued 24 miles to St. Johns. They had set fire to the fort and gone in their bateaus upon the lake 26 miles to the Isle aux Noix. Our army stayed there till the beginning of September repairing the fort and building near 200 bateaus to pursue them. We advanced in our bateaus; they kept retreating. From the Isle aux Noix we went up the river Lacolle. We continued our expedition over the Lake Champlain 250 miles from Quebec, 150 miles over the lake and there we over took them on the further side of the lake under Arnold. He was wounded and we destroyed several of their vessels. They were in schooners, floating batteries and gun boats; we had bateaus and gun boats. Then we followed them to Chimney Point, our old fort opposite Crown Point, which is 400 miles from Quebec. The river that parts them runs from Lake Champlain. There we encamped until October. The rebels went up to Ticonderoga to winter quarters. Now with winter approaching we were obliged to retreat down into Canada for winter quarters in different cantonments. The artificers stayed building ships, floating batteries, gun boats &c, two ships of 20 guns each *George, Maria, Carleton*, and a large floating battery carrying 16 guns and several gun boats. The remainder in country cantonments until the beginning of May 1777, when we were embodied at St. Johns under General Burgoyne.

Shipping floating batteries and gun boats before us to clear the lakes, the rest of the army (the principal part) went after in a few days in the bateaus, five men with their arms, ammunition, provisions &c in a bateau. We proceeded up the lakes until we came to Crown Point in 7 days. We encamped at Crown Point a few days, then one part embarked in the gun boats, the other landed, and we marched to where the shipping were 3 miles short of Ticonderoga. We encamped 2 or 3 days, and then advanced 1 1/2 miles further opposite to Ticonderoga. The shipping could not come up. When the rebels found we were so nigh they began cannonading upon us. The fire came so hot we were obliged to move our camp into the valleys; their balls then went over us. They had fortified Independent Hill joining the town strongly. We began to clear Sugar Loaf Hill a large hill southwest of the town and forts on the opposite side of the river that commanded the town and forts a mile distant, where they thought it was impossible for us to get any cannon up. It was so steep and high that it was with great fatigue with horses we got nine 32 pounders up. After clearing the hill and building a battery, we mounted two; we should have mounted the other seven in the morning and have given a hot fire, but they under General Schuyler left the fort, stores &c in the night. In the morning we took possession; they abandoned 100 pieces of cannon and all the heavy baggage with stores of provisions and spirits.

We followed them the same day, and before our shipping could pass the fort we had a bridge to break down that they built to hinder the shipping going up the river. They went up the river in their shipping and ours followed them to Skenesboro and destroyed them. Where they could not go any higher, one of their capital ships was blown up by a shell when it got among their powder; the report was heard for 25 miles and we saw the smoke above 20 miles away like a cloud in the sky. The rebels burnt their bateaus and took to the woods. Their provisions they had sunk and our men went down and saw there was a deal sunk, then we got our grappling irons to hook up the barrels of pork and flour, but we had such quantities of pork that we were sick at the sight of it. Then we encamped there.

At Ticonderoga the 9th and 21st Regiments went the other way up the river (it forks) to Fort George and took all the rebels' bateaus and destroyed them that went that way from Ticonderoga, of a distance 30 miles. The rebels had burnt the fort. The 21st took possession of the ground while the 9th pursued them through the woods to Fort Anne 24 miles away. The flying army pursued the rebels from Skenesboro to Hubbardton where they were encamped upon a hill and cooking in camp. Just leaving, they were surprised at that time. When we were at the bottom of the hill we engaged them. The fire was hot on both sides for three quarters of an hour. Our grenadiers and light infantry made a volley and a charge and took possession of the ground. The rebels retreated, not having time to take their knapsacks with them, with great loss of men—150 prisoners, 30 dined and retreated,[62] 35 killed. I was not there.

Just as we arrived at Skenesboro we heard the report of cannon and small arms at Fort Anne 18 miles from Skenesboro (there is a small river that comes from there to Skenesboro, part of the north river). *To arms* was beat for us to decamp and go to their assistance; before we could get there the 9th was cut off (to a few) by being overpowered. The rebels sallied out of the fort upon them, it being at dusk when the engagement began. The 9th had orders from Burgoyne that after they left the 21st at Fort George they were to follow the enemy and keep them in play until they were reinforced; because of that they durst not retreat, but after the rebels had gone into the fort the few of the 9th that were left coming down to Skenesboro we met at 9 o'clock at night, and had come two miles (very wet night). The 47th was sent to look after the wounded of the 9th Regiment; we brought them down to the first houses there were and doctors were appointed to attend them. A wet night and very dark, the roads were very bad so that in the morning our clothes could not be told what colour they were. We had this morning 1/2 pint of rum served out to each man. This night I carried an officer of a regiment named Lieutenant Torriano on my back to a private house where he gave me a guinea. The same day we returned and joined the army and encamped there again. We remained there until the road was repaired up to Fort Anne to bring up the heavy cannon. After that was completed we struck our camp and marched for Fort Anne and encamped there. The smell came so offensive off the hill that a party of us were ordered to go and bury the dead bodies of the 9th Regiment and the rebels.

They had evacuated the fort and set it on fire. We remained there a fortnight till the main army came up with the heavy cannon and baggage. We removed to Fort Edward 18 miles away. The flying Army went to Fort Miller 6 miles further on. We were at Fort Edward busied in making breast works and batteries for a fortnight. A detachment of the 47th and 62nd were ordered to a place called Jones' house 12 miles back. There we began building works, and were there four or five weeks. A detachment of our two regiments were sent to Fort George 24 miles away, 24 of us, 12 from each regiment, with 30 prisoners which went into Canada. When we came back to Jones' house we received 1/2 pint of rum for our trouble. Captain Law and 100 men were detached to Fort George to mend the road betwixt there and Fort Edward 25 miles, to bring up the heavy cannon and baggage, bateaus &c.

We remained at Fort Edward and Jones' house (a by pass) for 5 weeks until we got the cannon, bateaus, provisions &c up, then we removed to Fort Miller 6 miles from Fort Edward. There we pitched our camp. The flying Army moved after the rebels to Bennington 24 miles through the woods with the Regiment of Horse Hanoverians and Germans on foot. There they engaged the enemy and, surrounded, the whole fine regiment of Germans was killed and took prisoners, 5 or 6 escaping. The flying army suffered very much, a great many killed and wounded and the rest taken. Some made their escape to the main army.

We remained at Fort Miller until we built a bridge over the river, then we moved to Saratoga 5 miles from Fort Miller. There we encamped until the baggage &c came to us. In two days we made a movement of 18 miles. The flying army marched in front and took possession of Freeman's Farm 21 miles from Saratoga where they engaged the rebels. The grand army being three miles in the rear came up to their assistance, then a general engagement commenced by 7 o'clock in the morning and continued until sunset on the night of 19th September in which time there was a continued fire. Our loss was 1100 rank & file killed and wounded—no ground gained and darkness parted us. Their loss was more. Our general hospital, being large marquees, was full of wounded. The next morning a parley was beat by both parties to bury the dead. We had not more than 3000 engaged the whole day (at 1/2 mile distance from each), they had 4 times as many; the rest of our men were employed in raising works and bringing the baggage &c up. After burying the dead all men off duty were employed in making batteries (the rebels had works for three or four mile long of batteries and redoubts which they had raised before we came to them). The flying army all in front built a block house of 24 guns, 12 pounders, and several more block houses were made by the British and Germans (there being a wood between us). They had come out of their works 19th September.

After we had secured ourselves we built a bridge in the night and passed over in forage parties to get provender for the horses. We lay encamped expecting General Clinton would come up the North River and we should have the enemy between two fires. We lay till the 7th October displaying signals by fire rockets now and then. Clinton if he had been at Albany 35 miles away coming up the north River he might have seen them and found us. When we came out of Canada we brought 16 regiments of Indians with us but they were of very little use. They were employed in flanking parties and in the front; when they could espy their opportunity they would kill the rebel sentinels and scalp them, something which they would not part with. Amongst them, those that had the most scalps were accounted the best warriors. They were exceeding fond of rum; as for eating nothing that they could eat was refused. They were exceeding cruel; men, women and children they would scalp belonging to the enemy. They left us the latter end of September to go to their hunting for the winter which they would not neglect.

The army lay still until the 7th October (except a shell now and then) when our provisions began to get short. We began to cannonading about 8 o'clock in the morning which was continued an hour on each side before the small arms were fired, then they came out of their works. We advanced and the action began and continued until sunset at night, a constant fire. At last the rebels took the Germans works and they fled to our works and put the army in confusion. Night coming on we retreated a mile and lay upon our arms all night. Our killed and wounded were 900, General Fraser and Colonel Jones of the artillery both killed; the enemy lost 1500. We had not above 4000 engaged that day, the rebels were 3200 & above.

The next morning we retreated to Saratoga, 18 miles, by night and took possession of the old trench works. We began to cook our victuals by the fires, but they fired and killed several of our men so that we put out our fires and lay upon the ground all night. They having got upon an small island in the river a detachment was sent and drove them off the Island and kept guard all night. The next day we pitched our tents and all hands off duty were employed in making redoubts and breast works to preserve us from their shot that came across the river. They had three batteries playing upon us, which drove us out of our works and obliged us to retreat 100 yards back between two hills and all upon one another to screen us from their fire. Here a six pound ball took the bottom of my knapsack off. Our cannon played back with little effect. We continued in this situation four days wholly surrounded. At last General Burgoyne ordered the Commanding Officer of each regiment to ask the men whether they would start another general engagement at which they consented and gave three cheers, and we were drawn up in line of battle along the side of a wood 100 yards from the point of our first retreat. For ten days we lived on 4 biscuits per man per day and then we had some flour served out to us which we made dumplings of. We durst not go to our bateaus for the little beef and pork in them. The time that we first retreated we set fire to 72 barrels of rum and burnt the bridge and 450 bateaus, and cannon were sunk. General Riedesel went round to the German regiments to ask them whether they would stand, at which they answered no. With that he offered 3 guineas per man to stand another general engagement, but with one voice they answered no for they had no provision nor spirits and were badly used, so they grounded their arms so that we retired to our old post.

Then General Burgoyne ordered the 47th Regiment to attempt a retreat to Fort George. We started by 9 o'clock in morning; we got as far as Fort Edward, 19 miles, and just crossing the river we saw the rebels had taken possession of Fort Edward hill and had a large number of cannon planted to prevent our crossing over. General Burgoyne's aide-de-camp overtook us to turn back. At our retreat back they fired at us across the river (we were afraid they could have crossed it) at which we formed ourselves up in a line. A smart action for 1/2 an hour; by order of Colonel Sutherland the chief of the 47th Regiment the fire ceased with only one man wounded. We took up from the water 44 rebels killed besides their wounded. We retreated the same night to the army, all this day and only a drink of water. Just as we joined the army we set the barracks on fire, and lay at our post, they firing shells and balls all night.

Next morning they sent a flag of truce that if we did not surrender they would kill every man of us. General Burgoyne ordered a counsel to sit immediately. General Burgoyne went with a flag of truce to General Gates to his camp upon which they concluded upon the Articles of Convention. When he came back he acquainted us of a cessation of arms. The chief articles were as follows: All the stores &c &c that belonged to his Majesty, Officers and private men's property they were not to touch. We were not to ground our arms but to stack them.[63] In the bateaus were a barrel of pork and 2 1/2 of flour. After every thing was completed according to the Articles of Convention, the Canadians, artificers, the wagoners and drivers of cannons were permitted to go down to Canada without being molested. The soldiers were to march down to Boston to be sent to England and were not to serve again during the war. The articles were made on the 16th October 1777. We stacked our arms and marched 17 miles, the rebels formed themselves in two lines on each side the road and we marched through them in the centre. General Gates ordered that no man of his army was to cast any reflection as we passed. We were received by a strong guard of 500; they marched us to Freeman's Farm that night. Surrendered were 6572 Germans, 4000 regulars of the 9th, 20th, 21st, 24th, 47th and 62nd besides grenadiers and light infantry belonging to other regiments.

The next day from there to Stillwater, 13 miles, 200 miles from Boston. We had five days provision served out. The next morning we crossed the river and so were at Williamstown 26 miles, in New Hampshire. Next day we lay in the woods. 27 miles the next day, 27 next, 27 next, 27 next, 27 miles to Hadley in New England, next 6 Days provision served out. The middle of November we arrived at Prospect Hill near Boston 2 or 3 miles and went into wooden barracks and fortified works that they made for our men at Boston. There we remained all winter, good usage but very cold barracks. In the Spring General Burgoyne ordered us to exercise, then the shipping for us came round to Boston harbour, but the rebels thinking they wanted to take us to New York they would not let us go.

We remained there until the latter end of August, orders coming from Congress to remove to Rutland (in barracks) 72 miles into New England. We expected to have stayed all winter short of room but in the latter end of November an Order came from Congress to march us down to Virginia 732 miles to Albemarle County. Marched 27 miles per day under a guard, lay in the woods at night; when we were at towns we lay in gaols or Churches, when in the woods we had a blanket over us and lay round fires. A deal of snow both night and day. One night upon the Green Mountains there was snow upon us 1/2 yard deep. No place of any note in New England. We crossed Connecticut River, The Green Mountains are there, then to Rhode Island[64] and from thence to New York state, to New Jersey. Across the Pennsylvania River the first post town was Lancaster. Crossed the Susquehanna River, to Little York, to Manchester, Maryland, Taneytown, Maryland Fredericktown, Maryland; done this on Christmas day. Crossed the Potomac River within 7 miles of the line that parts Maryland and Virginia and we went into it 100 miles before we arrived at our journey's end. Then they put us into the woods and put a chain of sentinels round us and we had to build huts in a regular form with regular streets between every range of huts after the form of C. town in England.[65] Six men to a hut and so many huts for a regiment according to their strength, the Germans after the same manner; the main street parted them and us. We had no nails. After this we had to build our officers' huts, stables, gardens &c. Then a general hospital, a main guard house, sink wells and necessary houses. Mounted guard every day a serjeant, a corporal and 12 men, patrolling the streets to prevent disturbances and to keep good order as becomes a soldier.

General Burgoyne went on his parole to England. He left at Cambridge in New England; General Phillips commanded us after. After that General Phillips ordered all the British troops to make gardens and fence them in to produce vegetables of every kind to use with our salt provisions. After that we had a grave yard to make of an acre of land and fence it to prevent the wild beasts from breaking in. Then we had a church to build and had divine service every Sunday. Through the fatigue of officers the men deserted and went into the country several in a night. And the country people were allowed 1/2 Johannes per man that they brought in and they were confined under a rebel guard, and after they had got 300 they sent them under a guard to Winchester gaol 140 miles away. We remained in Virginia two and a half years. General Phillips and several of the principal officers we exchanged. The second winter there was a very severe frost, all the mills were frozen up. The Indians helped us with Indian corn &c &c. We pounded it between two stones. The women went into the country. 17 days together without flesh, 1 quart of Indian corn a day and that not regular, 10 days together without bread. There was plenty of beef and pork in the Continental store but it was salted by Negroes with oak and cherry ashes; when it came to be served out to us it stunk and was full of maggots. General Phillips ordered a jury of surgeons, 1 from every regiment, to examine if it was proper and fit to make use of to eat. It was condemned by that means, and the rebels were obliged to bury it in the woods by wagon loads. We got some of the best up again. The inhabitants begged some part of it to give to the Indians to make soup of.

A detachment from New York under Colonel Arnold landed at Richmond 99 miles away. The country was alarmed and an express came to the commanding officer to move us immediately. That night they marched us over the Blue Mountains, a range of mountains that begins in New England and runs by west and south 70 miles. From there to Winchester, a large market town. As soon as we got there we heard that some of our light horse had been at our barracks. Part of the army they put into the church, part in goal, part into the poor house, the others were gone to Fort Frederick on the other side of the Potomac in Maryland. We stayed here a fortnight. Then we were ordered to march into Maryland across the Potomac 26 miles and then to Fredericktown 70 miles. They put us into large barracks and a chain of sentinels round us. There we had to cut wood for our use. Several of our officers left us here. We remained here until the spring of 1782. It was a large market town. From there to Fort Frederick. Our prisoners were marched to Lancaster goal in Pennsylvania. They lodged us in the fort but the fort being so full the married people were allowed to camp on the green out side the fort and build themselves huts. We stayed there five weeks. Then we marched to Lancaster, the prisoners were taken to Philadelphia goal, and we at Lancaster were put into the stockades, and the married people and men of good character were permitted camp on the green outside. The men inside were put amongst several of the refugees that came out of Philadelphia goal. They brought the yellow fever; our men caught it and died like rotten sheep. The remaining part of our officers was exchanged here, and we had half a guinea per man advanced before our officers went. We remained there 9 weeks.

We crossed the Susquehanna River and went within four miles of Little York, and there they turned us into the woods and put a chain of sentinels round us. There we had to build huts. The ground was marked out for building regular streets. At Fredericktown we were drummed prisoners of war, and our provision were reduced to 10 oz. per day of beef and bread each. After the huts were built we sunk wells and made a grave yard 1/4 mile from the camp, railed and fenced 1/2 acre. We stayed there a year and 8 months. Several of us were bailed out the greater part of the time. I for one was from December 1781 until released; I was bound in a £30 bond to John Poke an Irishman 27 miles from the camp at a place called the Round Hill over Conewago River. I had two dollars per month and board working at his plantation; we hunted wolves. I stayed with him until May 1782. We received some clothing from New York. I left him, and he offered me 3 per month. Exceeding hot. Came to camp, remained there until August then was bailed out by Mr. John Ereman, a Dutchman, under-sheriff of Little York and Captain of a company of militia. 3 per month to cook, cut wood, and look after a horse and cow. I remained with him until April 1783. The latter end of that month the articles of peace were read in the town and the prisoners were called into camp in order to march to New York 180 miles from Little York. Our camps were called Security and Indulgence. We left them on the 10th May under a guard. We crossed the Susquehanna River the first night (we passed in scows),[66] the next day we went to Lancaster being 13 miles from our camp. We halted there two days. A pay master met us there from New York with two of our officers to take the command of us, the American guard being only a matter of form. The serjeants got 4 dollars and the rest two. From Lancaster to Philadelphia all through the woods 66 miles, there they put us into the goal. The prisoners that were there were marched to New York; they were our comrades that left us in Virginia. We remained there all night, a nasty place. From there we went to Elizabethtown Point. Our guard delivered us up there to Lieutenant General Clark of the 7th Regiment. There I sold a horse for a dollar. From thence we crossed the river to Staten Island being the 24th May. Here we received our provisions and 1/2 pint rum per man being the first that we had from our people for 597 miles.

The next day we marched to the flag staff and went on board some transports. We rode quarantine for several days waiting for an order.[67] On the 28th we left and arrived at New York and went on board transports that were bound for England; after we were settled at our different ships we petitioned to General Carlton for a little money. He gave us two dollars for serjeants and 1 for the rest, money being scarce. While we stayed there we had liberty to go ashore each day.

We stayed in the harbour 5 weeks and upwards.

We left on the 5th July and arrived at Gravesend in 5 weeks.

Epilogue

George Fox's narrative ends with his arrival in England in August 1783. The officers of the 47th Regiment had been paroled and returned two years before, and had already been at work reconstituting the regiment. The muster rolls that they kept initially show Fox as a corporal and prisoner of war in America, but he was struck from the rolls at the end of 1781. It is not known whether he rejoined the 47th or exactly when he received his discharge from the army. He went before the Chelsea commissioners on 20 November 1783 and was awarded an out-pension because eighteen years in the army had left him "unfit for service" at the age of forty.[68] He returned to the Stoke area to collect the five pence per day to which he was entitled; whether he supplemented this subsistence income with other work is not known. At some point in the next few years he narrated his recollections of service in America to a nephew. In 1790 he married a woman from Stoke and had five children during the next nine years.[69]

Among the things that did not occur in England was a reunion with his brother Thomas who he had enlisted back in 1770. Thomas Fox was among the British prisoners taken at St. John's in 1775. The experience of these captives was not nearly as rigorous as that of the Convention Army later in the war; an exchange was negotiated and they were repatriated in December 1776. The 7th Regiment went right back to work, campaigning in New Jersey in 1777. Although they remained in New York during the autumn campaign that saw the British occupation of Philadelphia, they soon were dispatched by sea to join the Philadelphia garrison. The evacuation of that city led to a march across New Jersey in 1778 and the Battle of Monmouth. The 7th was heavily engaged in raids along the Connecticut coast in 1779, then sailed with the expedition that seized Charleston, South Carolina, the following year. They remained in the south, and although they were not involved in major actions in 1780 after the taking of

Charleston, fate put them at the disastrous British defeat at Cowpens in early 1781. The regiment suffered heavy losses and most of the survivors were taken prisoner for a second time. They were exchanged within a few months but the regiment was now fragmented. A portion that was not taken at Cowpens served with Cornwallis's army, only to surrender at Yorktown in October; those exchanged after Cowpens were sent to garrison Savannah, Georgia, and a few others may have been scattered in other places. As British garrisons were evacuated in 1782 the survivors trickled into New York, and this battered regiment that had been in America before the war began was among the last to depart in November 1783. Thomas Fox, however, was not among them. The fragmentary muster rolls for the latter part of the war show that he became a prisoner of war some time after June 1779; we can assume that this occurred at Cowpens or Yorktown, but it could have been as early as Connecticut. Regardless, the rolls indicate that he died in May 1783.[70] It is possible that he died in captivity before that, with the May date—when the last British prisoners in America were repatriated—used because the actual date was unknown. It is unlikely that the Fox brothers saw each other after their separation in Quebec in 1775, and one wonders if George ever learned of Thomas's fate.

George Fox's pension obliged him to something more than just keeping his whereabouts known to the army. In 1796 the army was rapidly expanding due to a new war with France, and pensioners were called into invalid companies. Fox was sent as close to the war as any of these corps, joining a company on the island of Jersey in the English Channel close to the French shore. His wife, and presumably his children, went with him to this post where Fox was appointed corporal and served for another ten years. His fifth child was born there, his wife died there, and his oldest daughter married a soldier there.[71] Fox was finally discharged in Jersey in 1806 at the age of sixty-one,[72] still a corporal, after having served two stints in the army totaling just three months under twenty-eight years. He returned to the Potteries with his remaining children and died just three years later.

EIGHT

The Faithful Soldier

Alexander Andrew, 44th Regiment of Foot

Introduction

A pension was a fine thing compared to unemployment. The subsistence level income that it provided was similar to the subsistence portion of a common soldier's pay, enough to buy one's daily bread, but pensioners lacked other benefits earned in the army like clothing, opportunities for extra income working for the army, and the possibility of advancement. The pension provided subsistence but nothing more; it did not, however, restrict the recipient from earning extra money if he was able. The pension was granted on the premise that the man had given his all to the army and was no longer able to earn a living due to injury or infirmity, but some pensioners were able enough to do some jobs. Daniel Wright, for example, was discharged from the 22nd Regiment in 1784 after nineteen years as a soldier because he was "worn out" at the age of forty-four. Six years later the Argyle native was living in Glasgow and supplementing his pension by working as a cook on a herring boat. He was at sea when a call was published for pensioners to appear before an examining board; he missed the call and was struck from the rolls, and subsequently submitted a petition requesting that his pension be reinstated.[1] There were also many soldiers who, in spite of having been discharged due to incapacity and receiving pensions, reenlisted; fitness for service was subject to the opinion of officers whose judgment might vary depending upon the need for manpower. Reenlisting terminated the man's pension. Lacking any explicitly stated reasons why pensioners chose to return to active service, we can only guess whether the incentive was higher pay (including an enlistment bounty that could be several months' pay)[2] or a simple preference for the military environment.

There was an avenue through which soldiers could realize a more comfortable post-military life than a pension afforded. British society was more stratified than the strict dichotomies of upper and lower classes that existed in many European states,[3] but it was nonetheless very much a caste system which included servants and masters. The class division in the army was emphasized more than in civilian society—common soldiers and noncommissioned officers were inherently and unquestioningly subservient to their officers. Among the perquisites for officers was the provision to take a soldier from the ranks as a personal servant. Far from demeaning, being a servant to an officer could afford the soldier a more privileged and diverse life than duty in the ranks. But it was not an easy life, and not all soldiers were suited to it.

Soldier servants were required to remain fully capable of serving in the ranks; they were not supernumerary, after all, but part of the established strength of the regiment. Military writers recommended that only men with at least a year's service be taken for servants to insure that they had proper military training, and that each servant perform normal guard duty when his master was officer of the guard to insure that the servant maintained his soldierly capacity.[4] Most regimental officers were entitled to a single servant, while senior officers with additional responsibilities might retain another soldier as a bat-man to take care of his horse.[5] The servant's duties included tasks such as maintaining his officer's clothing, shaving him and helping him dress, packing and unpacking baggage, setting up a tent while on campaign, caring for his horse (if the officer could not retain a bat-man), running all manner of errands from delivering messages to purchasing necessities, and any other chores required by a busy officer and gentleman. Officers were encouraged to pool their resources to purchase food and dine together in a grouping called the officers' mess;[6] the servant, therefore, was not typically required to procure and prepare food but took on these chores when the officer was away from the mess. Senior officers, who bore the social obligation of inviting peers, junior officers, and influential civilians to dine with them, might retain yet another soldier as a cook. In return for these services, the officer paid his servant a shilling per week.[7] This was in addition to the soldier's regular pay; not only was it an increase in income of about 35 percent, it was also not subject to the withholdings built into the basic pay structure.[8] In addition, the servant might enjoy better food,[9] more comfortable quarters, extra clothing provided by the officer,[10] and some freedom of movement that went along with trust and responsibility. The advantages of such a position were made obvious by the story of Ebenezer Fox, related in Chapter 6; although not explicitly a servant to a single officer, Fox found that role as barber and hairdresser gave him access to information and freedom of movement, which he used to effect his escape from service that he had not willingly entered.

The term of servitude was up to the officer. If not satisfied with the work of one soldier, the officer could return him to the ranks and replace him with another. In spite of the recommendation to use men with some experience as servants, sometimes very young enlistees worked in this capacity before joining the ranks.[11] If the relationship was a good one, however, an officer could take the same soldier-servant with him throughout his career, transferring into whatever regiment the officer served.[12] In a society where the fortunes of a commoner could be greatly improved by the favor of a gentleman, servitude to an officer was a desirable function for soldiers with the appropriate disposition. Officers with a sufficient purse also could and did engage nonsoldiers in addition to (or, when manpower was at a premium, instead of) soldiers as servants; during the war in America the large number of slaves granted freedom in return for supporting the British cause provided a ready pool of labor and many were hired by British officers.[13] Faithful soldiers were nonetheless most likely to be the personal servants of officers, and as many as forty men in a regiment could expect to be so employed at any given time.[14]

Among many examples is William Goldthorp, a tailor from the London district of Lambeth. When he joined the 22nd Regiment of Foot in 1766 at the age of thirty-five he'd already been discharged from the army once after eight years of service.[15] He became the servant to Captain Christopher French, flamboyant commander of the regiment's light infantry company. The American war began badly for them; when the 22nd Regiment embarked for America in May 1775, French stayed behind and followed a few weeks later on a ship carrying clothing for his and another regiment. When they set sail, hostilities in America had only just begun and details of the situation there were not known. When the convoy carrying the regiment arrived off of New York a British warship diverted them to Boston, but French's ship, arriving off the coast two months later, made for Philadelphia. Fearful of being commandeered by rebels, they proceeded up the Delaware River with such caution that they even managed to evade a British warship that tried to warn them away.[16] Near Philadelphia the ship and its valuable military cargo were seized by colonial authorities; French and his servant Goldthorp, with a few other army officers on board, were made prisoners of war. French, who had just been promoted to major, was sent into captivity in Connecticut. He signed an affidavit for the Pennsylvania Committee of Safety that he would turn Goldthorp over to Washington's army and in the meantime prevent him from "misbehaving" and "giving any intelligence injurious to the American cause."[17]

The subsequent whereabouts of William Goldthorp are not clear. Although Major French kept a detailed journal of his sixteen months in captivity, he makes no mention of his servant. French himself made a daring escape in the last days of 1776 and boarded a British transport ship in Long Island Sound after ten days as a fugitive.[18] The muster rolls indicate that Goldthorp had already rejoined the 22nd Regiment by this time; whether by escape or exchange is not known.[19] It is clear that Goldthorp remained in the service of Major French, for when French transferred to the 52nd Regiment of Foot at the end of 1777, Goldthorp transferred too. When French retired from the army in October 1778, Goldthorp was discharged from the army. French returned to Ireland, arriving off the coast in mid-November; Goldthorp appeared before the commissioners of Chelsea Hospital on 18 December and was awarded an out-pension.[20] With their careers in lockstep, we assume that the faithful Goldthorp remained a member of the Christopher French household in his later years.

Other servants were not so fortunate. John Bolton of the 35th Regiment was brought to trial in Brooklyn on 30 July 1778 for desertion. It was the second offense for Bolton, who had been drafted into the 35th from the 20th Regiment in Ireland in early 1775. He had deserted in late 1776 and joined a newly raised Loyalist regiment called the New York Volunteers. In January 1778 he admitted being a deserter to avoid a punishment for an unknown infraction; he was returned to the 35th Regiment where the commanding officer pardoned him. That July, however, when he was entrusted to guard the regiment's baggage when the regiment changed locations, he absconded once again. Soon caught and brought to trial, he pleaded in his defense that "he never should have gone away, if he had been kept in the Ranks as a Soldier, but Captain Fitzgerald took him as a Servant, and ill treated him and beat him, particularly about two days before he went away, for losing a Key, and that he was also in liquor both the times that he went off."[21] The court was not sympathetic to this reasoning and sentenced Bolton to death.[22]

James Cairns of the 22nd Regiment suffered a different sort of misfortune. During the summer of 1775 his master, Lieutenant Charles Lane, fell ill. Lane left the encampment on Boston Common and took quarters in a local home, taking Cairns with him. The officer had already provided a greatcoat to his servant, and now Cairns's position afforded him better accommodation than the encampment, but the arrangements led to Cairns's undoing. Lane returned to Great Britain on recruiting service late in the year but Cairns remained in Boston with the regiment. Cairns was soon brought to trial, charged by the homeowner for having stolen "sundry goods" while he and his officer were quartered there. Although a piece of cloth from the home was found in Cairns's greatcoat pocket and other missing goods were discovered in the room where Cairns had stayed, the evidence was largely circumstantial. Lieutenant Lane was no longer in Boston to testify on his servant's behalf, and the court found Cairns guilty and sentenced him to four hundred lashes.[23] Two and a half years later Cairns was on trial again in Rhode Island for theft and desertion, and this time was executed for his crimes.[24]

For other soldier servants, favorable testimony from their officer masters was critical in determining their fates; in one case, even the wife of a soldier received a good character reference because she had made a good impression while her husband was a servant.[25] John Man (or Mann) of the 64th Regiment illustrates the dedication that a servant might have even in adverse circumstances. Man enlisted in the 64th on 9 February 1768 and like all recruits was attested and had the articles of war read to him. A year later the regiment sailed for Boston, and two years later Man became the trustworthy servant of an ensign. When his master was on leave in Great Britain, however, Man deserted. He was absent from the regiment from 5 April until 10 August 1773 when he returned to the regiment on his own volition. He claimed that "designing Bostonians" had coerced him "by their first making me drink to excess and then conveying me away in an obscure manner, lending & assisting all help and means to forward me from my Regt," a similar alibi to that given by Thomas Watson in Chapter 4. Man was tried by a regimental court martial and sentenced to receive six hundred lashes, but the regiment's commanding officer pardoned him. The following year Man's master returned. Whether he learned of Man's transgression or Man simply feared that he would is not clear, but Man's "sense of Shame ... for my ingratitude to so kind a Master" induced him to again succumb to the seduction of the inhabitants. He was reported as a deserter on 1 August.

About seven weeks later a sober man calling himself John Simmel enlisted in the 47th Regiment of Foot in New York. He took two New York shillings as bounty and went in the care of a sergeant to be attested before a magistrate. On the way to the magistrate's offices, however, the recruit stopped, saying he would not be attested because he was a deserter from the 64th Regiment. He was confined by the 47th Regiment, and soon after the 47th was ordered to Boston.

After arriving back at the city from which he had absconded, Man was put on trial once again for desertion. He gave an eloquent defense, reading from a prepared statement that it was his shame and the encouragement of designing citizens that had lured him away. He emphasized that he had returned voluntarily and confessed his transgressions; enlisting in the 47th was only a ploy to avoid being seized as a deserter. He called on his master, now a lieutenant, as a character witness who testified that "the Prisoner lived for a Year and a half as a Servant with Deponent and always behaved very well and at the time he deserted had the Care of all Deponent's things none of which Deponent missed." Although the court had no choice but to render a guilty verdict since Man had obviously deserted, his willing surrender and "the Exceeding good Character given him by his Officers" resulted in a sentence of one thousand lashes "at four several times in equal proportions" rather than execution. Unlike Valentine Duckett seen in Chapter 3, this two-time deserter had established a sufficiently good rapport with his officers to spare his life.[26]

The relative liberties that servants had did not escape the notice of other soldiers, and some occasionally tried to take advantage of them. One August evening in 1774, the 38th Regiment of Foot was among those camped on Boston Common and a young soldier named Luke Murphy was intoxicated. A fellow soldier had helped him clean his musket in the past in return for a promise of liquor; now Murphy was asked to make good on the promise but had no liquor to give. Knowing he was not allowed to leave the camp, he determined to have someone else obtain the liquor for him. He had already been drinking at the tent of a married friend in the 5th Regiment and knew that women had more freedom to leave the camp than soldiers did, so he went back there and asked the friend's wife to get some liquor for him. She "positively refused having observed that he was drunk when he came to the Tent." He then went to an officer's servant, knowing that he too was allowed to leave camp to run errands for his master. Servants, however, also knew their responsibilities and Murphy was again refused. Over the course of three hours he went to several tents begging of wives and servants to do his bidding; some he asked repeatedly and tried to bargain with, but all rebuffed the inebriated recruit. Determined to have his liquor, Murphy tried another tactic. A tailor by trade, he had been tasked with mending a brown frock coat belonging to an officer's servant and he had the coat in his tent, along with his own old "cut round hat" that he had worn on board ship. He donned these "colour'd Cloaths," put a canteen into his pocket, and attempted to leave the camp at around midnight. When a sentry stopped him, Murphy claimed that he was the servant of a captain in the regiment and had to go into town to find him. The sentry demanded the countersign, a password known only to those authorized to pass in and out of camp. Murphy, lacking this critical information, simply pushed by the sentry and tried to go on his mission, but the sentry quickly grabbed him and called out the guard. Although a general court-martial acquitted him of desertion, they sentenced him to one hundred lashes for disguising himself "contrary to the Custom of the Army and with Intentions to go out of Camp contrary to orders."[27]

Like many aspects of the military, officers having servants was a reflection of the stratified society from which military men were drawn. Service to gentlemen was a respectable form of employment which, like every occupation, had its benefits and drawbacks, its gracious masters and its tyrants. Unemployed servants, whether out of work due to misfortune, inability, or lack of inclination, were just as likely to join the army as men from any other profession. Although "servant" has not been encountered as a trade listed in military description books or on discharges, it is named as an occupation in many deserter advertisements in British newspapers.[28] For example, an advertisement for Alexander Hamilton, a recruit for the 22nd Regiment, noted that he "has been a servant to Mr. Robert Reeves, Attorney, and discharged his service but a few days before" and "requested no man will hire this Deserter, in case he should offer himself as a servant."[29] Professional servants might change jobs many times, as did Walter Urie; before he joined the 71st Regiment at age twenty-nine he "was formerly a servant to the Earl of Merchmont, and several men in Fifeshire, and when inlisted, was servant to James Stuart stabler in Grass market, Edinburgh."[30] Soldiers, too, might be servants to several officers during their careers, like George Patterson of the 44th Regiment who during six years had "lived with four different Officers as a Servant, with three of them, till they quitted the Regiment."[31]

The military career of Alexander Andrew was defined by two key events delivered upon him by others. Hailing from the parish of Inverkeithny, roughly between Inverness and Aberdeen in Banffshire, Scotland, he was twenty-one years old when he joined the army in unusual circumstances. His brother William, presumably older, was a soldier serving in the 44th Regiment of Foot.[32] A soldier who was fit for service could request his own discharge, but generally was required to either pay a substantial sum of money or find another man to take his place.[33] This "cunning" brother persuaded the "young and foolish" Alexander Andrew to take his place in the army. The 44th was posted in Ireland at the time, so we do not know whether this transaction was arranged by correspondence, if William was home on furlough or recruiting service, or if Alexander was for some reason in Ireland. The muster rolls show that William was discharged on 14 September 1772 and Alexander was "entertained" the next day.[34] The muster roll was prepared two months later at Dungarven in southeastern Ireland. Although perhaps an unwilling soldier, Andrew had the good fortune of being singled out by Lieutenant Colonel James Agnew. Perhaps the five-foot nine-inch soldier had good deportment or was particularly zealous in his duties, or he may have stood out because of the circumstances of his enlistment. Andrew had not acquired a trade before becoming a soldier, but he may have demonstrated useful skills or meticulous habits. Regardless of the reason, when the 44th was ordered to America in early 1775 Agnew took the twenty-four-year-old Scottish soldier for a servant.

The 44th Regiment sailed from Cork, Ireland, along with the 22nd, 40th, and 45th regiments in early May 1775; the four corps were divided among ten transport ships. They were bound for New York, but upon reaching the American coast in June the transports were intercepted by a British warship, which informed them of the rapidly changing situation in America and redirected them to Boston. They arrived piecemeal in late June and early July; by 3 August they were integrated with the Boston garrison and the commander-in-chief's secretary called the 44th "a prodigious fine regiment."[35] Agnew was given command of a grenadier battalion, an ad hoc formation of specialist troops which, had there been any more campaigning around Boston, would likely have been in the most active fighting. The assignment reflected favorably on Agnew's skill and experience and set the stage for further advancement. In March 1776 the British army removed to Halifax, Nova Scotia, to reorganize for a new campaign. Agnew was appointed aide-de-camp to the king with the rank of colonel in the army (although he remained the Lieutenant Colonel of the 44th Regiment) and was given the local rank of brigadier.[36] He took command of a brigade composed of three regiments that soon grew to four; in this role he played an active part in the campaigns of 1776 and 1777 that raged through New York and New Jersey.

Through these advances in responsibility and prestige the fifty-seven-year-old officer took his servant Alexander Andrew, who became a member of a large "family" of aides and servants. Agnew took on a second soldier as a cook while in Boston, a third apparently during the Philadelphia campaign, and also a freed slave, but retained Andrew as his principal servant. Because of the need to accommodate this entourage, brigadiers typically commandeered large houses for their quarters. Andrew, as Agnew's personal servant, was probably always close to the general and quartered with him. Although servants might not have the best accommodations in the house, occupying instead attics, garrets, or other nooks and crannies, they enjoyed greater comfort and privacy than sleeping five soldiers to a tent in encampments or a dozen or more in a barrack room. Interaction with the senior officers in the army surely made life interesting, and it was safer than standing sentry on the lines.

In battle Brigadier James Agnew was a leader who did not fear exposure to gunfire. Andrew, "by his side" throughout the campaigns of 1776 and 1777, was also exposed. He saw Agnew twice wounded, first on an expedition to destroy military stores at Danbury, Connecticut. This four-day raid in April 1777 was successful but incited fierce fighting during the British withdrawal. Agnew was hit in the shoulder by a musket ball with sufficient force to knock him down and leave a welt that remained visible for a month.[37] At the battle of Brandywine on 11 September Agnew led a brigade which was actively involved in the fighting. Leading from the center of his troops, Agnew was grazed by a cannonball but managed to remain at the head of his brigade for the rest of the day. These bold actions were sure to bring recognition and further promotion, which boded well not just for the officer but for the faithful servant who could be assured a place in the gentleman-officer's household when the war ended. A month after the great victory at Brandywine, however, a bold American attack threatened British forces in Germantown near Philadelphia, and forever changed Alexander Andrew's fortunes.

The complex battle on 4 October 1777 took the British by surprise and began as a rout. A combination of factors including weather, determination, and battlefield confusion turned the tide, and by late morning British troops had regained the initiative.[38] Brigadier Agnew took his brigade into the fray as part of a counterattack; in the audacious and heroic fashion that had served him in previous fights, he advanced ahead of his troops on horseback. A party of retreating Americans took advantage of buildings in the town to lay an ambush. As the general advanced they deployed into the street and opened fire. Agnew wheeled about in an effort to find safety but the American volley, although delivered at long range, found its lone target; a ball passed through Agnew from back to front, and another hit his hand. Andrew, following close behind and possibly also on horseback, was hit in the side by the same volley. The wounded servant nonetheless managed to prevent his master from falling from the horse. With the help of others, Andrew took the mortally wounded general into the safety of a nearby house and sent for a doctor. But there was no hope. Within a few minutes Brigadier James Agnew expired with his servant by his side, in the presence of a doctor and some others who had arrived on the scene.

Alexander Andrew continued to serve his master. He had the body taken to the general's quarters where he carefully dressed him one last time. He had a coffin made and oversaw the burial the day after the battle. He dutifully collected his

Alexander Andrew's work as a servant to a high-ranking officer gave him many perquisites but demanded a great deal of work. Here a servant busily polishes the black leather of a cartridge pouch, for his position did not except him from maintaining the ability to serve in the ranks when necessary.

Servants received the same regimental clothing as their fellow soldiers, but officers often added to their wardrobe. Andrew received a greatcoat from his master, a popular garment that military officers had privately made and for which there was no universal pattern. This soldier wears a dark blue greatcoat that is long enough to fully cover his body. Tailored to fit well for warmth without constraining movement, it has long cuffs and a cape that can be folded out for added warmth and features ample buttons so that it can be worn in various configurations. The soldier's red foraging cap has flaps folded down over his ears for warmth; the front flap is the yellow color of the regiment's coat lapels. In this informal setting the soldier has removed his shoes, and wears a handkerchief around his neck.

master's personal effects that were in the room and turned them over to an officer. The servant's duty was done.

The cash and other small items that General Agnew had with him were now in possession of the senior officer of the 44th Regiment. This officer recognized the dedication of Agnew's four attendants including Andrew by dividing these effects equally among them. Andrew received in addition a pair of silver buckles, presumably also the general's, as a reward for "good and faithful services." The general's other belongings, things like the marquee tent and campaign furniture that were in storage because houses were readily available to use as quarters, were sold at auction. This was a tradition in the British army;[39] it is not stated in this case whether the proceeds went to the general's widow or were divided among the servants. Andrew saw everything disposed of including a greatcoat that had been made for him. He felt slighted that the servants were, for the most part, rewarded equally when he himself was the principal among them, the general's close consort. In spite of receiving this immediate largess, Alexander Andrew had lost his patron and his prospects for a comfortable life in the household of a war hero. He had spent half of his military career in the service and company of senior officers, working dutifully but also enjoying a relatively high standard of living. Now he had no path before him but the life of a common soldier.

Andrew returned to the ranks but was soon recognized as uncommon. Whether in recognition of his servitude or as a direct result of his knowledge and skill, he was appointed corporal on 15 December 1777; clearly he had the notice and trust of his officers. His new rank afforded more pay and latitude than a common soldier but was a demanding position. He had significant responsibilities for the health and welfare of the private soldiers under his care. His service to a general officer may have prepared him well for the role, but after a few months he made a play to recoup some of the wealth, and perhaps the comfortable future, that he felt he'd lost. He penned a detailed letter to General Agnew's widow,[40] describing his service and dedication and her late husband's final moments. Although he stated his intentions as being dutiful, he was clearly seeking her patronage.

Alexander Andrew's Letter to Mrs. Agnew[41]

Philadelphia, 8th March, 1778.

Dear Madam, Though an entire stranger to your ladyship, yet, as I had the honour to wait on your beloved husband for a considerable time, which induced me to take the liberty of writing unto you, which I look upon as a duty of mine to you in memory of a good master, to whom I owe many obligations, is and will be always ready and willing to serve any of his if ever in my power. Dear madam, I came into the army in place of a brother of mine, who was cunning enough to persuade me, young and foolish enough, to go in his place. I joined the 44th in '72, then in Kilkenny, from which time I fancied Colonel Agnew took notice of me, and when the regiment embarked at Cork he took me to be his servant, with whom I had the honor to live very comfortably and happy until the day of his death. Being his principal servant, and the only one he would ever have to wait on him both in public and private, at home and abroad, and in all places wherever his person was exposed, I was there by his side, and an eyewitness to all his sufferings in Boston, in Halifax, Staten Island, Long Island, New York Island, on the expedition to Danberry, in the Jerseys, Maryland, Pennsylvania, and in three pitched battles, viz., 27th August, '76, the 11th of September, and 4th of October, '77, besides a number of skirmishes. On the expedition to Danberry, the general was knocked down by a ball, which left its mark for above a month. At the battle of Brandywine, the general had the misfortune to be grazed by a cannon-ball, but continued to head his brigade. It happened to be the last engaged that night, and, though he was very much indisposed, yet he commanded his gallant troops until they beat off and remained masters of the field. During the action the general remained at the head of the 64th, which regiment suffered more than any of the brigade.[42] The army then proceeded to that unfortunate place called Germantown, the 4th of October being the particular and fatal day of which your ladyship has cause to remember and I have much reason to regret. But to let you know the particulars of that day. Being between the hours of 9 and 12, as the brigade was following the 3d in an oblique advancing line, the general, with the piquet at their head,[43] entered the town, hurried down the street to the left, but he had not rode above 20 or 30 yards, which was the top of a little rising ground, when a party of the enemy, about 100, rushed out from behind a house about 500 yards in front, the general being then in the street, and even in front of the piquet, and all alone, only me, he wheeled round, and, putting spurs to his horse, and calling to me, he received a whole volley from the enemy. The fatal ball entered the small of his back, near the back seam of his coat, right side, and came out a little below his left breast. Another ball went through and through his right hand. I, at the same moment, received a slight wound in the side, but just got off time enough to prevent his falling,[44] who, with the assistance of two men, took him down, carried him into a house, and laid him on a bed, sent for the doctor, who was near. When he came he could only turn his eyes, and looked steadfastly on me with seeming affection. The doctor and Major Leslie just came in time enough to see him depart this life, which he did without the least struggle or agony, but with great composure, and calmness, and seeming satisfaction, which was about 10 or 15 minutes after he received the ball, and I believe between 10 and 11 o'clock. I then had his body brought to his former quarters, took his gold watch, his purse, in which there was four guineas and half a Johannes,[45] which I delivered to Major Leslie[46] as soon as he came home. I then had him genteelly laid out, and decently dressed with some of his clean and best things; had a coffin made the best the place could produce. His corpse was decently interred the next day in the churchyard, attended by a minister and the officers of the 44th regiment.[47]

He during his life, in his good humours, often told me that he would do better for me than being in the army; but, having no certificate from under his hand, I was ordered to join the regiment, which I am sure I never would have done. With regard to his effects that were present with him, were equally divided among all the servants, every thing being delivered over by Major Leslie to Major Hope.[48] Payne was cook, and came to the general in Boston; but the other man, Seymour,[49] was only part of one campaign, though he received an equal proportion of every thing the same as me. Agen,[50] even a pickt up negro received equal with me, who bore the burden and heat of the day, silver buckles excepted. Colonel Hope gave me them extraordinary as a reward (said he) for your good and faithful services to your master; and them I have, and am ready to part with them, if your ladyship or Captain Robert[51] chuse to send for them. All the rest of the things which was in store has all been lately sold by vendue, ye, even two great-coats made for me and Payne almost a year ago, was sold, with several other things too tedious to mention, such as remains of cloth, stockings, &c.

Dear Madam, I beg you will excuse this liberty; and if your ladyship please to sent me a few lines after the receival of this, I will be under a great obligation to you; and believe me to be, with sincerity and due respect, madam, your most obedient and humble servant while

Alex. Andrew.

Although clearly literate and elegant in relating events, Andrew had no talent for subtlety. He wrote under the guise of faithfully informing Mrs. Agnew of the events of her husband's demise and offering his services, but unabashedly shifted to pleading for remuneration. His appeal for reward is blatant, to the extent of complaining that all of the general's servants received an equal share of the proceeds from the sale of the general's effects even though he, Andrew, had served longer than the others. He suggests that the general had promised him a permanent position but had no proof of this. His tone suggests impoverishment which can hardly have been the case. Besides his pay as a private soldier he had been earning the additional wage of a servant for two and a half years; even if he was not receiving this as cash on a regular basis there can be no doubt that his accounts were settled out of the estate of the deceased. He probably had few expenses while a servant. He also received a share of the general's personal effects, and was now drawing higher pay as a corporal. If he was in financial straits, he must have brought it upon himself.

In the early nineteenth century a story began to circulate that General Agnew was shot by a lone sniper named Hans P. Boyer who took "deliberate aim at the star on his breast."[52] The story has been discredited, with the assertion that Boyer was "a half-witted fellow" who "claimed credit of the deed, but it is said to have not rightfully belonged to him"[53] but it nonetheless continues to be circulated. Setting aside the unlikelihood that Agnew wore a star on his uniform (there was no such emblem of rank for British general officers during this era, and Agnew had no title warranting such a device), Boyer's account seems to have originated well after the fact. Andrew's description is credible in that it was written fairly soon after the events occurred, he had nothing to gain by embellishing this detail of the day's events, and he was writing to someone who would have access to corroborating accounts.

It is unfortunate that we have no record of whether Andrew received a response from Mrs. Agnew. It is certain that she did not call him into her household. Andrew continued to serve in the 44th Regiment. That he did so without resentment is apparent in his appointment to sergeant on 25 October 1778, less than a year after becoming a corporal. This was a comfortable position attended with numerous opportunities and benefits—albeit also with significant responsibilities—and attaining it after only six years in the army was a noteworthy achievement.

The remainder of Alexander Andrew's career as a noncommissioned officer appears to have been successful and respectable. He was never reduced in rank, which indicates that his discipline and health remained good. He went with the regiment to Canada in September 1779, and he was not among those discharged when the regiment was reduced in size at the end of the war. The 44th Regiment returned to Great Britain in 1786. Around this time Andrew became the quartermaster sergeant which, while not a rank per se, was a position of great responsibility. After serving for three years in southern England and the island of Guernsey, the 44th

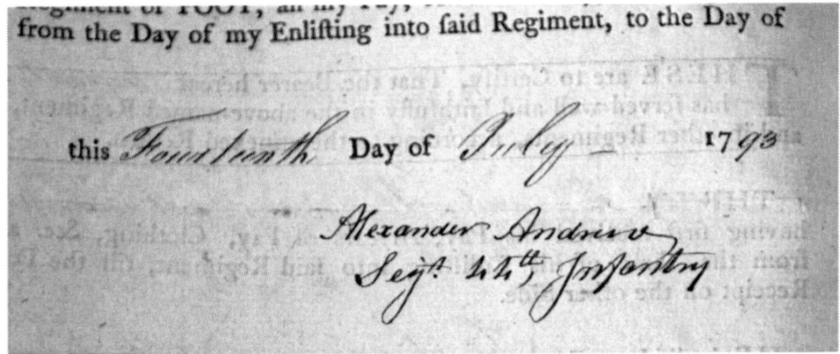
from the Day of my Enlifting into faid Regiment, to the Day of

this Fourteenth Day of July 1793

Alexander Andrew
Sergt 44th Infantry

Signature of Alexander Andrew on his discharge from the 44th Regiment. (*The National Archives. Photo by René Chartrand*)

moved to Scotland and the Isle of Man in 1789. Three years later, the regiment was ordered to Ireland where Andrew had joined it twenty years before. Soon after arriving in Dublin he took his discharge, having exceeded the twenty years of service customary for receiving a pension.[54] He was discharged "For his long and Faithful Service, also having been Wounded in the right side at the Battle of Germantown near Phillidelphia on the 4th Day of October 1777." His discharge indicates twenty-five years of service, overstating by three years his time as a private soldier and by one year his time as a corporal.[55] We cannot account for this discrepancy, but it made no difference in his eligibility. He nonetheless entered service as a sergeant in the Waterford Militia for at least a year before receiving an out-pension through Kilmainham Hospital.

EPILOGUE

Many aspects of Alexander Andrew's letter are typical of a genre of military writings called memorials. These depositions were usually written by officers seeking promotion and exist by the dozens among British army headquarters papers of the era.[56] Other memorials were written as letters of recommendation by senior officers on behalf of their juniors, again to help effect promotion. Far fewer are those written by soldiers, primarily long-serving sergeants who sought advancement into the officer ranks, a topic that will be further explored in the next chapter. A few sought other sorts of remuneration. John Hutton, a sergeant in the 10th Regiment of Foot who had been in the army for thirty-seven years when he wrote his memorial in 1782, explained that he had lost all of his worldly goods including 300 guineas in savings when the regiment's baggage was captured at sea at the end of 1777. He asked the commander in chief in America for "such provision for the remainder of a life spent in the service, as to your Excellency's Goodness and humanity" could provide.[57]

Widows of soldiers, although entitled to their husband's back pay, clothing, and any other possessions he might have had, also sometimes petitioned for relief. Mary Driscoll wrote that she became a prisoner of war after her husband was killed outside of Philadelphia in 1777; she was put in jail, escaped twice, and was retaken each time, and bore her late husband's twin children during her third stay in jail. She managed to escape yet again, with the children, and finally got into New York in late 1779. Her regiment long gone, she had no way to obtain her usual entitlement of her husband's back pay, clothing, and any other possessions; she sent a memorial to the commander in chief.[58] It is interesting that her husband, Cornelius Driscoll, was not in fact killed but had continued in service with the 10th Regiment through late 1778 when he was drafted into another corps and sent to the West Indies; his ultimate fate is unknown and there is no record of whether he and his wife were ever reunited.[59]

Alexander Andrew's memorial letter is distinctive in that, rather than being written to a senior officer, it is directed to a civilian whom he saw as a potential patron. More important, it is highly autobiographical, giving details of his life and service that have not been found in any other soldier's memorial. Because he wrote to his master's widow, Andrew lauded his deceased patron in a way that told as much about the servant as the master. His letter reveals not only the stated facts, but that he was well enough educated both to write and to present a forthright and succinct case, that he was polite in accordance with his caste, and that he had a clear understanding of social interactions, expectations, and obligations. These things are indicative of a man capable of succeeding in his career regardless of the success of this particular effort or the explicit patronage of any individual. His long and dedicated service is proof that the man who had entered the army because he was "young and foolish" was wise enough to make the most of his circumstances.

NINE

The Aspiring Soldier

William Burke, 45th Regiment of Foot

Introduction

While an army pension was a favorable and even generous benefit of long service in a society where few avocations offered any form of post-career security, it was probably not an explicit motivation for enlistment. Men who have left accounts of their reasons for joining the army were focused on the immediate benefits of employment and the romantic expectations of travel and adventure rather than the possibility of a modest income twenty or more years in the future. There is no reason to believe that most men had any specific long-term aspirations, whether for advancement in the army or for compensation after their discharge. During wartime, some may have been tempted by the possibility of land grants, but the large number that reenlisted rather than take discharges and land grants suggests that land was not an inducement for the majority.[1] Relatively few men ever advanced above the rank of private soldier,[2] so this too could not have been a common expectation of the majority of enlistees. There were, however, some men in the army who clearly enlisted with the expectation of advancement in rank and the commensurate improvement in compensation during and after their active careers.

It was possible for a common soldier to rise through the ranks to become an officer, but few careers saw such an outcome. Determining a precise number of men who achieved this rare result is challenging because there was more than one path through the ranks. It is a matter of interpretation whether each of these paths qualifies as a genuine rise through the ranks in recognition of talent and exceptional service; in many cases men already destined for commissions spent time in the ranks while waiting for an opportunity to advance. This may be counter-intuitive in the context of a society and military built upon a caste system, but the social order of the army was an extension of British society which was not as rigorously stratified as in other European nations.[3] It is outside the scope of this study to examine the officer class in detail. Suffice it to say that the social strata of the British army officer corps mirrored that of British society; far from being a dichotomy of upper and lower classes which provided the stock for officers and soldiers, British society during this era included a substantial and diverse middle class that yielded educated men who might seek commissions if their means, motivation, and connections allowed, but who might be equally disposed to enlist as common soldiers if any of these factors were lacking.

Much is made of the fact that army commissions could be purchased, giving the impression that only the wealthy could hold commissions and anyone who could afford a commission could become an officer regardless of abilities. These simplistic views overlook the attributes that made the system effective. Commissions were expensive, and young men were unlikely to have their own funds to purchase one; instead, the money generally came from a wealthy patron. Rather than a gift to the young officer, the purchase money was a sort of investment in the man's future. If the man served well he could eventually sell the commission and the investment was recouped, but poor performance could lead to a court martial and being cashiered, that is, forfeiting the commission money. In this way, purchase money was a sort of surety for the officer's diligent service. Also, commissions were sold only to those approved by the commanding officer of the regiment and then by the King; men with wealth but not character could not arbitrarily buy into the army. It also was possible to obtain a commission without purchase; in fact, about a third of commissioned officers did not purchase their ranks. Although there were opportunities for corruption and some inept men found themselves officers, overall the system worked well at producing an effective corps of officers highly invested in their careers.[4]

Promotion due to long and worthy service was awarded to soldiers who had become senior noncommissioned officers, that is, sergeants. While there are many individual examples, the proportion of men who achieved this advancement was extremely small. The officer corps of British infantry regiments included two staff positions, the quartermaster and the adjutant, responsible for logistics and administration, respectively. These posts, the adjutancy in particular, were sometimes filled by junior company officers acting in dual capacity, but they were also sometimes awarded to senior sergeants who had not only the service record but also the capacity to fill such positions. Shortly after the war began regiments in Ireland (many of which soon went to America) received a declaration from the King that "the proper Persons to be recommended for Quarter-Masters, are active Serjeants." This formally established the career path, but the order was not entirely complimentary since it was due to "His Majesty not thinking the Office very fit for Men of better Extraction."[5] At the beginning of 1777 the commander in chief in Canada broadened the scope to include adjutants, ordering "that he will not give the offices of Quarter Master or Adjutant, that may become Vacant in the Regiments to Commissioned Officers, but reserve them to excite the Emulation, and reward the merit of Non Commissioned Officers and private men; in conformity to which, The Commanding Officers of Regiments, are upon Vacancies of Adjutant or Quarter Master in their Corps, to recommend their most deserving and Capable Non Commissioned Officers or private Men to succeed to them."[6] Such advancement was in some measure a natural progression; one sergeant typically assisted the quartermaster in the aptly named roll of quartermaster sergeant, and was therefore groomed to take over the quartermaster's roll. Another sergeant, in the capacity of sergeant-major, assisted the adjutant. Although muster rolls are available for most regiments and reveal promotions from sergeant to adjutant and quartermaster, the rolls do not distinguish which sergeants held the specialized functions of sergeant major, quartermaster sergeant, paymaster sergeant, and others; the rolls simply list the two or three sergeants in each company with no further distinction among them.[7] This makes it impossible to say whether service in one of those specialties was a prerequisite for promotion. Skill at reading, writing, and bookkeeping were attributes necessary for all noncommissioned officers,[8] so we can assume that those selected for promotion were particularly talented in those areas in addition to being meritorious.

The 22nd Regiment of Foot, which arrived in America shortly after the battle of Bunker Hill in 1775 and was among the last regiments to leave New York in late 1783, provides a good example of the prospects for sergeants to become officers during the course of a long war which saw much attrition in the army. When the regiment disembarked in Boston, the posts of adjutant and quartermaster were both held by lieutenants who also served as company officers. Throughout the army it was routine for company officers to also have staff positions either within the regiment or in some other army function, so there was nothing unusual about this arrangement. Each of a (typical) regiment's ten companies had three officers and often functioned with only one present; besides staff duties, officers might be absent due to illness, leave for personal business, travel, detached duty, or myriad other reasons. Barely a year into the war, when the lieutenant serving as quartermaster of the 22nd transferred to another regiment, a long-serving sergeant named William Abercrombie assumed the post. Abercrombie held no other rank besides quartermaster at this time, but in 1778 obtained a commission as an ensign in the regiment, thus serving in a dual capacity as a company officer and as quartermaster; in 1780 he was promoted to lieutenant, continuing to hold the quartermaster's post until he retired in 1782.[9] Appointed in his place was thirty-two-year-old sergeant Henry Vennel, who had joined the army at the age of twenty and had become a corporal only in December 1778 and sergeant a year later. He remained in the singular role of quartermaster until obtaining an ensigncy in 1789.[10] Each regiment had men with careers similar to those in the 22nd. In a few instances men served as quartermasters while still holding the rank of sergeant, such as William Rushworth of the 33rd Regiment.[11]

Each (typical) regiment had a peace time complement of twenty sergeants, increased to thirty in wartime, but only one adjutant and one quartermaster. Clearly this limited the possibility of rising through the ranks by this avenue. War increased the opportunities for advancement, however, in the form of new-raised corps. The number of regular army regiments nearly doubled during the years of the American war, and large numbers of Loyalist regiments (as well as other military organizations such as independent companies) were raised in America. One other sergeant in the 22nd Regiment, Thomas Stewart, became quartermaster of the recently raised 76th Regiment in 1780 when that regiment's quartermaster, who was also a company lieutenant, was promoted to the command of a company and no longer able to hold the post typically assigned to a junior officer.[12] Another new-raised corps presented an opportunity for Joseph Hawkins, a man who had joined the 22nd Regiment in 1768 and become a sergeant in the relatively short span of six years. In May 1776 he was commissioned as an ensign in a newly raised Loyalist regiment called the Royal Highland Emigrants.[13] In January 1779 this corps became part of the regular army as the 84th Regiment of Foot; although it was disbanded at the close of the war, service in a regular regiment afforded Hawkins the security of being put on half-pay[14] at the end of his active career.

We see, then, four sergeants in the 22nd Regiment who became officers by attaining the post of quartermaster during an eight-year period of wartime service. This number is reasonably typical for regiments in America, including sergeants who became officers in both regular and Loyalist regiments. This sounds like reasonably good odds for a regiment with thirty sergeants, but thirty was the number of available positions at any given time during the war years. A total of seventy-three men served as sergeants at some time during this period, yielding odds of about 5 percent that a sergeant might become an officer. Also, a total of 1,005 men (not including officers) served in the regiment at some time during its service in America; with odds of only about 7 percent of even becoming a sergeant,[15] and just 5 percent of those who did so becoming officers, the odds of rising through the ranks in this manner were clearly very slim indeed. The proliferation of Loyalist corps raised during the American war opened many new opportunities, affording at least fifty-nine British sergeants (including Joseph Hawkins, discussed above) advancement in rank, but the percentages given here include that avenue of advancement.

Study of muster rolls gives the impression that many more private soldiers received commissions, but the muster rolls are deceptive in this regard. Each (typical) regiment had thirty-five officers, including three in each of ten companies plus five staff positions.[16] During the war, six more officers were added to each regiment serving in America for recruiting in Great Britain.[17] Of these forty-one established officer billets in a wartime regiment, however, only ten were for the most junior rank of ensign, the rank that most young men pursuing military careers first obtained.[18] Men who had the appropriate aspirations and connections had to wait for a vacancy before they could receive commissions, but that did not prevent them from serving with a regiment; indeed, active service brought the opportunity to distinguish oneself, recognition vital to obtaining a recommendation for entering the officer corps. So it was that young gentlemen joined the army as volunteers, learning their trade and integrating themselves into army society while receiving no pay and holding no formal rank. Modern writers frequently use the term "gentleman volunteer" when referring to these young men, but this term does not appear in period sources which instead use one word or the other; they were gentlemen by virtue of their social standing, and volunteers in the army.

The nuance for researchers is that some, but not all, of these men appear on the muster rolls among the private soldiers. There is no apparent distinction between those who appear on the rolls and those who don't; published announcements of promotions show men described as "gentlemen" and "volunteers" obtaining commissions, but muster rolls reveal no correlation between the terminology used in the promotion announcements and whether the man appears on the rolls. Cases in point are James Boyd, John George Hood, and Thomas Gage Bruce. The three were volunteers in the 54th Regiment of Foot in July 1781;[19] Boyd and Hood were commissioned as ensigns in September to replace officers lost at the storming of Fort Griswold, Connecticut, Boyd in the 54th Regiment and Hood in the 40th. Both are called "Volunteer" in the announcements of their promotions.[20] Boyd appears on the muster rolls of the 54th as having enlisted two months before his commissioning, while Hood never appears on the rolls; Bruce neither appears on the rolls nor ever received a commission.[21] Little is known about the day-to-day duties of these men; occasional mentions of volunteers in first-hand accounts suggest that they were among the officers learning the rudiments of their profession from that perspective,[22] while their appearance on the muster rolls suggests that they served in the ranks to obtain their military foundations; the latter view is supported by the admonition of military writers that young officers become expert in "the use of the firelock, in every position, manual exercise, &c."[23] Regardless of their duties, it would be a mistake to include these men among those who truly rose through the ranks, for they joined the army with the explicit expectation of becoming officers and were commissioned as soon as an opportunity arose and the appropriate approvals were obtained. They did not obtain promotions because their performance distinguished them from other common soldiers nor based on long and faithful service in the ranks. Muster rolls for any given regiment over the course of its service in the American war are liable to show a handful of volunteers; although the numbers are relatively few compared to the overall number of private soldiers, they are similar to the number of sergeants in a regiment that became officers and so would sorely skew the conclusions of an unwary researcher trying to understand the likelihood of enlisted men rising through the ranks.

There was yet another path of advancement through the ranks, discernible in the muster rolls but elusive to quantify or characterize. Some men joined the army as private soldiers and were appointed as corporals or sergeants very quickly, sometimes within less than a year, but then served in that capacity for several years before attaining an officer rank. A superb example is James Green, whose background is not clear. In 1772 he was twenty-one years old and living with a family friend in London. There is no indication of what career he'd had in mind until then, but when he ran out of money he turned to the military. He had missed an opportunity to join the East India Company because their ships had already set sail, and refused an offer for a situation in the Foot Guards because he did not wish to remain in London. He chose to join the 62nd Regiment of Foot, then quartered in Ireland, and enlisted as a private soldier. He wrote that he was "promoted gradually" but it took only four years for the young soldier to become sergeant-major of the regiment.[24] Such a rapid rise clearly illustrates that Green was not an ordinary recruit but had all of the qualifications for an officer. These qualifications were recognized in the form of a commission in the 26th Regiment of Foot in September 1777, but being on the ill-fated Saratoga campaign Green had to endure nearly a year of captivity before being able to actually assume this new roll. In the New York garrison Green received appointments including deputy judge advocate, barrack master, and paymaster for troops of the northern army who'd ended up in New York by escape or other means. These were positions of considerable responsibility for such a young officer, and are further testimony of Green's extraordinary ability. He returned to Great Britain with the 26th Regiment in 1780, but his post-war career took him back to Canada where he remained for the rest of his life serving in posts concerned with military finance and civilian banking until his death in 1835.[25]

James Green's career is not without parallel. Andrew Phair joined the 17th Light Dragoons as an eighteen-year-old common soldier when the regiment embarked for America in early 1775. He too became a corporal and then a sergeant within only four years, followed by an appointment to adjutant in a Loyalist regiment named the American Legion in 1781.[26] Others had similar quick advances, but they were few compared to the numbers of more conventional careers. With only a small number of such cases and absent any explicit explanation, it is not clear where these men fell in the military social order. Were they common recruits who happened to be so remarkable that they advanced on merit alone, or were they aspiring officers who lacked any influence whatsoever and could advance only by proving their capabilities and merit? Lacking direct information we can only guess. A few cases lead us to favor the latter conclusion, not because the men became officers, but because of their behavior when they didn't.

Where there was opportunity and advancement there was also bound to be disappointment and disillusionment. A military system that allowed men to distinguish themselves surely saw some who expected recognition and reward but did not receive it. An apparent case in point is Andrew Brown, who enlisted in the 47th Regiment in the early 1770s at around the age of thirty. This was an advanced age for a peacetime enlistment, suggesting that Brown was not a typical recruit. The Irishman arrived in America as a recruit for the 47th in August 1774; the regiment had come to the colonies the previous year. Brown deserted from Boston only half a year later, in February 1775. His subsequent pursuits indicate either that he was disappointed in his military career aspirations or simply did not have the temperament required for martial obedience; regardless of his original aspirations, he clearly had the education and talent required to become an officer. After his desertion he joined the fledging American army and became an officer in the Massachusetts militia, rapidly rising to the post of Deputy Muster Master General and assuming significant administrative and organizational responsibilities. He then became Town Major for the city of Boston, which in late 1777 put him in the embarrassing position of administering the confinement of the prisoners from Burgoyne's army that included his own 47th Regiment. After the war he opened a teaching academy for young ladies in Philadelphia, but abandoned the enterprise when it became clear that he lacked the patience required for a career as an educator; he then opened a newspaper called the *Federal Gazette* which later became the *Philadelphia Gazette* and gained notice for its editorial commentary on the newly established Constitution of the United States and debates in the fledgling Congress. Throughout his American military and postwar pursuits, it was no secret that Brown was a deserter from the British army and this fact was detrimental only during the brief period when he administered affairs associated with the Convention Army in Boston.

Joseph Dunkerley came to America with the 38th Regiment of Foot in 1774. Due to gaps in the muster rolls it is not known whether he was an experienced soldier when he set foot in America, or a relatively new recruit who had enlisted for the allure of traveling overseas.[27] He deserted from Boston in January 1776 and within three months was serving as a second lieutenant in Colonel Craft's artillery regiment.[28] A year later, he became the adjutant of Colonel David Henley's continental regiment. Such positions indicate that Dunkerley had education beyond basic literacy, and perhaps had enlisted in the British army with legitimate aspirations of rising through the ranks. When Henley's regiment was tasked with guarding British prisoners outside Boston, Dunkerley considered his potential fate if he continued serving as a Continental Army officer. He resigned on 3 May 1778 because of "The unequal chance I run, by appearing in the field: (If made a prisoner) according to the law of nations I must expect immediately death." He stated that he had deserted "through principle" and had tried to have friends in London obtain his discharge from British service but had received no response.[29] His military career over, Dunkerley turned to another pursuit that also attested to an uncommon background: he established himself as a painter of miniature portraits. His earliest surviving dated work is from 1776, and a December 1784 issue of the *Independent Chronicle* carried an ad in which Dunkerley stated that he "still carries on his Profession of Painting in Miniature at his house in the North Square." Around 1788 he moved from Boston to Falmouth, Jamaica, where he painted prominent members of the local society and played a role in the establishment of a Masonic lodge on the island. He died there in 1806.[30]

A more covert case is that of Thomas Machin, who also joined the army at the relatively late (for peace time) age of twenty-nine at the beginning of 1773.[31] He enlisted into the 23rd Regiment of Foot as that corps was preparing to embark for America; he may well have known Thomas Watson whom we studied in Chapter 4. Biographers claim that he was the son of British mathematician John Machin, but this is impossible as that accomplished scholar had no offspring. It is a logical conclusion, though, given that Machin was recognized by an officer in his regiment as being "a sensible intelligent fellow, with some knowledge of fortification and Gunnery."[32] When he deserted from Boston in July 1775 there was some rumor among the British army that he was deliberately sent by the British to the American lines to gather intelligence, false claims that nonetheless testify to his capabilities; he left behind personal effects including books and drawing instruments, items that further indicate his education and intellect. The reason for his desertion is not known, but his skills and personal effects strongly suggest that he was seeking advancement that he did not achieve. His subsequent career bolsters that supposition: he quickly distinguished himself as an engineer in the American army, where his work on the siege of Boston led General George Washington to call him "an ingenious Man." He was sent to assess the feasibility of building a canal across Cape Cod, and then to supervise the construction of chains across the Hudson River to block British shipping. He served in the field as an artillery officer in Colonel John Lamb's regiment, and after the war created a successful business minting coins for the New York government. Unlike Andrew Brown, however, Machin seems not to have acknowledged that he was a deserter from the British army, a fact that may have inflamed the jealousies of fellow officers who envied this rising star in the Continental service; his military career was dogged by controversy including a court martial for irregular management of recruiting matters. Machin's own ambitions probably contributed to his checkered popularity, for he was not beyond subterfuge—he claimed to have been a resident of Long Island so that he could put in claims to the government for losses suffered during the British occupation of New York even though he never actually lived there, and his postwar career was initiated by counterfeiting British copper coins. Hiding his British army service and desertion may have been his way of attempting to elevate his own character and gain acceptance in a societal class to which he clearly desired to belong. He hid his story well; virtually all biographies of him purport that he came to America as part of a mining venture. The timing of his arrival, however, and his movement through New York and New Jersey before traveling to Boston, correlate perfectly with the movements of the 23rd Regiment in prewar America, and there is no direct evidence of his presence in America before his desertion recorded on the muster rolls of the 23rd Regiment as well as by several diarists.

While we infer the disappointment of Brown, Dunkerley, and Machin at having failed to rise in the British ranks, William Burke stated his disaffection directly. Burke wrote an autobiographical memoir detailing his early life in Ireland and his service as a British soldier, clearly describing his experiences and aspirations in the army. As an orphan in western Ireland he had no initial aspiration to become an army officer. His parental misfortune brought the opportunity, at about ten years of age, to attend school, and he applied himself vigorously to learning. By his mid-teens he was able to take clerical jobs at which he seems to have done well. He is not clear on his reason for enlistment, saying only that he "had a wish to become a soldier."[33] There is no indication that he was discontent or in any sort of trouble like most of the other men we've met in this study; perhaps it was simply the wanderlust of young adulthood. Burke quickly showed his capacity for independent thought and leadership when, as a new recruit, he volunteered to assist in the pursuit and capture of deserters in the Irish west country. Bounty jumping—obtaining the army's enlistment bounty money and then disappearing into the countryside—was a common problem in Ireland where there was widespread dislike of the British government and the army that symbolized it. Recruiting officers in early 1776 gave laments like "I beg leave to inform your Lordship that the Recruiting here is not likely to be attended with much success. The men who Engage themselves ... unless very closely watched, desert as soon as they can find the opportunity" and "It is not possible for your Lordship to conceive the difficulty there is in getting Men in Ireland; Besides they are the very Scum of the Earth, and do their utmost to desert, the moment they are Cloathed."[34] This practice was expensive for the army not only in terms of the direct loss of the bounty money and any clothing that the recruits had been provided, but also in terms of effort required to enlist the men and then track them down after they deserted, and the embarrassment that it cost the service. Burke's upbringing in the region made him familiar with the ways of the native Irish and allowed him to track down the fugitives, recouping the army's investment. The commanding officer of the 45th Regiment, into which Burke had enlisted, had known Burke's family, no doubt the reason that Burke was trusted not to be just another designing deserter looking for an avenue to abscond from his enlistment contract. When Burke was twice successful in these manhunts, the commander of the regiment planted the idea in the young soldier's mind that he was destined for a commission.

That Burke made use of the Irish language reveals the multicultural nature of the British army in the 1770s. Although most British regulars were from the British Isles, this did not mean that they shared a common native language. Recruits from Wales, Ireland, and Scotland often spoke regional variants of Gaelic, and some could not speak English. Adding another dimension to this mix was the recruitment of some two thousand Europeans, mostly German, into the ranks of British regiments early in the war. Distinct from the German regiments that supplemented the British army in America, these "German recruits" arrived in America in late 1776 and were integrated into the ranks of the British infantry, some regiments receiving only a few and others receiving more than a hundred.[35] The result was regiments that included substantial numbers of men who had difficulty understanding English, adding an interesting challenge of command and management. It is unfortunate that we have no record of the numbers of non-English speakers in most regiments, making it difficult to quantify the extent of this linguistic divide. Military writers of the era are also strangely silent on the subject, leaving no explicit recommendations on how to deal with the issue. About 70 percent of the 76th Regiment of Foot, raised in 1778, were highland Scots, many of whom did not speak English; the soldiers were forced to learn English words of command so they could be trained in military drill, and "uncommon pains were taken by the major to explain to them the articles of war, and the nature of the duties required of them in Gaelic."[36] Proceedings of general courts-martial reveal that the language barriers were broken at least partially by bilingual soldiers in the ranks. While we might expect some officers to have been educated in foreign languages, and indeed many were, in trials of common soldiers it was usually other soldiers who were called as interpreters. When Murdock McLeod of the 42nd Regiment of Foot, the Royal Highlanders, was put on trial for plundering in December 1777, a sergeant involved in apprehending him testified that he had "pretended not to understand English," but the court learned that McLeod's linguistic limitations were genuine when he required a sergeant in his regiment to interpret his testimony "from the Erse to the English language."[37] In 1777 Sergeant John McKenzie of the 9th Regiment was called to the desertion trial of a British soldier, to "interpret faithfully" the testimony of two men from a German regiment who had discovered the deserter; McKenzie then interpreted the testimony of a German recruit in his own regiment who was also charged with desertion.[38] Sergeant Henry Klinge, a long-serving German in the 54th Regiment, performed similar service in the trial of a German recruit in the 22nd Regiment, interpreting both for the defendant and for soldiers of German regiments who testified.[39] The case of John Frederick Leo is ambiguous; when tried for desertion he mentioned his "ignorance of the English language" but he did not require an interpreter to deliver his testimony.[40]

Burke's account of his voyage to America includes the confusing claim that the 45th Regiment was initially ordered to Minorca but was diverted to America upon receiving news that war had broken out. This does not correlate with other contemporary accounts indicating that the 45th was ordered to America from the outset along with the 22nd, 40th, and 44th Regiments. These four corps were intended for New York but on arriving off the American coast their transports were redirected to Boston.[41] If we replace "Minorca" with "New York" Burke's account makes sense; this could be an indication that the soldiers of the 45th did not know their true destination, or it could be simply an error of recollection. Other than this apparent inaccuracy and some chronological mistakes Burke's recollections line up well with other primary sources, and Burke makes it clear that his ardor for soldiering quickly waned. It was displaced by fear, discomfort, and tedium. He endured storms at sea, hard labor at military duties, life-threatening illness, and the dangers of battle. All the while he retained hopes of obtaining a commission that would improve his lot both in the army and in society. He seems to have been prone to some of the deleterious behaviors that plagued soldiers like Valentine Duckett and Thomas Watson, but he nonetheless retained the favor of his officers. Although his hoped-for patron who commanded the regiment was detached to lead a grenadier battalion, a captain in the regiment appointed Burke as mess master for the officers. This role gave him access to those with whom he aspired to be peers as well as significant amounts of extra money. He was in a similar situation to Alexander Andrew, subject of the previous chapter; indeed, they had come to America in the same little fleet, and may have known each other. Like Andrew, William Burke's fortunes soon changed.

With his potential patron Lieutenant Colonel Monckton away on campaign, the death of the captain who had made him mess master left William Burke suddenly without a sponsor. Showing the same initiative that he had as a recruit, he obtained an offer of a commission from the commander of another regiment. This aspect of Burke's account is problematic because Burke refers to the officer as a "namesake," but there was no high-ranking officer named Burke in any British or Loyalist regiment in America at this time. The closest likely candidate is Lieutenant Colonel Samuel Birch who commanded the 17th Light Dragoons; this officer was in a position to grant Burke the favor of a commission and it is possible that the name was pronounced the same as Burke's. Burke had reason to be hopeful; he had seen three other men of the 45th Regiment become British officers since arriving in America, including two volunteers and one sergeant,[42] and he was probably aware that at least eight British sergeants had become officers in Loyalist regiments in 1777 alone. But local command of Burke's own regiment had devolved onto a captain who was not interested in Burke's aspirations. Rather than seeing a promising man seeking to better himself and the army, this officer perceived Burke's ambitions solely in terms of the loss of an able-bodied soldier from his own regiment. In keeping with frequently used conditions for breaking an enlistment contract, he required Burke to secure two other men in his place.[43] While this may have been practicable in his native country, it was an absurd demand for a young soldier in a foreign land where the limited British-held territory was already saturated with recruiters enlisting men for the proliferation of Loyalist corps being raised.

Denied his ambition, William Burke determined on a new path. His decisions are best related by himself, starting as he did from the beginning.

Memoir of William Burke

I was born in the county of Galway, Ireland, A.D. 1752, and by the death of both my parents, I was left an orphan nine or ten years old. My father died soon after my mother; they were, Roman Catholics. At the time of their death I knew no better than to go to the priest, and confess my sins and receive his absolution; he would tell me that I was then as free from sin as the child unborn. Soon after the death of my father I was sent to school. I became fond of going to school, and at the age of fourteen could read and write very well. About this time, Mr. James Morrison, a dancing master, came from England, and set up a school in the town where I then lived. I went to his school; he taught reading and writing, as well as dancing. I soon grew very fond of dancing, and made great proficiency in the art.

By this time, I had grown to the size of a man, was 16 or 17 years old, and went to live with Thomas Hudson, Esq., near the town of Aithlone, 65 miles west of the city of Dublin, in the capacity of steward. I collected his laborers, and kept accounts of the number of days they worked, &c. After living with this gentleman two years, I went to live with the Rev. Mr. Young, a clergyman of the Church of England, who lived in the town of Aithlone. With him I lived two years; my employment was the collection of his salary. From thence I went to live with Pierce Fitsgerald, Esq., of Baltimore, within 30 miles of Dublin. At this time the British officers were beating up for volunteers, and as I had a wish to become a soldier, I took a seat in the stage coach for Limerick, where was the 45th regiment of foot,[44] commanded by the Hon. Col. Henry Monckton, who was shortly to sail with his regiment up the straits of Minorca. When I arrived, I went to Col. Monckton and told him who I was, as he had some knowledge of my father's family. I joined his regiment, and soon after this, a soldier having deserted from the regiment, I offered to go as one of the four men whom the colonel was to send with the corporal in pursuit of the man. The colonel smiled and said I might go. So we took off our scarlet coats, and put on others, to prevent our being known by the deserter if we should come where he was. The corporal and the other three had but little knowledge of the customs and manners of the Catholic Irish, but I was well versed in their language, and well acquainted with their customs. The corporal gave up the command and the management of the business to me. We had sixty or seventy miles to go among the wild Irish, and meeting one of the king's tide-waiters,[45] he told us he believed he knew where the deserter might be found. We set off directly for the place which had been pointed out, and arrived there just at dark. Having lain by till the people in the house had all retired to rest, I then set a sentry at each door, and entered the house with the corporal and one of the men, lighted a candle, and went to his bed room, where the man of the house and his sons were lying, and told them if they made any noise they were dead men; instantly placed a sentinel over them, and went with the corporal, into the room where the deserter was in bed with a young woman who had ran away in his company. I sprung to the bed-side, put my bayonet to his breast, and told him he was my prisoner. We then took him, and set off for the river that runs from that place to Limerick; we had seven or eight miles to march to the place where we had seen the king's tide-waiter; we arrived at daylight, and embarked on board a sloop for Limerick, and arrived there the afternoon of the next day.

When we came to the castle the whole regiment flocked around us to see the deserter; they had thought that we should all have been killed by the Catholic Irish. The colonel ordered the sergeant of the guard to take the deserter to the guard house; he then thanked us for our faithfulness, and when he understood from all the party that young Burke was the sole means of taking the prisoner, he told me he would not forget me, and then put his hand into his pocket, and gave me a guinea.[46] Soon after this, I was sent to the town of Aithlone in pursuit of a deserter. I found him and enlisted three or four young men. When I returned the colonel was highly pleased, and told me that if I went on as I had begun, I should soon have a commission. This was in the autumn of 1774; early the next April we received orders to be ready for foreign service, and shortly afterwards we marched to the city of Cork. We tarried there six days. While there our regiment was ordered under arms to guard a man to the gallows; this was the first time that I had seen a man hung.

On the 12th of May, 1775, we embarked for Minorca; there were several transports employed to convey the whole regiment, which was one thousand strong, besides officers and women and children. Our voyage was very pleasant till we arrived in the bay of Biscay, where we had such a terrible storm for two days and nights that the captain ordered the hatchway closed down, and tarpauling nailed over it. My situation was now very unpleasant, as I had never been ten times on the salt water before. I would have given the whole world that I could be on shore, but I had *made my own bed and felt that I must lie on it.*

I begged and prayed for mercy, although I was very ignorant of that holy God upon whom I called. I had been taught to pray in the Catholic manner from a child, and always kept a prayer book. Soon the Lord was pleased to send us calm weather. The ship seemed to work regular; we sailed onward until we came near Gibralter, when one morning, to our great surprise a British man of war came in sight, and fired a great gun over our ship. We did not know what it meant. She soon came up with us and hailed. Our captain answered. She inquired where we were bound. Our captain replied "to Minorca." The commodore asked what troops were on board, and we answered the 45th regiment. "Who commands them?" "The Hon. Col. Monckton." "Tell him to come on board my ship." The colonel went on board the man of war, and was ordered to sail for New York, North America, as the king's colonies had rebelled. So we were all countermanded. The troops were all sorry, but could not help themselves. We arrived at Sandy Hook, and found the harbor of New York full of transports with British troops. The same day, as soon as we had dropped anchor, the Admiral hoisted signals for all the captains of the transports to come on board his ship to receive orders. In two hours they returned with orders to sail directly for Boston, as the British army had been defeated at Bunker Hill.

We weighed anchor, and set sail for Boston; arrived in three weeks, landed, and marched through the town to the *common* where we encamped. I was soon sent on guard to Bunker Hill, where the battle had been fought. Here I saw the destruction that had been made in the loss of lives and property, and it was here that I began to have trouble and sorrow. It was nothing but hard labor; working parties engaged in building batteries every day.[47] The weather being so much warmer than in Ireland, it overcame me, and brought on the camp distemper. I was very sick, and like to die; but he that has all power in heaven and earth, in his hand, was pleased to spare my life through the instrumentality of the surgeon general,[48] who visited me at the request of my worthy colonel. I soon began to get better. During my illness I had some convictions of sin, but as soon as I got my health again, I was as wild as ever. On the 17th of March following Boston was evacuated, and we sailed for Halifax, where we remained till the following June. We then received orders to embark for New York, and had not been at sea many days when we came up with 1200 troops from Hanover,[49] sailed in company with them till we came to Sandy Hook, landed on Staten Island, and encamped there until the 16th of August. Now, we were 32,000 strong; 20,000 British, and 12,000 Hanoverians. On the 17th of August we landed on Long Island, at day-break, and marched to Bedford, where the American troops lay. There I saw the first gun that I ever saw discharged in anger. We engaged the Americans first in a corn-field; had several skirmishes with them, till we at last attacked their main body. The foot attacked their front, but soon after the Prince of Wales' light horse came up,[50] and the action became general. We took two of their generals, and the troops they commanded, Lord Sterling and Gen. Sullivan. In this engagement my colonel was wounded. He had two balls shot through his body, and was taken from the field, supported by two drummers. The American army, by this time began to retreat, so that in the afternoon we encamped. The second day, if I mistake not, we understood that Gen. Washington was forming his whole force to give us pitched battle at Jamaica Plains. Twelve thousand of us were ordered to be ready at day-break. So we set off, and arrived there at night; lay all night upon our arms,[51] and as soon as the day was dawning, we saw a horseman coming up, who informed our general that Washington was crossing the East River into New York. We were ordered to march instantly, and we ran most of the way, twelve miles. The troops in front fired and wounded some of the Americans in the boats, as they were crossing the river. We marched from Brooklyn down the river to a place called hell-gate, where the Americans had a ten gun battery, and placed some mortars so that at day-break we were ready to lay siege to their battery. By throwing bombs and hot balls[52] we soon blew up their magazine, and dismounted their cannon, and burned the house of the Rev. Dr. Auchmuty, where their officers lodged. The way was then clear for our army to cross the river to York Island. As soon as all the troops were crossed, the line of march was formed, and we proceeded directly for New York. We expected to have hard work to take the city, but to our surprise the enemy retreated to Haerlem Ferry, fifteen lines north-east of the city. Soon after this, we got into barracks; the American army retreated still further into the country; our army pursued; but as we understood the Americans did not intend to meet us, if they could help it, we kept a strong guard out to Kingsbridge, and from the North to the East river.

During the fall, several battles were fought; the Americans built new works at White Plains; we sent a part of our army to Trog's Point,[53] where our front guard had a small engagement with them, but nothing of much consequence till we came to White Plains. Here we had a smart engagement; I expected every moment to be killed, as the shot, both great and small, flew in every direction. As soon as the action was over we encamped for the night, and the next day, our general sent a guard and waggons to pick up the dead and wounded. I was one of the guard, and it caused my heart to ache to see so many of the slain and wounded. When we picked up the wounded and buried the dead, we struck our tents,[54] and marched to Dobb's Ferry, on the creek east of Kingsbridge. Here we built an eighteen gun battery. This was in the last of October, 1776. Next we laid siege to Fort Washington; at three o'clock P.M., sent a flag of truce, and demanded the surrender of the fort, which was accordingly surrendered.[55] The fort was commanded by one Col. Magaw, an old farmer.[56] The troops in the fort were 2200 men. We could not keep possession of it any longer,[57] as there were three frigates in the North river, close to the fort, the Phoenix, the Glasgow, and the Rose, who fired constantly against it.

When the prisoners piled their arms,[58] they were marched a few rods from their arms, and kept under a strong guard till the next day, when they were marched to New York, and put in confinement in the sugar house,[59] and some into the prison ships. Now winter soon came on; we were put into winter quarters; the summer had been spent in arrangements to take Philadelphia, and when it was made known to me that my colonel was to have the command in that expedition,[60] it made me feel very bad, as I had expected whenever a vacancy should occur in his regiment to have had a commission. But I had several good friends among the officers of the army. One Capt. Nevins told me that though my colonel was gone, he would see that I would have a commission. This Capt. Nevins took the command of the regiment when my colonel went to Philadelphia. To do me kindness, Capt. Nevins made me mess-master of the regiment, to furnish the officers with dinner daily, at four o'clock. This was an easy berth; I soon became acquainted with all the officers in the regiment, and got a good deal of money; but it went as it came; I was so fond of money that I spent it freely.

In September, 1777, my worthy friend, Capt. Nevins died suddenly,[61] and the command was taken by one Capt. Wm. Graham.[62] He was a good soldier, but a very profane man; he took the command in the last of September, and in the month following, General Burgoyne was taken, when this news arrived at New York it struck a damp upon the army. I had a

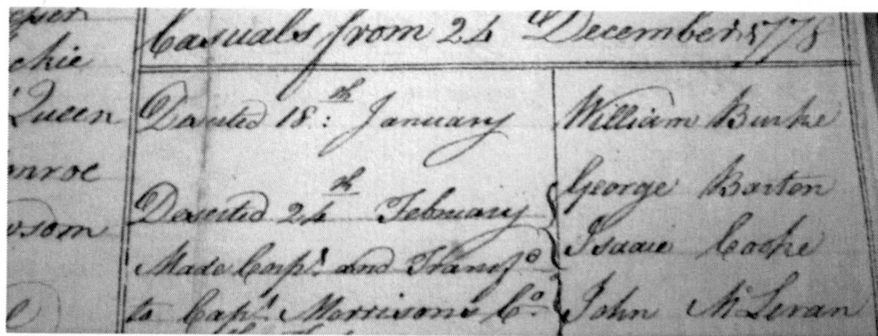
Casuals from 24 December 17[illegible]
Deserted 18th January — William Burke
Deserted 24th February — George Barton
Made Corpl. and Transf.d to Capt. Morrison's Co. — Isaac Cooke, John [illegible]

Detail from the muster roll of Colonel Henry Monckton's company, 45th Regiment of Foot, recording the desertion of William Burke (*The National Archives. Photo by Michael Barrett*)

namesake, one Col. Burke, in another regiment, who was acquainted with our regiment, and offered me an ensign's commission. Now I thought I was going to do well; but when I went to Capt. Graham with the news, he was much offended, and told me he could not let me go, unless I enlisted two men to supply my place. It was now about the 20th of December; at this time we had a guard of 1500 men at Kingsbridge; I was one of the number; we had eight redoubts with four pieces of cannon; these redoubts were on the east of the creek that separates York island from the main land. Here I began to think hard of getting away from the army. I found a Mr. Walker, a gunner, in the redoubt to which I was attached from the north of Ireland.[63] To him I communicated the treatment I had received from Capt. Graham, and told him I wanted to get to Hartford if I could get away safely. He fell in with my plan, and as I had the planting of the sentinels at night, I got the counter-sign.[64] We then made a solemn covenant that we would be true to each other, and agreed that we would start together the first chance we should get. Accordingly we set out for Col. Meigs, who commanded Gen. Washington's leather-cap regiment of foot,[65] on Sabbath night, the 12th of January, 1778.[66] The regiment which Col. Meigs commanded lay at Kings street, twenty miles from our lines at Kingsbridge. As we got three miles to the West Chester bridge, we met some people of color, going with fat turkeys to the British camp.[67] There were two men and two women, and they belonged to the tories. I had my bayonet in my hand, and ordered them to go back, or I would run them through. I took one of the men by the collar, and Walker knocked down the other. We then ran off almost with the speed of a horse. We were more afraid of the tories than the British; the night was very light; the black man begged leave to walk between us; so we put him between us, till we came to a village, where, as the snow was deep, we were passing very near the door of a house, when the black sprung from us into the house, and sung out that we were going to the American army. We ran with all the speed we had. I could then run very fast, but Walker was a large heavy man. However I was not going to leave him behind, for we had before promised to be faithful to each other, and had resolved not to be taken alive. We soon escaped out of the reach of the tories, and kept the main road; but were again in danger, because there were two regiments of British tories in the neighborhood. These wore collared coats, but we might not be able to distinguish them in the night.[68] I told Walker I would let no man challenge me first. Very soon, as we were on a highland west of Kingstreet, we saw a large party of men coming towards us. I told Walker I would challenge them, and would know if they were Americans. I placed Walker on my left hand, that they might think there were more of us than there really were. I wore a long scarlet coat, white pantaloons, and large cocked hat, which made the officer think, as he afterward told me, that I had a large party with me.[69] When they had come within about thirty rods of us, I roared out, "who comes there?" The officer answered "friends." I ordered him to halt his party, and to advance and give the counter-sign. It was but a few minutes before he advanced, and as soon as I was convinced he was an American officer, I took off my hat, and taking my bayonet by the point, I handed it to him. He immediately sprang, clasped his arms around my body, and asked me what office I held. I told him none. He then called his party; I found him to be a lieutenant in Col. Meig's regiment, who was himself stationed at King's street, only three miles from where we were.

The lieutenant was out on a patrole to see what he could learn of the movements of the British. He sent two or three men with us to the guard house, where we stayed till daylight. The colonel was then informed of us, who sent for us, to inquire what news we had brought from New York. So we told him all we knew, and what had happened to us on the road.

We found the colonel a very friendly man; he gave us all the counsel that was proper for our situation, and kept us over a great snow storm that came the next day. We then set off for West Point, to see Gen. Putnam. We found him at Fishkill; he received us very kindly; we gave him our side arms,[70] and he made each a present of some money; here I parted with Walker, as he chose to stay in Fishkill.

Now I was like Joseph in Egypt; my mind was bent on Hartford, in Connecticut. On my way there, I put off my red coat. Gen. Putnam had given me a pass, and I had to show it every where I stopped. When I came to Hartford, I looked around some; but I wanted to see New London, as I hoped it was a large place, where I could get into some sort of business. So I came to New London, but I did not like the place; I then went ten miles into the country, to the parish of which Rev. Mr. Jewell was preacher. I there hired out to work at farming, although I knew nothing of their method of working, and had not been used to work at much hard labor.

It was now planting season, and it came very hard to me, for I knew no more what way to go to work than a Guinea negro.[71] I soon grew tired of my work, and thought I would go to Albany; I set out, and came to Albany. Here I found Gen. Stark, and showed him my pass from Gen. Putnam. I told him I was in a strange land, with no money, and no trade, and no friends; I did not know how to labor as they do in this country, and did not know how I could support myself. The general asked if I could not go to Boston, as they wanted a man to get recruits for the Dean frigate, to form a marine company. She was the first Letter of Marque that went to France.[72] I told the general I should like to set up a fencing school, if he was willing. Some of the officers in the American army were in town, and wished to learn. The general gave his consent; So I went and procured my foils, and set up a fencing school; I did not continue it, however, but two or three days, on account of the British coming to Fort Stanwix.[73]

William Burke deserted from New York in January 1778. The regimental uniform was designed to be effective in all climates but required supplemental garments to bear the cold North American winters. Each year in each location winter clothing was produced and issued, sometimes based on orders from the local commander and sometimes specific to each regiment. There was no universal ensemble, but typical garments included woolen trousers (similar to the linen trousers worn in summertime, and sometimes fitted to be worn over breeches), woolen leggings (similar to gaiters and worn with breeches), and mittens. Since trousers and leggings were often made from locally procured cloth, color varied and style probably did too. Each company typically had a few heavy woolen watch coats for men to wear over their uniforms on sentry duty in inclement weather; while there is evidence that some regiments provided overcoats of some sort to all of their men, it is not known to have been a widespread practice.

The soldier depicted here wears his regimental coat buttoned against the cold weather. The green lapels have been unbuttoned, unfolded to show their red side, and buttoned across the chest; the cuffs and collar are unbuttoned and pulled over wrists and neck. British military buttons were cast from Britannia metal, a silver-colored alloy, and featured the regiment's number. The coat buttons for this regiment, the 45th, are spaced evenly rather than paired. Woolen leggings wrap the soldier's thighs and lower legs, fitted snugly for warmth and secured by garters below the knee and straps under each shoe to keep out dampness and debris. Typical of soldiers who were not on duty, he carries no musket or cartridge pouch but is armed with a bayonet. The waistbelt has been modified for permanent use as a shoulder carriage, a common adaptation in America.

2012

I then went and requested a letter from the general to the commander in chief at Boston. So he gave me a letter to Gen. Heath, and I accordingly set out for Boston. When I got to Worcester, it being court time, the public houses were all so full that I could not procure a lodging. I enquired who was the commanding officer there; they told me his name, and I went and found him a colonel in the army, showed him my pass from Gen. Putnam, and told him I had a letter from Gen. Stark to Gen. Heath, recommending me as a military man suitable to recruit for the Dean, Letter of Marque. The colonel treated me like a gentleman, as he was, and gave me a note to the last public house that had refused to take me in. They received me there, and the next day I set out for Boston.

I came to Gen. Heath, showed him my pass from Gen. Putnam, and Gen. Stark's letter. He told me he would give me forty dollars per month, while he wanted me. This was about dinner time; so the General ordered the waiter to set a small table, and I had dinner in the same room where they dined.

After dinner, I had a warrant as a recruiting sergeant, a sword and sash, and one drummer and fifer to attend me. I kept on recruiting till I enlisted the number they wanted. But before I got through, they began to offer me a commission. I told them I was willing to do all I could to help them, but that I could not join the army, because if I did, and should be taken by the British, I should suffer death. Therefore they did not insist upon it.

When the company which I had recruited was full, Gen. Hancock[74] ordered me to drill the company two hours in the morning, and two hours at night, which I did, and in three or four weeks, they were fit for action. The day was set for Gen. Hancock to come on board the ship, and see the men go through the manual exercise. The company had a captain and two lieutenants; they were paraded on the quarter deck; the officers took their places, and I did mine, but these gentlemen knew no more how to put their company through the manual exercise than children. Gen. Hancock knew so, and he ordered me to carry the company through the exercise. I stepped out in front of the company, drew my sword and carried the company through the exercise without the least mistake. The General then thanked the company for their good behavior, and thanked me also. Then he told me to dismiss the company, and to go to the purser of the ship, and get four gallons of spirits, and treat the company.

There was a French lieutenant on board the ship, a proud, haughty fellow, who could not bear to see what notice the general officers took of me.[75] As I was walking the quarter deck one afternoon, he ordered me off in something of a passion. I told him I thought I had a right to walk there; he then swore, and cursed me as an English rascal, and ordered one of the boatswains of the ship to put me in irons. The boatswain put a pair of irons on my hands. This threw me into a great passion; I called for pen and ink, and sent the lieutenant a challenge, telling him to lay down his commission, and I would show him British play; but he would not accept of it. The company then threatened to throw him overboard. Capt. Samuel Nicholson, who commanded the ship, then took me on shore, to prevent disturbance, and so the thing was dropped.

The officers now all wished me to accept of a commission; but I would not for fear of being taken. I then took leave of them, and went to New London, and began to live with a Mr. Darrow to learn the trade of making nails. I was to work for him eighteen months for what I could learn, and he was to board me. When I had lived with him one year, I could make as many nails as he could. I was then very active. I made 60,000 lath nails while I lived with him for Mr. David Trumbull.

After my time was out, I worked for wages; so now I began to get clothes, and to form acquaintances with the people. I also began to go to meeting, to hear Mr. Jewett,[76] of the north parish in New London, who was called a good preacher. Soon after this, the two deacons, Otis and Chester by name,[77] invited me to come to their houses, which I did, and they always gave me the best of counsel. By this time, I had seen the wickedness of the Roman Catholic clergy, and was rationally convinced that God only could forgive sins. Sometimes I thought I took a good deal of pleasure in the company of these good men.

Epilogue

The portion of William Burke's memoir presented here follows his life to the conclusion of his military service. Given his aspirations in the British army, it is surprising that Burke did not accept a commission so enthusiastically offered by the Americans. Besides his well-founded concerns about how he would be treated if captured, Burke may have had some genuine feelings of conscience about his decision to desert and the propriety of becoming an overt traitor by serving in an opposing army. Like Thomas Watson in Chapter 5, there is no way to know whether Burke's conflicts of conscience directly influenced his decisions or came into focus later in life when his memoirs were written.

William Burke's experience was similar to that of Alexander Andrew, in that both had won favor from senior officers who offered bright futures that were never attained. Had Burke gotten into Lt. Col. Monckton's family of servants, staking his future not on leadership but on servility, he would have ended up even more similar to Andrew: "his colonel" was killed at the battle of Monmouth, New Jersey, on 28 June 1778, leading a battalion of grenadiers in a valiant counterattack. Rather than being dutiful to his sovereign, nation, or cause, William Burke was loyal to gentlemen who treated him favorably; when those men were gone, so too was his ardor for the army.

Burke is one of two soldiers in this study who mentions carrying a prayer book. Given the paucity of information about personal possessions of common British soldiers, this is quite remarkable. While William Crawford carried his for convenience, Burke made use of his and found comfort in prayer in the face of danger. A few other soldiers are known to have relied on their religious texts. Thomas Cranfield of the 39th Regiment, discussed in Chapter 5, owned a Bible which he read and loaned to fellow soldiers.[78] An Irish corporal named John Graham of the 18th Regiment of Foot "commonly read the bible every day"; one day when an abusive officer in his regiment boarded a small boat to go from ship to shore, Graham held the Bible in his hand "and wished in the most solemn manner that the boat which took Capt.

Payne on shore might sink."[79] William Burke, like Thomas Watson, vacillated between morality and dissipation; their post-military experiences describe struggles with alcoholism that were finally extinguished by commitment to religion. Burke settled in Connecticut, outlived his first wife who bore him twelve children, and remarried. He spent a substantial part of his life traveling about the Northeast delivering Bibles and religious tracts to poor and destitute people, encouraging them to find the same peace in Christianity that he himself had. He died in Connecticut on 24 May 1836.

The memoir penned by William Burke traces his life and travels through 1816, but it is not clear when it was actually written.[80] It was published the year after his death, and no part of it is known to have been reprinted until the portion presented here. Burke's narrative of his early life and military service fill about a quarter of the total volume, while the remainder deals with his religious conversion and his evangelistic travels. His early aspirations of military achievement and social advancement were at first disappointed by others and then refused by him, leaving his purpose and satisfaction in life to be realized through modest charitable works. Although he saw his own success as having become a faithful and dutiful servant of God, his forthright record of a short career as a British soldier strengthens our understanding of the thousands of others who served with him in that capacity and thus provides invaluable service to history.

EPILOGUE

John Robert Shaw. William Crawford. Valentine Duckett. Thomas Watson. Robert Young. Ebenezer Fox. George Fox. Alexander Andrew. William Burke. Nine British regular soldiers, nine very different life stories. Common soldiers with little or nothing in common. Yet these were the men behind the numbers, the fabric of the armies that fought in America, the instruments of an eight-year war that grew from a political uprising, the soldiers whose endurance and many victories have been overshadowed by failures of policy and strategy that led to defeat in their war. The outcome of the conflict that they fought in has relegated them to being homogenized into a singular entity, the redcoats; and the outcome of the war has caused that entity to be sorely mischaracterized. The nine men examined here serve to deconstruct the entity, giving an accurate perspective on both the army as a whole and the individuals who served in it. It would be a mistake, however, to assume them to be a representative sample and extrapolate their lives and experiences to the entire army.

That all nine men volunteered for service is no surprise given the laws that governed the enlistment process. Their reasons for enlisting are consistent with those given by the small number of contemporaries who left written records of their intentions. The one man who enlisted under duress, the American prisoner Ebenezer Fox who was given the choice of remaining on a pestilent prison ship or becoming a soldier in the West Indies, is confirmation that criminals were allowed to join the army and for a brief period men were pressed into service, but all indications are that their numbers were few, as discussed in Chapter 6. The two men who volunteered to fight in America rather than remain in regiments in Great

Britain testify to the soldiery's sense of duty and verve for active service, but there is no way to know the actual proportion of such volunteers.

The mix of four Englishmen, three Irish, one Scot, and one American shows the diversity of national backgrounds in the army even though it does not accurately represent the proportionality; indeed, the national mix varied widely from one regiment to the next and over time within each regiment so that overarching statements about army demographics are difficult to make. Men like Thomas Watson, born in England and enlisted into the Royal Welch Fusiliers, demonstrate that regional recruiting was not yet the general practice in the British army. In most cases there was no correlation between a man's place of birth, place of enlistment, and service in the army. The number of men who transferred from one regiment to another—three of our nine, a number somewhat smaller than average but skewed by the fact that several in our study had careers foreshortened by death or desertion—calls into question assertions that soldiers were fiercely loyal to specific regiments and inherently disliked the practice of drafting (transferring from one regiment to another).

Even when experiences of these nine men are consistent with the army as a whole, it could be by chance rather than because they are a true representative sample. Two became noncommissioned officers, a proportion consistent with the army as a whole.[1] It happens, though, that those are also the only two of our sample who did not desert. Both also received pensions, a reward consistent with long service but not guaranteed and certainly not the purview only of men who rose above the rank of private soldier. Two of our writers are known to have been tried by military courts; both were found guilty but one had his punishment pardoned while the other twice suffered sentences. As discussed in Chapters 3 and 7, this is generally consistent with available quantitative information, but the dearth of regimental trial records makes it impossible to know for sure whether most of our men were tried; we know only that they did not mention it. In a strict sense, the fact that two men in this book were tried by general courts is wildly out of proportion with the overall rarity of these tribunals.

Many other aspects of this small sample of soldiers are wildly inconsistent with the majority. Seven of these nine deserted, a proportion that would have been unsustainable if it were anywhere close to typical; desertion also truncated careers that otherwise would certainly have included additional characteristic experiences. Three were executed for crimes, albeit only one while serving in the army; this is a reflection not of a tendency for soldiers to be condemned but for condemned men to leave autobiographical sketches. Two of the men studied here turned their lives to religion, as did two other contemporaries who left biographies;[2] this too is not representative of soldiers tending to become converts but of converts tending to write memoirs. A case could be made that men joined the army when faced with some type of desperation, and the rambling discontented spirit that brought on desperation eventually led either to conversion or condemnation. Such a conclusion, although a logical extrapolation of the memoirs presented here, is disingenuous to the majority of soldiers who led moderate lives as soldiers and civilians, never feeling the passion that led a few to leave testaments of either crimes or conversions.

Although seven of our nine soldiers wrote their own accounts, the literacy rate among soldiers remains difficult to quantify. With autobiographical material—either self-written or dictated—from so few soldiers, these accounts alone cannot be used to deduce anything about literacy in the army as a whole. The very nature of the material is biased in that only men who could write were likely to leave memoirs, for both the obvious reason of the ability to do so and the implied reason of having the intellect and insight to do so. Although other writings by soldiers survive in the form of memorials, letters, and military paperwork, the number of these is still far too small to use for analysis of literacy and too fragmented to constitute a reliable statistical sample.[3] If signatures alone are used as an indicator of literacy, where men either signed their name or made a mark, the results vary widely depending on the data sample used. Discharges retained for men who received out-pensions bear signatures at a rate of between 50 and 60 percent, consistent with estimates of the rate of male literacy in England;[4] on the other hand, pay receipts for two companies of regiments in America bear signatures for less than 35 percent of the men.[5] Both data samples could be biased, the former because literate men may have been more likely to apply for and receive pensions, the latter because both surviving paybooks concern soldiers from Scotland where overall literacy was lower.

Four of these soldiers became prisoners of war, a proportion significantly higher than the army in America as a whole. Even more disproportionate is the fact that three of these four deserted while prisoners of war.

Perhaps the greatest reason why these nine soldiers are not a good reflection of the army as a whole is that there are many attributes and experiences that they lack altogether. None of the prisoners of war, for example, escaped and rejoined the army like hundreds of others did—although William Crawford suggested an intention to do so. Not one of our nine soldiers was married, giving us no representation of the 10 to 20 percent in the army who had wives and children with them in America. None of our men was awarded a land grant at the end of the war, leaving us with no record of the thought process that led men to resettle, often with their families, on a new continent. There is no representation among our men of the several thousand continental Europeans who wore red coats and marched in the ranks of British infantry regiments, or of the struggles of those from many regions who did not speak English as their native tongue. No drummers, fifers, or regimental band musicians have left detailed accounts of American service, depriving us of insight on avocations that many men practiced for their entire military careers. We lack reminiscences from men who served in America in the British dragoons or artillery, branches of the army which while less numerous than the infantry played significant roles in many campaigns and provided different experiences for their soldiers.

In addition to the things that are not represented by the soldiers studied in this book, there is a wealth of experiences that they certainly shared but barely mention. Day to day military duties were apparently too mundane to warrant description even though they occupied much of the soldier's time. We learn nothing of their daily routine, hygiene, diet, or clothing. Information about the accumulation and disposal of income is absent from the memoirs. We hear of their personal interests and rapport with fellow soldiers only when those things were factors in their narratives; a few mentions of drinking and gaming leave details to the imagination. Opinions on the conduct of officers, military procedures, the course of the war, and the politics behind it are largely absent; we don't know if these men cared about such things at all. For all that these personal accounts reveal about the people who left them, the resulting pictures are only outlines of the lives that they represent, bare hints of the texture and complexity of military careers that lasted anywhere from a few months to a few decades.

If there is a common theme among these narratives, it is the reason why each was written. Six of these nine soldiers experienced life-changing events that led them to chronicle their lives, not for the sake of mundane recording but to illustrate how they came to be where they were when then they decided to tell their stories. William Crawford, Valentine Duckett, and Robert Young had led lives of dissipation that led to demise; their memoirs are a mixture of confession, explanation, and admonition. Thomas Watson and Andrew Burke had struggled with some of the same vices but found solid moral footings in religion; like Roger Lamb and Thomas Cranfield, whose writings are discussed throughout this book, their stories are foundations for spiritual awakening and religious devotion. Alexander Andrew had lost his patron and told his tale in a bid for sympathy, relief, and perhaps a chance to retain the future he'd envisioned. For Ebenezer Fox and George Fox the motive was simpler—they related their stories for the information and entertainment of young relatives, the former in writing and the later by dictation. Thousands of others, the vast majority of British soldiers who served in the American war, left no record of their experiences. Their careers can be pieced together from names on muster rolls and episodes recorded on other documents, but the human element of these men is lost. We are left to infer what we can from the few who told their stories, and wonder how they were the same, how they were different, and what they would have told us about their own lives.

That each of these nine soldiers had distinctive careers with few similarities, and the few additional contemporary narratives are equally distinct, shows the folly of generalities. While it is sometimes instructive to look for common elements to attain a better appreciation of the thousands of men that composed the army, the reality is that universally common factors are few. The British army that served in America was a haven of diversity, a population of different backgrounds and experiences brought together by a common career. The feats of arms that they accomplished were remarkable but have been largely lost in analysis of the leaders, strategies, and policies that determined the outcome of the war. They deserve greater recognition for their service than they have gotten. They were individuals, and they were soldiers.

APPENDIX I

The Poetry of Andrew Scott, 80th Regiment of Foot

Among the young men who answered the call for volunteers during the American war was a twenty-one-year-old farm worker from Bowden parish in the southeastern Scottish county of Roxburghshire, today part of Scottish Borders. Andrew Scott had a hobby of writing poetry, a pastime he'd begun as a herdsman at the age of twelve after he bought a pamphlet of Allan Ramsay's famous *The Gentle Shepherd: A Scots Pastoral Comedy* and was "charmed" by the melodic verses. He joined the new-raised 80th Regiment of Foot on 24 April 1778[1] for very similar reasons as other young men seen in this book, to satisfy a desire for adventure that he felt he otherwise might never experience. The regiment sailed to America the following year, initially garrisoning New York but joining the campaigning southern army in 1781. Scott survived through the siege of Yorktown and the captivity that followed, returning with the regiment to New York after the prisoners were released in 1783. At the end of the year the 80th returned to Great Britain where, like many of the new regiments, it was disbanded in 1784. Andrew Scott's days as a soldier were over.

Military service initially put him out of a poetic mood, but the soldier soon found his passion for verse rekindled and he wrote prolifically during his service. After his discharge he again laid aside his art, but began anew later in his subsequent life as an agricultural laborer.[2] He published a book of his poetry in 1811 which included, unfortunately, only two works written in America.[3] In his introduction he explains the sad circumstances of the loss of his other military compositions:

> This was about the end of the American war, and as I was tall enough for the service, I enlisted in a regiment, which was soon after called upon to cross the Atlantic. However wounding to my feeling the parting with my friends and

> native country was at the time, yet it afforded me an opportunity of seeing the world to an extent which, in another situation, I might never have had an opportunity of doing. This condition of life I found rather disagreeable, and for some time my rustic verse seemed averse to the life of a soldier's lady; but, by the time our regiment landed in Long Island, I had become more habituated to a military life, and the native scenery of so genial a climate altogether delighted me. Our wanderings through the vast woods, and over the varying face of such an extensive tract of country perfectly coincided with my feelings, to which new objects ever had a powerful charm. My attachment to verse-making again returned, and during the time I was in America, which was the five last campaigns that concluded the war, I wrote as many pieces as would have completed a small volume; some of them founded upon the varied scenery of the country, some on the manners and customs of the people, but most related to the incidents of military life, being wrote both from and to the feelings of soldiers. Many of them would have promoted risibility in a classical reader, not only from the vein of humour I had aimed at when I wrote them, but more from the whimsical warpings of my unbridled fancy, as I had seen no critical rules to restrain its extravagances. I cannot say that the pleasure I had in writing them at that time was all the benefit I derived from them; for, however trifling they in themselves were, they produced the good effect of securing me the favour of a number of my fellow-soldiers; they all, however, perished in oblivion, except two songs, the one on Betsy Rosoe, and that on the Oak Tree; these I particularly used to sing among my comrades, consequently preserved them in my memory till the time that I again visited my native shore.

Scott's two surviving wartime poems, along with his introductions and footnotes, appear below. The first, a delightful tribute to nature that reveals Scott's acuity for the pastoral, refers to a site on the Elizabeth River a few miles east of Norfolk that is today called Kempsville, Virginia. That Scott diverted his companions on this dangerous campaign by singing tributes to nature shows a sentimental aspect of soldiers that is too easily overlooked. The second poem recounts the tragic unrequited love of one of Scott's fellow soldiers. The sentimental tale, written from the perspective of the ill-fated suitor, contains references to well-known landmarks on Staten Island and Manhattan such as Cole's Ferry and Laurel Hill. The individuals involved in the tragic tale have not been identified with certainty, but likely candidates render the story completely plausible.[4]

The Oak Tree

Composed by the Author when a soldier in America, and when in the British army, under the command of Lord Cornwallis, were stationed at Kemp's Landing in Virginia, from whence they removed to the fatal station of Little York. —The tree alluded to is one of a very enormous size, but not so much for its height, as for the large circular space described by its shadow upon the ground, so that many of our tents were pitched under the shade of it.

Pray listen to me, an ancient oak-tree,
Tho' in my branches no fruit I bear,
Here in Kemp's Landing, I've had my standing
Since I was planted, this hundred year;
Nor rage of winter my growth could hinder,
Nor shocks of thunder e'er blasted me,
But still higher I aspire,
Till now arrived at maturity.
I thank dame nature, for this my stature,
An' bounteous Flora, that lovely queen,
Who in summer season, makes strangers gaze on
My lofty branches, clad all in green.
On this sweet plain, I stand here alone,
As one forsaken of company,
Yet of the forest, I am the fairest,
For spreading boughs none can equal me.

The pretty linnets, their vocal spinnets,
Among my branches tune ilk morn,

When fair Aurora bids all good morrow,
And bounteous Flora the fields adorn.
Once on a time, when peace o'er this clime,
Adorned ev'ry plain around,
My ancient master felt no disaster,
While here he laboured this fertile ground.

But when in rebellion his heart did dwell in,
He left his dwelling an' now he's gone;
T'escape a halter he's run for shelter
Under the banners of Washington.
You neighbouring trees, here me standing sees,
Your absence to me is no degrade,
While the British soldiers, my fellow lodgers,
Are here reclining below my shade.

I stand here distinguish'd to serve the British,
My boughs o'erhanging their heads at noon,
I'll them shade and shelter, till Phoebus alter
His course, and pass his meridian;
For now the summer is turning number,
The pretty cowslips I see decay,
Which is a token, my leaves tho' oaken,
Will shortly wither and fall away.

Cold frosty Saturn, I feel his return,
For to torment me with ling'ring pain,
While sweet zephyrs, like lovely Paris,
Transported far is out o'er the main.
Farewell sweet Flora and soft Aurora,
Farewell sweet arbours so fair to view;
Farewell ye flowers and lurking showers;
Farewell sweet Phoebus and morning dew.

Now cold November makes me remember
The shocks of winter I've undergone,
Cold Boreas bawling, my leaves are falling,
Few left my branches are now upon.
But December, colder, comes in far bolder,
My boughs clad over with fleaks of snow,

And heavy dashes against me clashes,
Of sleet and rain that most fiercely blow.

With January's repeated fury,
And February too makes me mourn,
Till March ensuing, my health renewing,
In hopes of summer's more sweet return.
Next comes April in, with aspect smiling,
When all my boughs they're again in bloom,
And when May's soft showers quicken the flowers,
My former glory I now resume.
Now ample Flora hath drenched my sorrow,
In the perfection of smiling June;
Cold winter scorning, the birds of morning,
Among my branches their voices tune.
Now the sweet warblers, in ilk green arbour,
Proclaim the glory of Nature's King;
While at my leisure I attend with pleasure,
An aged hermit in Kemp's Landing.

Betsy Rosoe

Air—The Cold Frosty Morning

The author composed the original manuscript of this Song in America, the scene of which is laid there, and the tragical event which it relates is founded upon reality.—When Lord Cornwallis's army were released from imprisonment, and had marched again into their own lines, the late 80th Regiment, in which the author served, was cantoned near to Richmond, in Staten Island, where this young woman's father and her uncle had their plantations, bordering to each other; and this young man, so unfortunate in his addresses to her, was a corporal in the same regiment with the author, and an intimate acquaintance of his. Betsy Rosoe had been expelled from her father's house, for putting too much confidence in an officer of a corps called the Queen's Rangers, being Continentals, and in the British service;[5] and was then living with her uncle: so that the author was intimately acquainted with both parties mentioned in this Song.

Adieu, ye sweet orchards in fair Statan Island,
Where the tree's drooping boughs are with fruit pressed down;
Ye lovely green arbours, where the negroes are toiling,
The once loved haunts of my dear Betsy Brown.
Alas! for my heart is now fixed on another,
Disdaining my suit, she's the cause of my woe,
Lamenting the day I was born of my mother,
I languish and sigh for fair Betsy Rosoe.

O Richmond, dear village, I'll never forget ye,
Where there in cantonment our regiment then lay;
Ye sweet-scented arbours, the haunts of my Betsy,
While life it enlivens my languishing clay.
Alas! for no longer here must we tarry,
Our route's for York Island, and hence we must go,
To cross the North River in boats to Chol's Ferry,
And leaving behind my sweet Betsy Rosoe.

Despairing of success, my love I concealed,
Still hoping that time would extinguish the flame,
Tho' anxious I was for to have it revealed,
My panting heart flutter'd to hear but her name.
'Twas on a fine evening, my charmer I spied,
Where the clust'ring fine cherries the boughs pressed low,
And this fine occasion I instantly plied,
Revealing my mind to fair Betsy Rosoe.

O Betsy, said, I, can you fancy a soldier,
Long time I have languish'd, your captive and slave;
For fear you deny me, my blood it runs colder,
O grant my request, and my life you will save!
If you are in earnest, young man, she replied,
I'm sorry I cannot,—I cannot, O no!
One of your profession he has me decoyed,
A false-hearted young man, that's brought me to woe.

My father and mother they both now disown me,
My dear little babe in the cradle now lies,
Altho' that my uncle's had pity upon me,

Yet still my hard fortune brings tears from my eyes.
I vowed, quo' she, and I purpose to keep it,
A soldier henceforth shall ne'er vanquish me so.
Thus saying, then instantly from me she tripped,
So this was my sentence from Betsy Rosoe.

Alas! for I had no design to wrong her,
Had love in return my poor bosom but blest;
Tho' hope was now gone, yet my passion grew stronger,
Her lovely dear image still haunted my breast.
O had I but died like a soldier in battle,
In honour's cold bed, by the hand of the foe,
My case then I would not have counted so fatal,
As slain by the charms of sweet Betsy Rosoe.

Oft times I have wander'd and vented my anguish,
Where she and I parted, by yon cherry tree;
I carv'd her name on it, and found it to languish,
And thus it afforded an emblem of me.
Now sleep to mine eyes is almost a stranger,
My appetite's gone, and my pulse beats low;
O cruel, false-hearted, deluding Queen's Ranger!
I suffer by you from fair Betsy Rosoe.

Tho' once like the pine-tree adorning the valley,
My person was handsome, both sprightly and tall,
But now I'm declining, my strength it goes daily,
Cold death its long slumbers shall soon on me fall:
Alas! Dr Pleydell*, thy art's unavailing,
And from thy prescriptions no comforts can flow:
Nor shall you e'er know the cause of my ailing;
Adieu then, vain world, and fair Betsy Rosoe.

Sequel.

So here this young soldier had fought for his country,
Bellona in battle his courage did prove:
But Cupid, blind urchin, he had the effrontry

*Surgeon in the 80th Regiment.[6]

To claim his sweet life as a tribute to love.
O Betsy, ye know not the power of your charms,
For now in York Island his dust it lies low;
Cold, cold he is sleeping in death's icy arms,
Who wish'd to have slept in thine, Betsy Rosoe.

O Betsy, had ye known that tragical story,
A tear o'er his urn would you dropped at least,
And wept o'er his dust, who so much did adore ye,
Requesting the turf to lie light on his breast.
Ye birds, as ye perch on the brakes of green laurel,*
Send wafted on zephyrs the accents of woe,
Melodious and melting his dirge for to carol,
Who thus died for love of fair Betsy Rosoe.

*The laurel grows a spontaneous shrub in some places of America; and near to the place alluded to, there is a rising height called laurel-Hill, from the abundance of laurel produced there.

APPENDIX 2

The Poetry of John Hawthorn, 6th (Inniskilling) Dragoons

A young cavalry trooper in Ireland used his poetic talent to describe aspects of military service that other writers apparently found too mundane. John Hawthorn, from Bannbridge in County Down, had been apprenticed to a linen weaver before heeding the call for recruits during the rapid expansion of the army in 1778. He joined the 6th Regiment of Dragoons, known as the Inniskilling Regiment, and rapidly trained in the ways of the horse soldier. Although his parents "could only afford him an education of Reading and Writing" he had a talent for verse and a keen knack for capturing his surroundings in whimsical rhyme. Less than a year after enlisting he published a book of verses, some probably written before becoming a soldier.[1] The first seven poems take a pastoral view on a variety of subjects: "The Journey of a Countryman" is a first-person account of traveling through rural Ireland that could be recollection, fiction, or a combination of the two; "On the River Bann" and "Combe Village" are tributes to beautiful landscapes while "Combe Camp" offers a sublime view of Hawthorn's English training ground; "The Choice" is a brief synopsis of a real or imagined romantic decision; "To a Benefactor" and "The First Chapter of Genesis Paraphrased" are musings on scriptural subjects.

It is Hawthorn's final three poems that complement the narratives in this book, providing enchanting insight on the tasks and concerns of British soldiers. While the camps of England and Ireland may have been more formal and regimented than the campaigns of America in details like hair powder and shoe blacking, Hawthorn's verses capture the disciplines that all recruits learned in order to maintain the personal hygiene and material serviceability necessary for overseas campaigning. In "The Drill" he compares martial demands with the easygoing life of a civilian; although he ascribes enlisting to "trading bad, and loss of different kind," it is not clear that his first-person poem is intended to be autobiographical. The extracts presented here omit extensive descriptions of country life and include only those parts describing the soldier's domain: the haversack for carrying a loaf of bread that was expected to last four days, the stick of rattan used by sergeants and officers to prod awkward recruits, the rigors of equestrian care followed by learning to march in ranks and files, and the manual of arms that ingrained proper handling of a musket. "On His Writing Verses" is a delightful account of the challenges faced by a literary man in a military environment, conveying in simple words the timeless banter of off-duty soldiers. Hawthorn's "Advice to a Recruit" describes the nuances of military life: avoiding quarrels and spending wisely on the "necessary items" of clothing that included shirts, shoes, and stockings; shunning the temptations of crap games and whores who could give the pox or clap; learning to clean oneself and dress the hair in the military style called a club; using blacking wax to waterproof the gaiters that kept damp and debris out of the shoes. He uses military terminology familiar to anyone who has studied texts and manuals of the period: dressing (aligning with the man on one end, or the center, to ensure a straight line of soldiers), flugal man (a well-trained soldier who stood in view of the others to demonstrate each position in handling the musket), advance arms (the musket held close on the right side of the body), rest and present arms (positions that were identical, but used at different times; present remains similar in modern manuals), poise arms (the musket held vertically with the lock in front of the face).[2] Adherence to his advice would not only avert punishment in the solitary confinement of the "black hole" but could win the favor of a pension—if the fate of battle did not intervene.

THE DRILL [extracts]

It is not many months ago, since I
Enjoy'd my freedom and my liberty,
Before I e'er took up a haversack,
Or bullying serjeant to rattan my back,

When on my stockings there might be a spot;
No matter if my shoes were black or not…

At first I thought it hard for to sustain,
The stir and the fatigue of a campaign;
Foraging first, then going to the longe,
Washing of manes and tails with comb and spunge.
The nose bags next, then sweeping with a broom;
Riding to water, twice a day, to Combe;
Then in a hurry for the drill prepare,
My shoes made black, and powder in my hair;
Then stepping forth, and falling in the ranks,
Filing off from the centre and the flanks,
Striving to march with a stout firm tread,
Push back my shoulders, and keep up my head;
My breast push'd out, and pressed back my thighs,
Then going o'er the manual exercise,
But, still I strove to learn, for truth is best,
An undisciplin'd soldier's but a jest;
And then, I have laid out a thousand ways,
To make my loaf to last me out four days,
But now, by plain experience I do see,
Its pinch'd enough, by Jove, to last me three.
Some of them damn my eyes and limbs, I'm sleeping,
Holla! make haste, damn you, you are always sleeping.
So many cry at once, by the God Cupid,
I do forget myself, and so seem stupid.

On His Writing Verses

Well may they write, that sit in parlours fine,
To raise their spirits can quaff luscious wine,
To keep out noise, the parlour door is shut,
The servants scarce dare speak, or budge a foot;
Under no fear, no terror, or no task,
But coolly can sit at a writing desk;
How different with me the time is spent,
Inclos'd with dragoons in a little tent;
Some darning stockings, others blacking shoes;
Some singing, others telling jests and news;

Their different sounds do ill confound my writing;
One should be solitary, when inditing,
Yet I must be a bard, nought less will do me,
And so write as nature dictates to me.

Advice to a Recruit

Humbly inscribed to his Quarter-Master.
Be not offended, sir, at what I do,
To dedicate this little piece to you;
Or think I am impertinent, or rude,
Because I on your leisure do intrude.
My little poems, you was the first to heed them,
And seem'd to take a pleasure for the read them;
Which was the reason that I made so free,
My soldiers counsel to inscribe to thee;
May blessings flow upon you, thick and soon,
It is the wishes of a light dragoon.
Once a recruit gave me a hearty gill,
To tell him how to manage at the drill;
How he might favour win, and anger miss,
The answer that I made to him was this:
If you intend a soldier's life to live,
Take this advice which here I to you give;
Never do you thro' ignorance, or price,
A wholsome counsel ever throw aside;
When you get your advance, do not abuse it,
But for to buy your necessaries use it;
For when you join your regiment, you will fret
To find yourself still running on in debt;
When you the regiment join, try if you can
Take up with some cool understanding man,
And keep from wicked, swearing, arrant raps,
Can talk of nothing but of w-s and c-ps;
Another thing be sure you don't forbear,
To learn your exercise with studious care;
But never go to drill, or to parade,
'Till you are clean, and decently array'd,
Your hair well club'd, and powder'd down your back;
Your stockings clean, with shoes and gaiters black;

Keep hands and face still clean with constant pains,
Nor wear a beard that's long by any means,
Keep your arms clean, without a bit of rust;
Brush well your clothes, and keep them free of dust:
When clothes and arms that you've made to shine,
Why then walk forth and form you up the line;
When on parade, pray play no foolish pranks,
By gazing round, or talking in the ranks,
For there is nought an officer more charms,
Than to see a soldier steady under arms,
Bring in your belly, and push out your breast,
Look o'er your right hand man's head, till you're drest;
Hold up your head, with a becoming pride,
And keep down your arms close by your side;
Keep down your hands from picking teeth or nose;
Keep close your heels, and turn you out your toes,
Press back your thighs and knees, with all you might,
And keep you eye fix'd steady to the right:
So when you march, see that you do labour,
To plant the left foot with the sounding tabor:
Against the word attention, don't transgress,
Whether you by the right or centre dress;
Strive all you can to never get a blame,
The plague it is to get a lazy name;
Upon the fleugal man keep fix'd your eyes,
When going o'er your manual exercise,
To the commanding word be close intent,
Nor advance your arms when you should present;
In shouldering, to the hip the piece is press'd,
Presenting, is the same thing as a rest,
Bring up your piece with vigour to the poise,
And bring your fingers level with your eyes,
Hold up your body, with becoming grace,
When to the right, or to the left you face,
Don't stand as if you were asleep or blunt,
Bring up your shoulders square quite to the front,
Be wise, look sharp, and always be alert,
Do what you will, still go about it smart,
And when you're going home, be free from noise,
Behave like soldiers, not like foolish boys;

When you are disciplin'd, mind what I say,
Be careful, wise, and manage well your pay,
From quarrelling, do a resolution make,
And drunkenness shun, as you would a snake;
Keep from the ale, let it be e'er so humbling,
A drunken soldier's very unbecoming,
Next due obedience to all orders pay,
And if you're scolded, don't an ill word say;
Keep silence still, tho' serjeants rage and curse,
Returning answers always make things worse;
Perhaps they'll call you dunce, or stupid ass;
Say not a word, but quiet let it pass.
Another thing, and mind it now be sure,
See that you follow no vile nasty w-e,
Nor ever do your constitution sap,
By following them, who'll give you p-x or c-p,
And bring upon yourself such loathsome pains,
With deadly poison trickling thro' your veins;
One thing observe, 'twill keep you from vexation,
Don't envy him that's in a higher station;
What if your toil is hard, why don't repine,
Things may grow better in a little time;
Envy not wealth, for if the truth you knew,
Rich men have troubles full as well as you,
Make a resolve, that happen you what will,
You'll not desert, stand to your colours still,
Think how deserters spend a life of dread,
Afraid of every one that's cloath'd in red;
If you are a dragoon, strive all you're able
To keep set hours, and punctual to the stable,
Bed well your horse, that he may easy lie,
And always rub his heels until they're dry,
Ne'er cause your serjeant to be check'd,
By your remissness, or by your neglect.
These rules observed, you'll find you'll favour win,
Nor the curs'd tag will ever touch your skin,
Or ever have occasion for to thole,
That most infernal region the black hole;
And when you were worn out, I will engage
You'll pension get, to keep you in old age,

What should be first, is now the latter thing,
I mean the duty that you owe your king,
If you be call'd where dreadful cannons roar,
'Midst clouds of smoak, and fields of purple gore,
Yet be assur'd that the all-seeing heaven
To ever, bullet has its billet given;
Fight bravely on, you have a noble cause,
Your king and country, liberties and laws,
And if you fall, each tongue your fame will tell,
There lies the man that for his country fell.

NOTES

The following abbreviations are used in the notes.

TNA The National Archives, London

WLC William L. Clements Library, Ann Arbor, Michigan

WO War Office

Introduction

1. This number is an approximation. Studies of the pay lists of two regiments, the 22nd and 33rd Regiments of Foot, show that almost exactly 1000 men served in each regiment while the regiment was in America; at any one time each regiment had about 500 men, but the arrival of new recruits and losses due to death, desertion, and discharge bring the total to 1,005 for the 22nd Regiment and 998 for the 33rd Regiment. Using these numbers as a baseline, and looking at the time that each of 56 foot regiments, two dragoon regiments, a composite battalion of Foot Guards, and detachments of the Royal Artillery spent in America between 1775 and 1783, we can estimate that around 50,000 men of the regular British army served in America. This figure includes Canada but not the West Indies, and does not include Loyalist or German regiments. Muster rolls, 22nd and 33rd Regiments of Foot, WO 12/3872 and WO 12/4803, The National Archives, London (hereinafter cited as TNA).
2. *A British Soldier's Story: Roger Lamb's Narrative of the American Revolution*, Don N. Hagist, ed. (Baraboo, WI: Ballindalloch Press, 2005). *From Redcoat to Rebel: The Thomas Sullivan Journal,* Joseph Lee Boyle, ed. (Bowie, MD: Heritage Books, 1997).
3. This book includes extracts from four such works: *The Life and Travels of John Robert Shaw* "Written by himself" (Lexington, KY: Daniel Bradford, 1807; reprinted and annotated as *John Robert Shaw: An Autobiography of Thirty Years*, Oressa M. Teagarden, ed. (Athens: Ohio University Press, 1992); *Memoir of William Burke, a Soldier of the Revolution* (Hartford, CT: Case, Tiffany and Co., 1837); *Some Account of the Life, Convincement, and Religious Experience of Thomas Watson*, "Written by himself" (New York: Daniel Cooledge, 1836); *The Adventures of Ebenezer Fox in the Revolutionary War* (Boston: Charles Fox, 1847; reprinted Bowie, MD: Heritage Books, 2008).

Chapter 1: The Volunteer Soldier

1. Trial of Edward Hall, 43rd Regiment of Foot, WO 71/79, TNA, 387–395.
2. The bounty offered to men for enlisting does not appear to have been

fixed in the years before 1775 but was typically on the order of one pound or one guinea (a coin valued at 21 shillings or £1 1s.). A template set of recruiting instructions directed that "no more than £1 11s. 6d. shall be given to each recruit as bounty-money" and also directed that a receipt be made "for the bounty-money agreed on" suggesting flexibility in the amount offered. In 1778 the government established a bounty of £3, and in 1779 to £3 3s. Edward R. Curtis, *The British Army in the American Revolution* (Gansevoort, NY: Corner House Historical Publications, 1998), 55, 57.

3. Trial of John Ingram. WO 71/83, TNA, 171–172.

4. Roger Lamb wrote two books: *A Journal of Occurrences during the Late American War* (Dublin: Wilkinson & Courtney, 1809) and *Memoir of My Own Life* (Dublin: privately published, 1811). Each book includes extensive material besides Lamb's own personal experiences; the two have been abridged into one volume containing only Lamb's firsthand experiences, in Don N. Hagist, ed., *A British Soldier's Story: Roger Lamb's Narrative of the American Revolution* (Baraboo, WI: Ballindalloch Press, 2005).

5. Hagist, *A British Soldier's Story*, 7.

6. Joseph Lee Boyle, ed., *From Redcoat to Rebel: The Thomas Sullivan Journal* (Bowie, MD: Heritage Books, 1997), 3.

7. Pell's Narrative, Grenadier Guards archives, London, as quoted in Glenn A. Steppler, "The Common Soldier in the Reign of George III," Ph.D. thesis, University of Oxford, 1984, 20–23.

8. P. A. Adair, "Sergeant Pell in London," *History Today* 21 (1971), 733.

9. That is, the soldier would receive a monetary bonus for enlisting Griffith.

10. W. Griffith, "Memoirs and Spiritual Experience of the late Mr. W. Griffith, Senior," *The Spiritual Magazine, and Zion's Casket* (London: E. Palmer and Son, 1848), 152.

11. Sometimes called "smart money" or simply "the smart," a fee of twenty shillings was required over and above the enlistment bounty for a man to buy himself out of an enlistment agreement. Four days were allowed for the man to raise this sum. The intent was to insure that men could not be enlisted while drunk or otherwise under duress, but it can be argued that twenty shillings was an unrealistic sum for many to raise in a short time. *The Annual Register, or a View of the History, Politics, and Literature, for the Year 1777* (London: J. Dodsley, 1794), 196.

12. Trial of John Ingram. WO 71/83, TNA, 171–172.

13. Orderly Book of Captain Henry Knight, Aide-de-Camp to General Howe. New-York Historical Society, 217, entry for 17 February 1777.

14. Trial of George Hartly. WO 71/83, TNA, 420–426.

15. Trial of John Walker, WO 71/85, TNA, 302–305.

16. Trial of John Alexander, WO 71/86, TNA, 185–189.

17. Trial of Charles Toomey, WO 71/86, TNA, 396–399.

18. Based on a survey of all of the general court trials for which proceedings survive. Proceedings of general courts martial, WO 71/80 through /98, TNA.

19. Most British foot regiments were given county titles in accordance with a royal warrant of 31 August 1782, but these designations did not mandate recruiting in their respective counties; rather, regiments were directed to "endeavour by all means in your power to cultivate and improve that connection so as to create a mutual attachment between the County and the Regiment." This text is from a form letter sent to each regiment informing them of their respective county titles; see, for example, George Noakes, *A Historical Account of the Services of the 34th & 55th Regiments* (Carlisle, England: C. Thurnam and Sons, 1875), 31–32.
20. Bennett Cuthbertson, *A System for the Compleat Interior Management and Œconomy of a Battalion of Infantry* (Dublin, 1768), 66–67.
21. At an annual inspection in July 1775, the last one before it departed for America, the 33rd Regiment consisted of 316 English, 5 Scottish, and 58 Irish soldiers. The inspection returns do not describe nativity in greater detail than nationality, and do not distinguish Welsh from other English. Inspection return, 33rd Regiment of Foot, WO 27/32. The records of 98 pensioners who had served in the 33rd Regiment during the American war show that 69 were English, 4 Scottish, 26 Irish, and 3 "Foreign" (2 from America and one from Gibraltar). Of the 69 English, 38 were from Yorkshire. Soldiers' discharges located in WO 97, WO 119, and WO 121, correlated with muster rolls, 33rd Regiment of Foot, WO 12/4803/1.
22. This is a very general figure based on the study of muster rolls for several regiments; actual figures vary significantly from year to year and regiment to regiment.
23. There was of course wide variation in the operational readiness of regiments in the army at any given time. For a detailed study of this topic, see J. A. Houlding, *Fit for Service: The Training of the British Army 1715–1795* (Oxford: Clarendon Press, 1981).
24. B. F. Stevens, ed., *General Sir William Howe's Orderly Book* (Port Washington, NY: Kennikat Press, 1980), 132, 302.
25. The initial order for creating the Additional Companies directed that each regiment was to have one complete company in England and one in Ireland; a subsequent order on 3 February 1776 directed that all men in Additional Companies be sent to America leaving only officers, NCOs, and drummers behind for recruiting. WO 4/96, TNA, 20.
26. Recruiting Accounts of Lt. Joab Aked, West Yorkshire Archives, Calderdale, SH17/A. Service Returns, WO 25/1126, TNA. Muster rolls, 22nd Regiment of Foot, WO 12/382, TNA.
27. Manningham, a village to the north of the town of Bradford, about nine miles west of Leeds. Shaw's family appears to have resided at nearby Baildon when he enlisted.
28. Shaw's journey appears to have begun at Bailden, now Baildon west of Leeds, then across the river Aire to the south to Shipley. He then headed east. "Windal" is probably Windhill on the way to "Coverly," probably now Calverley. Shaw continued east to Leeds.
29. James Shackelton was a sergeant in the 33rd Regiment who remained in Great Britain on recruiting service when the regiment went to America

in early 1776. Muster rolls, 33rd Regiment of Foot, WO 12/4803, TNA.

30. Samuel Coggill, from Leeds in Yorkshire, joined the 33rd Regiment in 1772 at the age of nineteen. He remained in Great Britain on the recruiting service when the regiment sailed for America. He became a sergeant and accompanied a party of recruits to America in 1780. He served forty years in the 33rd Regiment, receiving an out pension in 1812 at the age of fifty-nine. Muster rolls, 33rd Regiment of Foot, WO 12/4803; discharge of Samuel Coggill, WO 121/120/47, TNA.

31. Captain John Kerr of the 33rd Regiment remained in Great Britain on the recruiting service when the regiment sailed for America. He joined the regiment in America in 1780, and was killed during the siege of Yorktown in 1781. Muster rolls, 33rd Regiment of Foot, WO 12/4803, TNA.

32. The 59th Regiment of Foot had been sent to America in 1765, and returned to Great Britain at the end of 1775. Before returning to Britain, the able-bodied men were drafted into other regiments; see Chapter 2 for a discussion of drafting. Stevens, ed., *General Sir William Howe's Orderly Book,* 158, 163, 167.

33. Shaw's mention of the custom of soldiers sleeping naked is corroborated by a soldier in the 68th Regiment: "It should be observed, that it is usual for soldiers to lay without their shirts, both in camp and quarters; as in the former the straw wears them out very fast, and in the latter it is to avoid catching any distemper, as well as to save both the wash and the wear; as a soldier can ill afford to replace a shirt when worn out, and a man who is in the army, ought to have all his wits about him, to make his small trifle of pay to support him." Anon, *A Soldier's Journal, Containing a particular Description of the several Descents on the Coast of France last War, With an entertaining Account of the Islands of Guadaloupe, Dominique, &c., And also of the Isles of Wight and Jersey, To which are annexed, Observations on the present State of the Army of Great Britain* (London: E. and C. Dilly, 1770), 6–7. Officers may have encouraged this custom as a way of making desertion during the night more difficult. Also, this custom was not followed by soldiers on duties that might require a sudden call to action, whether in garrison or on campaign.

34. Lieutenant Colonel James Webster commanded the 33rd Regiment of Foot. Shaw makes frequent subsequent mentions of Webster; it is curious that he misstates the famous officer's first name. Steven M. Baule and Stephen Gilbert, *British Army Officers Who Served in the American Revolution* (Bowie, MD: Heritage Books, 2004), 184.

35. A cockade was an arrangement of ribbon worn on one leaf of the military cocked hat or cap, akin to a bow. Although the cockade that was worn with the regimental uniform was black, recruits did not receive full regimental uniforms. They only received uniform jackets and other clothing after arriving at a depot, so their clothing while still with the recruiting party was the responsibility of the recruiting officer. Hats were sometimes issued in order to have some look of uniformity among the recruits. Shaw's description indicates that recruiting officers had some latitude with the look of the recruits in their parties. This is consistent with some

illustrations of recruiting parties, but those illustrations are difficult to trust because they are often satirical. Recruiting Accounts of Lt. Joab Aked, West Yorkshire Archives, Calderdale, SH17/A. Letter, Thomas Gage to Cox & Mair agents, 26 July 1781, Thomas Gage Papers, WLC. Account of Capt. Michael Seix, Agent's ledgers, 22nd Regiment of Foot, A56e/102–103, Lloyds Bank Archives, London.

36. Shaw describes the Royal Hospital for Seamen at Greenwich.

37. That is, companies of recruits from eighty regiments.

38. The 1st Regiment of Foot, or Royal Scots; Shaw refers to a company of recruits from this regiment.

39. Firelock, the common term of the era for the musket carried by soldiers, so named for the flint and steel ignition system—the lock—that created a spark to ignite the gunpowder. The accoutrements consisted of a waist belt with a frog to hold a bayonet scabbard, and a cartridge box—a wooden block with eighteen holes, each holding a single cartridge, covered by a leather flap, and strapped onto the waist belt. When the recruits joined the regiments they also received a larger cartridge pouch that hung on the right hip by a leather strap over the left shoulder.

40. The cat-of-nine-tails, the whip used to inflict punishments.

41. As discussed in Chapter 7, long-serving soldiers no longer fit for campaigning often received pensions when they were discharged, with the caveat that they could be called back into service if needed. During wartime, pensioners were formed into companies to garrison forts, guard prisoners, and perform other relatively light duties. In this case they prevented men from deserting during the embarkation. This should not be construed as forcing the recruits into foreign service; rather, it was because embarkation provided an opportunity for recruits to desert knowing that their own corps would be departing and unable to apprehend them. The 44th Regiment of Foot, for example, enlisted fifty-five men in the first four months of 1775 as it was preparing to embark for America; during that same period, twenty-five men deserted including six of the new enlistees. Muster rolls, 44th Regiment of Foot, WO 12/5637/1. Other regiments had far less trouble with desertion before embarkation; the 54th lost only six deserters compared to 111 recruits; the 57th regiment enlisted thirty-two recruits and had no desertions. Muster rolls, 54th Regiment, WO 12/6398/1; and 57th Regiment, WO 12/6633, TNA.

42. It is difficult to imagine that Shaw didn't know when he enlisted that he would be sent to America, since the 33rd Regiment was already there.

43. A letter of marque was issued to privately owned ships authorizing them to act in a naval capacity. In general the Royal Navy did not operate its own transport ships, but instead hired private vessels to transport troops.

44. Although a bomb ketch was a type of naval vessel, Shaw uses the term as a slang to describe small boats carrying merchants that came alongside the shipping to sell provisions. David Syrett, "Living Conditions on the Navy Board's Transports During the American War, 1775–1783," *Mariner's Mirror* 55 (1969), 87–94.

45. Bedford, New York, another town on Long Island.
46. The raid on Elizabeth Town, New Jersey, that Shaw describes actually occurred on 23 February 1779. Shaw has recorded some of the events of his career out of the sequence in which they actually occurred.
47. Shaw refers to the Brigade of Guards, a composite corps formed of volunteer soldiers from the three regiments of British Foot Guards responsible for guarding royal persons and properties in London.
48. Lieutenant Colonel Thomas Stirling of the 42nd Regiment of Foot led the raid; there was no Colonel Frazer involved. Thomas Stirling to Sir Henry Clinton, 26 February 1779. Sir Henry Clinton Papers, volume 53, item 20, WLC.
49. American accounts of the raid do not indicate that men were in the barracks that were burned in Elizabeth Town. *New Jersey Gazette*, 3 March 1779. William Maxwell to George Washington, 27 February 1779, National Archives and Records Administration, Papers of the Continental Congress, M247, reel 169, item 152, volume 7, 139–141.
50. Shaw's memory is quite accurate—William Proctor and John Keith, private soldiers in the 33rd Regiment, were both killed on 23 February 1779. Both had been in the regiment since its arrival in America. Muster rolls, 33rd Regiment of Foot, WO 12/4803/1, TNA.
51. Shaw's garbled timeline has left it unclear which event he describes here.
52. The 28 September 1778 raid on Old Tappan, New Jersey, that included what came to be called the Baylor Massacre. Paul David Nelson, *Sir Charles Grey, First Earl Grey* (London: Associated University Press, 1966), 67–70.
53. The 3rd Continental Light Dragoons commanded by Colonel George Baylor.
54. Shaw plays on the patriotic ardor of his era; the British raid on Old Tappan was completely consistent with warfare conventions of the era.
55. Bomb proof, covered with a thick layer of earth that falling mortar bombs would not penetrate.
56. Six pounders, cannon that fired balls weighing six pounds.
57. The Loyal American Regiment commanded by Colonel Beverly Robinson.
58. The King's American Regiment commanded by Colonel Edmund Fanning.
59. Captain Patrick Ferguson of the 70th Regiment at this time commanded a small composite corps performing reconnaissance tasks along the Hudson River. M. M. Gilchrist, *Patrick Ferguson, A Man of Some Genius* (Edinburgh: NMS Publishing, 2003), 52.
60. Pickets, stakes, or poles driven into the ground as part of the defenses.
61. Pickets in this sense refer to soldiers posted at intervals as an advanced guard.
62. Swivels, small cannons mounted on walls that could be aimed and fired by hand.
63. Abattis, felled trees with their branches sharpened, arranged as a barrier.

64. Slow match, a length of cord infused with combustibles so that it smoldered with a slow-burning spark.
65. Lieutenant Colonel Henry Johnson of the 17th Regiment of Foot.
66. Shaw refers to the 16 July 1779 capture of Stony Point by American troops under General Anthony Wayne. He indicates that the Verplank's Point garrison, across the river, heard the initial firing but was unable to take any useful action. Don Loprieno, *The Enterprise in Contemplation: The Midnight Assault of Stony Point* (Bowie, MD: Heritage Books, 2004).
67. Chain shot, two cannon balls welded to either end of a length of chain designed to tear through the rigging of a ship. Adrian B. Caruana, *British Artillery Ammunition* (Bloomfield, Ontario: Museum Restoration Service, 1979).
68. Spiking a cannon was a way of disabling it by driving an iron spike into the touch hole, the small hole in the breech used to ignite the main powder charge.
69. It was typical for some wives and families of soldiers to accompany the army, enduring the same hazardous sea voyages as the men. Don N. Hagist, "The Women of the British Army During the American Revolution," *Minerva Quarterly Report on Women and the Military* 13, no. 2 (Summer 1995).
70. That is, to go to the ship leading the convoy to meet with the overall commander.
71. Bomb shells, hollow iron balls filled with gunpowder and fused to explode after landing, fired from mortars.
72. The British Legion commanded by Lieutenant Colonel Banastre Tarleton.
73. This occurred on 14 April 1780.
74. That is, the capitulation of the city of Charleston on 12 May 1780.
75. The muster rolls of the 33rd Regiment show that one officer and sixteen men were killed on 16 August 1780; the muster rolls do not indicate wounded men. Muster rolls, 33rd Regiment of Foot, WO 12/4803/1, TNA.
76. The 23rd Regiment of Foot was called the Royal Welsh Fusiliers (or Welch; the spelling varied). The 7th Regiment of Foot, also serving in the area, was called the Royal Fusiliers.
77. Here Shaw gives a lengthy description of the battle of Cowpens fought on 17 January 1781 where General Daniel Morgan defeated forces under Tarleton; because he did not experience it and it does not offer any new information about the event, it has been omitted.
78. Apparently Shaw means that he made bread for the men on guard and kept some for himself.
79. William Areton (as the name is spelled in the muster rolls; spelling variations are quite common in period military documents) came to America as a recruit in the 33rd Regiment in 1779, a year after John Robert Shaw. Areton served for the remainder of the war including time as a prisoner after the capitulation of Yorktown. He was discharged on 24 October 1783, a date typical of men who took land grants in Nova Scotia.

Muster rolls, 33rd Regiment of Foot, WO 12/4803/1, TNA. The correlation of 24 October 1783 with land grants is based on study of land grantees in the 22nd Regiment of Foot. To date, no comprehensive list has been found of British soldiers who received land grants.

80. On campaign British soldiers often constructed shelters out of brush, which they called wigwams. John U. Rees, "'We Are Now ... Properly ... Enwigwamed': British Soldiers and Brush Shelters, 1777–1781," *Brigade Dispatch* 29, no. 2 (Summer 1999), 2–9.

81. John Pyle attempted to bring a large party of Loyalists to join Cornwallis's army but was attacked and defeated on 24 February 1781. Lawrence E. Babbits and Joshua B. Howard, *Long, Obstinate, and Bloody: The Battle of Guilford Courthouse* (Chapel Hill: University of North Carolina Press, 2009), 38–39.

82. The Volunteers of Ireland, a Loyalist regiment.

83. Jägers, a corps of German troops armed with rifles and expert at scouting and skirmishing.

84. Richard Tattersdell joined the 23rd Regiment on 26 November 1770 and served throughout the war. Because he did not return from captivity at the end of the war, he was written off the muster rolls as a deserter on 24 June 1783. Muster rolls, 23rd Regiment of Foot, WO 12/3959 and /3960, TNA.

85. Jonny cake, a fried cornmeal cake.

86. Lieutenant Colonel Harry Lee commanded a mixed corps of cavalry and infantry known as Lee's Legion.

87. Subaltern, a commissioned officer below the rank of captain; that is, a lieutenant, ensign, or cornet.

88. Here Shaw gives a lengthy description of the battle; because he did not experience it and it does not offer any new information about the event, it has been omitted.

89. If Shaw gives his length of service accurately, he initially enlisted in late 1775.

90. The Portuguese half-Johannes or half-joe coin was worth 1 pound 16 shillings sterling. *Gaine's Universal Register, or, American and British Kalendar, for the Year 1776* (New York: Hugh Gaine, 1775).

91. Shaw's recollection is confusing in that he previously said his clothing had been taken from him.

92. Although regularly ordered to attend "divine service," British soldiers in general did not have a reputation for piousness. Indeed, one British officer famously wrote about the landing at Kip's Bay, New York, on 15 September 1776: "The Hessians, who were not used to this water business, and who conceived that it must be exceedingly uncomfortable to be shot at whilst they were quite defenceless and jammed together so close, began to sing hymns immediately. Our men expressed their feelings as strongly, though in a different manner, by damning themselves and the enemy indiscriminately with wonderful fervency." Francis Bickley, ed., *Report on the Manuscripts of the late Reginald Rawdon Hastings, Esq.* (London: Historical Manuscripts Commission, 1934), 183–184.

Although two of the soldiers presented in this book, Thomas Watson and William Burke, turned their lives to religion, both of their conversions occurred after leaving the army. The same was true of Roger Lamb, although Lamb was convinced that military discipline was a good avenue for "heedless, headstrong, and forward young men, too far gone in wickedness" to gradually become "not only moral, but truly pious." Orderly book, General Charles Grey's company, 26th Regiment of Foot. Special Collections / University Archives, Archibald S. Alexander Library, Rutgers, The State University of New Jersey; Roger Lamb, *Memoirs of His Own Life* (Dublin: privately printed, 1811), 69–70.

93. Necessary house, an outhouse or latrine.

94. Scantlings, narrow timbers placed laterally to hold adjacent stockade pickets together.

95. The Volunteers of Ireland commanded by Francis, Lord Rawdon.

96. Lieutenant John Anson Nutt; see Chapter 5.

97. Usquebaugh, a Gaelic term for whiskey.

98. Worsted, a woolen fabric woven from tightly spun yarn.

99. Long bullets, a game that involved throwing or rolling cannon balls to achieve the longest distance.

100. Shaw's desertion date is given as 24 August 1782. This is the date on which he was administratively written off, and has no relationship to actual events. It is very common for muster rolls to have arbitrary dates for the desertion or death of prisoners of war when their actual status was not known with certainty. Muster rolls, 33rd Regiment of Foot, WO 12/4803, TNA.

101. The study of men who deserted from one army and joined the other—some several times—is a recent one from which very little has yet been published. Of fifty escaped British prisoners of war who made claims for missed pay and clothing in New York in 1783, thirteen admitted serving for some time in the American army and others may have done so but not mentioned it in their claims. Board of Enquiry held at New York, British Headquarters Papers, PRO 30/55/6884, TNA.

102. Apparently Shaw did not know that his own enlistment, by royal proclamation in 1775, was only until the end of the war. After the war was ended by treaty in 1783 the British army was reduced from a wartime establishment to peace time strength; men who had enlisted after the war began were given the option of being discharged either in America or after returning to Great Britain. For the proclamation, see *London Gazette,* 16 December 1775; for orders describing the disposition of men at the close of the war in 1783, see General Orders, 17 August 1783; Sir Guy Carleton orderly book, Frederick Mackenzie Papers, Vol. F, WLC, 186–195.

103. An annotated edition was published as Oressa M. Teagarden, ed., *John Robert Shaw: An Autobiography of Thirty Years, 1777–1807* (Athens: Ohio University Press, 1992).

Chapter 2: Volunteering for American Service

1. Trial of John Riely and James Barry, 46th Regiment of Foot, WO 71/82, TNA, 388–402. Barry was found guilty and sentenced to receive one thousand lashes. He continued to serve in the grenadier company of the 46th Regiment until he died on 23 April 1778. Muster rolls, 46th Regiment of Foot, WO 12/5786, TNA.
2. Muster rolls, 2nd Regiment of Horse, WO 12/293, TNA.
3. The meaning is obvious from the usage in orders and other documents pertaining to drafts; the definition is the thirteenth sense of the word "Draught" as given in Samuel Johnson, *A Dictionary of the English Language* (London: W. Strahan, 1755).
4. See, for example, the drafting orders for the 18th and 65th Regiments; orders for other regiments are similar. Stevens, ed., *General Sir William Howe's Orderly Book*, 159, 165.
5. When the first reinforcement was sent to America in April 1775, no drafts were transferred into the three infantry regiments sent from Ireland (the 35th, 49th, and 63rd), but drafts were sent to strengthen the regiments already on service in Boston; for example, the 10th Regiment received nineteen drafts, and the 43rd Regiment received twenty. Muster rolls, 10th Regiment of Foot, WO 12/2750; and 43rd Regiment of Foot, WO 12/5561/1, TNA. The next four regiments that embarked the following month (the 22nd, 40th, 44th, and 45th) did receive drafts, including nineteen into the 22nd Regiment and sixteen into the 44th.
6. Regiments that were embarked at the end of 1775 for the abortive expedition against Charleston, South Carolina, received still larger numbers of drafts, the 54th receiving twenty-nine and the 57th receiving fifty-five, for example. Muster rolls, 54th Regiment of Foot, WO 12/6398/1; and 57th Regiment of Foot, WO 12/6633, TNA. When the 9th Regiment was preparing to embark for Canada a few months into 1776, they received eighty drafts, all from the 32nd Regiment. Orderly book, 32nd Regiment of Foot, MS 3750, National Library of Ireland.
7. Stevens, *General Sir William Howe's Orderly Book,* 132.
8. Muster rolls, 36th Regiment of Foot, WO 12/5025/1, TNA.
9. WO 34/144, f. 233, TNA.
10. Curtis, *The Organization of the British Army in the American Revolution*, 77.
11. Muster rolls, 52nd Regiment of Foot, WO 12/6240, TNA.
12. A British newspaper described the return of the 18th Regiment of Foot from America in March 1776 thus: "A few days ago the shattered remains of the 18th Regiment of Foot which was engaged in the action at Bunker's Hill and reduced to only twenty-five men, arrived at Maidstone." This gives the impression that the regiment was depleted as a result of rigorous service and battle, but in fact the able-bodied men in the regiment were drafted before it returned to Britain. The 18th had been in America since 1765; only one company—one tenth of the regiment—participated in the Battle of Bunker Hill. R. Frothingham, *History of the Siege of Boston*

and Bunker Hill (Boston: Little, Brown, 1903) 197. Frothingham does not identify the newspaper that carried this account.
13. See, for example, Curtis, *The Organization of the British Army in the American Revolution,* 77–80.
14. Cuthbertson, *A System for the Compleat Interior Management and Œconomy of a Battalion of Infantry,* 66–67.
15. Francis Grose, *Military Antiquities Respecting a History of the English Army from the Conquest to the Present Time* (London: S. Hooper, 1786), 186.
16. Of 1,005 men who served in America with the 22nd Regiment for some time between 1775 and 1783, at least 349 served in other regiments at some point in their careers; at least 54 served in at least two other regiments. In many cases it is difficult to determine a man's complete army career because service was not always continuous, and sometimes when men were drafted the muster rolls do not specify the regiment that they went into, making it impossible to trace subsequent service. Muster rolls, 22nd Regiment of Foot, WO 12/3871–3873, and muster rolls from other regiments in various WO 12 volumes, TNA; soldiers' discharges, WO 97, WO 119, and WO 121, TNA.
17. Grose, *Military Antiquities,* 186.
18. Orderly book, 32nd Regiment of Foot. MS3750, National Library of Ireland. Entry for 29 February 1776.
19. Between November 1774 and March 1775, John Pierce of the 3rd Regiment of Foot was tried and convicted three times by regimental courts-martial, and received a total of seven hundred lashes within that period. In May 1775 he was drafted into the 22nd Regiment of Foot and went with that corps to Boston; from which place he deserted in August 1775. He had been in the 3rd Regiment for eleven years in 1774, but no regimental court records survive before August 1774 so the total number of times he was tried and punished is not known. Return of Courts Martial held in Ireland, 3rd Regiment of Foot, 1 August 1774–10 January 1778, HL/PO/JO/10/7/544, Parliamentary Archives, Houses of Parliament, London; Muster rolls, 3rd Regiment of Foot and 22nd Regiment of Foot, WO 12/2104 and WO 12/3872, TNA.
20. For example, the 54th Regiment of Foot received 129 drafts when it prepared for embarkation for America in December 1775 and early January 1776. Three deserted from Rhode Island in 1777 and 1778, and two from New York in 1783. Two others were captured with the regiment's light infantry company and failed to return after being released at the end of the war. Muster rolls, 54th Regiment of Foot, WO 12/6398/2, WO 12/6399, TNA. The drafts on some of the company muster rolls are not denoted as such, but are evident by comparing the dates of their entry into the regiment with the dates given for drafts on other company rolls; for accounting purposes all drafts from one regiment were added to their new regiment on the same day, and it was typical to distribute drafts (and recruits) more or less equally among companies. Further confirmation is obtained by reviewing the muster rolls of the regiments that contributed the drafts, in this case the 3rd, 53rd, 66th, and 67th Regiments.

21. Col. Gavin Cochrane, 69th Regiment of Foot to the Secretary at War, 30 April 1776. WO 1/991, TNA, 33. The secretary's response leaves doubt about the quality of the drafts from the 69th, but nonetheless reinforces the point about volunteers being preferred: "By all accounts, I understand that your Drafts were not very fit for any Corps, as to their Morals. They are provided for, & I hope that you have not so many Sad Dogs left in the 69th. By their Accts they were Drafts, not Volunteers. This was not quite consistent with the Orders." Edward Harvey to Col. Cochrane, 9 May 1776, WO 3/6, TNA, 34.
22. Muster rolls for the 1st through 4th Regiments of Horse and the 1st through 18th Regiments of Dragoons, WO 12, TNA. 134 drafts have been identified on these rolls; missing rolls for some regiments leave the possibility that there were others. In addition, drafts were taken to complete the 16th and 17th Light Dragoons when they were ordered to America; those drafts have not been considered here.
23. While infantry regiments were divided into companies, cavalry regiments were divided into troops. The terms "company" and "troop" in this context are functionally equivalent.
24. Edward Harvey to Lt.-Colonel Smith, 7 September 1775. WO 3/5, 41.
25. John Matson, *Indian Warfare: or, the Extraordinary Adventures of John Matson the Kidnapped Youth, late of Kingsland Road, London; formerly of Bridlington Quay, in the County of York; Architect and Builder. Written by Himself* (London: Effingham Wilson, 1842), 10–86.
26. Muster rolls, 12th Light Dragoons, WO 12/1037, TNA.
27. The muster rolls for the 12th Light Dragoons show Crawford as having been drafted on 12 March 1776. WO 12/1037, TNA. The rolls for the 20th Regiment do not give a date for him joining the regiment, but he first appears on the rolls dated April 1776. WO 12/3676, TNA.
28. G. D. Scull, ed., *Memoir and Letters of Captain W. Glanville Evelyn, of the 4th Regiment, ("King's Own,") from North America, 1774–1776* (Oxford: Parker & Co., 1879), 70.
29. Richard Sampson's book *Escape in America: The British Convention Prisoners 1777–1783* (Chippenham, England: Picton Publishing, 1995) identifies some three hundred escapees from Burgoyne's captured army that rejoined other British regiments. The author relied on depositions and other sources that identify only a portion of these men; many more are revealed by examining muster rolls; for example, the muster rolls of the 22nd Regiment of Foot supplemented by other sources make it possible to identify at least thirty-three escapees from the Convention Army who joined the 22nd, only twelve of whom are listed in *Escape in America.* The muster rolls also reveal six escapees from regiments not in the Convention Army who joined the 22nd. It is impossible to get an exact count because escaped prisoners are not always annotated as having come from other regiments; in a few cases escapees who joined the 22nd are annotated simply as having "enlisted" rather than as being from another regiment. An example is John Overon, who had been in the 34th Regiment (but not the

companies in Burgoyne's army); after several years as a prisoner of war, he escaped and joined the 22nd Regiment but is annotated as having enlisted rather than having joined from the 34th. A copy of his discharge survives, verifying his service in both regiments. Muster rolls, 22nd Regiment of Foot, WO 12/3872, and 34th Regiment, WO 12/4866/2, TNA; discharge of John Overon, WO 97/423/141, TNA. The rolls of the 33rd Regiment of Foot make it impossible to directly identify escapees because all men who joined the regiment during the war, including returned deserters and prisoners of war from the 33rd itself, are annotated as "enlisted." Muster rolls, 33rd Regiment of Foot, WO 12/4803, TNA.

30. Lieutenant Colonel John Lind (or Lynd) commanded the regiment in America. Muster rolls, 20th Regiment of Foot, WO 12/3676, TNA.

31. Crawford's memory was clouded by old age. The assault on Quebec led by Generals Arnold and Montgomery had occurred months before the arrival of the 20th Regiment. Crawford did participate in the 1776 campaign led by General Carleton, which stopped short of taking Crown Point and Fort Ticonderoga.

32. The British army in America laid aside the formal linear warfare techniques practiced for European battles and adopted more rapid, fluid movements by lightly armed troops in open formations. The definitive study of the tactical discipline of the British army in America is Matthew H. Spring, *With Zeal and Bayonets Only: The British Army on Campaign in North America, 1775–1783* (Norman: University of Oklahoma Press, 2008).

33. This was the 1777 campaign led by Lieutenant General John Burgoyne.

34. Accounts vary as to the number of times the cannon changed hands, but Crawford's suggestion of twenty-four times is far greater than any other. While the opening shots of the battle were fired at around 12:30 P.M and the fighting ceased at darkness, around 7 P.M., the pitched portion of the battle began at around 3:30 P.M. There is no record of the commander of Crawford's company, Captain Lieutenant Paul Banks, having been wounded during the battle. The number of casualties in Crawford's company cannot be confirmed, but the entire regiment suffered 115 killed, wounded, and captured, and there is no reason to believe that half of that number was incurred by a single company. Brendan Morrissey, *Saratoga, 1777* (Oxford: Osprey Publishing, 2000), 59–61.

35. There is no record of Crawford having attained any rank above private, but muster rolls for the regiment are incomplete. The last surviving roll before the surrender at Saratoga is dated 1 March 1777, and pertains to the period 25 June–24 December 1776. Because the regiment was in captivity, there is a lacuna in the musters until 1782, when the regiment was recruiting in Great Britain. Muster rolls for the 20th Regiment of Foot, WO 12/3676.

36. Here Crawford mixes the 1776 campaign commanded by Carleton with the 1777 campaign commanded by Burgoyne. Carleton remained in Canada as commander in chief of the British forces in that province, a

position superior to Burgoyne's; that Carleton was not charged with leading the expedition south had more to do with his perceived performance in the 1776 campaign than with scheming by Burgoyne. Michael Glover, *General Burgoyne in Canada and America* (London: Gordon Cremonesi, 1976), 105–106, 123–124.

37. Crawford clearly has some bitterness about Burgoyne; opinions of his skill are varied but generally not as harsh as Crawford's. Glover, *General Burgoyne in Canada and America.*

38. That is, to break out of encirclement.

39. Crawford's recollection is dubious; there was a great deal of animosity between the British prisoners and the local inhabitants. Sampson, *Escape in America,* 56–81.

40. The Convention Army was cantoned in Charlottesville, Albemarle County, Virginia. The march there from Rutland took from November 1778 until January 1779. Sampson, *Escape in America,* 111–116.

41. Although large numbers of prisoners escaped from Charlottesville, there is no record of the singular breakout that Crawford describes. Sampson, *Escape in America,* 130–133.

42. This officer has not been positively identified.

43. Crawford quotes Shakespeare's *King Lear.*

44. Crawford quotes Shakespeare's *Othello.*

45. This is also from Shakespeare's *Othello,* albeit inexact.

46. This officer has not been positively identified.

47. *A Narrative of the Life and Character of William Crawford, of Fallowfield Township, Washington County, Who Was Executed at Washington, Pa., on Friday, the 21st February, 1823, for the Murder of His Son, Henry Crawford, on Tuesday, the 30th July, 1822; Related by Himself and Published by His Request* (Washington, PA: Reporter Office, 1823).

CHAPTER 3: WANDERLUST AND ROVING

1. For a detailed study of prisoners of war who escaped and made their way back into British lines, see Sampson, *Escape in America.*

2. Mark F. Odintz, "The British Officer Corps 1754–1783," Ph.D. diss., University of Michigan, 1988, 412–414. Sylvia R. Frey, *The British Soldier in America* (Austin: University of Texas Press, 1981), 90.

3. *The Useful Christian; a Memoir of Thomas Cranfield, for About Fifty Years a Devoted Sunday-School Teacher* (Philadelphia: American Sunday-School Union, n.d.), 8–10.

4. Griffith, "Memoirs and Spiritual Experience of the late Mr. W. Griffith, Senior," 119–120.

5. Punishment Book of the 44th Regiment of Foot. MG23, K6(2), Public Archives of Canada, Ottawa. This material is analyzed in G. A. Steppler, "British Military Law, Discipline, and the Conduct of Regimental Courts Martial in the Later Eighteenth Century," *English Historical Review* 102 (October 1987), 859–886. That study presents statistics pertaining to the crimes and punishments but does not consider the total number of men in

the regiment or the substantial number of repeat offenders. In 398 trials only 213 individuals were tried; 88 men were tried multiple times, including 37 tried twice, 28 three times, 10 four times, 6 five times, 3 six times, 3 seven times and 1 eight times. The number of men who served in the 44th during the years covered by the punishment book is estimated from the muster rolls, but several gaps make an accurate count impossible; a low estimate of 700 compared to 213 who were tried yields 30 percent brought to trial and 19 percent lashed. It is more likely that 800 or more men served in the regiment during these years, bringing the percentage tried into the same range as the other regiments. Muster rolls, 44th Regiment of Foot, WO 12/5637 and /5638, TNA.

6. Gaps in the muster rolls for each of the regiments make a precise count of the men who served during the years in question impossible. The percentages given here are estimates based on the assumption that attrition remained similar during the months for which we have no muster rolls. Return of Courts Martial held in Ireland, 1 August 1774–10 January 1778, HL/PO/JO/10/7/544, Parliamentary Archives, Houses of Parliament, London. Muster rolls, 3rd Regiment of Foot, WO 12/2105; 36th Regiment of Foot, WO 12/5025/1; 67th Regiment of Foot, WO 12/7537; 68th Regiment of Foot, WO 12/7623, TNA.

7. The exact number of men serving in the detachment over the entire time period covered by the punishment book cannot be determined due to insufficient surviving information on the 65th Regiment. A return for the detachment on one day shows 71 men of the 65th and 117 of the 18th, while the muster rolls of the 18th show 147 men serving during the entire period. The figure of 228 for the detachment is the sum of 71 known for the 65th and 147 for the 18th. Stephen Baule and Don Hagist, "The Regimental Punishment Book of the Boston Detachments of the Royal Irish Regiment and 65th Regiment, 1774–75," *Journal of Army Historical Research* 88 (2010), 5–18.

8. Using estimates to compensate for gaps in the muster rolls, the proportion of men who were punished in the 68th Regiment was between 18 and 23 percent, while that in the 3rd Regiment was between 23 and 30 percent; the 36th and 67th Regiments were 20 to 25 percent. Return of Courts Martial held in Ireland, 1 August 1774–10 January 1778, HL/PO/JO/10/7/544, Parliamentary Archives, Houses of Parliament, London.

9. A postilion rode one of the horses that was drawing a carriage, and assisted the driver in any way necessary. Nathan Bailey, *An Universal Etymological English Dictionary*, 20th ed. (London: R. Ware, 1765). For a good discussion of a youth learning to drive by working as a postilion, see John Macdonald, *Memoirs of an Eighteenth-Century Footman* (New York: Harper & Row, 1927), 17.

10. Duckett's enlistment date is not known, but appears to have been around August 1768.

11. The government did not regulate the minimum age for recruits, but some regiments did. For example, the 17th Regiment of Foot in 1767 gave

directions not to recruit "any man upwards of twenty-five or under fifteen years of age." Colonel Sir Bruce Seton, "Infantry Recruiting Instructions in England in 1767," *Journal of Army Historical Research* 4, no. 16 (April–June 1925), 84. Some specified a maximum age only, as in the 1775 order for the 71st Regiment to recruit no man "above 30 years of age." Bayard-Campbell-Pearsall Collection, Campbell Accounts and Papers, 1773–1781, Box 17, folder 2, New York Public Library. Height and general fitness for service were the overriding considerations rather than age per se; the above orders specified "none under five feet seven and a half high, except growing lads ... at five feet five inches" and "no man under 5 Feet four Inches without Shoes," respectively. A popular military text advised that "Young, active Men, from seventeen to twenty-five years of age, make the most tractable Soldiers." Cuthbertson, *A System for the Compleat Interior Management and Œconomy af a Battalion of Infantry*, 56.

12. Cuthbertson, *A System for the Compleat Interior Management and Œconomy af a Battalion of Infantry*, 56.

13. Oliver Morton Dickerson, ed., *Boston Under Military Rule (1768–1769): As Revealed in a Journal of the Times* (Boston: Chapman and Grimes, 1936), 112.

14. Gaps in the muster rolls of the 65th Regiment of Foot make it impossible to confirm this. Rolls from April 1769 and September 1770 confirm his presence on Castle Island and at Halifax, but there are no subsequent rolls until early 1775. Muster rolls, 65th Regiment of Foot, WO 12/7377, TNA.

15. Because desertion was a crime for which capital punishment could be sentenced, it required trial by a general court, that is, a court composed of officers of several regiments, a regulation that helped to prevent bias among members of the court. Variations of the crime were tried by regimental courts—those composed only of officers from within the soldier's own regiment—which could not impose capital punishment for the crime. For example, in the 67th Regiment of Foot between 1 August 1774 and 20 December 1777, one man was tried by a general court for desertion while two others were tried by regimental courts for attempting to desert. Return of Courts Martial held in Ireland, 67th Regiment of Foot, 1 August 1774—10 January 1778, HL/PO/JO/10/7/544, Parliamentary Archives, Houses of Parliament, London.

16. There is a listing of regimental courts for a detachment of the 65th Regiment in Boston between October 1774 and May 1775, but this post-dates Duckett's service. Stephen Baule and Don Hagist, "The Regimental Punishment Book of the Boston Detachments of the Royal Irish Regiment and 65th Regiment, 1774–75."

17. General Orders, America, WO 36/1, TNA, 17–18.

18. Among seven regiments in Boston during the period of the pardon, 9 July–10 August 1774, the 5th Regiment had 4 men desert; the 23rd 1; the 38th 5; the 43rd 4; the 47th 2; and the 64th 4; no men deserted from the 4th Regiment. Only one man returned from desertion during the pardon, Jonathan Richardson of the 43rd who had deserted on 18 June. Muster

rolls, 4th Regiment of Foot, WO 12/2194; 5th Regiment of Foot, WO 12/2289; 23rd Regiment of Foot, WO 12/3960; 38th Regiment of Foot, WO 12/5171/1; 43rd Regiment of Foot, WO 12/5561/1; 47th Regiment of Foot, WO 12/5871; 64th Regiment of Foot, WO 12/7313, TNA.

19. Winthrop Sargent, ed., "Letters of John Andrews, Esq. of Boston," *Proceedings of the Massachusetts Historical Society* (July 1865), 345. The bracketed text appears in the published version.

20. Trials of John Ragg, 5th Regiment, Luke Murphy, 38th Regiment, and William Pearson, 23rd Regiment, WO 71/79. The verdicts were made public in general orders on 11 August. General Orders, America, WO 36/1, TNA, entry for 11 August 1774.

21. The figures for desertion given above include only those men who deserted and did not return within the same muster period. The desertions of three men mentioned in the previous note are not recorded on the muster rolls because they deserted and returned within a muster period, and there may have been others.

22. "Dying Speeches & Bloody Murders: Crime Broadsides at the Harvard Law Digital Collection," accessed July 2011, http://broadsides.law.harvard.edu/home.php.

23. One of the broadsides with Duckett's speech is annotated as having been "Printed and Sold at the Printing House in School Street," while the other reads "Sold at the Printing-Office in School-Street, Price Six Coppers." No newspaper advertisements for it have been found.

24. One copy is in the American Antiquarian Society, Worcester, MA, cataloged as BDSDS 1774. Another is in the Massachusetts Historical Society, Boston, MA, catalogued as Broadsides 1774 Sept 9. The two copies differ slightly in format even though they were published by the same printer. Each copy has some words obscured by damage; the transcription presented here draws from both in order to discern the complete text.

25. That is, "took a boat." There are a number of grammatical and spelling errors in the original broadside.

26. Regimentals, that is, his British army uniform.

27. Packet, a small vessel that carried mail, passengers, and cargo on a regularly scheduled route.

28. Parry, a typographical error for "party."

29. The 60th Regiment of Foot, called the Royal Americans, was a regular regiment in the British army but was composed chiefly of foreign-born soldiers.

30. Shallop, a vessel designed for sailing in shallow waters.

31. Goal, an archaic spelling of jail.

32. Duckett appears to mean that it was obvious he had been living in the woods because of stains on his clothes, as opposed to a deliberate attempt to disguise himself.

33. Guinea, a gold coin worth 21 shillings.

34. Sea cowing, fishing for sea cows.

35. Bryan Island in the Gulf of St. Lawrence.

36. Officers of lesser rank, that is, ensigns, occasionally sat on courts in America when an insufficient number of other officers was available. Court Martial Proceedings, WO 71/80–98, TNA.
37. Matross, a gunner in the artillery.
38. Train, the train of artillery or Royal Artillery.
39. This is probably not the John Andrews who recorded Duckett's capture and execution, since that writer makes no mention of testifying at the trial.
40. The trial was actually in September; the month was written incorrectly in the trial record.
41. General Orders, America. WO 36/1, TNA, 38. The orders read: "Valentine Duckett, Private soldier in his Majesty's 65th Regiment, tried by the General Courtmartial of which Major Roger Spendlove of His Majesty's 43rd Regiment was president, for the crime of desertion, was found Guilty and sentenced by the said Court to suffer death. The Commander in Chief approves of the sentence and orders the same to be first in execution to morrow morning at 6 o'Clock, in the rear of the camp, by shooting said Duckett to death in the presence of the picquets of the line. The Field Officer of the day will pitch on a proper spot on the strand for that purpose, and order two men to be selected from each picquet for the execution."
42. "Letters of John Andrews," 357.
43. For example, fourteen men from the 65th Regiment were drafted into the 22nd Regiment which served in America for the remainder of the war. Of these, two were killed in battle, three died from other (unknown) causes), two deserted (one while a prisoner of war), and seven were discharged and received pensions. One of these seven was discharged during the war due to a wound, while the others were discharged some time after the war ended. Muster rolls of the 22nd Regiment of Foot, WO 12/3872; out-pension ledgers, WO 120; discharges, WO 121, all TNA.

CHAPTER 4: LITERACY AND EDUCATION

1. Documents have been found bearing signatures or marks by 145 men of the 22nd Regiment of Foot who served in America. Of these, 8 are ambiguous in that the men wrote their names on one document but made a mark on another, and one man wrote his initials. Of the remaining 136, 76 signed their names while 60 made marks. Most of the documents are discharges in WO 97, WO 119, and WO 121, TNA; other documents include Masonic warrants, personal letters, and a prize money receipt.
2. In 1767, officers of the 17th Regiment of Foot were given instructions that "No Miners or Welchmen to be inlisted." Colonel Sir Bruce Seton, "Infantry Recruiting Instructions in England in 1767," 84. A year later, a popular military author advised: "Sailors and colliers never make good Soldiers. Being accustomed to a more debauched and drunken way of life, than what a private Centinel's Pay can possibly admit of; and of course soon become disgusted with the Service, from which they speedily desert,

and are seldom again recovered, from the opportunities that the nature of their profession affords them, to remain concealed, in spite of the most diligent and active search." A collier, in this context, was a coal miner. Cuthbertson, *A System for the Compleat Interior Management and Œconomy of a Battalion,* 56.

3. Trades have been identified for 322 of the men who served in the 22nd Regiment in America between 1775 and 1783. Of 179 who had a trade other than "labourer," 4 were miners. Trades are identified primarily from soldier's discharges, WO 97, WO 119, and WO 121, TNA, supplemented by a wide variety of other sources.

4. References to the regiment from the 1770s and 1780s use both the spelling "Welsh" and "Welch," with "Welsh" being somewhat more common. In 1920 the regiment officially adopted the spelling "Welch" in order to have uniform spelling.

5. When inspected in 1772 the 23rd consisted of 357 English, 26 Irish, 43 Scottish, and 2 "Foreign" soldiers (Welsh are not distinguished from English in the annual inspection returns). Inspection return, 23rd Regiment of Foot, 1772, WO 27/24, TNA. A sampling of 69 Chelsea out-pensioners who served in America with this regiment includes 45 English, 2 Welsh, 10 Scottish, 10 Irish, and 2 Germans. Chelsea Hospital out-pension lists, WO 120, TNA.

6. Allen French, ed., *A British Fusilier in Revolutionary Boston* (Cambridge, MA: Harvard University Press, 1926), 3–23.

7. For example, in early 1776, three companies of the 42nd and 71st Regiments were captured at sea or when the ships that they were on sailed into Boston harbor unaware that the British army had evacuated the city. William James Morgan, ed., *Naval Documents of the American Revolution* Vol. 5 (Washington, DC: Government Printing Office, 1970), 619–620. In early 1779 the *Mermaid* transport, carrying two companies of the 82nd Regiment, ran aground off the coast of New Jersey. One officer, 112 soldiers, 13 women, and 7 children of the regiment perished, while 5 officers and 25 soldiers were saved. *Edinburgh Advertiser,* 18 June 1779. One popular source, in discussing the sickness that could befall soldiers during the long passage from Great Britain to America, cites a few examples without mentioning the majority of cases where soldiers arrived in acceptable health. Edward E. Curtis, *The Organization of the British Army in the American Revolution* (New Haven: Yale University Press, 1926), 125–126.

8. Rather than a misspelling of "Highlanders," "Scotch Hollanders" refers to a brigade of Scottish regiments that were part of the Dutch army. *Papers Illustrating the History of the Scots Brigade in the Service of the United Netherlands, 1572–1782* (Edinburgh: Scottish History Society, 1901).

9. Bennett Cuthbertson, *A System for the Compleat Interior Management and Œconomy of a Battalion*, 9.

10. Thomas Simes, *The Regulator* (London, 1780) 2. The same author restated this in *A Military Guide for Young Officers* (London, 1776), 164.

11. Orderly book, 32nd Regiment of Foot, MS 3750 (Belfast: National Library of Ireland) entries for 21 March, 13 and 14 May 1776.

12. Regulations for doing Duty, 37th Regiment of Foot, Eyre Coot Papers V27/4, WLC, undated entry circa 1774.
13. Orderly book, 47th Regiment of Foot, Eyre Coote papers V22/15, WLC, entry for 19 September 1782.
14. Don N. Hagist, ed., *A British Soldier's Story*, 9.
15. "School with Joseph Rhodes Eq.," Item 999, George Chalmers collection, Peter Force manuscripts (Washington, DC: Library of Congress).
16. Thomas Watson, *Some Account of the Life, Convincement, and Religious Experience of Thomas Watson, Late of Bolton, Massachusetts* (New York: Daniel Cooledge, 1836).
17. Trial of Thomas Watson, WO 71/83, TNA, 30–41. The court that tried Watson sat from 30 September through 4 October and heard six cases involving eight soldiers.
18. That is, with a bayonet belt and scabbard, cartridge pouch, or other accessories to indicate that he was a soldier.
19. Firelock, the common term for the military musket.
20. Paulus Hook, New Jersey, adjacent to Manhattan and Staten Island.
21. That is, cannons.
22. Lt. Col. Charles Mawhood Orderly Book, 11 October–28 December 1776, New-York Historical Society.
23. That is, told a man that it was time for him to go on duty.
24. For example, Alexander Gray joined the 22nd Regiment in March 1770. In November 1779, the officer commanding the regiment in America wrote to the adjutant-general of the army in America requesting permission to discharge Gray because "he was inlisted for six years only at the expiration of which period he was to be discharged." It is not stated why Gray didn't request his discharge sooner. Archibald Erskine to John André, 20 November 1779. Sir Henry Clinton Papers, WLC.

Chapter 5: Free Time for Industry and Mischief

1. Comparing discharges to muster rolls for men in the 22nd Regiment of Foot allows the age at the time of enlistment of 211 men to be determined. Of these, 100 enlisted between the ages of 20 and 23, 59 enlisted in their teen years, and 55 enlisted between the ages of 24 and 29. Eight enlisted over the age of 30, including 3 over the age of 35. Most of these enlistments occurred during peace time, with only 24 occurring during the years of the American war. Royal Hospital Chelsea Soldier Service Documents, WO 97; Royal Hospital Chelsea Out-Pension Admission Books, WO 116; Royal Hospital Kilmainham Pensioners' Discharge Documents, WO 119; Royal Hospital Chelsea Discharge Documents of Pensioners, WO 121; Muster rolls, 22nd Regiment of Foot, WO 12/3871 through /3873, all TNA. Of 67 men recruited for the 46th Regiment of Foot between 23 December 1775 and 9 February 1776, 11 were between the ages of 16 and 19, 18 were between 20 and 23, 20 between 24 and 26, 14 between 27 and 30, and 5 between 30 and 35. Four other men have no age listed. List of Recruits Rais'd for the 46th Regiment of Foot, WO 1/992, TNA.

2. Sylvia R. Frey, *The British Soldier in America*, 10–15.
3. For example, bakers from fourteen regiments were called to work at the commissary in January 1776; carpenters "most used to fitting up transports" were called to the deputy quartermaster general in April 1776. Stevens, ed., *General Sir William Howe's Orderly Book*, 197, 252.
4. Don N. Hagist, ed., *General Orders, Rhode Island* (Bowie, MD: Heritage Books, 2001), 38, 41.
5. *Thomas Cranfield, The Useful Christian*. The memoir refers to Cranfield in the third person, but in its detail seems to have been written or narrated by him. The information in these two paragraphs comes from pages 5 through 29 of the memoir.
6. *Thomas Cranfield, The Useful Christian*, 17, 24.
7. See, for example, John Pringle, *Observations on the Diseases of the Army* (London: 1775), 87–88.
8. Although there was no regulated limit on the number of sutlers that a regiment could license, one popular author recommended no more than five. Thomas Simes, *The Regulator*, 156. For an interesting discussion of the challenges faced by commanders in regulating the liquor trade, see Don N. Hagist, "The Women of the British Army During the American Revolution," 29–85.
9. Bennett Cuthbertson, *A System for the Compleat Interior Management and Œconomy of a Battalion*, 20–24.
10. Paul E. Kopperman, "'The Cheapest Pay': Alcohol Abuse in the Eighteenth-Century British Army," *Journal of Military History* 60:3 (July 1996), 445–470.
11. Trial of Luke Murphy, 38th Regiment, WO 71/79, TNA, 367–374. Murphy was convicted and sentenced to receive 100 lashes; he deserted on 4 January 1775. Malcolm Campbell died on 20 September 1775 of unknown causes. Muster rolls, 38th Regiment of Foot, WO 12/5171/2, TNA.
12. British regimental coats had false pocket flaps on the outside which reinforced voluminous pockets cut into the inside. "His Majesty's Warrant for the Regulation of the Colours, Clothing, etc. of the Marching Regiments of Foot. Miscellany Book: Clothing Correspondence. 19 December 1768." WO 30/13B, TNA, as quoted in Hew Strachan, *British Military Uniforms 1768–1796: The Dress of the British Army from Official Sources* (London: Arms and Armor Press, 1975), 174. Trial of Benjamin Doran and William Lamb, 23rd Regiment, and John Cox and John Woods, 63rd Regiment, WO 71/81, TNA, 405–430.
13. Drunkenness figured in about two-thirds of the regimental courts-martial in a detachment of the 18th and 65th Regiments in Boston in late 1774 and early 1775. Stephen Baule and Don N. Hagist, "The Regimental Punishment Book of the Boston Detachments of the Royal Irish Regiment and 65th Regiment, 1774–75," *Journal of Army Historical Research* 88 (2010), 5–18. Regimental courts in four regiments in Ireland between August 1774 and January 1778 charged men with alcohol-related crimes (usually drunkenness, but occasionally related crimes like steal-

ing liquor) between a quarter and a third of the time; in the 3rd Regiment of Foot, there were 91 alcohol-related trials out of 294 altogether; in the 36th, 70 out of 219; in the 67th, 57 out of 200; and in the 68th, 63 out of 270. The surviving list of trials for these regiments includes only the charges, not the actual proceedings; it is possible that alcohol was a factor in a host of other charges such as "rioting in town," "being insolent," and "being out of barracks all night." Return of Courts Martial held in Ireland, 1 August 1774–10 January 1778, HL/PO/JO/10/7/544, Parliamentary Archives, Houses of Parliament, London. Proceedings of general courts-martial held in America show that alcohol was often a factor in cases of desertion, theft, mutiny, and other disorderly behavior among both soldiers and officers. Court Martial Proceedings and Board of General Officers' Minutes, WO 71/80–97, TNA.

14. Paul E. Kopperman, "'The Cheapest Pay.'"

15. Bennett Cuthbertson, *A System for the Compleat Interior Management and Œconomy of a Battalion,* 152–153.

16. Hiller B. Zobel, *The Boston Massacre* (New York: W. W. Norton, 1970), 182.

17. Trial of Evan Evans, 52nd Regiment of Foot, WO 71/84, TNA, 48–51; Muster rolls, 52nd Regiment of Foot, WO 12/6240, TNA.

18. Don N. Hagist, "Soldier's Games," *The Brigade Dispatch* 31:4 (Winter 2001), 13–15.

19. Trial of Bartholomew Gilmore, 22nd Regiment of Foot, WO 71/90, TNA, 26–34. Gilmore had assaulted Richard Hallum of the same regiment while the latter was on his way to go fishing in Rhode Island.

20. Trial of Murtoch Laughlan, Charles Neal, and Robert Pearce, 22nd Regiment of Foot, WO 71/85, TNA, 159–161. They had stolen and butchered several sheep, some of which they kept for themselves and some of which they gave to a soldier's wife in payment for liquor.

21. Trial of John Sinclair, 76th Regiment of Foot, WO 71/91, TNA, 22–27. Other examples appear in Chapter 9.

22. Joseph Lee Boyle, ed., *From Redcoat to Rebel,* 4.

23. Robert M. S. Pasley, ed., *Private Sea Journals, 1778–1782, kept by Admiral Sir Thomas Pasley* (London: J. M. Dent and Sons, 1931), 204.

24. Muster rolls, 2nd Regiment of Foot, WO 12/2020, TNA. The surviving rolls begin in 1768.

25. The 2nd Regiment muster rolls for the first half of 1776 are missing. The roll for the last half of 1775 was prepared in England in March 1776, and Young is shown on that roll; the next roll, covering 25 June–24 December 1776, does not include him. Muster rolls, 2nd Regiment Foot, TNA.

26. Eight regiments had departed Ireland on 10 February 1776 accompanied by warships and arrived off the Carolina coast on 3 May. An attempted coordinated attack by the army and navy against Fort Moultrie, protecting the seaward approach to Charleston, SC, failed and the operation was abandoned. Clinton was successful in his second attempt to take the city in 1780.

27. For a detailed discussion of this recruiting effort, see Don N. Hagist, "Forty German Recruits: The Service of the Von Scheither Recruits in the 22nd Regiment of Foot, 1776–1783," *Journal of the Johannes Schwalm Historical Association* 6:1 (1997), 63–66.
28. Don N. Hagist and Eric H. Schnitzer, "German Recruits in Lt. George Anson Nutt's Detachment of the 33rd Regiment of Foot on Burgoyne's Campaign," *Journal of the Johannes Schwalm Historical Association*, 8 (2005), 42–44.
29. Lord George Germaine to General Sir Guy Carleton, 17 February 1776, in Horatio Rogers, ed., *Hadden's Journal and Orderly Books: A Journal Kept in Canada and Upon Burgoyne's Campaign in 1776 and 1777, by Lieut. James M. Hadden, Roy. Art.* (Albany, NY: Joel Munsell's Sons, 1884), lxix.
30. Drafting recruits into other regiments occurred frequently during the war. While it was a matter of practicality when the recruits' intended regiment was in a distant location, it was also done sometimes simply to balance the strength of regiments. Later in the war, a corps of British recruits was maintained in New York composed of recruits for regiments that were captured at Yorktown, but this corps did not see service outside of the New York garrison.
31. Carleton to Barrington, 24 November 1776, WO 1/11, TNA 19–20. Carleton to Barrington, undated [29 November 1776], WO 1/11, TNA 21–22. This shows that the 33rd was at the forefront of the trend to recruit from a particular area, which led to the establishment of county titles for regiments in 1782; also, the quality of the clothing made it too expensive for another regiment to reimburse the 33rd for a transferred recruit.
32. Barrington to Carleton, 25 March 1777, CO transcripts, Q series, v. 13 (Ottawa: Public Archives of Canada), 239.
33. Several sources suggest that the German recruits did not receive military clothing until they arrived with their regiments in America. See, for example, the trial of George Hundredmark, WO 12/84, TNA, 181–186.
34. Horatio Rogers, *Hadden's Journal and Orderly Books*, lx.
35. Horatio Rogers, *Hadden's Journal and Orderly Books*, 67.
36. John Burgoyne. *A State of the Expedition from Canada as Laid Before the House of Commons, by Lieutenant-General Burgoyne, and Verified by Evidence, with a Collection of Authentic Documents, and an Addition of Many Circumstances Which were Prevented from Appearing Before the House by the Prorogation of Parliament* (London, 1780), 97.
37. Charles W. Snell, *A Report on the Strength of the British Army Under Lieutenant General John Burgoyne, July 1 to October 17, 1777 and on the Organization of the British Army on September 19, and October 7, 1777* (Stillwater, NY: Saratoga National Historical Park, 1951), 38.
38. William Digby. *The British Invasion From the North: The Campaigns of Generals Carleton and Burgoyne from Canada, 1776–1777, with the Journal of Lieut. William Digby* (Albany, NY: Joel Munsell's Sons, 1887), 324.
39. Don N. Hagist, *A British Soldier's Story*. "Liste des Recrués Anglois embarqués á Stade pour Spithead en Irlande ce 14me de Mai 1776." WO, Class 43, vol. 405, TNA; Autobiography of John Philip Aulenbach, in D.

Luther Roth, *Acadie and the Acadians,* 3rd ed. (Utica, NY: L. C. Childs, 1891), 360–363.

40. Thomas Cranfield, *The Useful Christian.* John MacDonald, *Autobiographical Journal of John MacDonald: Schoolmaster and Soldier, 1770–1830* (Edinburgh: Norman MacLeod, 1906).

41. *Londonderry Journal*; 19 August 1777. *Manchester Mercury*, 20 February 1776.

42. McGregor was examined by the Chelsea Out-Pension board on 18 December 1778; he does not appear on the muster rolls of the 54th Regiment. Out-pensions Admission Books, WO 116/7; Muster rolls, 54th Regiment of Foot, WO 12/6398, TNA.

43. The British regiment in which Woodward served has not been identified; the information above comes from an advertisement for his desertion from the American army. *Carlisle Weekly Gazette*, 9 September 1795. Walter Graham was standing guard at the headquarters of General Richard Prescott on the night of 10 July 1777 when he, the general, and another officer were captured in a daring American raid. Graham deserted from captivity; one of the American raiders recorded in his pension application that "This same sentinel afterwards taught school in Pownal, Vermont, and claimant sent a member of his family to school to him." This has not been verified from other sources. Pension application of Abel Potter, Rhode Island militiaman, in John C. Dann, ed., *The Revolution Remembered* (Chicago: University of Chicago Press, 1980), 24.

44. Ellis had been on a guard post on a raft in the river by Boston with another soldier; when he fell asleep in the canoe used to get to the raft, the other man rowed them to the American lines. In 1777 he was captured in a house in New Jersey with a number of American militiamen. In spite of his testimony that he had not willingly absconded, he was tried and convicted for desertion. Trial of William Ellis, 10th Regiment of Foot, WO 71/83, TNA, 192–194.

45. For the complete story of this event see Deborah Navas, *Murdered by His Wife: A History with Documentation of the Joshua Spooner Murder and Execution of His Wife, Bathsheba, Who was Hanged in Worchester, Massachusetts, 2 July 1778* (Amherst: University of Massachusetts Press, 1999).

46. *Thomas's Massachusetts Spy Or, American Oracle of Liberty* (Worcester, 9 September 1779).

47. Proceedings from his trial have not been located.

48. An example is Patrick McMullen of the 38th Regiment of Foot. After two desertions from the British army and several from the American army, he was hanged in Philadelphia on 4 September 1778. "He was so hardened and insensible to his unhappy situation that when the executioner put the rope about his neck, he smiled and said it was strong enough to hang any man, and behaved with the same unaccountable indifference to the last moment." Muster rolls, 38th Regiment of Foot, WO 12/5171/1; *Pennsylvania Gazette*, 4 September 1778.

49. Andrew Scott. *Poems, Chiefly in the Scottish Dialect* (Kelso, Scotland: Andrew Leadbetter, 1811), xi.

50. John Hawthorn, *Poems* ("Printed for the author and sold by E. Easton [Salisbury, England], J. Dodsley, and J. Wilkie [London], 1779). *The Critical Review: Or, the Annals of Literature. Volume the Forty-Eighth* (London: A. Hamilton, 1779), 76.

51. The first edition was published in Worcester on the day of the execution, as evidenced by the title. Quite possibly it was composed in the days prior and available for sale at the execution. An edition appeared soon after in New London with the title modified from "this day" to "Thursday last." It has some variations in spelling and punctuation but not in content.

52. That is, drinking with friends; alcohol was often consumed from a shared bowl or pot.

53. The New London edition has several minor differences in wording and spelling; the only significant difference is these six lines, which read: "When it was dark I met the little fair,/ (Great God forgive, and hear my humble pray'r)/ And, O! dear Jane, wilt thou forgive me too,/ For I most cruelly have used you./ I took advantage of the dark'ning hour,/ (For beasts always by night their prey devour)."

54. "The last Speech, Confession and dying words of James Andrew, who was executed in the Grassmarket of Edinburgh, upon Wednesday the 4th day of February 1784 for the horrid crime of Highway Robbery," in R. C. and J. M. Anderson, *Quicksilver: A Hundred Years of Coaching 1750–1850* (Newton Abbot, England: David & Charles, 1973), 174–177.

55. Courts Martial Proceedings and Board of General Officers' Minutes, WO 71/80–98, TNA.

56. Don N. Hagist, *General Orders: Rhode Island* 14.

57. Francis Bickley, ed. *Report on the Manuscripts of the late Reginald Rawdon Hastings* (London: Historical Manuscripts Commission, 1934), 179.

58. William Bell Clark, ed., *Naval Documents of the American Revolution* vol. 5 (Washington, DC: Government Printing Office, 1970), 936.

59. Sir William Howe's Orderly Book, 30 June–4 October 1776, Morristown National Historical Park. A soldier in the 40th Regiment was tried for murdering another soldier who had assaulted his wife, but this case involved men and women of the army rather than inhabitants of Staten Island. Trial of William Norrington, 40th Regiment of Foot, WO 71/82, TNA, 377–388.

60. Regimental court martial records for the 3rd, 36th, 67th, and 68th Regiments, Return of Courts Martial held in Ireland, 1 August 1774–10 January 1778, HL/PO/JO/10/7/544, Parliamentary Archives, Houses of Parliament, London. Punishment Book of the 44th Regiment of Foot. MG23, K6(2), Public Archives of Canada, Ottawa. Steven Baule and Don N. Hagist, "The Regimental Punishment Book."

61. Trial of Corporal Charles McKenny, 5th Regiment of Foot, *Boston Gazette*, 29 August 1774.

62. Walter Hart Blumenthal, *Women Camp Followers of the American Revolution* (New York: Arno Press, 1974).

63. The often-repeated number of six wives per company refers only to the number for which shipping was typically allocated when regiments embarked for America; there was no regulated number of wives allowed in general, although the number allowed to accompany a regiment on campaign was often restricted and the remainder left behind in garrisons. Don N. Hagist, "The Women of the British Army." The remainder of this paragraph is taken from this article.

Chapter 6: Unwilling Volunteers and Criminals

1. Edward R. Curtis, *The Organization of the British Army,* 56.
2. Among the acts of Parliament providing the option of military service are the 1744 Salt Duties Act, 17 Geo. II, c. 5; the 1776 Insolvent Debtors Relief Act, 16 Geo. III, c. 38; and the 1776 Natural-born Children of Aliens Act, 18 Geo. III, c. 52.
3. See the reference below.
4. Stephen R. Conway, "The Recruitment of Criminals into the British Army, 1775–81," *Historical Research* 58 (May 1985), 46–58.
5. Eileen A. Robertson, *The Spanish Town Papers* (New York: Macmillan, 1959) 73–75. Berrepo's name does not appear on muster rolls for the 18th Regiment during this era.
6. "The Voluntary Confession of James Aitken, Commonly Called John the Painter," *Universal Magazine of Knowledge and Pleasure* 60 (March 1777), 148–150.
7. *Sherborne and Yeovil Mercury*, 21 March 1777.
8. Edward R. Curtis, *The Organization of the British Army,* 57–59.
9. Edward R. Curtis, *The Organization of the British Army,* 57.
10. Francis Grose, *Military Antiquities Respecting a History of the English Army, from the Conquest to the Present Time,* vol. 1 (London: S. Hooper, 1786), 100.
11. Edward R. Curtis, *The Organization of the British Army,* 66; Stephen R. Conway, "The Recruitment of Criminals into the British Army," 48.
12. This number is an approximation based on studies of the muster rolls of two regiments, the 22nd and 33rd. Almost exactly 1,000 men served in each regiment during the time the regiment was in America; at any one time each regiment had about 500 men, but the arrival of recruits and losses due to death, desertion, and discharge bring the total who served during the war to 1,005 for the 22nd Regiment and 998 for the 33rd Regiment. Muster rolls, 22nd Regiment of Foot and 33rd Regiment of Foot, WO 12/3872 and WO 12/4803, TNA.
13. Edward R. Curtis, *The Organization of the British Army,* 66; Stephen R. Conway, "The Recruitment of Criminals into the British Army," 48.
14. A return of the British recruits prepared in New York on 1 September 1779 listed 976 private soldiers fit for duty and 285 sick, and noted that 43 had died on the voyage. Among these recruits were 63 men for the 22nd Regiment, of whom almost all were listed as sick on the next muster roll and of whom 26 died within their first year of service. "State of the

Troops which arrived in the fleet from England under the Command of Vice Admiral Arbuthnot, New York 1st. Septr. 1779," CO 5/98, TNA, 493; Muster rolls, 22nd Regiment of Foot, WO 12/3872. Two deserters from the 23rd Regiment noted of the 1779 recruits that "several whereof were sick many of them old and pressed men." Lewis Nicola to John Jay, 10 September 1779. Papers of the Continental Congress, M247, r180, i163, National Archives, 132.

15. Lt. John Ridout to Barrington, 10 August 1776. WO 1/993, TNA.

16. Muster rolls, 46th Regiment of Foot, WO 12/5797/1, TNA.

17. Paul H. Silverstone. *The Sailing Navy, 1775–1854* (New York: Taylor & Francis, 2006), 18.

18. Fox's name is among some 8,000 recorded as having been incarcerated on this prison ship during the war. *A Christmas Reminder, being the names of about eight thousand persons, a small portion of the number confined on board the British prison ships during the war of the revolution* (Brooklyn, NY: Eagle Print, 1888), 26.

19. A list of surviving accounts of life on the *Jersey* appears in David Swain, ed., *Recollections of Life on the Prison Ship Jersey* (Yardley, PA: Westholme, 2010), xix.

20. So great was the importance of protecting the island's rich trade from French, Spanish, and American aggression that Jamaican plantation owners and merchants provided funds to pay British soldiers an extra five shillings per week, and sums between two and four shillings per week to wives, children, widows, and orphans. Recruiting advertisement for the 88th Regiment of Foot, *Royal Gazette* (New York), 30 December 1780. Recruiting advertisement for the 99th Regiment of Foot (Royal Jamaica Volunteers), *Belfast Newsletter*, 3 March 1780.

21. Unfortunately no muster rolls for the 88th Regiment survive from the time during which Fox was enlisted, so neither his own service nor the overall attrition rate of the regiment can be corroborated. When the 88th Regiment was inspected in England on 12 October 1779 there were 762 men present. A return dated 1 March 1782 in Jamaica indicates only 394 men remaining, of whom 142 were sick. Although the nominal strength had been reduced from 782 to 662 in the interim, this nonetheless suggests that at between 368 and 488 men had been lost during this twenty-eight-month period, not including replacements like Fox who were also lost. These numbers include noncommissioned officers, drummers, fifers, and private soldiers. Inspection return, 88th Regiment of Foot, WO 27/44, TNA; Monthly Return of His Majesty's Troops in Jamaica 1 March 1782, WO 34/133, fol. 84, TNA.

22. *Royal Gazette* (New York), 10 January 1781.

23. Fox actually refers to two regiments, both of which were serving in Jamaica. The Loyal American Rangers were raised in 1780 and the Duke of Cumberland's Regiment commanded by Lord Montague was raised in 1781; both were composed largely of American prisoners of war. In 1783 the Loyal American Rangers were disbanded, and many of the men were incorporated into a new battalion of the Duke of Cumberland's. Fox may

have perceived them as a single regiment because they were serving together. Fox provides the only known reference to blue coats faced with white, so it is not clear which of the two regiments wore them. Todd W. Braisted, *The Loyalist Corps: Americans in Service to the King* (Trenton, NJ: FoxAcre Press, 2011), 35, 57.

24. The prescribed uniform for the 88th Regiment consisted of a red coat with green lapels, cuffs and collar. A 1779 deserter advertisement described a uniform consisting of "a white Jacket, white Waistcoat, and Breeches, faced with green." It was quite common for new regiments to wear white jackets with various color trim only during the first year that they were raised while contractors were producing the prescribed uniforms. The white binding that Fox refers to was a strip of white fabric that lined the edge of the military cocked hat, preventing the felt from fraying as well as giving a decorative appearance. *Bell's Complete and Correct List of the Army* (London: John Bell, 1782), 7. *Manchester Mercury*, 28 September 1779.

25. The 79th Regiment of Foot, titled the Royal Liverpool Volunteers, was also sometimes known as the Liverpool Blues. Information on the uniform of this regiment is scarce; the nickname apparently stems from the blue lapels, cuffs, and collars on their red coats.

26. "Buckra men" was a common term used by the natives for white men, as Fox explains in one of his own footnotes.

27. Biscuit was the dried, hard bread widely used by the army and navy because it kept well for long periods of time. In the nineteenth century it came to be called hardtack.

28. Ebenezer Fox, *Adventures of Ebenezer Fox in the Revolutionary War* (Boston: Charles Fox, 1847). There have been several reprint editions including Heritage Books (Bowie, MD, 2008).

CHAPTER 7: THE PENSIONER

1. Muster rolls of this era were kept for each individual company within a regiment, usually semi-annually. They typically record the date on which a man began receiving pay from the company; because men often enlisted with recruiting parties operating away from the regiment, actual enlistment dates are seldom found on the company muster rolls (this is verified by the smattering of men for whom actual enlistment dates are known from other sources). When regiments were serving in Ireland, they included each man's nationality on the muster rolls, but only in the general terms of "British" (that is, English, Scottish, or Welsh), "Irish," and "Foreign" (which included men born in America and other places). The rolls also carry annotations for men being "sick," "on duty," "on command," and similar terms which are very difficult to interpret. Desertion is typically recorded only when the man remained missing at the time the muster roll was prepared; if he deserted and returned during a muster period, the rolls seldom record it (this is verified by deserter advertisements and courts-martial). Dates recorded for discharge or transfer to other regiments are

actually the date through which the men were paid, usually a few weeks after the date on which they actually departed (verified by discharges which survive, primarily for pensioners). Muster rolls for various regiments, WO 12, TNA.

2. Bennett Cuthbertson, *A System for the Compleat Interior Management and Œconomy of a Battalion of Infantry*, 147.

3. Of 1,005 men who served in the 22nd Regiment in America from 1775 through 1783, 90 deserted never to return; a few others deserted and were either captured or returned of their own volition. Another 12 men who were prisoners of war did not return when repatriated and were written off as deserters. Muster rolls, 22nd Regiment of Foot, WO 12/3872, TNA. Of 998 men who served in the 33rd Regiment, 100 deserted and 25 prisoners of war did not return; This does not include the men of Lt. Nutt's detachment on Burgoyne's expedition. Muster rolls, 33rd Regiment of Foot, WO 12/4803, TNA. These figures pertain only to service in America; desertion rates from recruiting parties in Great Britain cannot be determined because no comprehensive muster rolls are known to exist for them.

4. General Orders, 27 June 1783. Sir Guy Carleton orderly book, Frederick Mackenzie Papers, vol. F, WLC. The 23d Regiment of Foot wrote off 35 men who did not return; the 33rd Regiment wrote off 25. Muster rolls, 23rd Regiment of Foot, WO 12/3960, and 33rd Regiment of Foot, WO 12/4803, TNA.

5. For example, James Caffrey and John Overon of the 34th Regiment became prisoners of war after 1779 in unknown circumstances. They came into New York and joined the 22nd Regiment on 1 January 1782, but continued to be carried on the muster rolls of the 34th as prisoners of war until they were struck off at the end of the war. Muster rolls, 22nd Regiment of Foot and 34th Regiment of Foot, WO 12/3872 and WO 12/4866/2, TNA.

6. A striking example is Owen Smith of the 63rd Regiment who deserted in Dublin two years before the regiment sailed for America; he changed his sentiments, made his own way to America, was persuaded to enlist in the American army, then deserted to rejoin the 63rd Regiment in November 1776. The regiment's muster rolls show him as having enlisted in 1776, but his trial for desertion reveals the full story. Court Martial of Owen Smith, WO 71/82, TNA, 429–434. Another likely case is John King of the 33rd Regiment, deserted on 29 March 1782 and then "enlisted" on 23 February 1783, a date on which no other men enlisted. Muster rolls, 33rd Regiment of Foot, WO 12/4803, TNA.

7. Discharge of Alexander Brice, 7th Regiment of Foot, WO 121/2/145; discharge of George Friskin, 7th Regiment of Foot, WO 121/6/184, TNA.

8. The David Library of the American Revolution has an index of general court proceedings in America, 1774–1783, drawn from the material in WO 71/80 through /98. This collection includes most, but not all, trials conducted on the New York establishment, which included Nova Scotia,

the eastern seaboard, and the West Indies but not the army headquartered in Quebec.
9. Trial of Evan Evans, WO 71/84, TNA, 48–51. At the time of this statement Evans had served twenty years and had never before been brought before a court-martial.
10. Trial of John Fisher, WO 71/85, TNA, 290–307. At the time of this statement Fisher had served five years.
11. Trial of William Lamb, WO 71/81, TNA, 405–430.
12. A total of 241 men were discharged from the 33rd Regiment of Foot between September and December 1783, of whom 68 reenlisted in the regiment immediately. From the 22nd Regiment, 220 men were discharged between September and December of whom at least 109 reenlisted immediately, 40 back into the 22nd Regiment and 69 into other regiments. Muster rolls, 33rd Regiment of Foot, WO 12/4803; 22nd Regiment of Foot, WO 12/3872, TNA.
13. Refer to the notes for the next paragraph for details on how this figure was determined.
14. General Orders, 17 August 1783. Sir Guy Carleton orderly book, Frederick Mackenzie Papers, vol. F, WLC, 186–195.
15. Muster rolls, 22nd Regiment of Foot, WO 12/3872 and /3873, TNA; additional muster rolls were consulted for those men who went into other regiments before ending their careers. Royal Hospital Chelsea Soldier Service Documents, WO 97, TNA; Royal Hospital Chelsea Out-Pension Admission Books, WO 116, TNA; Royal Hospital Kilmainham Pensioners' Discharge Documents, WO 119, TNA; Royal Hospital Chelsea Discharge Documents of Pensioners, WO 121, TNA. At this writing, 251 men of the 22nd Regiment are known to have received pensions and 85 to have received land grants, leaving 275 with no known reward. It is possible that some of those 275 received pensions that have not yet been identified; the available pension information sometimes records only the last corps in which a man served, and discontinuities in both the muster rolls and in actual service can make it impossible to determine a given pensioner's complete service record.
16. Charles Mathew Clode, *The Military Forces of the Crown: Their Administration and Government,* vol. 2 (London: John Murray, 1869), 280.
17. Disability and Royal Artillery Out-Pensions, Admission Books, WO 116, TNA.
18. These discharges form the bulk of the WO 97, WO 119, and WO 121 collections, TNA. Most are printed forms with individual details filled in by hand, and the richness of detail varies widely. Age, place of birth, and trade are consistently recorded. Years of service are usually recorded, and sometimes the years in each regiment are enumerated. The reason for which the man is recommended for a pension vary from brief terms such as "wounded," "rheumatic," or the catch-all "worn out" to verbose descriptions of specific maladies or the date and place where a wound or injury was received. The soldier either signed or made his mark on the document, providing some insight as to whether the soldier could write. Most of those

dealing with soldiers who served in America are from the 1790s and early 1800s, often pertaining to discharges from corps other than those with which they served during the American war; many nonetheless include details of wounds, injuries, and maladies resulting from service in America.

19. *Report of the Commissioners Appointed to Inquire into and to State the Mode of Keeping the Official Accounts in the Principal Departments Connected with the Receipts and Expenditure for the Public Service* (London: Printed for His Majesty's Treasury, 1829), 266–267.

20. For this reason, some of the documents in WO 121 are petitions by pensioners who had been struck off the rolls because they missed their appointments due to illness or other reasons.

21. Charles Mathew Clode, *The Military Forces of the Crown,* 281.

22. Charles Mathew Clode, *The Military Forces of the Crown,* 81.

23. Discharges of men receiving pensions through Kilmainham are in WO 119, TNA.

24. See, for example, the notice directed "To the Out-Pensioners of Chelsea-College," *Edinburgh Advertiser,* 17 March 1775.

25. For example, John Corbett joined the 22nd Regiment in America in December 1777; although discharged only two years later due to a wound, he continued to serve in veteran battalions until 1814 when he was discharged at the age of fifty-four after thirty-six total years of service. Muster rolls, 22nd Regiment of Foot, WO 12/3872, TNA; discharge of John Corbett, 1814, WO 121/178/96, TNA. At least forty-six soldiers who served in the 22nd Regiment in America later served in veteran battalions, as evidenced from subsequent pensions. Royal Hospital Chelsea Discharge Documents of Pensioners, WO 121, TNA.

26. Roger Lamb's "commonplace book" is owned by a family descendant; digital images of it are in the National Army Museum, London, Saratoga National Historical Park, New York, and the David Library of the American Revolution, Pennsylvania. Don N. Hagist, "Unpublished Military Writings of Roger Lamb, Soldier in the 1775–1783 American War, Part 2," *Journal of the Society for Army Historical Research*, 90 (Summer 2012), 79.

27. Comparing discharges of soldiers who served in the 22nd Regiment of Foot during the 1775–1783 period (in WO 97, WO 119, and WO 121) with service in the muster rolls (WO 12) shows that discrepancies of one or two years are common, but this is to be expected because WO 12 typically does not record actual enlistment dates but the date that recruits joined the main body of their regiment. Among the soldiers of the 22nd Regiment, there are too few large discrepancies to suggest that the inflated service records described by Lamb were common. A similar study of the WO 12, WO 97, WO 119, and WO 121 material for men of the 23rd Regiment might corroborate Lamb's assertions.

28. Incidents in Dublin are reported in the *Freeman's Journal* (Dublin) of 1 January, 4 February, 30 March, 1 April, and 19 August 1775. In cases where perpetrators were caught, they were executed. *Freeman's Journal*, 7 and 28 March 1775.

29. At least one of eight soldiers known to have been houghed in 1775 received an out-pension. *Freeman's Journal* (Dublin) of 6 January 1776. Discharge of Anthony Dunlavy, 24th Regiment of Foot, WO 97/435/135, TNA.
30. This occurred in Cork. *Freeman's Journal* (Dublin), 31 August and 2 September 1775.
31. Evidenced by numerous discharges in WO 119 and WO 121, TNA.
32. These towns were incorporated into the city of Stoke-on-Trent in 1910. George Fox was baptized in Stoke-on-Trent on 17 March 1745. Percy W. L. Adams, ed. *Stoke-upon-Trent Parish Register, Part 3, 1734–1797* (Staffordshire Parish Record Society, 1925), as cited in J. A. Houlding and G. Kenneth Yates, "Corporal Fox's Memoir of Service, 1766–1783: Quebec, Saratoga, and the Convention Army," *Journal of the Society for Army Historical Research* 68 no. 275 (Autumn 1990), 146–168.
33. "Description of Lord Robt. Berties Company Royal Fuziliers," Journal of Walter Home, Peter Force MSS, George Chalmers Collection, Library of Congress.
34. Muster rolls, 7th Regiment of Foot, WO 12/2474, TNA.
35. Fox's recollection was that this occurred in March rather than February.
36. Muster rolls. 7th Regiment of Foot, WO 12/2474, TNA.
37. The writer refers to the price of rum at 21 shillings per gallon. A. M. W. Stirling, *Annals of a Yorkshire House, from the Papers of a Macaroni & His Kindred,* vol. 2 (London: John Lane, 1911), 340.
38. *Quebec Gazette*, 12 May 1774.
39. "Journal of the Most Remarkable Occurrences in Quebec," *Collections of the New-York Historical Soceity* (1880), 189.
40. John Joseph Henry, *Account of Arnold's Campaign Against Quebec* (Albany, NY: Joel Munsell, 1877), 135.
41. "Journal of the Siege from 1st Dec. 1775," *The Blockade of Quebec in 1775–1776* (Quebec: Library and Historical Society of Quebec, 1906), 22.
42. "Journal of the Most Remarkable Occurrences in Quebec," 231.
43. Don N. Hagist, ed. *A British Soldier's Story.*
44. Eight soldiers of the 29th Regiment were tried for the shootings that occurred in Boston on 5 March 1770. John Carrol, William McAuly, William Warren, and Hugh White were still on the regiment's rolls prepared in Canada during the war. Gaps in the surviving rolls introduce the possibility that not all are the same men who were in Boston in 1770. Muster rolls, 29th Regiment of Foot, WO 12/4493, TNA.
45. The 22nd, 23rd, and 33rd Regiments were also sent to theaters where their colonels held senior commands (General Thomas Gage, General William Howe, and Lt. General Charles Cornwallis, respectively). There were cases where colonel's regiments were not sent to serve under them, as in Sir Henry Clinton's 12th Regiment of Foot which spent the war years in Gibraltar.
46. The muster rolls of the 47th Regiment confirm that fifty-three men of the 7th, including George Fox, were drafted in May 1776.

47. Don N. Hagist, ed., *A British Soldier's Story.*
48. Muster rolls, 47th Regiment of Foot, WO 12/5871, TNA.
49. Precise numbers are not available. Returns of the numbers of men surrendered at Saratoga vary slightly. A collection of returns of prisoners from 1781 in Lancaster, Pennsylvania, lists seventy-one men of the 47th including George Fox, but there may have been a few men held in other places. "List of British Prisoners Brought to Lancaster by Major Baily the 16th June 1781." "Roll of the Men's Names of Brittish Prisoners of War and the Numbers of the Regiments they Belong to in Lancaster Barracks Agust the 15th 1781." Peter Force Papers, Series IX, Reel 106, LOC.
50. J. A. Houlding and G. Kenneth Yates, "Corporal Fox's Memoir of Service, 1766–1783."
51. Newcastle-under-Lyme.
52. This was Lt.-Col. Allen McLean of the Royal Highland Emigrants, a regiment that would later become the 84th Regiment of Foot. Upon its formation in 1775 it was sometimes called the 71st Regiment because it was incorrectly assumed that it would acquire that designation.
53. Again Fox refers to the Royal Highland Emigrants as the 71st.
54. The original text says "rode currenteen." The meaning of this is not clear. It could be interpreted as meaning "rode with the current." We have interpreted it as "rode quarantine" because this phrase was used with some frequency in period literature, while "rode current" was not. Fox probably did not mean that they were isolated for medical reasons, but simply that they were confined on the vessels and unable to go on shore.
55. That is, cannon that fired 12-pound balls.
56. Fascines were bundles of saplings, branches, and brushwood tightly bound together, used to quickly create field fortifications. George Smith, *An Universal Military Dictionary* (London, 1779), 87.
57. A canister shot was a can or canister filled with smaller balls that was loaded into a cannon; when fired, the canister broke open and the balls scattered like a shotgun blast. Canister shot was used at short range against infantry.
58. The light infantry and grenadier companies were formed into separate battalions; there were, however, no companies from other regiments besides those that Fox listed.
59. The transfer of men from the 7th to the 47th is recorded on the muster rolls as 21 May 1776. Muster rolls, 47th Regiment of Foot, WO 12/5871. The phrase in the manuscript appears to say "the 52 were ordered to be drafted into the 47 reg the 24 to 76 reg." Since Fox refers all along to only 52 men from the 7th, and all were transferred to the 47th, the phrase "24 to 76 reg" appears to be an error by the copyist for "24 March 76."
60. The manuscript reads "then proceeded to the three rivers 100 men and we lay at Anchor for four days." This appears to refer to 100 men of the 47th Regiment.
61. Brigadier General William Thompson was among the captured at the battle of Trois Rivières or Three Rivers. L. Edward Purcell, *Who Was Who in the American Revolution* (New York: Facts on File, 1993), 473.

62. It is not clear what "dined and retreated" means.
63. Stacking arms refers to propping up muskets in groups of three, teepee-like, with their ramrods interlocked. It was a point of honor to stack the arms rather than lay them down on the ground.
64. The Convention Army did not pass through Rhode Island; Fox's recollection of the geography is somewhat garbled.
65. We do not know the town in England that Fox refers to.
66. The manuscript appears to read, "we passed N. Scows." We have assumed that Fox dictated "in scows" and the copyist wrote it incorrectly.
67. Here, again, Fox probably means simply that they could not go on shore.
68. Disability and Royal Artillery Out-Pensions, Admission Books, WO 116/8, TNA.
69. J. A. Houlding and G. Kenneth Yates, "Corporal Fox's Memoir of Service," 148.
70. Muster rolls, 7th Regiment of Foot, WO 12/2474, TNA.
71. J. A. Houlding and G. Kenneth Yates, "Corporal Fox's Memoir of Service," 148.
72. His discharge from the Invalids in 1806 gives his age as sixty-three; discrepancies in age of a few years are not unusual in surviving discharge documents. Discharge of George Fox, WO 121/165/232.

Chapter 8: The Faithful Soldier

1. Petition of Daniel Wright, WO 121/140/157, TNA.
2. The typical peacetime enlistment bounty was one guinea and a half, or one pound (£1), 11 s. and 6 p. During the American War it was raised to £3 in 1778 and again to £3, 3 s. in 1779. Some regiments raised regionally only during, and for the duration of, the war used even greater bounties. Bruce Seton, "Infantry Recruiting Instructions in England in 1767." Edward R. Curtis, *The British Army in the American Revolution,* 57, 59, 76.
3. Mark F. Odintz, *The British Officer Corps, 1754–1783* (Ann Arbor: University of Michigan Press, 1988), 180–181.
4. Bennett Cuthbertson, *A System for the Compleat Interior Management and Œconomy of a Battalion of Infantry,* 156; Trial of James Cairns, WO 71/82, TNA, 241–250.
5. George Smith, *An Universal Military Dictionary,* 21; Bennett Cuthbertson, *A System for the Compleat Interior Management and Œconomy of a Battalion of Infantry,* 154–156.
6. A mess was any group of men who dined together. For common soldiers it was typically a group of five men who also shared a tent. Officers in a regiment or any ad hoc formation usually formed a mess for economy, efficiency, and camaraderie. George Smith, *An Universal Military Dictionary,* 175. Bennett Cuthbertson, *A System for the Compleat Interior Management and Œconomy of a Battalion of Infantry,* 25–31.
7. There was no regulated wage for servants, but military texts recommended a uniform wage of one shilling per week regardless of the rank of

the officer, to ensure fair treatment of all of the regiment's servants. Bennett Cuthbertson, *A System for the Compleat Interior Management and Œconomy of a Battalion of Infantry,* 155.

8. The base pay of soldiers during this era was eight pence per day, but withholdings from it were used to pay for the soldier's food, clothing, washing, medical treatment, and other services. It was the responsibility of the company officers to manage the soldiers' accounts and allow only those men who had proven capable of it to handle their own budgets directly. This eight pence per day, however, was only a base wage; the army offered many opportunities to earn additional money for soldiers with skills as tailors, wagon drivers, shoemakers, and other trades. Labor at building barracks, fortifications, roads, and other infrastructure was regularly provided by the army and compensated by the government. Soldiers were allowed to hold jobs outside of the army as long as those jobs did not interfere with their duty. Bennett Cuthbertson, *A System for the Compleat Interior Management and Œconomy of a Battalion of Infantry,* 152–154. Opportunities such as these could be quite lucrative. For example, in 1782 seven soldiers of the 22nd Regiment worked as boat men at Paulus Hook near New York City, each earning one shilling per day for eighteen days. This amounted to £3 12 s. for each man, a sum greater than a quarter of their annual base pay for just eighteen days' work. "Abstract of Pay due for Men employed in the Boat at Paulus Hook, from 27th May to 30th June 1782, being 35 days." PRO 30/55/4964.

9. When an officer was with the regiment, servants were generally expected to dine with the other soldiers in their mess unless the officer was willing to take responsibility for the soldier eating and in general living "in a regular and proper manner." Bennett Cuthbertson, *A System for the Compleat Interior Management and Œconomy of a Battalion of Infantry,* 29.

10. Bennett Cuthbertson, *A System for the Compleat Interior Management and Œconomy of a Battalion of Infantry,* 155–156. The commanding officer of the 65th Regiment went so far as to order officers to provide their servants with frock coats. Standing orders, 65th Regiment of Foot, A/1958/Z, Barnsley Archives, Barnsley, England.

11. As seen in Chapter 1, when the young John Robert Shaw was enlisted the recruiting officer suggested that he would become a servant.

12. For example, when Lieutenant Charles Laton of the 22nd Regiment took a captaincy in the 64th Regiment in 1776, he took a thirty-two-year-old soldier named William Graham with him, and a soldier from the 64th joined the 22nd Regiment. Muster rolls, 22nd Regiment of Foot, WO 12/3872, TNA.

13. William Hale, a Lieutenant in the grenadier company of the 45th Regiment of Foot, wrote the following from Head of Elk, Maryland, in August 1777 at the beginning of the Philadelphia campaign: "I write this under a tree, while my black is making a fire to boil my pork, and my white servant pitching my tent." W. H. Wilkin, ed. *Some British Soldiers in America* (London: H. Rees, 1914), 229. Service to British officers is men-

tioned in several newspaper advertisements for runaway blacks, including one each in the *New York Gazette* of 7 July, *Pennsylvania Packet* of 1 September 1778, *New Jersey Gazette* of 23 September 1778, and New York *Royal Gazette* of 8 September 1781.

14. Most regiments of foot had established positions for thirty-five officers including thirty company officers and five staff. It was common for a few of these positions to be vacant or, in the case of the adjutancy, filled by a company officer doing double duty. With most officers having one servant and a few having two, we can expect between thirty and forty servants in a regiment at any given time.

15. When he received an out-pension in 1778 he had twenty years of service, but no details on his career before joining the 22nd Regiment have been found. Regimental Registers of Pensioners, WO 120/15, TNA.

16. William Bell Clark, ed., *Naval Documents of the American Revolution,* vol. 2 (Washington, DC: Government Printing Office, 1966), 21.

17. *Minutes of the Provincial Council of Pennsylvania: from the organization to the Termination of the proprietary Government* (Harrisburg, PA: Theo. Fenn & Co., 1852), 306.

18. Sheldon S. Cohen, "The Connecticut Captivity of Major Christopher French," *Connecticut Historical Society Bulletin* 55–56 (Summer/Fall 1990) 223–229.

19. The semiannual muster rolls often denote men as "Prisoner with the Rebels" but do not indicate the dates on which men entered captivity; similarly, when a man returned from captivity he no longer is denoted as a prisoner but his date of return is not given. This reflects the muster rolls' purpose of reconciling the pay of each man; time as a prisoner of war did not affect pay, whereas events like enlistment, death, desertion, or transfer did. Muster rolls, 22nd Regiment of Foot, WO 12/3872, TNA.

20. The date of Goldthorp's pension examination, 18 December 1778, appears to conflict with the date shown on the muster rolls for his discharge, 24 December 1778; clearly he was not examined in London a week before he was discharged in New York. The muster rolls, however, reflect the date through which a man was paid, not his actual date of departure; it was typical for soldiers to receive a few weeks of additional pay to provide for their journey home. Chelsea Hospital Admission Books, WO 116/7; Muster rolls, 52nd Regiment of Foot, WO 12/6240, TNA.

21. Trial of John Bolton, WO 71/86, TNA, 216–218.

22. A gap in the muster rolls has made it impossible to determine whether Bolton was executed or pardoned. Muster rolls, 35th Regiment of Foot, WO 12/4949, TNA.

23. Trial of James Cairns, WO 71/82, TNA, 241–250.

24. Trial of James Cairns, WO 71/86, TNA, 84–98; "Newport in the Hands of the British: A Diary of the American Revolution," *Historical Magazine* 4 (March 1860), 71.

25. See, for example the trial of John and Sophia Sinclair, 76th Regiment of Foot, WO 71/91, TNA, 22–27.

26. Trial of John Man, 64th Regiment of Foot, WO 71/79, TNA, 407–413.
27. Trial of Luke Murphy, 38th Regiment of Foot, WO 71/79, TNA, 367–374. It is not known whether Murphy received the punishment or was pardoned, but he deserted the following January. Muster rolls, 38th Regiment of Foot, WO 12/5171, TNA.
28. A survey of 307 deserter advertisements in British newspapers includes eight men who were servants before joining the army. Many of these ads describe more than one deserter. The sample is a random collection of ads that this author found interesting, from a number of different newspapers. A study of 161 deserters identified three servants. William P. Tatum III, "Deserted! Opportunism and Desertion in the British Army, 1763–1783," Senior Honors Thesis, College of William & Mary, May 2003.
29. *Hibernian Chronicle*, 24 October 1776.
30. *Edinburgh Advertiser*, 9 January 1776.
31. Trial of George Patterson, 44th Regiment of Foot, WO 71/87, TNA, 348–361.
32. A gap in the muster rolls makes it impossible to determine when William Andrew joined the 44th Regiment. He was in the regiment on 1 October 1771, but not on the previous rolls from 1765. Muster rolls, 44th Regiment of Foot, WO 12/5637, TNA.
33. Bennett Cuthbertson, *A System for the Compleat Interior Management and Œconomy of a Battalion of Infantry,* 137. It appears that regiments could set their own terms for allowing a man's discharge; sometimes two men were required, as will be seen in Chapter 9.
34. Muster rolls, 44th Regiment of Foot, WO 12/5637, TNA.
35. "Journals of Lieut.-Col. Stephen Kemble," *Collections of the New York Historical Society for the Year 1883,* 52.
36. The rank of brigadier was used only in wartime; brigadiers were usually lieutenant colonels or colonels, appointed to command brigades. George Smith, *An Universal Military Dictionary,* 36. The term "brigadier general" was and is widely used.
37. *The London Magazine, or, Gentleman's Monthly Intellegencer for the Year 1777,* vol. 45 (London: R. Baldwin, 1777), 335.
38. For a full account of the battle see Thomas J. McGuire, *The Surprise of Germantown* (Gettysburg, PA: Thomas Publications, 1994).
39. See, for example, orders of 5 July 1775 and 10 August 1775, B. F. Stevens, *General Sir William Howe's Orderly Book*, 33, 65–66.
40. James Agnew had married Elizabeth Sanderson in 1747. Charles Mosley, ed., *Burke's Peerage, Baronetage & Knightage*, Vol. 1 (Wilmington, DE: Genealogical Books, 2003).
41. Benson J. Lossing, *The Pictorial Field-Book of the American Revolution; or, Illustrations, by Pen and Pencil, of the History, Biography, Scenery, Relics, and Traditions of the War for Independence,* vol. II (New York: Harper and Brothers, 1852), 319. Lossing writes, "This letter, and several written by Agnew himself to his wife at various times, are in the possession of his grandson, Henry A. Martin, M. D., of Roxbury, Massachusetts."

42. The brigade that Agnew commanded included the 33rd, 37th, 46th, and 64th Regiments. It was typical to form brigades with the lower numbered regiments on the flanks and the higher numbered in the middle, so that Agnew's brigade probably was usually formed with the 33rd Regiment on the right flank, the 37th on the left flank, the 46th in the center right, and the 64th in the center left. Right and left is from the perspective of standing in the ranks looking forward. This meant that Agnew, to be at the center of his brigade, was also in front of the right flank of the 64th Regiment. "Fieldwork: Order of Battle of the British Flank Battalions," *The Brigade Dispatch* 23, no. 2 (Spring 1992), 26–27.
43. A picquet, or picket, was a formation of soldiers spaced at wide intervals usually in advance of another formation or a defensive position. George Smith, *An Universal Military Dictionary,* 202.
44. Andrew's phrase suggests that he was also on horseback, and "got off" to attend to Agnew.
45. A guinea was a gold coin worth £1 1 s. sterling; the Portuguese half-Johannes or half-joe coin was worth £1 16 s. sterling. *Gaine's Universal Register, or, American and British Kalendar, for the Year 1776* (New York: Hugh Gaine, 1775).
46. Captain William Leslie of the 46th Regiment of Foot, who was serving as extra major of brigade in America. He had been in the 44th Regiment until May 1776. *A List of the General and Staff Officers, and of the Officers in the several Regiments serving in North America* (New York: Macdonald and Cameron, 1777), 4.
47. James Agnew was buried in the Lower Burial Ground in Germantown. Before the British evacuated Philadelphia in 1778, Agnew's and other British officers' remains were moved to the De Benneville Family Burial Grounds in Philadelphia.
48. Henry Hope of the 44th Regiment was promoted from major to lieutenant colonel after Agnew's death. Steven M. Baule and Stephen Gilbert, *British Army Officers,* 92.
49. John Payne and Henry Seymour were both in the 44th Regiment when it arrived in Boston in 1775. They both served through the end of the American war. Muster rolls, 44th Regiment of Foot, WO 12/5637, TNA.
50. Andrew appears to have misspelled "again."
51. This probably refers to General Agnew's son, Robert Agnew, an officer in the 58th Regiment of Foot; there was no officer in the regular army with the surname Robert at this time. Calling him "Captain Robert" is incongruously familiar for a servant, but this may be the way that Andrew had heard the general refer to his son. Charles Mosley, ed., *Burke's Peerage,* 47.
52. John F. Watson. "Notes of the Early History of Germantown," *Register of Pennsylvania* 1, no. 19 (10 May 1828), 290.
53. Daniel K. Cassel, *History of the Mennonites* (Philadelphia: Daniel K. Cassel, 1888), 113.

54. The muster rolls show Andrew's discharge date as 14 July 1792, which agrees with his discharge. Muster rolls, 44th Regiment of Foot, WO 12/5638/2.
55. Discharge of Alexander Andrew, WO 119/1/4.
56. Examples can be found in the Guy Carleton Papers, PRO 30/55, TNA; in Headquarters Papers, WO 28, TNA; and other collections.
57. Memorial of John Hutton. Guy Carleton Papers, PRO 30/55/6918, TNA.
58. Memorial of Mary Driscoll. Guy Carleton Papers, PRO 30/55/2452a, TNA.
59. Driscoll was drafted into the 5th Regiment of Foot, but a gap in the rolls of that regiment leaves his fate a mystery. Muster rolls, 10th Regiment of Foot and 5th Regiment of Foot, WO 12/2750 and WO 12/2289, TNA.

Chapter 9: The Aspiring Soldier

1. When the 22nd Regiment of Foot prepared to leave America in 1783, eighty-five discharged men took land grants and at least sixty-nine reenlisted in regiments that were sent to Canada. The number who reenlisted is difficult to determine exactly because the men were actually discharged from the 22nd, and usually appear as enlistees on the rolls of other regiments (primarily the 17th and 54th Regiments of Foot) with no annotation that they'd been in another regiment. The sixty-nine have been identified by comparing names, discharge dates, and enlistment dates supplemented by pension data and other available records. Muster rolls, 22nd Regiment of Foot and other regiments, WO 12, TNA.
2. About 20 percent of the men who served in the 22nd Regiment of Foot in America between 1775 and 1783 became corporals or sergeants at some point in their careers. Muster rolls, 22nd Regiment of Foot, WO 12/3871 through /3873, and for other regiments in which those men served during their careers, TNA.
3. Mark F. Odintz, *The British Officer Corps, 1754–1783,* 180–181.
4. John A. Houlding, *Fit for Service*, 102–115.
5. Orders dated 17 July 1775, and repeated 9 June 1779. *Standing Orders and Regulations for the Army in Ireland* (Dublin: George, Grierson, 1794), 65.
6. General Orders of Sir Guy Carleton, 6 January 1777. Orderly book, 8 May 1776–29 June 1777, Lloyd W. Smith Collection, Morristown National Historical Park.
7. Before the war began the established strength of each company included two sergeants; in 1775 this was increased to three for the duration of the war. There were no sergeants in a regiment besides these company sergeants, and their ranks included the sergeant-major, quartermaster sergeant, and other specialties. Muster rolls of marching regiments, WO 12, TNA.
8. Thomas Simes, *The Regulator*, 15; Bennett Cuthbertson, *A System for the Compleat Interior Management,* 8–9.

9. Muster rolls, 22nd Regiment of Foot, WO 12/3872, TNA.
10. Muster rolls, 22nd Regiment of Foot, WO 12/3872, /3873, TNA.
11. Muster rolls, 33rd Regiment of Foot, WO 12/4803, TNA.
12. Muster rolls, 22nd Regiment of Foot, WO 12/3872, TNA.
13. Joseph Hawkins's date of rank is given as 25 December 1775, but the muster rolls of the 22nd Regiment show that he was "promoted" from sergeant on 19 May 1776. Such inconsistencies of dates are common on documents that reflect administrative considerations rather than "ground truth." Hawkins joined the Royal Highland Emigrants when the British army under General Sir William Howe was reorganizing in Halifax in May 1776, but his commission was back-dated so that he would have the appropriate seniority in his new capacity. Muster rolls, 22nd Regiment of Foot, WO 12/3872, TNA; Steven M. Baule and Stephen Gilbert, *British Army Officers,* 87.
14. Half-pay, a sort of reserve status for officers that kept them on half of their normal military pay when there were no active positions available for them. It was common for officers to go on half-pay when the size of the army was reduced, and to receive full-pay postings when an expansion occurred again.
15. Besides the 73 men who served as sergeants in the 22nd Regiment in America between 1775 and 1783, there were men in the regiment who became sergeants later on in their careers; in other words, the odds of becoming a sergeant at some time in one's career were slightly greater than the 73/1005 that the period of American service indicates. None of the men who became sergeants later in their careers are known to have subsequently become officers. Muster rolls, 22nd Regiment of Foot, WO 12/3872, TNA.
16. Within an infantry regiment of ten companies, five of the companies had one captain, one lieutenant, and one ensign. Two of the companies were commanded one each by the lieutenant colonel and the major. One company was nominally commanded by the colonel, but because that officer was often absent on other service the actual command fell to the next senior officer who, instead of being a lieutenant, was called captain-lieutenant; his rank and duties were effectively the same as a captain. The grenadier and light infantry companies each had a captain and two lieutenants; because these companies were composed only of experienced men they had no ensigns who were by definition inexperienced officers. The adjutant, quartermaster, surgeon, surgeon's mate and chaplain were carried on the muster rolls of the colonel's company but were not for operational purposes members of any company; the post of adjutant was often held by one of the lieutenants.
17. Additional Companies, discussed in Chapter 1, were established in 1775 and disbanded at the end of the war. Note that officers did not stay permanently in the Additional Companies, but were liable to be rotated to America and back.
18. The figure of ten ensigns includes eight in the companies in America and two recruiting in Great Britain. In cavalry regiments, the junior offi-

cer was called a cornet; in fusilier regiments, which had historical connections with the artillery but by the time of the American war were the same as other infantry regiments, the junior officers were called second lieutenants. Although the titles varied, the ranks of ensign, cornet, and second lieutenant were effectively the same.

19. Return of Volunteers serving with the following Corps 1 July 1781. Frederick Mackenzie papers, WLC.

20. "Volunteer John George Hood to be Ensign, vice John Grant," *London Gazette,* 4 December 1781; "Volunteer James Boyd to be Ensign, vice Henry Overing," *London Gazette,* 11 December 1781.

21. Muster rolls, 40th and 54th Regiments of Foot, WO 12/5318 and /6398/2; Steven M. Baule and Stephen Gilbert, *British Army Officers,* 19, 92.

22. William Proctor, a volunteer who came from Halifax to Boston with the 65th Regiment, appears to have led a small party that drove back an American advance against a British advanced post on 28 August 1775. He received a minor wound, and soon after was appointed as an officer in the first loyalist corps raised in America, the Royal Fencible American Regiment (his commission was back-dated to 1 August). He received an ensign's commission in the 22nd Regiment of Foot the following year, and was mortally wounded at the battle of Rhode Island on 29 August 1778. Lt. Gen. Howe to Gen. Gage, 29 August 1775 and Lt. Col. George Clark to Gen. Gage, 2 September 1775, Thomas Gage Papers Volume 134, WLC; Return of Officers in the Royal Fencible American Regiment, WO 1/681, TNA, 57; Muster rolls, 22nd Regiment of Foot, WO 12/3872, TNA.

23. Thomas Simes, *The Regulator,* 125.

24. Extracts from letters of James Green. Ms. 7201–36–1, National Army Museum, London.

25. Frances G. Halpenny, ed., *Dictionary of Canadian Biography*, vol. 6, 1821–1835 (Toronto: University of Toronto Press, 1966).

26. Muster rolls, 17th Regiment of Light Dragoons, WO 12/1306, TNA.

27. Dunkerley's name is spelled various ways in different sources. The muster rolls between 1769 and May 1774 are missing for this regiment. Muster rolls, 38th Regiment of Foot, WO 12/5171, TNA.

28. A second lieutenant in the artillery was the equivalent of an ensign in the infantry. *Massachusetts Soldiers and Sailors of the Revolutionary War*, Vol. 5 (Boston: Wright & Potter Printing, 1899), 52.

29. Theodore J. Crackel, ed., *The Papers of George Washington*, Revolutionary War Series vol. 15 (Charlottesville: University Press of Virginia, 2006), 171–172.

30. Carrie Rebora Barratt and Lori Zabar, *American Portrait Miniatures in the Metropolitan Museum of Art* (New Haven: Yale University Press, 2010), 168.

31. Muster rolls, 23rd Regiment of Foot, WO 12/3959, TNA.

32. Richard Williams, *Discord and Civil Wars* (Buffalo, NY: Easy Hill Press, 1954), 26.

33. The date on which Burke joined the 45th Regiment is not known. He first appears on the muster roll prepared in Limerick on 17 April 1775; he is not on the previous roll prepared in January. Muster rolls, 45th Regiment of Foot, WO 12/5718/1, TNA.
34. Capt. Richard Drakeford, 26th Regiment of Foot, to the Secretary at War, 7 January 1776; Col. Robert Cunningham, 14th Regiment of Foot, to the Secretary at War, 19 May 1776, WO 991/1, TNA, 9, 119. Unfortunately no comprehensive recruiting records for any regiment have been found, so it is not possible to quantify the problem. Capt. William Cowley of the 22nd Regiment of Foot reported, on 5 January 1776, that of 116 recruits raised 39 had deserted. WO 991/1, TNA, 106. Of 71 men enlisted for the 46th Regiment of Foot between 17 December 1775 and 4 February 1776, 15 deserted. WO 1/992, TNA.
35. Don N. Hagist, "Forty German Recruits," 63–66.
36. Colonel James J. Graham, ed. *Memoir of General Graham* (Edinburgh: R. & R. Clark, 1862), 10–11.
37. Trial of Murdock McLeod, 42nd Regiment of Foot, WO 71/85, TNA, 151–154.
38. Trial of Patrick McDonald, 47th Regiment of Foot, WO 71/84, TNA, 178–181. Trial of George Hundredmark, 9th Regiment of Foot, WO 71/84, TNA, 181–186.
39. Trial of Hubertus Römer (Hubert Reimar), 22nd Regiment of Foot, WO 71/87, TNA, 241–243. Henry Klinge was not among the German recruits described here; he was already in the 54th Regiment when the war began. Muster rolls, 54th Regiment of Foot, WO 12/6398, TNA.
40. Trial of John Frederick Leo, 22nd Regiment of Foot, WO 71/86, TNA, 97–98.
41. William Bell Clark, ed., *Naval Documents of the American Revolution,* vol. 1, 556–557.
42. James Richardson was promoted from sergeant to quartermaster in the 45th Regiment on 11 January 1777; George Gillespie was promoted from private in the 45th to surgeon of the 4th Regiment of Foot on 5 July 1777; Samuel Wogan entered the 45th and was promoted from private to ensign on 30 September 1776. Muster rolls, 45th Regiment of Foot, WO 12/5718, TNA.
43. Thomas Simes, *The Regulator,* 153. Sometimes only one man was required as a replacement, as in the case of Alexander Andrew discussed in Chapter 8.
44. The original publication says 5th regiment, but clearly this is a typographical error; the Lieutenant Colonel of the 45th Regiment was Henry Monckton, and Andrew Burke appears on the muster rolls of that regiment at the appropriate times.
45. A tide waiter was a customs officer who boarded ships to insure that customs laws were followed.
46. Guinea, a gold coin worth 21 shillings.
47. Batteries, fortifications for artillery.
48. It is not known to whom Burke refers when he says "surgeon general."

49. This is probably supposed to read 12,000, as suggested by the subsequent text.
50. Burke's description of the Battle of Brooklyn on 27 August 1776 is difficult to understand, as might be expected from his view as a private soldier. The 45th Regiment was part of the 1st Brigade, in the right wing of the British army that marched around the American flank and turned the battle into a rout. The only British dragoon regiment in America at this time was the 17th Regiment of Light Dragoons, which was in the advance guard of the column that included the 45th Regiment; the 12th (Prince of Wales') Light Dragoons never served in America. Some sources put the 16th Light Dragoons as participating, but they did not arrive in America until the following month.
51. That is, slept in uniform with their weapons at hand.
52. Bombs were hollow spherical shells filled with gunpowder and a fuse; when fired from a mortar, the mortar's ignition lit the fuse which was formulated to burn for approximately the duration of flight so that the shell exploded on, or soon after, impact. Hot balls were solid iron balls heated to a high temperature before they were fired, in the hope of setting fire to the target. Adrian B. Caruana, *British Artillery Ammunition.*
53. Throgs Neck.
54. That is, took down the tents and packed them.
55. Burke glosses over the bitter battle that was fought at Fort Washington before the surrender occurred.
56. Colonel Robert Magaw of Pennsylvania was actually a lawyer. Charles Francis Himes, *Colonel Robert Magaw, the Defender of Fort Washington* (Carlisle, PA: Hamilton Library Association, 1915), 7.
57. It appears that Burke speaks as an American when he states that "we" were unable to keep possession of Fort Washington.
58. That is, turned over their weapons to their captors by laying them down in one location.
59. The Sugar House was a large storage house in New York that was converted into a prison.
60. Lieutenant Colonel Monckton was put in command of the 2nd Battalion of Grenadiers, formed from grenadier companies detached from several British regiments. In this passage, Burke refers to the operations in New Jersey at the end of 1776 that advanced as far as the Delaware River but did not actually advance to Philadelphia. Monckton remained in the command of the grenadier battalion in the autumn 1777 campaign to Philadelphia, and it is possible that Burke simply garbled the timeline.
61. Captain Hugh Nevin of the 45th Regiment actually died on 11 January 1777. Muster rolls, 45th Regiment of Foot, WO 12/5718/1, TNA.
62. Captain William Graham was born in Scotland in 1743 and served as a volunteer before receiving an ensign's commission in the 45th Regiment of Foot in 1760; he retired in August 1778. Muster rolls, 45th Regiment of Foot, WO 12/5718, TNA.
63. That is, Walker was from the north of Ireland.

64. By "planting sentinels," Burke means posting sentries. A unique countersign was given out each night as a way for sentries to distinguish friend from foe. If a sentry detected someone in the dark, he would ask the unknown person to give the countersign. Only sentries and parties authorized to be outside of the lines at night knew the countersign. Burke chose to desert on a night that he knew the countersign so that if British sentries challenged him he could give the impression that he was authorized to be passing through the lines.
65. The 6th Connecticut Regiment commanded by Colonel Jonathan Meigs wore distinctive leather caps. Philip Katcher, *Uniforms of the Continental Army* (York, PA: Geo. Shumway, 1981), 75; John C. Fitzpatrick, ed., *The Writings of George Washington,* vol. 21 (Washington, D.C.: Government Printing Office, 1937), 83.
66. The muster rolls show Burke's date of desertion as 18 January 1778. Muster rolls, 45th Regiment of Foot, WO 12/5718/1, TNA.
67. That is, African Americans who were loyal to the British government bringing in turkeys for food.
68. Burke's unusual terminology seems to mean that the tories wore uniforms that could be distinguished by their colored collars, a typical style for uniform jackets widely used during the war. The phrase "collared coats" is, however, unusual; "colored coats" or clothing was a phrase widely used to describe nonmilitary clothing, but this would not make sense in the context used by Burke.
69. Burke's crude terminology describes the typical British private soldier's uniform consisting of a red regimental coat, white breeches, and a black cocked hat. Why this clothing on a single man would suggest to the American officer that Burke had a large party with him is not clear; the officer's subsequent question indicates that he took Burke to be an officer rather than a private soldier.
70. Their side arms were their bayonets, carried in scabbards typically suspended on the soldier's left side from a belt worn either under the coat around the waist or over the coat around the right shoulder. Apparently the first officer to whom Burke had offered his bayonet had returned it.
71. Burke refers to Africans brought to America and put to work as slaves on farms and plantations in spite of having no knowledge of western agricultural practices.
72. A letter of marque was an authorization for a private naval vessel to seize enemy ships at sea; it allowed private owners to operate vessels as privateers. The frigate *Deane* was built in France and arrived in Boston in May 1778 to fit out as part of the new Continental navy.
73. The British assault on Fort Stanwix occurred in 1777, months before Burke deserted. His mention of it here is unexplainable.
74. John Hancock took leave from the Continental Congress and returned to his native Massachusetts in July, where he took command of the state militia.
75. A French fleet had put into Boston in late August 1778 to refit after being devastated by a storm during the abortive siege of Rhode Island.

The presence of a French lieutenant on the *Deane* suggests that this incident occurred during August or September 1778.
76. Reverend David Jewett, pastor of North Parish church in present-day Montville, Connecticut. D. Hamilton Hurd, *History of New London County, Connecticut* (Philadelphia: J. W. Lewis, 1882), 577.
77. Deacon Joseph Otis and Deacon Joseph Chester of North Parish church. D. Hamilton Hurd, *History of New London County,* 572, 573.
78. *The Useful Christian,* 16.
79. Trial of Captain Benjamin Charnock Payne, 18th Regiment of Foot, WO 71/81, TNA, 2–165. Discharge of John Graham, WO 121/18/146.
80. William Burke, *Memoir of William Burke, Soldier of the Revolution* (Hartford, Conn.: Case, Tiffany and Company, 1837).

EPILOGUE

1. The proportion of men who became corporals or sergeants at some point in their careers has been estimated by using muster rolls to trace the careers of the 1,005 men who served in the 22nd Regiment of Foot in America between 1775 and 1783. About 20 percent of these men spent some part of their careers as corporals or sergeants. Muster rolls, 22nd Regiment of Foot, WO 12/3871 through /3873 and for other regiments, TNA.
2. Besides Thomas Watson and William Burke, Roger Lamb (who served in America from 1776 through 1783) and Thomas Cranfield (who served in Gibraltar from 1777 through 1783) turned their lives to religion as headmasters of religious schools. Don N. Hagist, *A British Soldier's Story*; *Thomas Cranfield, The Useful Christian.*
3. In other words, regardless of how many written documents survive, we don't know whether other soldiers could not write or if we simply lack surviving examples of their writing.
4. Kenneth Lockridge, *Literacy in Colonial New England* (New York: W.W. Norton, 1974) 87.
5. Sylvia R. Frey, *The British Soldier in America,* 68.

APPENDIX I

1. Muster rolls, 80th Regiment of Foot, WO 12/8454, TNA.
2. Scott was described later in life thus: "While under these feelings one winter evening, an old woman observed-'Dear me, ye're aye singin' sangs. I never hear any o' ye sing "The Oak Tree," a fine sang, made by Andrew Scott when he was a sodger in the American war.' 'Who is Andrew Scott, Peggy?' inquired I. 'Bless me! do ye no ken Andrew Scott o' Bowden, wha thrashes at Whinfield, barnman there this winter? He stops there a' the week, and gangs home on Saturday nights. Has made mony a bonnie sang, and nice poems, too, and is a kindly, quiet man as ye ever saw—aye sae blythe and weel pleased. If ye wad gang up in the fore-supper time, an' crack wi' him about poetry, his heart wad rise, for he'll ha'e naething to amuse him at nights yonder but a book, for he's aye readin' or writin', or

tweedlin' on the fiddle.' This conversation occurred early on a winter's evening. So out I sallied, and flew like a meteor over a mile of ground to Whinfield, dropt in to the farmer's kitchen, and found Andrew Scott, my friend to be, sitting on a form seat, tailoring his old grey coat, which had got very poetically out at the elbows. Though I felt abashed to tell my errand in the hearing of the rest of the inmates, yet at one glance I saw he was just the very thing for me—a tight, handy-like man, of middle age and stature, with a face kind and inviting." John Younger, *Autobiography of John Younger*, Shoemaker, St. Boswell's (Kelso, Scotland: J. & J. Rutherfurd, 1881), 180-181.

3. Andrew Scott; *Poems, Chiefly in the Scottish Dialect* (Kelso, Scotland: Andrew Leadbetter, 1811).

4. Three corporals of the 80th Regiment died around the time the poem was written, one each in August, September, and October 1783. "Betsy Rosoe" was probably Elizabeth Rezeau, daughter of Jacob Rezeau of Staten Island.

5. By "Continentals" Scott means they were from the American continent. The Queen's Rangers was a Loyalist regiment in the British army.

6. Samuel Pleydell was actually the surgeon's mate of the 80th Regiment, subordinate to the surgeon. The term "surgeon" was used for military doctors and did not denote any medical specialty.

APPENDIX 2

1. John Hawthorn, *Poems* (Printed for the author and sold by E. Easton [Salisbury, England], J. Dodsley, and J. Wilkie [London], 1779).

2. *New Manual, and Platoon Exercise: with an Explanation. Published by Authority* (Dublin, 1768); *containing the description of a Firelock, Position of a Soldier under Arms, Directions for the Manual Exercise, &c.* (Dublin: W. Collis, 1784).

BIBLIOGRAPHY

Primary Sources

Manuscripts

American Antiquarian Society, Worcester, MA
  BDSDS 1774: Broadsides
Archibald S. Alexander Library, Rutgers, The State University of New Jersey
  Orderly book, General Charles Grey's company, 26th Regiment of Foot
Library of Congress, Washington, DC
  George Chalmers collection, Peter Force Manuscripts
Lloyds Bank Archives, London
  Cox & Company: Regimental Ledger Books
Massachusetts Historical Society
  Manuscripts: Broadsides
Morristown National Historical Park
  Lloyd W. Smith Collection
National Archives and Records Administration
  Papers of the Continental Congress
National Archives, Kew, London
  Domestic Records of the Public Record Office (PRO)
    PRO 30/55: Guy Carleton Papers
  War Office (WO)
    WO 1: Secretary-at-War and Commander-in-Chief, In-letters
    WO 12: General muster books and pay lists
    WO 25: Service Returns
    WO 27: Inspection Returns
    WO 34: Jeffrey Amherst Papers
    WO 36: Entry Books, American Revolution
    WO 71: Judge Advocate General's Office: Courts Martial Proceedings
    WO 97: Royal Hospital Chelsea: Soldiers Service Documents
    WO 116: Disability and Royal Artillery Out-Pensions, Admission Books
    WO 119: Royal Hospital, Kilmainham: Pensioners' Discharge Documents

WO 120: Royal Hospital, Chelsea: Regimental Registers of Pensioners
WO 121: Royal Hospital, Chelsea: Discharge Documents of Pensioners
National Army Museum, London
Ms. 7201–36–1: Extracts from letters of James Green
National Library of Ireland
MS 3750: Orderly book, 32nd Regiment of Foot
New-York Historical Society
Orderly Book Collection
New York Public Library
Bayard-Campbell-Pearsall Collection, Campbell Accounts and Papers
Parliamentary Archives, Houses of Parliament, London
HL/PO/JO/10/7/544: Return of Courts Martial held in Ireland
Public Archives of Canada, Ottawa
CO transcripts, Q series
MG23, K6(2): Punishment Book of the 44th Regiment of Foot
West Yorkshire Archives, Calderdale
SH17/A: Recruiting Accounts of Lt. Joab Aked
William L. Clements Library, University of Michigan
Eyre Coote Papers
Frederick Mackenzie Papers
Henry Clinton Papers
Thomas Gage Papers

Newspapers

British
Belfast Newsletter, 1780
Edinburgh Advertiser, 1775, 1776
Freeman's Journal (Dublin), 1775, 1776
Hibernian Chronicle, 1776
London Gazette, 1781
Londonderry Journal, 1777
Manchester Mercury, 1776, 1779
Sherborne and Yeovil Mercury, 1777

North American
New Jersey Gazette, 1778, 1779
New York Gazette, 1777
Pennsylvania Packet, 1778
Quebec Gazette, 1774
Royal Gazette (New York), 1780, 1781
Thomas's Massachusetts Spy Or, American Oracle of Liberty, 1779

Published Primary Sources

Andrews, John. "Letters of John Andrews, Esq. of Boston." Winthrop Sargent, ed. *Proceedings of the Massachusetts Historical Society* (July 1865).

The Annual Register, or a View of the History, Politics, and Literature, for the Year 1777. London: J. Dodsley, 1794.

Anon, *A Soldier's Journal, Containing a particular Description of the several Descents on the Coast of France last War, With an entertaining Account of the Islands of Guadaloupe, Dominique, &c., And also of the Isles of Wight and Jersey, To which are annexed, Observations on the present State of the Army of Great Britain.* London: E. and C. Dilly, 1770.

Aulenbach, John Philip. Autobiography of John Philip Aulenbach, in D. Luther Roth, *Acadie and the Acadians,* 3rd ed. Utica, NY: L. C. Childs, 1891.

Bailey, Nathan. *An Universal Etymological English Dictionary*, 20th ed. London: R. Ware, 1765.

Boston Under Military Rule (1768–1769): As Revealed in a Journal of the Times, Oliver Morton Dickerson, ed. Boston: Chapman and Grimes, 1936.

Burgoyne. John. *A State of the Expedition from Canada as Laid Before the House of Commons, by Lieutenant-General Burgoyne, and Verified by Evidence, with a Collection of Authentic Documents, and an Addition of Many Circumstances Which were Prevented from Appearing Before the House by the Prorogation of Parliament.* London, 1780.

Burke, William, *Memoir of William Burke, Soldier of the Revolution.* Hartford: Case, Tiffany and Company, 1837.

Cranfield, Thomas. *The Useful Christian; a Memoir of Thomas Cranfield, for about Fifty Years a Devoted Sunday-School Teacher.* Philadelphia: American Sunday-School Union, Philadelphia, no date.

Crawford, William. *A Narrative of the Life and Character of William Crawford, of Fallowfield Township, Washington County, Who Was Executed at Washington, Pa., on Friday, the 21st February, 1823, for the Murder of His Son, Henry Crawford, on Tuesday, the 30th July, 1822; Related by Himself and Published by His Request*. Washington, PA: Reporter Office, 1823.

The Critical Review: Or, the Annals of Literature. Volume the Forty-Eighth. London: A. Hamilton, 1779.

Cuthbertson, Bennett. *A System for the Compleat Interior Management and Œconomy of a Battalion of Infantry*. Dublin, 1768.

Digby, William. *The British Invasion From the North: The Campaigns of Generals Carleton and Burgoyne from Canada, 1776–1777, with the Journal of Lieut. William Digby*. Albany, NY: Joel Munsell's Sons, 1887.

"Dying Speeches & Bloody Murders: Crime Broadsides at the Harvard Law Digital Collection," accessed July 2011, http://broadsides.law.harvard.edu/home.php.

Evelyn, W. Glanville. *Memoir and Letters of Captain W. Glanville Evelyn, of the 4th Regiment, ("King's Own,") from North America, 1774 –1776*. G. D. Scull, ed. Oxford: Parker & Co., 1879.

Fox, Ebenezer. *The Adventures of Ebenezer Fox in the Revolutionary War.* Boston: Charles Fox, 1847.

Gaine, Hugh. *Gaine's Universal Register, or, American and British Kalendar, for the Year 1776*. New York: Hugh Gaine, 1775.

General Orders, Rhode Island, Don N. Hagist, ed. Bowie, MD: Heritage Books, 2001.

Graham, Colonel James J., ed. *Memoir of General Graham* (Edinburgh: R. & R. Clark, 1862), 10–11.

Green, Fleet. "Newport in the Hands of the British: A Diary of the American Revolution." *The Historical Magazine* 4, March 1860.

Griffith, W. "Memoirs and Spiritual Experience of the late Mr. W. Griffith, Senior." *The Spiritual Magazine, and Zion's Casket*. London: E. Palmer and Son, 1848.

Hadden, James M. *Hadden's Journal and Orderly Books: A Journal Kept in Canada and Upon Burgoyne's Campaign in 1776 and 1777, by Lieut. James M. Hadden, Roy. Art*, Horatio Rogers, ed. Albany, NY: Joel Munsell's Sons, 1884.

Hastings, Reginald Rawdon. *Report on the Manuscripts of the Late Reginald Rawdon Hastings, Esq*., Francis Bickley, ed. London: Historical Manuscripts Commission, 1934.

Hawthorn, John. *Poems.* Printed for the author and sold by E. Easton [Salisbury, England], J. Dodsley, and J. Wilkie [London], 1779.

Henry, John Joseph. *Account of Arnold's Campaign Against Quebec*. Albany, NY: Joel Munsell, 1877.

Howe, William. *General Sir William Howe's Orderly Book*, B. F. Stevens, ed. Port Washington, NY: Kennikat Press, 1980.

Johnson, Samuel. *A Dictionary of the English Language*. London: W. Strahan, 1755.

"Journal of the Most Remarkable Occurrences in Quebec." *Collections of the New-York Historical Society*, 1880.

"Journal of the Siege from 1st Dec. 1775." *The Blockade of Quebec in 1775–1776*. Quebec: Library and Historical Society of Quebec, 1906.

Kemble, Stephen. "Journals of Lieut.-Col. Stephen Kemble." *Collections of the New York Historical Society for the year 1883*. New York, 1884.

Lamb, Roger. *A British Soldier's Story: Roger Lamb's Narrative of the American Revolution*, Don N. Hagist, ed. Baraboo, WI: Ballindalloch Press, 2005.

———. *Memoirs of his Own Life*. Dublin: privately printed, 1811.

A List of the General and Staff Officers, and of the Officers in the several Regiments serving in North America. New York: Macdonald and Cameron, 1777

The London Magazine, or, Gentleman's Monthly Intellegencer for the year 1777, vol. 45. London: R. Baldwin, 1777.

MacDonald, John. *Autobiographical Journal of John MacDonald: Schoolmaster and Soldier, 1770–1830*. Edinburgh: Norman MacLeod, 1906.

———. *Memoirs of an Eighteenth-Century Footman*. New York: Harper & Row, 1927.

Mackenzie, Frederick. *A British Fusilier in Revolutionary Boston*, Allen French, ed. Cambridge, MA: Harvard University Press, 1926.

Matson, John. *Indian Warfare: or, the Extraordinary Adventures of John Matson the Kidnapped Youth, late of Kingsland Road, London; formerly of Bridlington Quay, in the County of York; Architect and Builder. Written by Himself*. London: Effingham Wilson, 1842.

Minutes of the Provincial Council of Pennsylvania: from the organization to the Termination of the proprietary Government. Harrisburg, PA: Theo. Fenn & Co., 1852.

Naval Documents of the American Revolution. 11 vols. William James Morgan et al., eds. Washington, DC: Government Printing Office, 1964–2005.

New Manual, and Platoon Exercise: with an Explanation. Published by Authority. Dublin, 1768.

Pasley, Thomas. *Private Sea Journals, 1778–1782, kept by Admiral Sir Thomas Pasley*, Robert M. S. Pasley, ed. London: J. M. Dent and Sons, 1931.

Pringle, John. *Observations on the Diseases of the Army*. London: 1775.

Scott, Andrew. *Poems, Chiefly in the Scottish Dialect*. Kelso, Scotland: Andrew Leadbetter, 1811.

Shaw, John Robert. *John Robert Shaw: An Autobiography of Thirty Years, 1777–1807,* Oressa M. Teagarden, ed. Athens: Ohio University Press, 1992.

———. *The Life and Travels of John Robert Shaw.* Lexington, KY: Daniel Bradford, 1807.

Simes, Thomas. *A Military Guide for Young Officers.* London, 1776.

———. *The Regulator.* London, 1780.

Smith, George. *An Universal Military Dictionary.* London, 1779.

Standing Orders and Regulations for the Army in Ireland. Dublin: George Grierson, 1794.

Sullivan, Thomas. *From Redcoat to Rebel: The Thomas Sullivan Journal,* Joseph Lee Boyle, ed. Bowie, MD: Heritage Books, 1997.

"The Voluntary Confession of James Aitken, commonly called John the Painter." *The Universal Magazine of Knowledge and Pleasure* 60 (March 1777), 148–150.

The Volunteer's Companion; containing the description of a Firelock, Position of a Soldier under Arms, Directions for the Manual Exercise, &c. Dublin: W. Collis, 1784.

Watson, Thomas. *Some Account of the Life, Convincement, and Religious Experience of Thomas Watson.* New York: Daniel Cooledge, 1836.

Williams, Richard. *Discord and Civil Wars.* Buffalo, NY: Easy Hill Press, 1954.

Younger, John. *Autobiography of John Younger, Shoemaker, St. Boswell's.* Kelso, Scotland: J. & J. Rutherfurd, 1881.

SECONDARY SOURCES

BOOKS

Anderson, R. C. and J. M. Anderson. *Quicksilver: A Hundred Years of Coaching 1750–1850.* Newton Abbot, Devon, England: David & Charles, 1973.

Babbits, Lawrence E. and Joshua B. Howard. *Long, Obstinate, and Bloody: The Battle of Guilford Courthouse.* Chapel Hill: University of North Carolina Press, 2009.

Barratt, Carrie Rebora and Lori Zabar. *American Portrait Miniatures in the Metropolitan Museum of Art.* New Haven: Yale University Press, 2010.

Baule, Steven M and Stephen Gilbert. *British Army Officers Who Served in the American Revolution.* Bowie, MD: Heritage Books, 2004.

Blumenthal, Walter Hart. *Women Camp Followers of the American Revolution*. New York: Arno Press, 1974.

Braisted, Todd W. *The Loyalist Corps: Americans in Service to the King*. Trenton, NJ: FoxAcre Press, 2011.

Caruana, Adrian B. *British Artillery Ammunition*. Bloomfield, Ontario: Museum Restoration Service, 1979.

A Christmas Reminder, being the names of about eight thousand persons, a small portion of the number confined on board the British prison ships during the war of the revolution. Brooklyn, NY: Eagle Print, 1888.

Clode, Charles Mathew. *The military forces of the crown: their administration and government*, vol. 2. London: John Murray, 1869.

Crackel, Theodore J., ed. *The Papers of George Washington*, Revolutionary War Series, vol. 15. Charlottesville: University Press of Virginia, 2006.

Curtis, Edward R. *The British Army in the American Revolution*. Gansevoort, NY: Corner House Historical Publications, 1998.

Dann, John C. ed. *The Revolution Remembered*. Chicago: University of Chicago Press, 1980.

Fitzpatrick, John C., ed. *The Writings of George Washington,* vol. 21. Washington, DC: Government Printing Office, 1937.

Frey, Sylvia R. *The British Soldier in America.* Austin: University of Texas Press, 1981.

Frothingham, R. *History of the Siege of Boston and Bunker Hill.* Boston: Little, Brown, 1903.

Gilchrist, M. M. *Patrick Ferguson, A Man of Some Genius.* Edinburgh: NMS Publishing, 2003.

Glover, Michael. *General Burgoyne in Canada and America.* London: Gordon Cremonesi, 1976.

Grose, Francis. *Military Antiquities Respecting a History of the English Army from the Conquest to the Present Time*. London: S. Hooper, 1786.

Hale, William. *Some British Soldiers in America*, W. H. Wilkin, ed. London: H. Rees, 1914.

Halpenny, Francess G., ed., *Dictionary of Canadian Biography*, vol. 6, 1821–1835. Toronto: University of Toronto Press, 1966.

Himes, Charles Francis. *Colonel Robert Magaw, the Defender of Fort Washington.* Carlisle, PA: Hamilton Library Association, 1915.

Houlding, J. A. *Fit for Service: The Training of the British Army 1715–1795*. Oxford: Clarendon Press, 1981.

Hurd, D. Hamilton. *History of New London County, Connecticut.* Philadelphia: J. W. Lewis, 1882.

Katcher, Philip. *Uniforms of the Continental Army.* York, PA: Geo. Shumway, 1981.

Loprieno, Don. *The Enterprise in Contemplation: The Midnight Assault of Stony Point.* Bowie, MD: Heritage Books, 2004.

Lossing, Benson J. *The Pictorial Field-Book of the American Revolution; or, Illustrations, by Pen and Pencil, of the History, Biography, Scenery, Relics, and Traditions of the War for Independence.* Vol. II. New York: Harper and Brothers, 1852.

Massachusetts Soldiers and Sailors of the Revolutionary War. Boston: Wright & Potter Printing, 1899.

Morrissey, Brendan. *Saratoga, 1777.* Oxford: Osprey Publishing, 2000.

Mosley, Charles ed., *Burke's Peerage, Baronetage & Knightage,* Wilmington, DE: Genealogical Books, 2003.

Navas, Deborah. *Murdered by his Wife: A History with Documentation of the Joshua Spooner Murder and Execution of His Wife, Bathsheba, Who was Hanged in Worchester, Massachusetts, 2 July 1778.* Amherst: University of Massachusetts Press, 1999.

Nelson, Paul David. *Sir Charles Grey, First Earl Grey.* London: Associated University Press, 1966.

Noakes, George. *A historical account of the services of the 34th & 55th Regiments.* Carlisle, England: C. Thurnam and Sons, 1875.

Purcell, L. Edward. *Who Was Who in the American Revolution.* New York: Facts on File, 1993.

Report of the Commissioners Appointed to Inquire into and to State the Mode of Keeping the Official Accounts in the Principal Departments Connected with the Receipts and Expenditure for the Public Service. London: Printed for His Majesty's Treasury, 1829.

Robertson, Eileen A. *The Spanish Town Papers.* New York: Macmillan, 1959.

Sampson, Richard. *Escape in America: The British Convention Prisoners 1777–1783.* Chippenham, England: Picton Publishing, 1995.

Silverstone, Paul H. *The Sailing Navy, 1775–1854.* New York: Taylor & Francis Group, 2006.

Snell, Charles W. *A Report on the Strength of the British Army Under Lieutenant General John Burgoyne, July 1 to October 17, 1777 and on the Organization of the British Army on September 19, and October 7, 1777.* Stillwater, NY: Saratoga National Historical Park, 1951.

Spring, Matthew H. *With Zeal and Bayonets Only: The British Army on Campaign in North America, 1775–1783*. Norman: University of Oklahoma Press, 2008.

Stirling, A. M. W. *Annals of a Yorkshire House, from the Papers of a Macaroni & his Kindred.* Vol. 2. London: John Lane, 1911.

Strachan, Hew. *British Military Uniforms 1768–1796: The Dress of the British Army from Official Sources*. London: Arms and Armor Press, 1975.

Swain, David, ed., *Recollections of Life on the Prison Ship Jersey*. Yardley, PA: Westholme Publishing, 2010.

Zobel, Hiller B. *The Boston Massacre*. New York: W. W. Norton, 1970.

Articles and Theses

Adair, P. A. "Sergeant Pell in London." *History Today* 21 (1971).

Baule, Steven M. and Don N. Hagist. "The Regimental Punishment Book of the Boston Detachments of the Royal Irish Regiment and 65th Regiment, 1774–75." *Journal of Army Historical Research* 88 (2010) 5–18.

Cassel, Daniel K. *History of the Mennonites*. Philadelphia: Daniel K. Cassel, 1888.

Cohen, Sheldon S. "The Connecticut Captivity of Major Christopher French." *Connecticut Historical Society Bulletin* 55–56 (Summer–Fall 1990), 223–229.

Conway, Stephen R. "The Recruitment of Criminals into the British Army, 1775–81." *Historical Research* 58 (May 1985), 46–58.

Hagist, Don N. "The Women of the British Army during the American Revolution." *Minerva Quarterly Report on Women and the Military* 13, no. 2 (Summer 1995), 29–95.

———. "Fieldwork: Order of Battle of the British Flank Battalions." *The Brigade Dispatch* 23, no. 2 (Spring 1992), 26–27.

———. "Soldier's Games." *The Brigade Dispatch* 31, no. 4 (Winter 2001), 13–15.

———. "Forty German Recruits: The Service of the Von Scheither Recruits in the 22nd Regiment of Foot, 1776–1783." *Journal of the Johannes Schwalm Historical Association* 6, no. 1 (1997), 63–66.

Hagist, Don N. and Eric H. Schnitzer. "German Recruits in Lt. George Anson Nutt's Detachment of the 33rd Regiment of Foot on Burgoyne's Campaign." *Journal of the Johannes Schwalm Historical Association* 8 (2005), 42–44.

———. “Unpublished Military Writings of Roger Lamb, Soldier in the 1775–1783 American War, Part 2.” *Journal of the Society for Army Historical Research*, pending publication.

Houlding, J. A. and Kenneth G. Yates. “Corporal Fox’s Memoir of Service, 1766–1783: Quebec, Saratoga, and the Convention Army.” *Journal of the Society for Army Historical Research* (68, no. 275), 146–168.

Kopperman, Paul E. “‘The Cheapest Pay’: Alcohol Abuse in the Eighteenth-Century British Army.” *Journal of Military History* 60, no. 3 (July 1996), 445–470.

McGuire, Thomas J. *The Surprise of Germantown.* Gettysburg, PA: Thomas Publications, 1994.

Odintz, Mark F. “The British Officer Corps 1754–1783.” Ph.D. diss., University of Michigan, 1988.

Papers Illustrating the Hstory of the Scots brigade in the service of the United Netherlands, 1572–1782. Edinburgh: Scottish History Society, 1901.

Rees, John U. “‘We Are Now... Properly... Enwigwamed’: British Soldiers and Brush Shelters, 1777–1781.” *The Brigade Dispatch* 29, no. 2 (Summer 1999) 2–9.

Seton, Colonel Sir Bruce. “Infantry Recruiting Instructions in England in 1767.” *Journal of Army Historical Research* 4, no. 16 (April–June 1925).

Steppler, Glenn A. “British Military Law, Discipline, and the Conduct of Regimental Courts Martial in the Later Eighteenth Century.” *English Historical Review* 102 (October 1987) 859–886.

———. “The Common Soldier in the Reign of George III.” Ph.D. thesis, University of Oxford, 1984.

Syrett, David. “Living Conditions on the Navy Board’s Transports During the American War, 1775–1783.” *Mariner’s Mirror* 55 (1969), 87–94.

Tatum, William P. III, “Deserted!: Opportunism and Desertion in the British Army, 1763–1783.” Senior Honors Thesis, College of William & Mary, May 2003.

Watson, John F. “Notes of the Early History of Germantown.” *Register of Pennsylvania* 1, no. 19 (10 May 1828).

ACKNOWLEDGMENTS

I started learning about British soldiers when I was a teenager. During thirty-five years of research, I've had the remarkable good fortune to receive information, help, and encouragement from far more people than I can recount. This book draws on information from all of them, but unfortunately it is only possible to acknowledge those who provided direct input to the material in these pages.

Stephen D. Rayner made this book possible. I had long been considering a compilation of soldiers' narratives but hadn't taken the initiative to get started. Steve brought to my attention several that I hadn't been aware of; these not only provided enough volume to make the book viable, but more importantly rounded out the diversity of accounts to allow for a complete and flowing narrative. His remarkable ability to ferret out information and his earnest generosity turned what would have been a dry compilation into a broad, rich study.

Todd W. Braisted has been my friend and research colleague from the beginning, and constantly challenges me to pursue new sources and avenues of inquiry; he freely shared a wealth of information used in these pages. Donald M. Londahl-Smidt has been consistently generous in sharing his own research as well as providing guidance on manuscript collections. William P. Tatum III took time from his own research expeditions to find material for me, and more importantly encouraged me to write and publish. Katherine Ludwig, librarian at the David Library of the American Revolution, has been quick to find last-minute items and has endured the hijinks of Todd, Don, Will, and myself on many long days at the library. Eric H. Schnitzer contributed not only his great artistic talents but also his extensive knowledge of period culture gleaned from primary-source artwork to create the original drawings that illustrate each chapter. Michael F. Barrett provided research skills and hospitality during visits to the National Archives in Kew. Steven M. Baule, Eric H. Schnitzer, Alexander John Good, Paul L. Pace, and Brendan Morrissey all shared their research and analysis of individual regiments that served in America, as well as general insights on the service of soldiers. J. A. Houlding answered innumerable queries about service records of British officers in addition to being instrumental in presenting George Fox's narrative. Andrew Cormack offered invaluable insight on the army pension system and related topics. Gilbert V. Riddle shared a great deal of research over the years and provided proofreading expertise. Gregory J. W. Urwin and John A. Nagy gave tremendous encouragement and assistance in the process of writing and publishing. René Chartrand assisted with photographs and other guidance from his extensive experience in publishing works on military uniforms. J. L. Bell, T. F. Mills, and Todd Post provided insight and information that allowed me to decode various details in the narratives. And Katie Williams believed in my writing.

Thanks to you all.

INDEX